Culture of Daʿwa

Culture of Daʿwa

ISLAMIC PREACHING IN THE MODERN WORLD

EDITED BY
ITZCHAK WEISMANN AND JAMAL MALIK

THE UNIVERSITY OF UTAH PRESS
Salt Lake City

The Defiance House Man colophon is a registered trademark of The University of Utah Press. It is based on a four-foot-tall Ancient Puebloan pictograph (late PIII) near Glen Canyon, Utah.

Library of Congress Cataloging-in-Publication Data

Names: Malik, Jamal, editor. | Weismann, Itzchak, editor. Title: Culture of daʿwah : Islamic preaching in the modern world/edited by Itzchak Weismann and Jamal Malik.
Description: Salt Lake City : The University of Utah Press, [2020]
Identifiers: LCCN 2019040610 (print) | LCCN 2019040611 (ebook) | ISBN 9781607817451 (paperback) | ISBN 9781607817468 (ebook)
Subjects: LCSH: Daʿwah (Islam) | Islam—21st century.
Classification: LCC BP170.85 .C85 2020 (print) | LCC BP170.85 (ebook) | DDC 297.7/4—dc23
LC record available at https://lccn.loc.gov/2019040610
LC ebook record available at https://lccn.loc.gov/2019040611

Errata and further information on this and other titles available online at UofUpress.com

Printed and bound in the United States of America.

Contents

Acknowledgments

This book has come a long way since we joined hands in studying and reflecting on the role and manifestations of *daʿwa* in modern Islam. In this endeavor, two important landmarks were workshops we held at Erfurt University, Germany, 9–13 April 2012, and at the Center for the Study of Developing Societies (CSDS) in New Delhi, 16–18 January 2013, under the title "The Daʿwa Phenomenon in International Comparison: Islamic Missions from 1920 to the Present." These were followed by a three-day conference at Haifa University in Israel, 6–8 January 2015, entitled "Modern Preaching of Islam: Salafis, Islamic Movements, Muslim States." The present collection consists of selected papers from that conference, augmented by invited papers aimed at providing as comprehensive a treatment of the subject as possible.

The authors would like to thank the Volkswagen Foundation and the Israel Science Foundation (ISF) for their generous seed grants, and Erfurt University, Haifa University, and the Center for the Study of Developing Societies (CSDS) in New Delhi for hosting the respective two workshops and the conference. Michael Asbury and Murray Rosovsky did a wonderful job in editing the chapters. We also thank Patrick Hadley and the wonderful team at the University of Utah Press for taking care of the manuscript and preparing it for publication.

Finally, and most importantly, we are thankful to the contributors for joining us in this precious endeavor to present various facets of modern Islamic preaching and for their patience with our wishes and attentiveness to the overall framework we had in mind.

A Note on Transliteration

We have employed a simplified form of the Arabic (and other Muslim languages) transliteration system used by the *International Journal of Middle East Studies* (IJMES). Throughout the book, we have avoided dotted consonants and long-vowel marks and wherever applicable opted for the common English usage of foreign terms and standard names (e.g., Quran and ulama, Hussein and Khaled, al-Jazeera or al-Qaeda). We have also omitted the ayn [ʿ] at the beginning of names (e.g., Abd rather than ʿAbd), but retained it in the notes and references, while maintaining the hamza [ʾ] and the ayn in the middle of words..

Introduction

ITZCHAK WEISMANN AND JAMAL MALIK

THE FAST-GROWING SCHOLARSHIP on the contemporary resurgence of Islam has paid relatively little attention to *daʿwa*. Preaching Islam, to both non-Muslims (proselytization) and Muslims (re-Islamization), is overshadowed by Islamist militancy and terrorism epitomized in the concept of jihad. Still, the remarkable revival and expansion of the meaning and practice of *daʿwa* in the course of the twentieth century makes it an important key to understanding the evolution of Islam in modern times in general, and its more recent violent mutations in particular. In the longer perspective, we believe it is *daʿwa*—now directed primarily at Muslims themselves—rather than jihad, which forms the backbone of modern Islamic collective action.

The concept of *daʿwa* appears frequently in the Quran and the Prophet's Sunna.[1] It has a wide semantic range, rendered into English by such terms as "invitation" or "summons" to Islam, religious call and outreach, propaganda, mission, and proselytization. *Daʿwa* thus denotes both the means for the spread of Islam and the message, which is ultimately Islam itself. Quran 12:108 affirms that *daʿwa* is a divine commandment: "Say thou: This is my way: I do invite unto Allah [*adʿu ila allah*]—on evidence clear as the seeing with one's eyes—I and whoever follows me. Glory to Allah! and never will I join gods with Allah!" Another often quoted verse, Quran 3:104, further clarifies that this commandment be associated with the upright of society: "Let there arise out of you a band of people inviting to all that is good [*yadʿuna ila al-khayr*], enjoining what is right, and forbidding what is wrong [*al-amr bi'l-ma'ruf wa'l-nahi 'an al-munkar*]: They are the ones to attain felicity."

There is a close affinity between the concept of *da'wa* and that of jihad. The two are both competing and complementary strategies to disseminate Islam. According to some hadith, holy war against non-Muslims may be waged only after they have been offered the choices of accepting the invitation to Islam, paying a poll tax (*jizya*), or preparing to fight. On the other hand, some later jurists regarded Islamic conquests as designed to facilitate the preaching of Islam.[2] In contemporary Islamist writings, one can find composite expressions such as *al-da'wa ila al-jihad* and *jihad al-da'wa* or *da'wat-e jihad*.

Still, despite its prominence in the scriptures, the concept of *da'wa* seems to have been little used in premodern Islamic history. This may have to do with the political connotation it acquired in the Abbasid propaganda against the Umayyad dynasty in the mid-eighth century and with its appropriation by the missionary propaganda of the Shi'i Isma'ili sect after the ninth century.[3] Subsequently, conversion to Islam was carried out primarily by Sufi masters and holy men, often as a long processes and in compromise with local beliefs and customs,[4] while edification of the Muslims was the preserve of mosque preachers (sing., *khatib*) and popular storytellers.[5] *Da'wa* resurfaced in an aggressive form in the mid-eighteenth century in conjunction with the puritan Wahhabi movement, which portrayed "straying" Muslims as infidels (*takfir*) and waged jihad against its neighbors in the Arabian Peninsula and the Ottoman state.[6]

In modern times, *da'wa* has evolved into a piety movement propelled by the perceived threats of the intruding Western secular culture and challenges posed by Christianity and other missionary religions. Its theology/ideology found roots in new concepts of religious renewal and reform that substituted traditional Sufi and juristic conceptualizations of guidance and conversion. Its organization entailed transformation of Sufi brotherhood practices and mosque sermon conventions.[7] The mission was first taken up by socioreligious movements intent on re-Islamizing society from below. Other Islamic actors soon joined in, from governments bent on imposing docile forms of Islam from above and propagating it abroad to individuals attuned to the changing spiritual and material needs of elites and common people alike.

Meanwhile, new forms of summoning to Islam have arisen in the context of the formation of public sphere(s) and the rise of mass politics. Spreading the message has been facilitated by the expansion of official education systems, the resulting increase in literacy, and by the development of new means of communication, from the printing press to the internet and social media. In the process, *daʿwa* has spread into new fields of activity such as social welfare and education, politics and sports, and more recently gender relations, self-help advice, and interfaith dialogue.

Modern *daʿwa* has been closely associated with political evolution in the Muslim lands in the past century. Its emergence in the 1910s and 1920s reflects the appalling state of the Muslim community (*umma*): disintegration of the Ottoman Empire following World War I, subsequent abolition of the Caliphate, and imposition of colonial rule over the greater part of the Muslim world. The call to Islam thrived in colonial settings such as British India and Egypt and in Arab monarchies that drew national and transnational legitimacy from religion. That call was repressed in surviving independent Muslim states—notably Turkey and Iran, which adopted aggressive policies of secularization—and later in postcolonial Arab and Muslim republics, where authoritarian-populist regimes subjected religion to the secular ideologies of nationalism and socialism.

Since the 1970s, the invitation to Islam has become an integral part of the Islamic resurgence, which sometimes followed "the retreat of the state," as in Egypt or Tunisia, at other times was led by the state, as in Saudi Arabia, Pakistan, and Malaysia, or even overtook the state, as was the case with Iran and temporarily Sudan. Today, the call to Islam continues to be both enhanced and constrained by the forces of globalization, neoliberalism, Muslim immigration to the West, and above all the appeal of global jihad.[8]

Modern *daʿwa* took shape in parallel in two of the core regions of the Muslim world: the Arab Middle East under the leadership of Egypt, where Muslims constituted the vast majority, and the South Asian subcontinent, where although they comprised one third of all Muslims in the world, they were still a beleaguered minority. It sprang respectively out of the modernist Salafi orientation and the Deobandi school network. The earliest call movements begotten by these reformist trends—and the most enduring—have been the Muslim Brotherhood, the foremost Islamic movement in the Arab countries, and the British-Indian-originated Tablighi Jamaʿat, arguably the largest Islamic organization on earth. From them, the Islamic call movement spread, separately and in various combinations and adaptations according to specific local conditions, to other Muslim countries and beyond. Their work was then augmented and diversified by a plethora of more or less explicit *daʿwa* organizations, from the modernist

Turkish Nur and Gülen movements to the messianic Ahmadiyya and Sufi-based Daʿwat-e Islami of India and Pakistan. These socioreligious movements, along with Islamic states such as Saudi Arabia and Iran, learned jurists and scholars, and lay preachers from these core regions and from other Muslim majority and minority environments, recognize no internal borders within the *umma*. In cooperation and in competition, they have systematized, popularized, and universalized the call of *daʿwa* in their societies and thence worldwide.

THE STUDY OF *DAʿWA*

Despite the obvious importance of *daʿwa* for the contemporary Islamic resurgence, academic research on the subject has not really taken off. Works dedicated to Islamic preaching as such are rare, whereas those dealing with Islamic activism at large, just like the general public, are naturally focused on the spectacular deeds of the jihadis much more than on the long-term, low-pitched effort of the *duʿa*. Echoing neglect of the term in premodern juristic and theological writings, some of the major studies of Islamic preaching and conversion fail to mention it altogether.[9] On the other hand, recent scholarship of Islam is only beginning to engage new theoretical insights gained in the field of religious studies by disentangling the term mission (from *missio*, to send) from its specifically Christian context and applying it to all convert-seeking religions.[10]

Of course, *daʿwa* is by no means absent from the scholarly literature of modern Islam—sometimes it even trickles down to the media and the public sphere. One of the most comprehensive treatments of the subject to date, itself a sign of the state of the art, is Egdunas Racius's unpublished 2004 dissertation, previously cited. Adopting an essentially textual approach, Racius begins with an exploration of the meanings of *daʿwa* in the scriptures and its theological and practical implications for today. There he makes important distinctions between what he calls extra- and intra-ummaic *daʿwa* on one hand and state and nongovernmental re-Islamization on the other.[11] This is calibrated by Henning Wrogemann's typology of *daʿwa* movements, which distinguishes five forms of calling: reformist-organizational, revolutionary-procedural, purifying-individualistic, cooperative-pragmatic, and puritan. As a theologian, Wrogemann is particularly interested in the usefulness of these various types for interreligious dialogue.[12]

Few other academic works mention the term in their title. These include the monographs of Larry Poston, who examines the spread of *daʿwa* from "the East" to "the West," Nina Wiedl, who focuses on the European arena, and Matthew J. Kuiper, who studies the Indian scene. The first two have also contributed to the present volume. Poston refers to *daʿwa* primarily as Islamic pietism and distinguishes external-institutional from internal-personal strategies of proselytization.[13] Wiedl dwells mainly on the discourse of individual thinkers, emphasizes the differences between *daʿwa* and mission, and positions it within modern Islamic revival.[14] Kuiper's work revolves around two case studies—one principal call movement and one principal contemporary activist preacher—examining their teachings and practices in the context of global interreligious relations.[15]

Several anthropological and ethnographic studies have moved beyond the discursive level to a contextual examination of the actual organization of *daʿwa*, the various motivations behind it, its structures of mobilization, and its channels of communication. Typically, they deal with the performance of the practice by the *daʿi* but also with its reception by the *maduʿ*. The trend was set by Dale Eickelman and James Piscatori, who refer to the Islamic call briefly within the general framework of the invention of tradition in Muslim politics.[16] Here too belong the works, mostly on Egypt, of Carrie Wickham on Islamist ideological outreach;[17] and in parallel those of Richard Gauvain (also a contributor to this volume) on the purist Salafi call;[18] Janine Clark on re-Islamization activities of middle-class social welfare networks;[19] Saba Mahmood on the Egyptian grassroots women's piety movement;[20] Charles Hirschkind on the culture of the cassette sermons;[21] Chanfi Ahmed on missions of conversion in East Africa;[22] and Florian Harms and others on Islamic proselytization on the internet.[23] Of special importance on the historical side is Reinhard Schulze's study of the Saudi-sponsored World Muslim League and the internationalization of Islam.[24]

Many scholars have tackled *daʿwa* in reference to particular movements, states, and individual thinkers—the agents of modern Islamic revival and reform. *Daʿwa* is obviously present in research on Islamic call movements, though here too the findings are often clouded by the political and militant aspects of their activities. This bias is particularly apparent in the case of the manifestly political organizations: the Muslim Brotherhood in the Arab world[25] and the Jamaʿat-i Islami in South Asia.[26] Islamic preaching moves to center stage in apolitical movements that bear explicit missionary names, as is the case with the Tablighi Jamaʿat[27] and

Daʿwat-e Islami.[28] The same caveat holds for Islamic thinkers. Those who have been identified in one way or another with Islamic political movements: the Muslim Brotherhood-associated Yusuf al-Qaradawi and Muhammad al-Ghazali[29] and Jamaʿat-i Islami's founder and leader Abu al-Aʿla al-Mawdudi, are known as scholars/ideologues and activists rather than as *duʿa*.[30] In contrast, independent and nonpolitical figures such as the traditional popular preacher Muhammad Mutawali al-Shaʿrawi, the revivalist Abd al-Hamid Kishk, and the "new preacher" Amr Khaled, are recognized primarily as such.[31] A few studies have been devoted to the role of states in promoting *daʿwa*, most notably in relation to Saudi Arabia, Libya, and Iran,[32] but also Zia ul-Haq's Pakistan and Mohamad Mahathir's Malaysia.[33] Here, the political connection is obvious. Still, much remains to be done.

STRUCTURE OF THE BOOK

This book seeks to provide a broad and updated picture of the complex, multifaceted phenomenon of Islamic *daʿwa* within the political, social, and cultural contexts of modernity. The fifteen contributions to the volume examine the preaching of Islam to Muslims as well as non-Muslims from various angles, by many of its major agents, and in many of its principal regions. Accordingly, Parts I and II of the book's four parts focus on the two core regions in the formation of modern Islamic *daʿwa*, the Arab Middle East and South Asia, analyzing the major discourses and the main movements that put them into practice. Part III charts the evolution of *daʿwa* in the context of globalization, with particular focus on Southeast Asia, Western Europe, and North America. Part IV turns attention to recent developments in *daʿwa* and some of its strategic transformations, considering the new challenges of globalization in general and global jihad in particular.

Part I dwells on the *discourses of daʿwa*. In the opening chapter, Itzchak Weismann provides an overview of the emergence and spread of *daʿwa* as a discourse and practice in the Arab-Muslim world over the past century. He identifies three principal phases in the evolution of modern *daʿwa* and analyzes the writings of major proponents in each: (1) the formative period in the first half of the twentieth century, which includes the modernist Salafi Rashid Rida and his successors in the Muslim Brotherhood and the Salafi Ansar al-Sunna al-Muhammadiyya; (2) the midcentury era of systematization and transnationalization dominated by scholars associated with the Muslim Brotherhood or Salafi-Wahhabi organizations such as the Muslim World League; and (3) the contemporary age of Islamic revival and globalization in which *daʿwa* has been adopted by a variety of proponents—from popular to intellectual preachers, and from neoliberal to radical jihadi preachers.

Turning to the other major region in the development of modern *daʿwa*, South Asia, in Chapter 2 Hilal Ahmed tackles the general problems facing Muslims seeking to propagate their faith in the secular context of India, particularly in view of the Indian constitution. Focusing on two leading movements (Tablighi Jamaʿat and Jamaʿat-e Islami Hind) and three prominent religious figures (Wahiduddin Khan, Abu al-Hasan Ali Nadwi, and Zakir Naik), he shows that their evolving positions and ideas have moved between two extremes. On the one hand are ideal/textual interpretations of Islam, which reinforce the sense of Islamic supremacy. On the other hand there is the legal/constitutional framework of postcolonial India, within which the *duʿa* have to work. Their attitudes to the question of religious preaching and conversion have been determined by their various responses to this internal conflict between the effort to reconceptualize the normative sphere of Islam and the necessity of mutual coexistence—and dialogue—among all religions.

In Chapter 3 of this section, Nina Wiedl examines the role that *daʿwa* has filled in the emergence of Salafism as a global religious movement and the changes it has undergone in the process. More particularly, she asks whether the preaching of Islam to non-Muslims in "the West" today may be regarded as a modern surrogate for jihad. Following Wiktorovicz's seminal distinction between quietist and jihadi Salafis, Wiedl analyzes the formulations of major transnational Salafi thinkers such as Nasir al-Din al-Albani and Abu Muhammad al-Maqdisi, as well as European lay Salafi *duʿa* such as the German convert Pierre Vogel. She also explores the interconnection between the establishment of Salafi movements in the Western diaspora, and the adjustment of *daʿwa* strategies on the one hand, and the relation between the methods and strategic priorities of different trends of the Salafi movement on the other.

Part II of this volume, *Preaching in Movement*, sheds light on the practices, methods, identity formation, and propagation of *daʿwa* by the major socioreligious Islamic call movements. In Chapter 4, Jamal Malik traces the prototypical manifestations of Islamist *daʿwa* in the strategies of Hasan al-Banna and Abu Aʿla al-Mawdudi and charts the trajectories of their respective movements: the Muslim Brothers and Jamaʿat-e Islami. He is particularly keen to demonstrate how Islamic proselytization has been integrated and harmonized with the initial ideology and early practices of these two major organizations of political Islam. Malik claims that building on the intrinsic plurality of *daʿwa*, Islamists have eventually produced a new field in an attempt to standardize the diverse array of contesting proselytizing endeavors and endow them with some legal superstructure—the field of *fiqh al-daʿwa* (jurisprudence of the mission).

In Chapter 5, Richard Gauvain draws on fieldwork done before and after the Arab Spring to explore the gradual rise and recent fall of Egyptian Salafi *daʿwa* from its beginnings in the early twentieth century to its present "televangelists." He argues that while the core Salafi messages have changed little during this time, the political contexts in which they operated earlier, and the preaching strategies they employed, have necessarily evolved. Such strategies have come to incorporate both the apocalyptic rhetoric of Sayyid Qutb and the hadith-saturated, ritual-focused scholarship of Nasir al-Din al-Albani and the global Wahhabi-Salafi movement. However, following disputes and scandals that affected the Salafi *duʿa* in post–Arab Spring Egypt, especially between the Nour party and the apolitical preachers, they have lost much of their credibility in the eyes of the public.

Thomas Gugler, in Chapter 6, explores and compares the two major rival South Asian call movements: Tablighi Jamaʿat and Daʿwat-e Islami. He points out that Tablighi missionary journeys began in the 1920s among the lowest classes, and in the late 1960s began to expand globally. Daʿwat-e Islami followed suit in the 1980s, developing an alternative system of "Medina rewards" designed to maximize salvation advantages in a neoliberal fashion. Both movements have thus focused on piety and self-improvement by turning their members into volunteer itinerant preachers, and both developed in the latter part of the twentieth century into transnational, tradition-bound faith-revival movements.

In Chapter 7, the last chapter of this part, Amatzia Baram turns our attention to the exigencies of Shiʿi proselytization, which traditionally vacillated between the activist drive to expand through conversion and the quietist tendency toward self-preservation in hostile Sunni environments. The bulk of the chapter is devoted to the Iraqi Islamic Daʿwa Party and its progenitor and ideologue Muhammad Baqir al-Sadr. Baram contends that the foundation of the party in 1957 was a response to the effective Communist propaganda among the Shiʿi youth, as well as a reflection of the influence exerted by the Sunni radical Sayyid Qutb among local Shiʿi Islamists. Its influence waned under the heavy hand of Saddam Hussein's regime and did not recover even after the U.S.-led invasion of 2003 and the subsequent election of Shiʿi governments.

Part III, *The Global and the Local*, examines the spread of Islamic preaching into other Muslim majority and minority societies, pointing to the dynamic between national and transnational settings. Julia Day Howell contrasts the stances taken by the national governments of Indonesia and Malaysia on revivalist *daʿwa* since the 1970s, as both countries were undergoing rapid economic development and social modernization. She avers that in Malaysia revivalist *daʿwa* came to be predominantly state-driven and state-constrained, whereas similar Indonesian initiatives, while also state supported, were largely civil-society generated and less constrained by government policy or surveillance. This difference resulted in a broader spectrum of revivalist thinking and organization in Indonesia, and more recently, in the postauthoritarian era, in a variety of educational and commercial *daʿwa* initiatives.

The next two chapters in this part focus on the transmission of *daʿwa* to the West. In Chapter 9, Uriya Shavit examines how the concept of spreading the word of Islam to non-Muslims provided legitimization for the massive migration to Europe in the period following World War II. Beginning with the juristic debate since Islam's early centuries about the permissibility of permanent Muslim residence in non-Muslim countries, he traces the roots of its more recent acceptance by scholars concerned with Muslims in the diaspora growing distant from their faith. Focusing on the Islamist and Salafi camps, he then charts the gradual development of the concept of *daʿwa* by Middle Eastern and, increasingly, European scholars as a means of community preservation, unity, and empowerment. Shavit finds, however, that as proselytization is ill-received in the secular European public spheres, the numerous articulations of *daʿwa* are hardly being actualized.

Elysia Guzik and Larry Poston chart similar difficulties in Chapter 10 with *daʿwa* work on the North American continent against the background of political events in the Middle East, Islamic terrorism that reached American soil on 9/11, and widely held negative perceptions of Islam in general. The chapter gives a brief history of the development of *daʿwa* in the United States and Canada and details the various Islamic outreach initiatives and the many current philosophies and strategies underlying them. As in Europe, one of these trends is the growing interest in the concept of "being witnesses for mankind," which often substitutes direct propagation. Guzik and Poston pay particular attention to the roles played in *daʿwa* activity in North America by gender distinctions, prison ministries, and the internet and conclude with predictions for the future of Islamic outreach in the Western hemisphere.

In the concluding chapter of this section, Chapter 11, Dietrich Reetz takes up the discussion of the move of the Tablighi Jamaʿat onto the global stage. He notes that the beginnings of *daʿwa* in the subcontinent were associated with the agitation of the transnational Khilafat movement in the aftermath of World War I. By contrast, the foundations for the rapid expansion of the Tabligh movement outside South Asia were laid in the 1940s and 1950s, with the extension of the travel itineraries of its preaching groups to England, the Hijaz, and Southeast Asia. Carried both by South Asian Muslim diaspora networks and by local indigenous adherents, today Tablighi *daʿwa* activity covers most countries and is arguably the largest Muslim missionary movement in the world. Reetz further emphasizes the doctrinal flexibility of the organization and examines its different roles in such diverse contexts as the Taliban's Afghanistan, Kyrgyzstan, Germany, South Africa, and Gambia.

Part IV turns to *New Directions* in the performance of *daʿwa*, whether by innovative means of outreach or novel strategies of interaction within the Muslim community and without. Aaron Rock-Singer deals in Chapter 12 with the rise in the early twenty-first century of a group of educated lay preachers, soon to become known as the "New Preachers" (*al-duʿa al-judud*). Through satellite television and the internet, they drew large audiences, while challenging both religious scholars and political elites. Their innovative message, according to Rock-Singer, was the tie between preaching, piety, and economic prosperity through a mantra of "development by faith." He traces the rise of neoliberal *daʿwa* in the Middle East by examining the vision and programs of its leading figure, the Egyptian accountant-turned-preacher Amr Khaled. Particular attention is paid to the increasing claims of religious mobilization projects benefiting economic productivity. These neoliberal projects of religious piety are compared with Islamist, Salafi, and state competitors.

Jakob Skovgaard-Petersen's chapter (13) analyzes the public perception and reflection of the *daʿi*'s role in contemporary Arab TV dramas—apparently the most influential form of cultural expression in the Arab world today. Noting that the character of the television preacher has itself become the subject of fictional treatment, Skovgaard-Petersen investigates what is considered the way to deliver *daʿwa* and how a *daʿi* should look and behave. He compares three influential fictional portraits of a *daʿi* in contemporary Egypt as a means to explore the evolution of the *daʿi* representation as religious, political, and personal role model from the late Mubarak period to al-Sisi's military takeover in 2013.

Another major direction in *daʿwa* is presented in Muhammad Al-Atawneh's chapter (14), which examines recent developments and changes in the Wahhabi doctrine and practice of Islamic dissemination. He argues that following 9/11 official Wahhabi *daʿwa* broke from its traditional monolithic discourse of exclusivism toward recognition of other cultures and nations. Al-Atawneh analyzes the official statements and websites of established Saudi-sponsored call organizations such as the World Muslim League, as well as new initiatives such as the King Abdulaziz Center for National Dialogue (KACND) and King Abdullah bin Abdulaziz International Centre for Interreligious and Intercultural Dialogue (KAICIID), to demonstrate Saudi Arabia's new approach to the (Muslim and non-Muslim) Other. The new Wahhabi message is that it no longer subscribes to simply delivering "the truth" to the ignorant Muslim and non-Muslim but stands for mutual understanding.

In the last chapter of the book (15) Adam Hoffman examines the changing importance of *daʿwa* in Salafi-Jihadi discourse since the Arab uprisings of 2011. He maintains that the new political opportunities that presented themselves in the Middle East and North Africa following the events of the Arab Spring led many Salafi-Jihadis to reconsider their rejection of *daʿwa* and to incorporate it in their activities. Focusing on the two organizations of the Islamic State (ISIS) and Jabhat al-Nusra, al-Qaeda's arm in Syria, Hoffman shows that while ISIS focused entirely on jihad and presented a harsh and uncompromising interpretation of Islam, Jabhat al-Nusra used "soft power" to enhance its outreach and integrate the group into the local population. While leading ideologues such as Usama bin Laden and Ayman al-Zawahiri argued for years that "the jihad movement must come closer to the masses" and engage in civic activities, it was only after the regional events of the Arab Spring, and the resulting regional instability, that such public preaching by Salafi-Jihadi organizations could be effected.

FURTHER RESEARCH

We cannot purport to have covered all aspects of such a broad topic as modern Islamic *daʿwa*. Neither could we refer to all regions of the Muslim world, all its call movements, and all individual preachers. However, we do hope that this book will provide an impetus for research in a hitherto relatively neglected field and spark a scholarly and public debate over the symbolic and material processes through which a religiously inspired citizenry negotiates its politics, modernity, and globality. It is our belief that a systematic, multidimensional, and comparative study of *daʿwa* such as this is bound to elucidate the role of inward and outward propagation in the overall religious economy of Islam.

Examining the workings of the Islamic culture of preaching in the public sphere will enhance our understanding of the assortment of ideologies, strategies, organizations, and networks that together constitute the contemporary resurgence of Islam against the backdrop of the major questions of the compatibility of religion, modernity, secularism, identity, and agency. A perspective study of Islamic *daʿwa* in conjunction with missionary work in other religions, most notably Christianity and Hinduism, or the Jewish Teshuva movement, will yield further significant results regarding the role of politics, neoliberal economy, and social media in the ongoing deprivatization of religion and "the return of the gods." Weighing the balance between the elements of *daʿwa* and jihad in local and global Islamic arenas may also assist politicians in the core Muslim regions as well as in Western Europe and North America to adopt more reliable policies toward various Islamic organizations. It may even be of some use for those Muslims engaged in *daʿwa* by making them aware of the dangers of overzealous preaching and pointing to more agreeable and peaceful methods through intra- and interfaith dialogue.

PART I

Discourses of Daʿwa

CHAPTER 1

The Making of the Modern Arab Daʿwa Discursive Field

ITZCHAK WEISMANN

DAʿWA—THE "CALL" or missionary work in Islam—reemerged as a major Islamic strategy at the beginning of the twentieth century. Its renewal was a product of the Muslim encounter with the West in general and its engagement with Christian missionary activity in particular. While proselytization among non-Muslims was never relinquished, the modern variants of *daʿwa* have more often focused on Muslims themselves, a shift of gravity that reflects anxiety over the influence of the secular West and a desire to bring straying Muslims back into the fold of Islam.[1] The means employed were greatly expanded to include not only preaching and persuasion but also education, propaganda, and social work.[2] By the end of the twentieth century, with the introduction of cassette tapes and then satellite TV, the internet, and social media, a plurality of *daʿwa* forms had become ubiquitous in both the Muslim world and Muslim diasporas in the West.[3] Though habitually overshadowed by the violent excesses of jihad, Islamic preaching remains the backbone of modern Islamic collective action.

The present chapter seeks to trace the emergence and evolution of *daʿwa* as a socioreligious discursive field in the Arab-Muslim world over the course of the past century. Taking a chronological approach, I analyze and compare the utterances of major participants in the *daʿwa* discourse in each of its three principal phases: the founding generation of Islamists and Salafis (ca. 1910s–1950s); the transnational scholars and organizations of the 1950s and 1960s; and the variety of proponents of the call in the contemporary global Islamic revival from the 1970s to the present.

THE FORMATIVE PERIOD, CA. 1910S–1950S

The early modernist Islamic reformers struggled to assimilate Western ideas and institutions without losing their religious identity and authenticity. For them, propagating Islam—*daʿwa*—either to non-Muslims or within the Muslim community was not a priority.[4]

Rashid Rida, editor of the famous pan-Islamic journal *al-Manar*, belonged to that generation but lived long enough to witness the disintegration of the Ottoman Empire, the catastrophe of World War I, the imposition of colonial rule over the Arab world, and the abolition of the Caliphate. Rida's new conceptualization of *daʿwa* was spelled out in *al-Manar*'s exegesis on Quran 3:104: "Let there arise out of you a band of people inviting to all that is good, enjoining what is right, and forbidding what is wrong: They are the ones to attain felicity." In it he stresses that in the present situation, *daʿwa* has become a personal duty imposed on each and every believer (*fard ʿayn*) and that it must be directed not only at non-Muslims but first and foremost at fellow Muslims.[5]

Not content with mere words, in 1912 Rida founded Dar al-Daʿwa wa'l-Irshad (Institute of Preaching and Guidance), which, modeled on missionary lines, was designed to create a body of *duʿa* knowledgeable in both religious and contemporary sciences. He hoped they would attain official posts in the state apparatus and be consulted by policy makers. The Institute operated for two years but eventually failed to achieve its goals.[6]

Rida was a major source of inspiration both for Hasan al-Banna, founder of the Society of the Muslim Brothers, who frequented his circle in Cairo,[7] and for Muhammad Hamid al-Fiqi and his associates in the Salafi association Ansar al-Sunna al-Muhammadiyya most of whom had attended Dar al-Daʿwa wa'l-Irshad.[8] Banna's principal achievement was to give Rida's ideas a modern organizational form and to mobilize people behind them. For him the concept of *daʿwa* defined his organization, its methods of propaganda for the re-Islamization of society, the ideology that animated it, and ultimately Islam itself.[9] Fiqi's work institutionalized Rida's alliance with the House of Saud and helped to rehabilitate Wahhabism. From their point of view, the Wahhabi call was indeed the prototype of Islamic *daʿwa*.

Banna's concept of *daʿwa* was consolidated through his actual experiences in Ismailiyya, where he was posted after graduating from teachers' seminary in Cairo. In his autobiography, he relates how after school he would frequent coffee houses and street corners and call on the people to return to Islam.[10] From this, the Society of the Muslim Brothers was founded in 1928, and within a decade it would become the largest political organization in Egypt. The theme of *daʿwa* was further elaborated and disseminated among the rank and file through Banna's authoritative collection of edited sermons, *Majmuʿat Rasaʾil*, which were basic reading in the society's meetings.

In *Our Mission*, his programmatic essay from the mid-1930s, included in *Majmuʿat Rasaʾil*, Banna emphasizes that the Muslim Brothers' call is pure and unselfish, animated by feelings of faith in God and love for the people, and demanding self-sacrifice with no compensation. It is embedded in a unifying, comprehensive Islamic ideology, set against the other ideologies (also defined as *daʿawat*) of modern times—patriotism (*wataniyya*), nationalism (*qaumiyya*), and their like, which are partial and divisive. In order to reach the hearts and minds of the people, Banna warns, the Islamic *duʿa* must stand up to the educated, well-equipped, trained, and professional propagators of the competing ideologies and employ the most advanced means of propaganda, from books and magazines to theaters and radio. It is time, then, for the Muslim Brothers to treat the ills of the *umma* through an adequate program carried out by faithful activists under a reliable and resolute leadership.[11]

In another epistle from this period—*To What We Call the People*—Banna further explains that the Muslim Brothers' goal is to bring happiness in this world by guiding humanity to the correct order, which is the sound teachings of Islam. He has no difficulty admitting that this is a political call, so long as it is based on the Quran, "the book of God," and the Sunna, the way of the Prophet. Here we find the first component in Banna's famous multidimensional definition of the Muslim Brothers as *daʿwa salafiyya*.[12] Yet he also points out, "God ordained waging jihad for His sake in spreading and universalizing this *daʿwa* among the people by demonstration and proof, and if they persist in their injustice, oppression, and rebelliousness, then by the sword and the spearhead." The Muslim Brothers' call for united and dedicated action on the basis of the principles of Islam is, therefore, the foundation of its modern revival.[13]

Reflecting on these ideas, and in light of the rise of fascism and the eruption of World War II, Banna asserts in his 1942 essay *Our Mission in a New Stage* that the Muslim Brothers' *daʿwa* is designed to reestablish the spiritual connection between man and his Lord against the failing materialism of the West and to create a just human brotherhood without regard for race or color. Referring to the ideological ferment in Egypt at this time,[14] he likewise stresses the comprehensive nature of this call, which encompasses Egyptian patriotism, though not the pharaonic ideology; Pan-Arabism; Oriental solidarity despite its ephemerality as merely a designation of the non-Occident; and the unity of mankind, which is Islam's ultimate goal. The fundamental principle of Islamic *daʿwa* according to Banna is free thinking within the framework of Islam rather than imitation of the West. It must begin with the individual and the family before turning to the nation and humanity at large. Its practical means is in service to the people by building schools and libraries, establishing running clubs and sports teams, commemorating Islamic holidays, and engaging in social work and arbitration.[15]

Muhammad Hamid al-Fiqi's concept of *daʿwa* was shaped in reference to the Wahhabi mission. The pre–World War I modernist Salafis shared the Wahhabi critique of the Islamic tradition in general, and of popular practices associated with Sufism in particular. Indeed, the beginnings of this trend were closely related to the rediscovery of the medieval Hanbali theologian Ahmad ibn Taymiyya (1263–1328), and the rehabilitation of his premodern Wahhabi followers. Still, the concept of *daʿwa* rarely comes up in the works of early Salafis.[16] This changed in 1926 when Fiqi, together with other students of Rida, founded Ansar al-Sunna al-Muhammadiyya association. Its leading members, most of them ulama graduated from al-Azhar, were invited during the 1920s and 1930s to assist in modernizing Saudi Arabia's religious and educational systems and thereafter maintained close ties with the Wahhabi scholars.[17]

For Fiqi, Wahhabism presented the ideal type of modern-day *daʿwa*. This is conveyed in the very title of his major treatise: *The Effect of the Wahhabi Call on Religious and Cultural Reform in the Arab Peninsula and Beyond*, published in 1935 and based on his lectures and discussions at the Ansar al-Sunna al-Muhammadiyah club in Cairo.[18] It is likewise apparent in the association's stated principles and goals from its semiofficial history, which are practically identical to those of the Wahhabis. They include the call to accept God's absolute unity (*tawhid*) purified of all forms of polytheism (*shirk*), to love the Prophet and follow his example, to rely solely on the Quran and Sunna, and to eschew innovations and novelties (*bidaʿ wa-muhaddathat al-umur*).[19]

Through his treatise, Fiqi aims to "clarify the truth of the Wahhabi mission and its leader, followers, and supporters . . . and remove the delusions, falsehoods, errors, and lies that surround them."[20] He accordingly begins with an exposition of the major Wahhabi teachings, then moves to

Ibn Abd al-Wahhab's (1703–1792) biography, and concludes with the contribution of the House of Saud to the cause. Within this general framework several observations are in order for the assessment of Fiqi's concept of *daʿwa*. One is his remark that in view of the principles of the Wahhabi mission it is more appropriate to give its *daʿwa* the title of Salafiyya Muhammadiyya.[21] Another is that Fiqi describes the endeavors of previous ulama such as Ibn Taymiyya and his disciple Ibn Qayyim al-Jawziyya (1292–1350) to advance these same teachings as jihad, in its general sense of effort, rather than as *daʿwa*.[22] This seems to imply that for him *daʿwa* applied to religious movements rather than individual preachers. On the other hand, the ulama who opposed the Wahhabi mission are depicted as *duʿa al-su'*—the callers of evil—and their incitement of the Ottoman government to fight it as *diʿaya siyasiyya*—political propaganda. From Fiqi's viewpoint *daʿwa* has thus come to denote a pietist Islamic movement, the best example of which is the Central Arabian Salafi Wahhabi movement.[23]

SYSTEMATIZATION AND TRANSNATIONALIZATION, 1950S AND 1960S

The takeover by revolutionary Pan-Arab regimes in the wake of independence spelled persecution for the Society of the Muslim Brothers in Egypt, Syria, and Iraq and a political threat to conservative kingdoms such as Saudi Arabia. The Muslim Brotherhood was consequently divided between radicals, who in the footsteps of Sayyid Qutb adopted the course of jihad against tyrannical rule at the expense of *daʿwa* and moderates who stuck to the original call of Hasan al-Banna.[24] To the latter camp belonged the Egyptian ulama Muhammad al-Ghazali and Yusuf al-Qaradawi who strove to fortify the *daʿwa* by establishing it as a modern scientific field. The Saudi reaction to the rise of Nasser's Arabism was to foster an Islamic counterideology, centered on the Wahhabi-Salafi creed, and to sponsor an array of transnational *daʿwa* organizations, most notably the Islamic University in Medina and the World Muslim League, which were designed to spread the call throughout the Muslim world.[25]

Both Ghazali and Qaradawi had joined the Muslim Brotherhood during their studies at al-Azhar, were very active in the organization in their youths, and remained sympathetic to the cause and its ideas for the rest of their lives. Ghazali, however, was expelled from the organization in 1953 due to disagreements with Hasan al-Hudaybi, Banna's successor as General Guide, and he established himself as an independent *ʿalim*.[26] The decade-younger Qaradawi relocated to Qatar in 1961, where he gradually built a reputation as the "global mufti."[27] The popularity of the two in Egypt and internationally was largely based on the balance they had managed to strike between the role of the *ʿalim* and that of the *daʿi*.

In *On the Procession of the Call*, Ghazali's first work dedicated to Islamic *daʿwa*, the concept itself is still indeterminate.[28] Published in 1954, two years after the Free Officers' revolution and one year after his break with the Muslim Brothers' leadership, the book was directed against what he regarded as Hudaybi's timidity. The *duʿa*, Ghazali declares, must advance proposals for Islamic reform and lead the struggle against the political and social heresy embodied in the injustice of the rulers and the feudal lords. Derisively likening the Brothers' "procession of the Islamic *daʿwa*" to a frivolous Sufi parade, and those at the helm of the organization to a fifth column for other ideologies (*nahadat*), Ghazali sought to clarify the Islamic view on the various issues facing the Muslim Brotherhood. None of these, however, referred to Islamic *daʿwa* as such.[29]

In contrast, the 1965 *With God: Studies on the Call and the Callers* is a systematic exposition of the scientific field of *daʿwa*.[30] In the preamble, Ghazali explains that this is a professional book designed for *duʿa*, rather than the common people, and that it is based on his lectures in the law faculty at the University of al-Azhar.[31] For Ghazali, the formation of the Islamic *umma* depends on the formation of its *duʿa*. He likewise stresses, in line with the earlier work, that the dangers surrounding Islam and the might of its rivals concern him less. What terrifies him is deviation and the weakening of faith among the Muslims themselves.[32]

Befitting a religious, scientific work, Ghazali begins with the definition of *daʿwa* on the basis of its repeated mention in the Quran and the logic of the messages of the prophets, especially Muhammad's. Accordingly, it is "a comprehensive program (*barnamaj*) encompassing all the knowledge men need for realizing the purpose of their lives and seeking out the signposts (*maʿalim al-tariq*) that will put them on the right path."[33] Such a program has become particularly urgent in modern times, in which the circulation of different materialist ideologies that deny or ignore God has brought devastating wars, anxiety, and senseless hedonism. It is therefore incumbent upon the Muslim *umma*, who received the message from the Prophet, to spread it to all mankind. Consonant with modernist ideology, Ghazali maintains that this was the practice of the righteous ancestors (*al-salaf al-salih*), which was later neglected due to several factors that must be corrected: lack of adequate organs of propaganda (here he has Christianity and its missionaries in mind), neglect of Arabic language and literature, and divisive scholarly disagreements.[34]

The Muslim science of *daʿwa* is posed against that of the Orientalists, who claim that Islam was spread through conquest and persecution. This even holds true for T. W. Arnold, whom Ghazali singles out for his fair treatment of the subject, but who still maintained that along with preaching there has also been oppression.[35] Arnold was indeed ready to admit that similar cases of violence occurred in the Christian mission (also referred to as *daʿwa*), but for Ghazali this does not justify the assertion that it happened in Islam too.[36] According to him, the Muslim preacher is characterized by his bond to Allah, self-correction, and accurate understanding of both religion and worldly affairs. He must act out of sincere devotion, audacity, and wide knowledge. His principal means are setting a good example through moral deeds, education and reiteration of the truth of Islam, preaching in the mosque and in the classroom, relating religious stories that attract hearts, and writing directed at minds. His provisions are the Quran, the Sunna of the Prophet, and the example of the Rightly Guided Caliphs and other Muslims great and small.[37]

These ideas are complemented by Qaradawi's *The Culture of the Caller*, which focuses on the *daʿiya* himself.[38] The book is based on a lecture he gave at the first international conference on the direction of *daʿwa* and preparation of *duʿa* organized by the Islamic University in Medina in 1977. For Qaradawi, *daʿwa* is the mission of the prophets and their heirs, the righteous ulama. It is second in importance only to belief in God and therefore requires strong *duʿa*, well equipped with faith, morality, and appropriate knowledge and culture.[39] This is to be derived not only from Islam's authentic sources—the Quran, the Sunna, and the religious sciences—but also history, the humanities, modern science, and the contemporary world should also be considered. The *daʿiya* must procure intellectual and spiritual support from the Quran, pay particular attention to the Prophet's practical example in the sound hadith, have some knowledge of Islamic Law, theology, and Sufism. Moreover, the *daʿiya* should study in depth the Islamic order (*al-nizam al-islami*), namely the view of Islam as a comprehensive and all-encompassing system, as taught by Banna and other Islamist thinkers and activists.[40] Likewise, he must, with all due precaution and in Islamic spirit, study the history of the worldwide and Arab *jahiliyya* (pre-Islamic era of barbarity); the Islamic renewal and reform movements and the role of Islam in anticolonial movements; take an interest in psychology, sociology, pedagogy, and the natural sciences; and last but not least be aware of the present realities of the Muslim world, the international forces opposing it, the different religions and ideologies it faces, and the various Islamic movements and institutions and their *daʿwa*.[41]

The Islamic University of Medina and the Muslim World League were founded in quick succession in 1961 and 1962. Both sought to spread Islam in general—and its Wahhabi-Salafi version in particular—around the globe. Presiding over them were the heads of the Saudi religious establishment: the Grand Mufti Muhammad ibn Ibrahim and his successor, the president of the Committee of Senior Scholars (*Hayʾat Kibar al-ʿUlama*) Abd al-Aziz ibn Baz. In both institutions, however, non-Wahhabis played a conspicuous role. Most of the faculty at the Islamic University of Medina—dominating all disciplines apart from theology—belonged to various Islamic trends worldwide, including Muslim Brothers and other Islamists.[42] Most members of the Constituent Council of The Muslim World League—initially to be named the World League for the Islamic Daʿwa—were well-known Islamist public figures such as the South Asians Abu al-Aʿla al-Mawdudi and Abu al-Hasan al-Nadwi, the Moroccan Allal al-Fasi, and Hasan al-Banna's son-in-law Saʿid Ramadan, who had settled in Switzerland.[43]

The main feature of the concept of *daʿwa* represented by these and similar successive organizations, such as the World Assembly of Muslim Youth founded in 1972, was their emphatic transnationalism. The official declaration of the foundation of the Islamic University of Medina by King Saud in May 1961 read,

> I am duty bound to serve the two Holy Mosques and start to extend the message of Islam to all areas of the globe. In pursuance of this objective, I have ordered the establishment of the Islamic University at al-Madina al-Munawara, the burial-ground of the Prophet, may God bless him. I have ordered that all means be made available to enable this University to carry out its eminent message, and I have brought in several Muslim ulama from several countries to draw up all the necessary programs, regulations, and curricula for the University.

The charter of the Muslim World League, which asserted its role as a popular organization, likewise states: "We, the members of the Muslim

World League representing the Muslim world with respect to belief and faith, obligate ourselves with God—most exalted—to fulfill the duty God has imposed on us to teach his message (*tabligh risalatihi*) and spread it in all parts of the world."[44]

ISLAMIC REVIVAL AND GLOBALIZATION, 1970S–PRESENT

The decline of Arabism in the aftermath of the Six Day War on the one hand, and the establishment of Muslim communities in Western Europe and North America on the other, precipitated the revival and universalization of the Islamic call. In Egypt, though not in Syria or Iraq, the mainstream Muslim Brotherhood was allowed to renew its activity around its new magazine, *al-Daʿwa*,[45] while in Saudi Arabia the Committee of Senior Scholars struggled to define in its fatwas the rules for preaching Islam domestically and abroad. In the space between the Muslim Brotherhood and the Committee of Senior Scholars, Muhammad Qutb strove to reestablish *daʿwa* through merging a pragmatic interpretation of his brother's teachings with the original Wahhabism, while Abdallah Azzam and Abu Muhammad al-Maqdisi opted for a radical interpretation that subordinated *daʿwa* to the requirements of a global jihad.

In contrast, the successive popular Egyptian preachers Muhammad Mutawali al-Shaʿrawi and Amr Khaled exploited the emerging new media to enhance Islamic civil life at home. Their more academic counterparts Ismaʿil al-Faruqi and Tariq Ramadan used *daʿwa* to shape the attitudes of Muslim communities toward their host societies in the West. And Hasan al-Banna's grandson Jamal reinvented *daʿwa* as a unique liberal Islamic strategy.

The resumption of *daʿwa* as the cornerstone of the mainstream Muslim Brotherhood was indicated by General Guide Hudaybi in his 1969 legal/theological response to the Qutbists under the telling title *Preachers . . . Not Judges* [of fellow Muslims].[46] The leading ideologues of the movement then shouldered the programmatic task of charting the guidelines for renewal. Giving considerable thought to the organizational flaws that made the Muslim Brothers easy prey to oppressive governments, and partially appropriating Qutb's vocabulary of jihad against today's *jahiliyya*, these authors nevertheless reconfirmed their loyalty to Banna's original teachings and explored the means for adapting them to the new realities in their diverse respective countries, as well as the Arab-Muslim world at large.[47]

The Egyptian Mustafa Mashhur, a major contributor to *al-Daʿwa* and a future General Guide, reminded his readers that Banna had clarified the signposts—another critical reference to Qutb's contested manifesto—and stressed that they should not be transgressed. According to Mashhur, Banna had forewarned against the twist of *takfir* (labeling other Muslims unbelievers) decades before the radicals adopted it and against attempts to win quick results without due preparation.[48] From the Society's bitter experience under the Nasserist regime he further emphasizes that the way of *daʿwa* demands forbearance and sacrifice.[49] In the series of articles entitled "The Youth Ask: What Are We Required to Do Now," Mashhur answers, "Our motto at this stage is: correct yourself and call others." The caller to God must be aware of the obligatory nature of *daʿwa*, preach from a position of strength and knowledge, and be a model in his behavior, lenient and considerate in his method, and truthful in his word.[50]

For Fathi Yakan, the founder and leader of al-Jamaʿa al-Islamiyya in Lebanon, *daʿwa* in the current circumstances is not just a duty incumbent on each Muslim (*fard ʿayn*). Yakan also contends that the trials and tribulations (*mihna*) surrounding it are actually necessary and the guarantee of its success.[51] Addressing the organizational weaknesses of the Islamist *daʿwa*, Yakan translates Banna's threefold scheme of action into individual phases that proceed from inculcating faith, the establishment of an Islamic way of life, and recruitment for the movement.[52]

Saʿid Hawwa, chief ideologue of the Syrian Muslim Brothers under the Hafiz al-Asad regime, suggested establishing a network of *daʿwa* study circles to deliver a comprehensive program combining the religious sciences—scholarly and Sufi—with the realities of the contemporary world. Summing up his comrades' renewed commitment to *daʿwa*, he wrote,

> If the *daʿwa* to God is in itself the goal, it is also the means to all other goals such as purification of the soul, constitution of the Muslim personality, [and] existence of the Muslim family, the Muslim society, and the Islamic state, locally and worldwide. All these depend on *daʿwa* and on its success. The rightful efforts exerted on its path determine the measure of fulfillment of the goals that glorious and exalted God imposed on his servants. Therefore, *daʿwa* must be given priority like no other thing.[53]

The accelerated opening of the Saudi state to the outside world in the wake of the oil boom, and the concomitant rising challenge of Islamic radicalism, have likewise led to new emphases in the Wahhabi-Salafi concept of *daʿwa*. Ibn Baz and his colleagues on the Committee of Senior Scholars repeat time and again in their fatwas that the call to God must be performed with knowledge and wisdom and through pleasant speech rather than harsh words, anger, and violence. In their judgment, *daʿwa* and its corollary of commanding right and forbidding wrong, is a collective duty (*fard kifaya*), rather than an individual one, and entails such great responsibility that only rulers, ulama, and people of religious distinction may engage in it. In apparent contradiction, they also stress that a good Muslim should never miss an opportunity to perform this duty, and that it is particularly important to take *daʿwa* to the newspapers and magazines to counter secular ideas and object to the abominable pictures of women they publish.[54]

A mediating position between the Islamist and Salafi conceptualizations of *daʿwa* is represented in the work of Sayyid Qutb's younger brother Muhammad. Leaving Egypt following the amnesty given to the Muslim Brothers by President Sadat, Muhammad Qutb found refuge in Saudi Arabia, where he was appointed as a professor at Umm al-Qura University in Mecca. He educated generations of students on the combination of a moderate interpretation of Sayyid's radicalism and the Wahhabi creed, which earned him the sobriquet *shaykh al-sahwa* (spiritual leader of the [Saudi Islamic] awakening).[55] Through this combination, the performance of *daʿwa* is subject to pragmatic considerations. In *How to Invite the People to Islam* (2001), Muhammad Qutb embraces his brother's concept of *jahiliyya*, though for him this includes not only human-made Western laws but also the Wahhabi *bête noire* of visiting tombs.[56] The text likewise considers secularism as well as the theological doctrine of *irjaʾ* (suspension of judgement), to which Banna's followers subscribe but the Hanbali tradition vehemently rejects.[57] Qutb maintains that the Islamic movement's situation today resembles, indeed is even graver than, that of the early Muslim community in Mecca and must therefore follow the precedent of the pious forefathers in enduring persecution with patience and forbearance and concentrate on *daʿwa*—with wisdom and good admonition—rather than on violence and *takfir*. Rebellion in the present situation, he warns, is illegitimate in the eyes of the public and will lead to destruction. Yet jihad will come when circumstances change, just as it did after the emigration to Medina, when Islamic teachings crystallized, the solid base was formed,[58] and a firm unitarian community was established.[59]

In the thought and action of the Palestinian radicals Dr. Abdallah Azzam and Abu Muhammad al-Maqdisi, jihad takes center stage. Azzam, father of the Afghan jihad and spiritual mentor of Osama Bin Laden, joined the Muslim Brotherhood as a youth in the West Bank and came under the influence of Sayyid Qutb's teaching while completing his studies in Islamic law at al-Azhar. Settling in Peshawar, with Bin Laden's help he set up the Bureau of Services, which organized, trained, and indoctrinated the Arab volunteers.[60] Maqdisi, the erstwhile mentor and colleague of ISIS's progenitor Abu Musʿab al-Zarqawi, grew up in a Salafi environment in Kuwait, and acquainted himself with Wahhabi teachings at the Islamic University of Medina. He too went to Peshawar where he engaged not in combat but in teaching.[61] For both men, however, *daʿwa* is an integral component of jihad.

Azzam stresses in *Words from the First Front Line* that both the call to Islam and actual fighting are necessary for the success of global jihad.[62] Contrary to Muhammad Qutb, his main lesson from the Prophet's example in Mecca and Medina is that *daʿwa* may endanger the Muslim community when unaccompanied by physical struggle, though for him too waging jihad without proper Islamic education is conducive to crime and self-destruction. Moreover, unlike Fathi Yakan and his fellow Muslim Brothers, Azzam believed that *daʿwa* itself involves not mere passive suffering but active self-sacrifice, just as jihad does. In *The Religion of Abraham* (1984), Maqdisi is more concerned with the reluctance of preachers to confront un-Islamic rulers—among whom he counts the Saudi royal family—on such grounds as preventing disorder (*fitna*) and damaging the interests of the community.[63] Following Juhayman al-Utaybi, leader of the messianic group that took over the sanctuary of Mecca in 1979, Maqdisi calls his fellow *duʿa* to take an example from Abraham's argument with his polytheist people and declare "open enmity and disavowal (*al-baraʾ*) toward the disbelievers and their deities and their false legislations."[64] For him, *daʿwa* is an important tool in the struggle against disbelieving Muslim rulers and the means to consolidate the achievements of jihad.

In their *daʿwa*, the popular Egyptian preachers Muhammad Mutawali al-Shaʿrawi and Amr Khaled, and also Qaradawi in his later years, combine personal charisma with skillful utilization of the new media. Shaykh Shaʿrawi, a graduate of al-Azhar who served as minister of religious affairs under Sadat, gained enormous fame in the 1970s due to his frequent appearances on national radio and television. Amr Khaled, an accountant by profession and the most prominent figure among "the new lay preachers" (*al-duʿa al-judud*), followed suit in the 1990s.[65] Influenced by both Shaʿrawi and Ghazali, he expanded his appeal beyond Egypt to other Arab countries and the United Kingdom through satellite television and the internet.[66] For both preachers, *daʿwa* was largely "disobjectified" in the sense that they were less interested in the conceptualization of *daʿwa* and more in its actual practice.[67] Shaʿrawi's appeal to the masses lay in his treatment of the problems of daily life in simple terms and colloquial language and in his endorsement of popular "traditional" beliefs and practices such as the reality of miracles and *jinn*.[68]

Amr Khaled's popularity rests on his endorsement of a combination of personal piety and economic prosperity, and on his eloquent use of *taswir*, a style of communication that brings to life historical scenes from the Quran and the hadith.[69]

In Shaʿrawi's *Foundations of the Call*—his only explicit treatment of the subject—*daʿwa* is ultimately synonymous with Islam.[70] The book begins with a brief definition of Islam, followed by a detailed exposition of such basic issues as the five pillars, the principal articles of faith, and legal punishments (*hudud*), along with various contemporary issues of political, socioeconomic, and gender import. In between, a few chapters are dedicated to *daʿwa* in its more specific meaning. Like Ghazali, Shaʿrawi dismisses the claim, which he attributes to the enemies' machinations, that Islam was spread by the sword, while sharing the Islamists' belief that its weakness today is a result of the forces of oppression and the estrangement of Muslims from their religion.[71] To convey the importance of *daʿwa*, Shaʿrawi refers to the Quranic story of "the inhabitants of the city" (*ashab al-qariya*; Quran 36:13–32), one of the peoples that rejected the prophets sent to warn them. He points out that it was the men of influence and power who led the fight against God's messengers,[72] that although the call was proclaimed peacefully and without coercion it was met with threats of torture and death, and that despite all difficulties the procession of *daʿwa* on God's path (*manhaj*) will never stop.[73] The discussion concludes with the properties of the *daʿiya* in the Quran: clear-sightedness and tenderness, patience and uprightness, modesty and bravery.

Daʿwa is mentioned even more rarely in Amr Khaled's publications; the only time the term occurs in a major work is in the Ramadan 2007 TV series, *The Call to Live Together*, where it bears a peculiar meaning. Rather than a call to Islam as such, the twenty-four-part series relates episodes from the lives of the founders of the four schools of law, aiming to promote common values among family, friends, and society, as well as coexistence with the West.[74]

The late American scholar Ismail Raji al-Faruqi and the British-based professor Tariq Ramadan combined their academic credentials with active participation in conferences and interfaith meetings to adapt *daʿwa* to the new realities of the Muslim diaspora in the West.[75] Faruqi, a Palestinian refugee from 1948, earned his doctorate in philosophy at the University of Indiana in 1952, following which he studied Islam at al-Azhar. He settled in the United States, where he was appointed professor of Islamic studies and the history of religions at Temple University.[76] Tariq Ramadan, a grandson of Hasan al-Banna and son of Saʿid Ramadan, founder of the influential Islamic Center in Geneva, was born in Switzerland, studied philosophy and French literature, and wrote his doctoral dissertation on his grandfather at the University of Geneva in 1998. Considered one of the most prominent, as well as controversial, Muslim intellectuals in the West, he is presently Professor of Islamic Studies at St. Antony's College, Oxford.[77] Both present conceptualizations of *daʿwa* that are designed to give meaning and provide guidance for the Muslim communities in Western Europe and North America.

For Faruqi, *daʿwa* constitutes the only justification for Muslims to immigrate to and stay in the West. The concept of "the call unto the path of Allah" in his posthumously published collection of essays with the telling title *Islam and Other Faiths* is nevertheless equivocal.[78] On the one hand, Faruqi likens *daʿwa* to "a kind of academic seminar," or rather a public sphere, "in which men are free to present and argue their religious causes with one another" through a critical rational process of intellection. But on the other hand, his understanding of interreligious relations is based on the theological proposition that Islam is *din al-fitra*—the original and first religion, against which all other religions are to be judged. Islam thus represents the ultimate truth, and its *daʿwa*, although described as ecumenical, is nothing but "the call of man to return to himself, to what is innate in him."[79] From this angle, Faruqi can declare condescendingly that "the marvel of the spread of Islam" testifies to a divine plan for the salvation of the West from its spiritual bankruptcy, while the Islamic vision of the Muslim immigrants is apt to free them of their identity crisis and guilt complex, give them a sense of mission, and make them realize that they are instruments for calling non-Muslims to Islam.[80]

By Ramadan's formulation, *da'wa* is turned into the main tool in the integration of Western Muslims into their societies. In his 2004 essay, *Da'wa in the West*, he reminds his coreligionists, "Bearing witness to the truth" is especially important in the secular West and must begin with one's own family and relatives who live in this environment.[81] To Faruqi's statement about Islam as the human being's original state, Ramadan adds an emphasis on human brotherhood. Thus, "We should develop in our heart an affection towards every man and woman even if they are not Muslims" and avoid "being judge but rather genuine callers, *du'at*," which brings to mind Hudaybi's stricture against Qutb's radicalism. Ramadan is certain that knowledge will lead to people freely choosing Islam, and that in the circumstances prevailing in the West, which, like the Prophet's Mecca should be defined as *dar al-da'wa*, the best call is to bear witness (*shahada*) to the truth and act as a model of love and justice rather than to speak much. For this purpose, Ramadan concludes, "We need to live among the people, to be in touch with them and not to be isolated from the society we live in."[82]

Last but not least, Hasan al-Banna's younger brother, Jamal, rejects all present forms of *da'wa* in favor of a liberal version of the call. An extremely prolific writer who lived his entire life in Egypt, Jamal al-Banna augmented his basic religious education with vast reading in the traditional as well as modern sciences. In *Strategy of the Islamic Call in the Twenty-First Century*, he accepts the general view of the bleak condition of the Muslim world, more especially of the Islamic call, which is forced to fight both the Western powers and its own people.[83] Lumping the conservatives of al-Azhar, the Shi'i institutions of learning (*hawza*), and the Saudi universities together with Islamic movements such as the Muslim Brotherhood, he argues that all have failed because they are oriented toward the past instead of the future.[84] Against them, and apparently in reference to Sayyid Qutb's *taswir*, Banna bases his *Call for Islamic Revival* on *tathwir*, a style of "provoking" using the Quran as a tool for the enlightenment of man and the building of a new society. This will generate a new understanding of Islam, which, in the spirit of Islamic Modernism and its *wasati* (middle way) sequence, will make room for the civilizational values of science, justice, freedom, and gender equality, while adhering to the fundamental Quranic values that the Salafis and the conservatives have distorted.[85] It is to be propagated through the public sphere rather than by political revolution, and should address a popular audience in simple language, rather than focus on academic niceties or religious disputations.[86]

CONCLUSION

Daʿwa has established itself over the past century as a major strategy in the revival of Islam. The roots of today's Islamic call lie in the work of the Modernist-Salafi Rashid Rida at the beginning of the twentieth century. His ideas were taken up after World War I by students and followers who were responsible for establishing the two major trends of the modern Arab-Islamic revival: the Society of the Muslim Brothers and the Wahhabi-allied Salafiyya. *Daʿwa* received a further boost after independence, with the rise of authoritarian-populist regimes and the eruption of the Arab Cold War, as Azharite ulama associated with the persecuted Muslim Brotherhood and Saudi-sponsored transnational organizations elaborated and systematized the call. *Daʿwa* became universal following the Islamic awakening, starting in the 1970s, as the partly rehabilitated Muslim Brothers and Wahhabi-Salafis were joined by official and independent ulama, radical jihadists, and popular lay preachers, as well as Western academics abroad and liberal activists at home. Together, and in constant debate over questions of content and methodology, such Islamic preachers and activists continue to shape the ongoing discursive field of modern Islamic *daʿwa*.

CHAPTER 2

Discourse(s) of Daʿwa in Postcolonial India

HILAL AHMED

THE DOMINANCE OF the secularism/communalism debate in postcolonial India has resulted in a static and fixed official imagination of Islam as the religion of a constitutionally protected minority. The minoritization of Islam in independent India has not only paved the way for a different kind of legal-constitutional Muslim politics but has also reshaped current Islamic religious discourses. Within this framework, ideas of *daʿwa* have been redefined and reconstituted in a variety of ways in order to adjust to the limits set by the evolving discourse of minority rights.

This chapter addresses two related principal questions. First, how is it possible to make sense of an Islamic religiosity that concentrates mainly on the propagation of Islam among Muslims while deliberately dissociating itself from the controversial issue of religious conversion of non-Muslims? Second, how has the normative sphere of Islam been reconceptualized in light of this stated adherence to a restricted form of *daʿwa*? To answer these questions, we must consider some broader conceptual and empirical issues. One concerns the possibility of reconstituting Islamic *daʿwa* projects in a national society based on the broad principles of mutual coexistence envisioned respectively by M. K. Gandhi and Abul Kalam Azad. Another issue is the relation of such *daʿwa* projects to the ideal secular imagination of the political sphere. Finally, we need to examine the view of postcolonial *daʿwa* movements and thinkers regarding the question of conversion in the Hindu-majority state.

Rather than discuss the various postcolonial Indian Islamic *daʿwa* projects, however, this chapter focuses on the notion of *daʿwa* as a discourse. It examines the ongoing positions of two leading Sunni *daʿwa* movements—Tablighi Jamaʿat and Jamaʿat-e Islami Hind (JIH), along with the ideas of three prominent Sunni religious figures: Mawlana Wahiduddin Khan (b. 1925), Mawlana Abul Hasan Ali Nadwi (also known as Ali Mian) (1914–1999) and Zakir Naik (b. 1965). These organizations and religious scholars have had a profound impact on contemporary Indo-Islamic religious traditions, especially among Sunnis.

The widely spread Tablighi Jamaʿat professes commitment to apolitical *daʿwa*, but its presence has always been felt in public life, particularly in relation to communally targeted violence against Muslims.[1] The JIH, which essentially functions as a pressure group, has had a problematic relationship with the Indian state but nonetheless was able to engage successfully in *daʿwa*.[2] Wahiduddin Khan, head of the *al-Risala* (Mission) organization, criticizes the inward-looking attitude of Islamic religious leaders and argues for a humane, peace-oriented, rational approach to propagating Islam. Abu al-Hasan Ali Nadwi, the former rector of the Dar al-Ulum Nadwat al-Ulama and who wrote extensively on Islamic *daʿwa* in India, argues for a contextual operation within the realm of the constitutional right to religion. The controversial Zakir Naik promotes a more direct and radical *daʿwa* project aimed at religious conversion using various media channels.[3]

These practitioners seem to follow a common, unspecified impulse with certain ideas, if not an ideology, of *daʿwa*. Ali Mian, at one time a member of the Tablighi Jamaʿat, wrote about its founder, Muhammad Ilyas Kandhalawi (1885–1944). Wahiduddin Khan was a member of JIH at one point and has likewise been sympathetic to the work of Muhammad Ilyas. Even Zakir Naik, who follows the South African writer and public speaker of Indian origin, Ahmed Deedat (1918–2005), shares some of the most fundamental understandings of *daʿwa* with other Islamic scholars. Still, there are serious debates and differences of opinion among these scholars concerning the methods of mobilization for *daʿwa* work as well as regarding the question of religious conversion.[4]

CONTOURS OF *DAʿWA* DISCOURSE IN COLONIAL INDIA

Nineteenth-century debates on the propagation of Islam emerged from the long process of reconstituting Islamic religiosity—codifying Islamic principles on a modern basis and searching for an ideal practice that could rejuvenate Islam as a way of life. Religious revival was manifested in a variety of ways in response to two crucial questions: (1) how should Islamic supremacy be reestablished as the ultimate religion in a colonial context? And (2) how should Muslims be invited to give up un-Islamic practices and embrace the ideal Islam? In these debates, the fall of Muslim rule in India was conceived as an inevitable consequence of the un-Islamic values and cultural practices adopted among Muslims.

The argument that Muslims have given up the true path of Islam dominated religious discussions of late-nineteenth- and early twentieth-century India. Although the nature of the true Islamic path and what methods should be used to achieve it have always been highly contested issues, there was a consensus that return to the original, ideal Islam would be the ultimate solution.

Such collective self-evaluations were compatible with the demands imposed by the colonial state, especially in the post-1857 period, after the great rebellion. The pro-empire Muslim elite, led by the modernist Sayyid Ahmad Khan (1817–1898), founder of Aligarh Muslim University, evoked the inherent liberal and scientific spirit of original Islamic principles to carve out a political space for Muslims in the colonial institutional framework.[5] This religious reinterpretation would later legitimize the reform agenda of modern education. On the other hand, the antiempire Muslim elite, especially the ulama associated with the Deoband school network, highlighted the revolutionary potentials of "original" Islam. This radical elucidation of Islam produced a powerful conceptualization of *muttahida qawmiyyat* (unified/composite nationalism)—an assertion that true Islam permits Muslims to make collaborations with other religious groups for the sake of territorial nationalism.[6] These seemingly different Islamic explanations focused primarily on the reconversion of Muslims—the assertion that in order to establish Islamic supremacy there was a need to make better Muslims.

In the late colonial period, three main theses were advanced with regard to the objective of *daʿwa*. The dominant view was that Islam should be presented as capable of answering the challenges posed by modernity. The purpose of *daʿwa* according to this thesis was twofold: Muslims should be educated to appreciate the universal spirit of Islam; and non-Muslims should be introduced to Islam to widen the scope for rational intellectual debates. The emphasis on education found a different expression among the ulama. This second influential thesis of *daʿwa* relied heavily on ideas and practices related to purity and advocated the spread of religious education through a network of mosques and traditional schools (*madrasas*). Institutionalization was seen as a means for *daʿwa* among Muslims.[7] The third thesis, advocated mainly by Muhammad Ilyas, founder of Tablighi Jamaʿat, suggested a clear separation of religion from overtly political affairs so as to build commitment and resolve among Muslims.[8]

The contours of *daʿwa* discourse in colonial India, broadly speaking, revolved around these three contesting positions: the top down approach toward *daʿwa* to make Muslims religiously civic and ostensibly modern; institutionalized *daʿwa* to make Muslims religiously Islamic; and grassroots *daʿwa* to make committed, exemplary Muslims. Postcolonial *daʿwa* discourse inherited these contestations while responding to the challenges posed by the postcolonial legal-constitutional discourse of secularism.

THE LEGAL-CONSTITUTIONAL FRAMEWORK: PROPAGATION VERSUS CONVERSION

The Constituent Assembly of India held an extensive discussion on the question of religious conversion. After a fierce debate, the assembly agreed to accept conversion as an important aspect of the freedom of religion. Article 25(1) of the constitution decreed, "Subject to public order, morality and health and to the other provisions of this Part, all persons are equally entitled to freedom of conscience and the right freely to profess, practise and propagate religion." Article 25 is a fundamental right protected by the judiciary, and therefore the commitment expressed in relation to religious freedom in this article (and for that matter, the propagation of religion) constitutes the basic structure of the constitution itself.

The word "propagation" has itself been a highly contested issue in the postcolonial legal-constitutional discourse. A variety of laws have been legislated to deal with what is often referred to as "forced conversion." In fact, "public order, morality and health" are often given precedence over the "right to profess and propagate religion" in various anticonversion laws and the court rulings upholding them. Some states even have separate anticonversion laws. These laws empower the state to control the activities of those organized religions that employ different means (including force) to convert people, especially those sections of society perceived as weaker, such as Scheduled Castes (SC), Scheduled Tribes (ST), and women.

This conversion-versus-propagation binary has produced a special typology of religions. Those faiths born in India are classified as intrinsically Indian; those originating outside are described as foreign.[9] In this sense, the territorial boundaries of the postcolonial Indian republic are recognized as the ultimate marker for determining the Indian-ness of a particular religion.[10] In fact, the nineteenth-century discovery of the Hindu religion as the most authentic and fundamental religious tradition of India is taken up conceptually to evaluate the notion of religious propagation.

The judiciary has employed the "Indian origin of religion" as an explanatory template on many occasions. In *Rev. Stanislaus v. State of Madhya Pradesh* (1977), the Supreme Court had to consider two questions: (1) what is the meaning and scope of the word propagation? And, (2) since freedom of religion is a fundamental right, can a state legislature (assembly) enact a law that might aim at governing religious issues?

Citing the Oxford English Dictionary, the court made a distinction between freedom of conscience and the right to propagate religion. It argued,

> Art 25(1) guarantees "freedom of conscience" to every citizen, and not merely to the followers of one particular religion, and that, in turn, postulates that there is no fundamental right to convert another person to one's own religion because if a person purposely undertakes the conversion of another person to his religion, as distinguished from his effort to transmit or spread the tenets of his religion, that would impinge on the "freedom of conscience" guaranteed to all the citizens of the country alike.[11]

The judgment's second finding was more problematic. It upheld the authority of state legislatures to enact such anticonversion laws with the justification that forced conversions might affect public order, partly because it would affect the sentiments of the majority community (read: those belonging to religions of Indian origin) and partly because the weaker sections of society would become more vulnerable given their lack of independent judgment.[12]

The preoccupation of various judicial explanations with the conversion of weaker sections of society is inextricably linked to the modern history of Indian religions, which found a very different political manifestation after partition.[13] The weaker sections—tribal communities, as well as communities considered to be lower in the caste hierarchy—were defined essentially as Hindus. In fact, a political consensus emerged in the 1950s that through legal intervention the state should play an active role in dealing with social problems such as untouchability and Hindu caste-based discrimination. The social stratification in non-Hindu religions, especially among Muslims and Christians, was completely ignored in these discussions. As a result, citing "backwardness" (being part of a socially disadvantaged group) for providing "reservation" (preferential treatment in selection for jobs and educational institutions as well as seats in parliament and state assemblies) actually emerged as one of the most crucial components of the state's Hindu social reform agenda.

To elaborate this point, Presidential Order 1950, which has already been amended twice, is a relevant example. The order argues that "the castes, races or tribes or parts of, or groups within, castes or tribes ... shall, in relation to the States to which those Parts respectively related, be deemed to be Scheduled Castes." The next paragraph of the order notes, "No person who professes a religion different from the Hindu, the Sikh or the Buddhist religion shall be deemed to be a member of a Scheduled Caste."[14] This clearly implies that, in order to avail the benefit of reservation, members of the identified Scheduled Castes would have to stay within the Hindu fold.[15] Further, socially disadvantaged Muslims and Christians are not entitled to reservation as part of a Scheduled Caste.[16]

Conversion among the weaker sections to Christianity and Islam is thus interpreted as a serious challenge to the very nature of affirmative action policies, at least in a legal-constitutional sense.[17] The Dissent Note of the Member Secretary, Misra Commission 2007, is a case in point. Describing the objective of affirmative action as a way of addressing Hindu social problems, this note evokes the Indian origin of religions theory. It argues, "Both Islam and Christianity are religions, which originated outside India and came from foreign lands ... along with traders, invaders and preachers." Since these foreign religions do not recognize caste, the argument goes, it is very difficult to determine the exact numbers of "the progeny of such traders/invaders/preachers/settlers from foreign lands and Scheduled Castes who converted in the present population of Muslims/Christians in India."[18]

This observation clearly establishes that those communities that had left their original Hindu religion in the past are not entitled to positive discrimination for two reasons: (1) embracing Islam or Christianity means accepting a faith that is intrinsically alien to caste-based Indian social order; and (2) leaving Hinduism means the end of exploitation based on untouchability. In this sense, freedom of religion, both in terms of the "propagation of religion" as well as conversion to another religion, is understood with reference to an unstated order of religion. Thus, the religions of Indian origin—Hinduism, Sikhism, Buddhism, and Jainism—constitute the core of Indian religiosity, while Islam and Christianity are seen as floating external ideas.[19] Islamic *daʿwa* movements operate within a legal-constitutional framework in which the freedom to propagate Islamic ideas is *not to be aimed* at converting people of other religions.

DAʿWA IN THE (RE)PUBLIC: PURPOSES, MODES, AND IMAGINATIONS OF POSTCOLONIAL ISLAM(S)

In a programmatic speech delivered on 26 April 1947—a few months before the partition of South Asia—Jamaʿat-e Islami leader Abu'l-Aʿla al-Mawdudi (1903–1979) explored the possibilities of *daʿwa* in the future Republic of India and offered a blueprint for what he considered a peaceful Islamic revolution. He made four proposals. The first two dealt with the creation of a conducive environment for *daʿwa*—a trust-building endeavor so as to carve out a space for spreading the message of Islam in India. The other two proposals concerned the practicalities of *daʿwa*: preparing Islamic intellectuals and translating Islamic literature into Indian languages. Mawdudi advised, "Our workers . . . should learn . . . Indian languages. . . . If Muslims restrict themselves only to Urdu due to their religious prejudice, they will become strangers to the general population of the nation."[20]

This blueprint involved three central aspects of *daʿwa* discourse that would prevail in postcolonial India: its meaning and purpose, the constituency for religious mobilization, and the putative methods by which the message of Islam could be effectively disseminated. Islamic scholars, religious movements, and Muslim political elites have offered a variety of different (and usually conflicting) responses to these fundamental issues. Nor are these responses fixed: arguments change, positions are modified, and sometimes completely new resolutions are proposed. To map out this varied and flexible discourse, I concentrate on context-specific contestations and issue-based consensus. In the following discussion, I identify five different responses and read them in relation to the freedom of religion, especially the propagation versus conversion debate, explored in the previous section.

DAʿWA FOR THE SAKE OF *DAʿWA*

For Muhammad Yusuf Kandhalawi (d. 1965), Muhammad Ilyas's successor as second amir of Tablighi Jamaʿat, *daʿwa* is an end in itself.[21] In his definition, "The manner in which the Prophet Muhammad lived his life and worked for the *din* of Allah is *tabligh*."[22] Taking the cue from God's messenger he reasons,

> The Roman and Persian empires were like spider webs at the time of the Prophet Muhammad. The Prophet worked on building the commitment of Muslims and preparing pure believers. Because of the sheer presence of these pure believers, Allah cleaned out the webs of Rome and Persia with his *azab* [punishment]. This will eventually happen with the superpowers of our time: Russia and the USA.[23]

Din (religion) in this framework of *daʿwa* is juxtaposed with *dunya* (world). It is an expression of faith and commitment to Allah, which can only be completed by absorbing the message of the Prophet. Muslims need to consolidate *din* if they want to be successful in this life and in the hereafter.[24] Therefore, Muslims should not endeavor to establish Islamic dominance (in direct political terms) in this world; they should act to consolidate *din* through *daʿwa*. In Kandhalawi's words, "The purpose of *tabligh* is not to disseminate any particular form of knowledge; instead, the aim is to breathe life into the very idea of *din* that the Prophet introduced and made possible for the prosperity of Muslims. If this very idea were to triumph as part and parcel of everyday life, the Almighty would shower his kindness on us."[25]

To understand the nature of this "*daʿwa* for *din*," one must keep in mind the six principles of the Tablighi Jamaʿat: *kalima* (profession of faith), *salat* (or *namaz*, the five obligatory prayers), *ilm o dhikr* (knowledge and remembrance of God), *ikram-e Muslim* (respect for all Muslims), *ikhlas-e niyyat* (sincerity of intention), and *tafrigh-e waqt* (sparing time).[26] The first three principles focus on the universally accepted norms of Islamic religiosity. One must profess his faith, pray five times a day, and recite the Quran (and for that matter any other religious text). The other three principles are more innovative. They call upon Muslims—particularly those involved in the Jamaʿat's *daʿwa* work—to show respect toward all forms of Islamic religious practice and to avoid argument and confrontation. Respecting all Muslims is necessary if one intends to participate in the activities of the Jama'at. Sparing time is an extension of the purity of intention and tells us how to put words and intentions into action.

The six principles offer a conceptual outline for the purpose of *da'wa*, that is, the endeavor to (re)create an environment of *din*. Its focus is on actions (*'amal*). The Jama'at makes a persuasive argument for abandoning the given understanding of Islam as an individual-centric spiritual experience, offering instead a systematic plan of action for collective involvement in worldly affairs in order to prepare Muslims for the hereafter. This unequivocal appeal for religious transformation is an appropriate example of the "propagation of religion" in the legal-constitutional sense discussed in the previous section. In fact, this form of *da'wa* moves away from social and/or political intervention and seeks to protect the faith of those who have already recognized themselves as Muslims.[27]

DA'WA AS AN ASSERTION OF ISLAMIC IDENTITY

Jama'at-e Islami Hind's conception of *da'wa* is more overtly political. Departing from Mawdudi's original formulations, JIH presents *da'wa* as a way of intervening in the postcolonial public sphere.[28] In a speech delivered as early as 1952 at Hyderabad, Abul Lais Islahi Nadwi (1913–90), its then amir, outlined the key features of their *da'wa* project. He argued,

> JIH is not a religious organization in the restricted sense of the term; nor is it a political group in the way politics is popularly understood. . . . We invite people to worship the Almighty. We have not only given *da'wa* to Muslims but have made a serious endeavor to introduce it [Islamic teachings] to each and every community of India. For this purpose we have started producing literature in languages other than Urdu. . . . We do not desire a large congregation—or crowd—in our meetings; our aim is to achieve a wider acceptability—conformity of those ideas and values that we cherish. When they [people] recognize the truthfulness of our message, they would redesign their lives accordingly.[29]

JIH recognizes the centrality of *da'wa* as an important aspect of Islamic religiosity. Yet, in contrast to Tablighi Jama'at, it shows an active interest in the ongoing political debates and issues that concern Muslims. In fact, it identified the dissemination of Islam as a means for direct engagement in political discussions. To work out a practical design for this seemingly difficult project of *daʿwa*, especially in the postpartition, anti-Muslim environment of the 1950s–1970s, JIH took the language question very seriously. Mawdudi's foreword for the 1970 Hindi translation of the Quran states, "It had been felt for a long time that there was a need for translating the Quran and other Islamic literature into Hindi, which is the national language of India . . . so that the vast majority of [Indians,] the Hindi speaking population, can become acquainted with the fundamental essence of Islam."[30]

To better realize the value of Mawdudi's argument, one must consider the manner in which the question of language and translation is debated in postcolonial Islamic *daʿwa* discourse. The Calcutta Quran case of 1985 is an example. A writ petition was filed in the Calcutta High Court demanding that "the publication of the Koran in the original Arabic as well as in its translations in various languages . . . amounts to commission of offences . . . and accordingly each copy of the book must be declared as forfeited."[31] The petition, as expected, was dismissed by the court on the grounds that the Quran is the basic text of Islam. Hindu fundamentalist groups, however, continued to use this politically grounded reading of the Quran to aid in their mobilization efforts.

The Hindi translation of the Quran, published by the Jamʿiyat-e Ulama-ye Hind, a religiopolitical body established by Deobandi ulama in 1919, responded to this debate directly. In the preface, the translators argue that their purpose is primarily to expose the anti-Muslim propaganda of Hindu fundamentalists and that "the essentialist and anti-Muslim conclusions are quite possibly due only to substandard Hindi translations of the Quran."[32] In order to maintain the purity of Hindi, this translation was sent to several Hindi experts, who happened to be non-Muslims, for their approval.

The evolution of Hindi as a possible language of Islam in postcolonial *daʿwa* discourse is apparent in the wider Hindi/Urdu politics of the 1970s.[33] The protection of Urdu, which eventually emerged as a "minority issue," is creatively reconceptualized by *daʿwa* movements, especially by JIH. While determination to protect Urdu was profoundly expressed in this case, the other Indian languages, especially Hindi, were seen as tools for spreading the message of Islam. This reordering of languages helped JIH communicate with various actors—the state, non-Muslims, and non-Urdu-speaking Muslim communities within the framework of the constitutionally granted freedom of religion.

DAʿWA AS AN EVOCATION OF RATIONALITY

Wahiduddin Khan describes *daʿwa* as the natural expression of faith (*iman*) and offers a nuanced perspective on conversion. Adopting a historical viewpoint, he emphasizes the outcome of the "sacred performance" that has brought large numbers of non-Muslims to Islam. In Khan's opinion,

> conversion in Islamic thought is not synonymous with proselytism in the formal sense. It is an event, which takes place in a person's life as a result of intellectual revolution or spiritual transformation. It is not simply leaving one religious tradition for another. The Islamic ideal of conversion is for the individual to discover the truth after an exhaustive search for it and then by his own choice, abandon one religion for another.[34]

But what are the possibilities for this kind of intellectual change of hearts today? Khan argues that modern rationality has become a way of life in the contemporary world. He recognizes a number of rational truth seekers, individuals who are exploring all sorts of possibilities in their search for solutions to the challenges of modern life. In his view, the intellectual revolution of our times has favored Islam because "all other religions have been subjected to human interpolation and have been rendered historically unauthentic. . . . Islam enjoys the exceptional position of having the authentic version of the revealed religion."[35] Therefore, there is a need to convert this rational search for truth into consciousness, as "all the people of the present day have potentially become Muslims" and thus, "the need of the hour is to do *daʿwa* work . . . so that this potential may be turned into a reality."[36]

The conducive environment mentioned by Mawdudi in his 1947 speech is interpreted differently by Wahiduddin Khan. He envisages an environment of rationality and identifies "potential Muslims" in this rational world. Khan seems to suggest that conversion in the given and formal sense of the term disrupts the argument for the propagation of Islam as *daʿwa*—primarily because conversion is not an event or rupture but a continuing quest for rationality. In this constellation, Muslims function as *du'a* (who have been given the responsibility to invite others to Allah and the truth), while non-Muslims are *mad'u* (who are *called* by Muslims). Khan argues that in their role as *du'a*, Muslims must tolerate the oppression and injustice of other nations, since without such forbearance, "That atmosphere cannot be produced which is required for the effective performance of *da'wa*."[37] This appeal to the rational spirit in people of all faiths represents a clear adherence to the constitutional expression of the freedom of religion, in which conversion is always understood as a rational choice.

DA'WA AS AN EQUILIBRIUM BETWEEN FAITH AND RIGHTS

A different version of rational *da'wa* is offered by Abul Hasan Ali Nadwi, who argues that the methods of *da'wa* are contingent upon the sociocultural formation of society. He thus emphasizes that there are no "fixed rules and regulations" for *da'wa* work.[38] This context-sensitive mode of *da'wa* is supplemented by two other required components: linguistic clarity and purity of intention. Nadwi writes, "Linguistic competence is of the utmost importance for the purpose of *da'wah*. . . . And the most important ingredient is sincerity and an earnest urge to persuade others."[39] Confident of the inner strength of *da'wa*, he declares, "The powerful nations like USA or Soviet Russia will never be able to win the hearts of the people as Islam has won them. The call of true Islamic faith which draws hearts of Muslims unfailingly is like a magnet that pulls iron chips toward it. Nothing in the World but faith (*iman*) has such a power."[40] Still, in view of the present situation in India, Nadwi prefers not to elaborate on the crucial relationship between the propagation of Islamic ideas and the conversion of non-Muslims.

Nadwi emerged as a key figure in the debates on Muslim Personal Law in the 1970s and in the Babri Masjid-Ram Temple dispute of the 1980s.[41] His take on overtly political issues helped him develop a clear perspective on the expected role of the state with regard to religious and cultural minorities. He asserted, "If minorities exist in the country, then safeguarding and keeping secure their religions, their places of worship, their Personal Laws and . . . language . . . is necessary. . . . This is the primary duty of every government and no government . . . deserves to be called a government . . . if it cannot provide this."[42]

Nadwi's understanding of Islamic *daʿwa* in the secular-constitutional context of India was rooted in his historical view and political activism. He maintained that Islam had not come to India to destroy Hinduism and that Muslim Indians recognized India as their motherland. They established great empires, which played a pivotal role in the cultural advancement of Indian civilization, rediscovered the ancient sciences and philosophy of India, and introduced them to the wider world. Still, today they suffer discrimination. Nadwi describes the unjust and partial Indian system of education, the decline of Urdu, and other socioeconomic disadvantages borne by Indian Muslims, thereby questioning the policies of the state. This is despite the fact that "Muslims are not only citizens of an equal status with anybody in India; they are among its chief builders and architects, and hold a position second to none among the people of the world for selfless service to the motherland."[43]

This historically imbedded argument underlies Nadwi's conception of *daʿwa*, which he sees as not only the propagation of Islam to non-Muslims but also as a self-awareness of the constitutionally granted rights of Muslims. He traces the compatibility of Islamic principles with democratic norms to conceptualize the Muslims of India as an identifiable minority community with distinct culture and religion. Here, the purpose of *daʿwa* is to spread the message of this distinctiveness to Muslims, non-Muslims, and above all to the state.[44]

DAʿWA BEYOND ISLAMIC REFORM

Zakir Naik's *daʿwa* began in the 1990s, making him one of today's most visible Muslim religious faces in India—online and off-line. Unlike other postcolonial Sunni *daʿwa* practitioners, Naik makes a direct appeal to using the Quran and hadith to invite primarily non-Muslims to Islam. For him, "*daʿwah* means a 'call' or 'invitation' . . . to invite non-Muslims to Islam as well as the Muslims to the true understanding and practice of Islam."[45] His *daʿwa* project is therefore critical of inner reformist projects such as that of the Tablighi Jamaʿat. He explains, "Many Muslims . . . doing Islaah [reform] . . . have completely ignored *Daʿwah*. . . . Therefore, it is . . . our responsibility to concentrate on *Daʿwah* in order to fill this vacuum."[46] In this sense, Naik is more concerned with the modes by which his interpretation of Islam can be adequately propagated and disseminated—for reforming Muslims as well as converting non-Muslims.

Naik's direct form of *daʿwa* openly rejects other religious traditions. Replying to a question regarding the use of the term *kafir* (infidel) for non-Muslims, Naik explains, "*Kafir* is derived from the word *kufr*, which means one who conceals . . . the truth of Islam . . . if any non-Muslim considers the word *kafir* as an abuse, he may choose to accept Islam and then we will stop referring to him as a *kafir*." Similarly, when asked about freedom of religion in Islamic regimes, he retorted that since Islam is the only true religion and Muslims believe in it, the propagation of other religions is not permissible in an Islamic country. By the same logic, Naik supports prohibiting non-Muslims from entering Mecca and Medina since "the primary condition required for any human being to enter Makkah or Medina is to say . . . there is no God but Allah and Muhammad (PBUH) is his messenger."[47]

Concomitantly, Naik asserts that the most appropriate method for comprehending Islam is to "understand the authentic sources of Islam—the Quran and the authentic hadith." His strict textuality helps him draw legitimacy for his explanations. Naik rejects the claim that the Hindu gods Rama and Krishna might be recognized as Allah's prophets, as there is no direct reference to these names in the Quran. In addition to disapproving of music, he opposes customary practices such as the wearing of a *mangalsutra* (a black thread worn by married Hindu women) by Muslim women because he finds it offensive to the Islamic dress code.

Making ample use of the new media, Naik was able to extend his appeal to migrant Muslim communities living in the West, the Middle East, and throughout Asia. These communities are experiencing different trajectories of modern life but together become inseparable components of what might be called an online *umma*. This is constituted when Naik delivers speeches before large congregations but even more so when the images of such gatherings are disseminated through the internet and mobile apps. Naik, in this sense, addresses a community that follows his image—an image of an English-educated, well-dressed (he typically wears Western-style business suits), skull-capped Muslim doctor, who relies primarily on his exceptional memory and scientific knowledge.

Naik's *daʿwa* is highly provocative and often described as "tempered jihad" because of its seemingly sympathetic attitude toward Islamic "fundamentalism." Naik does not find this allegation problematic, maintaining, "A fundamentalist is a person who follows and adheres to the doctrine or theory he is following."[48] In this sense, he and all practicing Muslims are fundamentalists. The same logic is used to justify terrorism. Naik argues,

"A true Muslim should be a terrorist to selective people, i.e., antisocial elements, and not to the common innocent people."[49] These refined, commonsensical explanations contribute to his image as a prominent Muslim figure and place him in the top ranks of various lists of "influential Muslims."

Naik's *daʿwa* departs from the dominant religious discourse in postcolonial India, as his project does not entirely respond to the minority rights-centric framework of the law. He disregards the thin line between propagation and conversion, offering instead polemical, straight, and ready-to-use Islamic responses. Yet this straightforward approach has not worked in Naik's favor when in recent years his NGO and TV channel were closed by the Indian government, and access to his website was restricted. His effort to take advantage of the legal-constitutional discourse should be seen in the context of these restrictions. As he now explains,

> The system and agencies have been used to suit a premeditated result set by the government of India, a government that took an oath to uphold the Indian Constitution, the same Constitution that allows me the freedom to profess, practice, and propagate my religion. Let us not be gullible to think this was just an attack on me. It is an attack on whom I represent, the Indian Muslims. It is an attack on peace, democracy, and justice.... India is my home, my roots, and I will fight this ban come what may.[50]

CONCLUSION

In this chapter, I suggest that the secular legal-constitutional framework in postcolonial India determines representations of Islam as a religion. The Indian Muslim scholars discussed here have been preoccupied with the cardinal questions of how to reinterpret the secular law without compromising their belief in Islamic supremacy and how to reconfigure *daʿwa* without crossing the line between propagating the religion and converting non-Muslims. In this endeavor, they celebrate the discourse of minority rights but also actively engage it, interpret it, and offer new and creative articulations of *daʿwa*.

Our discussion has shown that Tablighi Jamaʿat's expressed commitment to apolitical *daʿwa* functions within this framework. The agenda of preparing Muslims for *din* never poses any challenge to secular law, allowing the Jamaʿat to operate in a closed sphere of religion. Jamaʿat-e Islami Hind, by contrast, seems to use the "propagation versus conversion" debate as a vantage point to reinterpret the project of *daʿwa* and disseminate an activist version of Islam. Wahiduddin represents *daʿwa* as a rational interpretation of Islam, which he finds compatible with Indian secularism. For Nadwi, law and secularism have been deeply ingrained in the social values of Muslims. He argues that reasserting Islamic sovereignty as a form of *daʿwa* in the postcolonial period is a legitimate constitutional right. Zakir Naik is the only figure in our discussion to frequently cross the propagation-versus-conversion line. His image-centric identity allows him to speak of the conversion of non-Muslims more directly on TV shows. However, his attitude changed radically as soon as he was interrogated by Indian authorities. Like other postcolonial Indian Islamic scholars, Naik now evokes the discourse of minority rights and asserts his Indian identity to justify his Islamic adherence.

This brings us to the main argument of this chapter: postcolonial Islamic *daʿwa* discourse in India is highly multilayered. Functioning like a pendulum, the ideal-textual interpretations of Islam and the concept of Islamic supremacy are at one end of the pendulum's swing, while the legal-constitutional considerations and assertion of minority rights are at the other.

CHAPTER 3

Contemporary Salafi Discourses on Daʿwa from a Transnational Perspective

NINA WIEDL

WITH THE GLOBALIZATION of the Salafi version of the call to Islam (*daʿwa*) and the importance of *daʿwa* for the emergence of Salafism as a global religious movement, the Salafi discourse on *daʿwa* has intensified and changed.[1] In addition to classical issues, such as the question of how the Quran and hadith literature depict the concept of *daʿwa*, now Salafi ulama and preachers also discuss whether *daʿwa* has turned from a communal to an individual duty in our times and in specific regions or whether preaching Islam to non-Muslims in the West may be regarded as a modern surrogate for initial jihad (*jihad al-talab*).[2]

The term *salafiyya*, commonly translated as Salafism, denotes a pronounced loyalty to *al-salaf al-salih* (the righteous predecessors), pious Muslims of the first three generations of Islam.[3] In accordance with the now-prevailing definition, Salafism is used in this chapter to describe a scripturalist, literalist, puritanical approach to the Quran and the traditions that is rooted in the ninth-century traditionalist school of the Ahl al-Hadith and builds on (among other things) the teachings of Ahmad ibn Hanbal (d. 855) and, particularly, Taqi al-Din Ahmad ibn Taymiyya (d. 1328). Both scholars had a profound influence on the eighteenth-century revivalist movement of Muhammad ibn Abd al-Wahhab (d. 1792) and subsequently on the *ulama* of Saudi Arabia. The Salafi approach is characterized by a comprehensive understanding of the oneness of God (*tawhid*)—which they divide into the oneness of lordship (*tawhid al-rububiyya*), of worship (*tawhid al-ʿibada*), and of God's names and attributes (*tawhid al-asma' wa'l-sifat*)[4]—as well as a struggle to purify Islamic belief and rituals from aberrations and innovations (*bida*ʿ).[5]

Though largely united in creed, Salafis differ in their methods of dealing with state and society.[6] Quietists disapprove of political involvement under the current circumstances and aim to "Islamize" societies gradually by means of *daʿwa*, *tarbiya* (education), and *tasfiya* (purification). Political Salafis involve themselves additionally in politics by means of statements, parliamentary politics or extraparliamentary protest. Salafi-Jihadis are, broadly speaking, divided into one strain that focuses on global jihad and another that approves of military jihad in Muslim lands (against so-called "apostate" Muslim regimes or "infidel" occupying forces), while confining themselves to *daʿwa* and education in the West.

This chapter presents and compares ideas on *daʿwa* that are voiced by Salafis from different regions and trends (quietists, political Salafis, and Salafi-Jihadis). The focus is on the ideas of renowned quietists and pivotal actors in transnational Salafi movements—scholars from the Saudi Arabian religious establishment and the hadith scholar Muhammad Nasir al-Din al-Albani (d. 1999)—as well as global Salafi-Jihadi scholars such as Abu Muhammad al-Maqdisi (b. 1959) and prominent preachers representing the three main trends of the Salafi movement in Europe. An analysis of Salafi texts (including fatwas) and lectures on *daʿwa*, supplemented with interviews conducted with Salafi lay *duʿa* in Germany, serves as the basis of the discussion.[7] It examines views on how to define *daʿwa*, who is obliged and qualified to perform it, which target group should be addressed first, and how it is related to the concept of jihad. Special attention will be given, on the one hand, to the interconnection between the establishment of Salafi movements in the Western Diaspora and the adjustment of *daʿwa* strategies to new environments, and on the other, to the relation between the methods (sing. *manhaj*)[8] and strategic priorities of different trends of the Salafi movement and their respective views on *daʿwa*.

DEFINITIONS OF *DAʿWA*

The term *daʿwa* has a wide range of meanings in the Quran and Sunna. It denotes, among other things, an act of prayer, an appeal, a call, and a missionary activity. In some Quranic verses it takes the meaning of an appeal to other ("false") gods than Allah, a call to the fire, or a call by Satan. The Quran makes it very clear, however, that *daʿwa* to any other god than the True God is in vain.[9] In modern Salafi publications, *daʿwa* commonly denotes a verbal "call" or "invitation."[10] Accordingly, in translations of Salafi tracts into European languages and non-Arabic Salafi publications, the term is rendered as "call"[11] or "invitation"[12] (also less frequently as "preaching"[13]). The *daʿi* calls/invites people "to Allah"[14] or—equivalently—to "the truth,"[15] "the true creed,"[16] "what people were created for,"[17] "the good and the guidance,"[18] or "the straight path of Allah,"[19] all of which are Quranic synonyms for Islam. The prevalence of these synonyms reflects the authors' close orientation toward the Quran, which Muslims consider to be the preserved speech of God.

In this respect, Salafi scholars and prominent preachers differ from lay Salafi *duʿa* from Germany and, supposedly, other European countries, some of them recent converts without any command of Arabic. These lay preachers define *daʿwa* as "the spread of Islam," "the call to Islam," "information about Islam," or "enlightenment about Islam."[20] Such definitions seem to be based on their aims and experience as *daʿwa* activists rather than on studies of the scriptural sources of Islam and, as such, may provide us with information about their image of modern *daʿwa* in Europe.

Some Salafis also use the term *daʿwa* for a call to the "falsehood."[21] The late Grand Mufti of Saudi Arabia, Abd al-Aziz ibn Baz (d. 1999), warned against "*daʿwa* to destructive principles and ... atheism."[22] Abu Abdullah (Brahim Belkaid), a popular Salafi preacher in Germany, refers to the Christian mission as the "Soldiers of Satan's ... *daʿwa* for the falsehood."[23] References to this "false" *daʿwa* are commonly used as a tool of rhetoric that creates the impression of a competition between "true Islam" and "false" religions and ideologies, such as Christianity, communism, atheism, or Islamic modernism. Often they are combined with appeals to Muslims to spread the call to "the true creed."[24] In line with the Salafi doctrine, Muhammad Nasir al-Din al-Albani emphasizes that this "true *daʿwa*" is based on three fundamental foundations: Quran, Sunna, and an understanding of *al-salaf al-salih*."[25]

THE TARGET GROUPS

Non-Muslims were the primary target group of the Prophet's call, and early Islamic traditions also discuss *daʿwa* predominantly in the context of an offer to non-Muslims to embrace Islam.[26] Many Quranic verses on *daʿwa* likewise define it as an invitation to unbelievers to accept a message about the truth (i.e., Islam). Neither religious instruction nor dealing with hypocrites and renegades among Muslims are shrouded in *daʿwa* terminology in the revelation.[27] *Daʿwa* to Muslims as a call to "convert" to a specific group claiming to represent "true Islam" only emerged after the *umma* had split into different sects and strains. The Khawarij sect in the second half of the seventh century may be regarded as one of the first groups engaged in this form of *daʿwa*.[28] The early Wahhabi call in the mid-eighteenth century is a more recent example.

With the global spread of Salafi *daʿwa*, particularly since the 1970s, the target audience of non-Muslims gained new importance, not least because non-Muslims in the Muslim Diaspora proved to be promising subjects and—after conversion—committed preachers of the Salafi call.[29] At present, most Salafis agree with Ibn Baz, that *daʿwa* has to be transmitted to Muslims as well as non-Muslims.[30] In order to support this view, Ibn Baz stresses that Allah created the *jinn* and humankind to serve Him.[31] The German convert preacher and political Salafi Pierre Vogel, alias Abu Hamza, explains why *daʿwa* to non-Muslims should not be postponed until all Muslims have returned to the "pure" faith.

> The Prophet ... did not say "you should first engage in *daʿwa* to this person and then to that person." How many non-Muslims went to Hell in the meantime? ... Moreover, we will never manage to achieve having all Muslims practice religion to one hundred percent.[32]

Salafi-Jihadis generally share the view that the message of Allah should be conveyed to Muslims and non-Muslims alike,[33] yet they do often focus on Muslims. The German preacher Abu Ubayda justifies this by stating, "They [non-Muslims] know what Islam is, if they want to convert to Islam they would do it."[34] The late Bahraini scholar Turki ibn Mubarak al-Binali, alias Abu Sufyan al-Sulami (d. 2017), a former student of al-Maqdisi and, later, ideologue of The Islamic State (IS), argues that *duʿa* who distribute translations of the Quran to non-Muslims neglect the divine order to disavow (*al-baraʾ*) infidels[35] and should instead use their funds to support Muslim (i.e., Salafi-Jihadi) prisoners.[36] The fact that Jihadis often prefer to give *daʿwa* from a position of superiority and believe that non-Muslims may just as well convert after their countries have been conquered, seems to be an additional reason for the lower priority given to *daʿwa* toward non-Muslims.[37]

DA'WA AS A RELIGIOUS OBLIGATION

According to the majority opinion among Islamic scholars, including Salafis, practicing *da'wa* is a religious obligation and an act of worship that is based on textual evidence from the Quran and Sunna.[38] Salafis, as well as other Muslims, often refer to Quranic verses that contain verb forms derived from the root *d-'-w* as a basis for their understanding of *da'wa*, such as Quran 16:125 ("Invite [*ud'u*] to the Way of thy Lord with wisdom and beautiful preaching. . . .[39]); Quran 3:104 ("Let there arise out of you a band of people inviting [*yad'una*] to all that is good, enjoining what is right, and forbidding what is wrong. . . .[40]); Quran 12:108 ("Say you: This is my way: I do invite [*ad'u*] unto Allah—on evidence clear as the seeing with one's eyes—I and whoever follows me. . . .[41]); and Quran 41:33 (Who is better in speech than one who calls [*da'a*] to Allah . . . ?[42]). They also cite the prophetic saying, "Convey [*balaghu*, root: *b-l-gh*] from me even if it is a single verse,"[43] which indicates that they consider *da'wa* as being closely related to or even identical with the principle of *tabligh* (conveyance of Islam).

Based on Quran 3:104, *da'wa*—at least in its organized and public form—is considered by most ulama to be a collective duty (*fard kifaya*).[44] As Ibn Baz writes, this means that the burden is lifted from the rest of the *umma* if it is correctly performed by a sufficient number of people in their respective regions.[45] However, based on prophetic sayings on *tabligh*, many ulama agree with the former member of the Saudi Arabian Council of Senior Scholars, Muhammad ibn Salih al-Uthaymin (d. 2001), that conveying the message of Allah is also an individual obligation upon every Muslim, according to each person's level of ability and knowledge.[46]

The question of which group of the *umma* should be entrusted with the communal duty of *da'wa* at present is disputed among Salafis. Any given scholar's or preacher's particular response to it reflects his own view of who the "true believers" and their legitimate leaders are, a position which is likely influenced by the trend of Salafism he adheres to and by his socio-political environment. Ibn Baz writes that all ulama and Muslim rulers are responsible for fulfilling this duty.[47] Needless to say, as a Saudi regime loyalist, he above all refers to Saudi state ulama. As a Salafi-Jihadi, al-Maqdisi dismisses these scholars, asserting that Saudi loyalist ulama are "evil scholars who have given the pledge for the *taghut*[48] . . . and utilized their knowledge to secure its throne." Rather than attaching value to the position and formal education of *duʿa*, he emphasizes their "correct" methodology and attitude and writes, "The distinguishing feature of our *daʿwa* is the public declaration of the creed of Ibrahim, by practicing disavowal of infidels and their false deities and creeds."[49] In another publication, he stresses that this, and nothing else, was the way of the Prophet and the root of his *daʿwa*.[50]

Salafis further disagree as to whether *daʿwa* has turned into an individual duty in modern times or in specific regions. Dissent exists even among Saudi state ulama. Another former member of the Council of Senior Scholars, Abdallah ibn Jibrin (d. 2009), states, "*Daʿwa* is an optional act of worship in these times because there are those working in this field."[51] Alternatively, Ibn Baz writes that *daʿwa* is an individual duty (*fard ʿayn*) in most regions today because ignorance and evil are prevalent and there is a lack of *duʿa*.[52] In his opinion, the responsibility lies "on everyone from among this *umma*—scholars, leaders, tradesmen, and everyone else."[53]

Among European Salafis, we find the same range of opinions. Eager to enlist followers as multipliers of their message, political Salafis often argue that practicing or at least supporting *daʿwa* is an order today for everybody because "*jahiliyya* (ignorance) and wickedness is widespread and not many people engage in *daʿwa*."[54] Quietists, who give more emphasis to protecting Muslims from the influence of "infidel" society, sometimes hold that *daʿwa* is a collective duty because it is performed by a sufficient number of people.[55] Salafi-Jihadis sometimes combine the quietists' emphasis on isolation from disbelievers with a strategy that links armed jihad in Muslim countries and *daʿwa* (primarily, but not exclusively to Muslims) in the West.[56] Many of them concur with al-Maqdisi that jihad is more important than *daʿwa*, but Muslims who cannot emigrate and join the armed struggle should nevertheless "busy themselves with the call to *tawhid*."[57]

An article by the Egyptian-British Salafi-Jihadi preacher Mustafa Kamel, alias Abu Hamza al-Masri (b. 1958), illustrates that a Salafi's view on this matter is also influenced by his definition of *daʿwa*. Al-Masri classifies *daʿwa* as a collective duty, but he does not then infer that individual Muslims are exempted from making the call to Islam. Rather he claims that a person who merely calls to Islam performs *tabligh*, as contrasted with a *daʿi*, who also has to coordinate between preachers, *mujahidin*, and practitioners of enjoining right and forbidding wrong to assess when preaching has to be supported or replaced with force.[58]

Muslim residence in a non-Islamic country is another condition that may transform *daʿwa* into an individual duty.[59] In particular, quietists and Salafi-Jihadis often stress that residence in *dar al-kufr* (the abode of disbelief) is prohibited or undesirable unless Muslims have a legitimate reason for it, such as practicing *daʿwa*.[60] Political Salafis in Europe, who are more pragmatic and focus currently on consolidating Salafi movements in the West, discuss this prohibition (that aims at encouraging emigration to Islamic countries, rather than *daʿwa*) less frequently.

THE QUALITIES OF A *DAʿI*

According to the majority view among Islamic scholars, and among Salafi scholars in particular, the Quran and the traditions indicate that *duʿa* need specific qualities. They require wisdom and (religious) knowledge (Quran 12:108 [*basira*], Quran 16:125 [*hikma*]); a lawfully earned sustenance (Quran 11:88); and must personally practice the virtues to which they call (Quran 11:88, 2:44, 61:3).[61] They should be honest and sincere[62] and only practice *daʿwa* for religious reasons—to worship Allah.[63] Scholars and preachers further claim that a *daʿi* needs to speak mildly (Quran 20:44) and must be gentle (Quran 3:159) and patient (Quran 16:125–127).[64] He should not deter his interlocutor and openly attack his belief (Quran 6:108)[65] and must be merciful in his dealings with non-Muslims.[66] However, if the invitee refuses to accept the *daʿwa* and remains "stubborn and unjust," the *daʿi* should be severe, "As Allah said: O Prophet, strive hard against the unbelievers and the hypocrites, and be harsh with them" (Quran 66:9).[67] Some European Salafis add qualities to this list, such as eloquence[68] and self-assurance,[69] but do not claim any evidence in the Quran or the Sunna. Rather, they argue that these qualities are necessary in order to attract and convince the audience.[70] This indicates that they consider *daʿwa* to be, among other things, a method of marketing Islam.

Nevertheless, most Salafis also hold that a lack of such qualities should not deter Muslims from practicing *daʿwa*. They stress that a *daʿi* can make do with knowledge of those things that he calls to[71] or about the specific verse or hadith that he transmits.[72] Moreover, Ibn Baz writes, "Benefit can be derived from him even if he has some deficiencies in his character,"[73] nor should he cease spreading the call if he fears he does it primarily "to earn people's praise"[74] because Satan would surely love him to stop.

DAʿWA AND JIHAD

The views of contemporary Salafis on the relationship between *daʿwa* and jihad vary depending on their respective definitions of jihad. Corresponding to the range of meanings that the term takes in the Quran, Ibn Baz and many Arab ulama describe jihad as a struggle that may be performed with one's body (physically fighting), one's wealth, one's heart (hating evil), one's tongue (preaching, teaching, and guiding) or by helping to do good in any way. They consistently define *daʿwa* as an aspect or (lower) form of jihad.[75] Many European Salafi preachers, by contrast, use the term jihad in a narrower sense to describe armed struggle for the sake of Allah or struggle by the sword (*jihad biʾl-sayf*), the form of jihad considered in many chapters in the hadith collections.[76] These same preachers also use the term *daʿwa* to denote preaching Islam. Such definitions are compatible with the meaning that both terms have for many Europeans.

Salafi views on the relation between *daʿwa* and jihad are also influenced by a scholar's or preacher's particular strategy for the spread of Islam. In this regard, we can differentiate between a "Meccan" and a "Medinan" strategy. Ibn Baz explains that the first approach was chosen by the Prophet Muhammad in Mecca, when Muslims were weak. Therefore, "It was of the wisdom of God to prevent his messenger and Muslims from *jihad biʾl-yad* (jihad by the hand, physical struggle) and [He] ordered them to … [practice] *jihad biʾl-lisan* [striving with the tongue] and *daʿwa*."[77] It was only after they had gained strength that more bellicose verses (e.g., Quran 9:36 and 2:190–191) were revealed. First, Allah "permitted Muslims to perform jihad. Then, He … ordered them to fight those who fought against them, and … after that Allah prescribed the … initial and defensive jihad."[78] According to the traditions, the Prophet still sent letters and emissaries to foreign rulers in order to call them to Islam when Islam enjoyed a position of power and authority, but he and his successors (the rightly-guided caliphs) also sent out Muslim warriors who "invited" non-Muslims to accept Islam, sometimes pay tribute, or face a decisive battle.[79] In the context of these expeditions, *daʿwa* constitutes a brief invitation extended to an enemy to accept Islam that must precede the fight (*daʿwa qabla al-qital*).[80]

With reference to the paradigm of the Prophet's call, many Salafi scholars, even quietists like Ibn Baz, argue that *daʿwa* is generally more effective when supported by force.[81] Though the Saudi religious establishment has distanced itself more clearly than before from global jihad following 9/11,[82] Saudi governmental institutions still publish texts that praise initial (armed) jihad, such as Ibn Baz's fatwa stating that Allah "prescribed jihad to pave the way for *da'wa*"[83] and made it obligatory if Muslims are strong. One reason for the reluctance of Salafi ulama to declare initial jihad as outdated is certainly the fact that neither Medinan verses nor the traditions from this period support this view. According to the Islamic idea of progressive revelation, normative provisions of the Quran that have been revealed later may abrogate earlier ones, but not vice versa. Classical Muslim interpretations of the Quran have even "regarded the Sword Verses, with the unconditional command to fight the unbelievers, as having abrogated all previous verses concerning the intercourse with non-Muslims."[84] Many contemporary Salafis, however, hold that Medinan and Meccan verses on *da'wa* and jihad should be combined and brought into alignment. Ibn Baz writes that some scholars, whose views he does not dismiss, believe that, when Muslims are weak, they may abstain from initial jihad and adapt their conduct toward people of other religions to the verses revealed in Mecca.[85] European Salafis (except Jihadis) generally share this view and hold that due to their weakness, among other reasons, Muslims in Europe should not, at present, fight against non-Muslims.[86] Hence, for most Salafis the suspension of initial jihad remains a conditional and second-rank strategy for exceptional circumstances, at least in theory.

Yet some quietist and political Salafis in present-day Europe present *da'wa* (in its meaning of preaching and education) as a modern surrogate for initial jihad that is equal in value or even superior to it. In order to justify this view in religious terms, Pierre Vogel argues that the armistice of Hudaybiyya[87] establishes that periods of peaceful relations between Muslims and non-Muslims—when *da'wa* is practiced without force—are more conducive to gaining converts than periods of expansive warfare and fighting.[88] Additionally, he contextualizes Medinan verses on fighting infidels (Quran 9:29, 2:192) and concludes that they neither imply a general permission to fight non-Muslims nor are they applicable to the present state of Muslim life in Europe.[89] He further asserts: "The defense of the Sunna [which he defines as verbal refutations of modernist interpretations of Islam] is better than fighting in the way of Allah."[90]

As would be expected, Salafi-Jihadis reject most of these arguments. The late U.S.-Yemeni jihad ideologue Anwar al-Awlaqi (d. 2011) depicts military conquest, followed by the establishment of Islamic rule and the teaching and preaching of Islam from a position of superiority, as Prophet Muhammad's preferred method, the exclusive paradigm of the *da'wa* of the Companions, and an eternally viable model for the spread of the Islamic faith. He explains,

> The Prophet's Companions went in with armies. . . . They did not knock at everybody's door and say, "Please become Muslim." The Companions would take over the land, take over the government, and then they would go to the masjid [mosque] and everybody who is interested in learning Islam would find us in the masjid. . . . The Companions were not missionaries . . . talking in the streets as people are just passing by and not listening to them.[91]

Abu Hamza al-Masri adds that *daʿwa* without force can never succeed because "fifty percent of the population will only listen to Muslims if they take their possessions from them." Still, many Salafi-Jihadis seem to have recognized the importance of *daʿwa* (by word) for gaining followers and recruiting fighters. At present, most advocate a strategy that combines preaching, teaching, and fighting.[92] Al-Masri claims that rulers may be fought if they "declare *haram* to be *halal* and *halal* to be *haram,*" while "*daʿwa* to the ordinary man on the street"[93] should be practiced in the form of preaching and teaching. Shahid Janjua, alias Abu Waleed, calls for connecting armed jihad in Muslim countries to *daʿwa* in "the West,"[94] and al-Maqdisi argues that Muslims in the Diaspora must carefully consider whether "confrontations with the [Western] regimes" bring more benefit or harm for them. If the latter is the case and they cannot emigrate and join the jihad abroad, then they should focus on teaching and preaching Islam until they gain strength.[95]

This pragmatic and flexible approach provides leeway for adjusting *daʿwa* strategies to changing environments and state repression and explains why Salafi-Jihadi groups may appear as *daʿwa* networks in one region or at one stage and as militants in or at another. For example, the German branch of the transnational Salafi-Jihadi group Millatu-Ibrahim (MI) initially focused on preaching and teaching Islam and its militant ideology in Germany until a ban on the group (following riots at a rally it organized)[96] significantly restricted their opportunities to practice public *daʿwa* and led many group members to emigrate to Egypt (later joining the jihad in Syria and Iraq). Only then did its former leader, Mohamed Mahmoud, alias Abu Usama al-Gharib, claim in reference to Quran 16:125 that "the time for *daʿwa* with good words and wisdom is over," followed by his enjoining Muslims to "rise up for Allah" in order to "live or die in honor."[97]

CONCLUSION

This chapter demonstrates that Salafis discuss *daʿwa* as a Quranic concept, a path or methodology of the Prophet(s), an act of worship, a religious obligation, and a method for marketing and spreading Islam. As such, their discourses are shaped by religious dogmatism and strategic pragmatism, by interpretations of Quranic verses and traditions, and by assessments of the current situation of Muslims and Islam. They are also characterized by continuity and change. Salafi views on *daʿwa* are as complex and heterogeneous as the Salafi movement itself. Dissent not only occurs among adherents of different trends of the movement or among scholars living in different regions but also among Salafis from within the same trend and region.

Salafis agree on most general and "timeless" aspects of *daʿwa* that are related to this concept in the Quran and the Sunna. They define "true" *daʿwa* according to these sources as a call or invitation to Allah and to the belief in God and his religion that generally constitutes a collective duty. They hold that *duʿa* need specific qualities, such as knowledge and patience but need not be scholars or of perfect character. Most Salafis—including Saudi state ulama—likewise share the view that *daʿwa* is more effective when it is supported by force.

Disagreements arise when Salafis apply this general knowledge on *daʿwa* to contemporary situations. Differing opinions are often a product of various situational assessments leading to different strategies for the "establishment of *tawhid*." Quietist and political Salafis believe that at present Muslims should spread Islam globally by means of *daʿwa* or a combination of *daʿwa* and political activism. Most of them consistently hold the view that preaching to non-Muslims is just as important as preaching to Muslims. By contrast, Salafi-Jihadis currently focus on revolutionary or global jihad and often hold that promoting jihad and disavowal of infidels is more important than *daʿwa* to non-Muslims.

Other conflicts of opinion appear to be a result of the fact that Salafis live in diverse sociopolitical environments. Saudi state ulama openly proclaim (in Arabic texts) that the current suspension of initial jihad remains a temporary and revocable exception. European non-Jihadi preachers, who live as minorities within countries that are potential targets of initial jihad, express concern lest such statements lead to a ban on their activities and sometimes depict *daʿwa* as a superior alternative.

Finally, Salafis may change their attitudes toward *daʿwa* and its importance for Muslims according to changing circumstances. If state repression increases, propagandists of the Salafi-Jihadi ideology may declare the "*daʿwa* phase" in Muslim minority contexts over and opt instead for militant activism (at home or abroad). Conversely, *daʿwa* seems to gain importance for Salafis when they consider nonviolent relations with "the Other" to be conducive to reaching their aims, such as in minority contexts, when there is little state repression of Salafi *duʿa*, and/or when Salafis assess that the preconditions for armed struggle or political activism are not met.

PART II

Preaching in Movement

CHAPTER 4

Ideology, Practice, and Law in the Daʿwa of the Muslim Brothers and Jamaʿat-e Islami

JAMAL MALIK

WITH THE EMERGENCE of Islamic movements during the first half of the twentieth century, preaching of Islam (*daʿwa*) has surfaced as a trend that redefines or reinvents religious practices and serves as a vital mechanism for ensuring support to new political objectives. Subsequently, activities in this missionary field have gained additional dimensions, theoretically by introducing new definitions and accompanying jurisprudential references, and practically by changing its content, tools, and outer frame. Acquiring resources, organizing publication, arranging recruitment, and engineering schooling are of prime concern to organizations and individuals practicing *daʿwa*. In so doing, they have developed differing agendas and strategies depending on cultural circumstances.

The prototypical manifestations of Islamist *daʿwa* can be seen in the strategies of Hasan al-Banna (1906–1949) and Abu'l-Aʿla al-Mawdudi (1903–1979). Both went beyond the mere formulation of a new Muslim political theory by seeking to put their schemes into practice through political and social action and by establishing political movements. But while Banna's Muslim Brotherhood (founded in 1928) was crushed in its premature bids for power (Banna was assassinated in 1949, and many movement leaders perished under the Nasser regime), Mawdudi and his party, Jamaʿat-e Islami (the Community of Islam, established in 1941), survived several similar clashes with Pakistani authorities in the early 1950s. Under Zia al-Haqq's military regime (1977–1988), Jamaʿat-e Islami emerged as a dominant political force.[1]

This chapter traces how Islamic proselytism has been integrated and harmonized with the ideology and early practices of the Muslim Brotherhood (MB) and Jamaʿat-e Islami (JI). It argues that these parties have the potential to reevaluate and reorganize normative structures handed down over time and across space with specific patterns of reinventing the past to serve the future. This is especially true since meanwhile *daʿwa* has gone global, building on its intrinsic plurality.[2] Against the backdrop of a multiplicity of *daʿwa* efforts and the emergence of *daʿwa* as an agent of power-discourse across society, Islamists such as the Ikhwan and the Jamaʿatis have also produced a new genre that attempts to standardize the diverse array of contesting proselytizing endeavors and to assert their justifications for how to propagate their notion of Islam—*fiqh al-daʿwa*.

THE ORIGIN OF ISLAMIST PROSELYTISM AND ITS SEMANTIC EXPANSION

Initially *daʿwa* meant propagation, peaceful invitation to non-Muslims and Muslims alike to convert or improve their behavior and become righteously guided Muslims. Over time, this outer and inner *daʿwa*, and the missionary *(daʿi)* involved in it, underwent systematic changes[3] when different ideas of *daʿwa* were adopted in reaction to the external threats of Western cultural hegemony and the missionary work of other faiths among Muslims. It seems beyond dispute that the Wahhabiyya played a major role in focusing on the inner *daʿwa*,[4] but by the late nineteenth century Islamist proselytism had become equated with the Christian concept of missionary work and the realm to be proselytized: *terrae missionum*. It was subsequently awarded a powerful genealogy, originating from the Prophet and passed down through the champions of Islamic revivalism, from Ibn Taymiyya to Mawdudi. Soon, *daʿwa* was turned into a key concept for religious propagation among Muslims worldwide.[5]

Preaching, social activities and education were and still are the prime vehicles in this venture. One of the first groups to start formulating ideas about *daʿwa* was the Ahmadiyya in British northern India. It has since become a major proselytizing force far beyond the borders of South Asia and has also acquired official status in some Western nations but has been dubbed heretical in Muslim majority areas.[6] Similarly, the Tablighi Jamaʿat in the late 1920s evolved into a major player in the field of *da'wa*, mobilizing hundreds of thousands of people.[7]

In the face of these more or less rural ventures, others turned toward urban strata, and soon after to university circles as well, using the social and communicative structures of the cities of Egypt and the Punjab. In the Arab context, credit usually goes to Rashid Rida (1865–1935), editor of the widely-circulated *al-Manar*, who in 1912 established an institution for the training of missionaries (*du'a*), Dar al-Da'wa wa'l-Irshad.[8] Banna and his associates are reported to have studied at his feet for a while and Shibli Nu'mani (d. 1914) even had the honor of hosting Rida at the Nadwat al-'Ulama in Lucknow.[9]

Soon, another actor entered the stage: Mawdudi with his first book *al-Jihad fi'l-Islam*, published in 1930 in Urdu.[10] Even a revisionist short version of that 600-page book in Arabic entitled *Jihad fi Sabil Allah* (1939) made a major impact in the Arab world, rendering Mawdudi into one of the most prominent Islamist reformers worldwide.

Putting *da'wa* into practice required the shedding of some of its discursive shackles in order to highlight the activist proselytism so important for Islamic reform movements and its instigator, the *da'i*. The discussion on "commanding right and forbidding wrong" (Quran 3:110) fills whole libraries, and Rida himself made use of this verse in the context of proselytism.[11] Such semantic expansion of *da'wa* led the Lebanese Shi'i scholar Husayn Fadlallah (1935–2010) to affirm this nexus[12] and thus provide Islamists with a normative device for intervention and surveillance, especially since the first part of the verse considers Muslims the chosen people. This encouraged Mawdudi to toy with the notion of man being the representative of God (*khalifat allah*).

Another semantic device of political *da'wa* pertained to whether it was *fard 'ayn* (individual duty) or *fard kifaya* (collective duty). Some Islamists take on a wider definition that is not limited only to advising and encouraging goodness but also considers acting as a good Muslim role model to be a kind of *da'wa*. Accordingly, *da'wa* is an individual responsibility that every Muslim should carry out, each according to his expertise and capacity.[13] Yet, other Islamists adopt a narrow meaning for *da'wa*, stressing that it is only religious scholars who must bear this responsibility,[14] while traditional ulama argue that *da'wa* is both an individual and collective duty.[15] Thus, it is a relative issue, according to the effectiveness and sufficiency of those who perform *da'wa* in society, an issue that has become a major point of contention in the struggle of activists and intellectuals for agency and authority.

THE SOCIOHISTORICAL CONTEXT OF POLITICIZING *DAʿWA*

The reevaluation of Islam as a political ideology was initiated between the two World Wars. This can be understood as both a reaction to colonial encroachment and a demarcation against inherited religious traditions, augmented by the abolition of the Caliphate in 1924. Oscillating between indigenous and colonial contexts, the societal basis of this urban version of Islam yielded to new social formations that had developed under colonial rule. Representing the educated lower-middle class, as well as skilled labor, students, lawyers, physicians, engineers, journalists, and new professionals bound up in the (post)colonial system, Islamists adopted and adapted its major terms, making them part of their own biographies but in Islamic garb. This normative replacement enabled these Islamists to transcend traditional boundaries and legitimize modern developments within Islamic semantics. In this process of reinventing tradition, code- or identity-switching is most important because it provides reciprocal translation of symbols and terms enabling action on different societal levels and makes meaningful the contest over acquiring religious social capital. Political Islam is thus provided with its particular dynamics for which the image of an enemy is essential.[16]

Both Banna and Mawdudi perceived the present system as morally deviant and politically corrupt, its leaders being the embodiment of illegitimate innovation (*bidʿa*). The resulting social pathologies, they decried, had developed from modernization and were often cited as evidence of a Machiavellian strategy employed by the West in order to seize power. The purpose of such rhetoric is to produce a normative consensus, to increase cultural self-confidence, and to mobilize the masses.

Islamists, however, lack the socioreligious capital usually held by traditional religious scholars and their networks. Not generally trained in traditional religious institutions, they keep references to purely Islamic symbols to a minimum, continuously playing on Islamic semantics. One such symbol is the notion of the *taghut*, the iconic villain and embodiment of the contemporary tyrannical system. The other is *jahiliyya*, no longer a historical period of ignorance in Arabia prior to Muhammad's revelation but a condition that can occur in any era and now seen as modern barbarity. Hence, it is the most important duty of all Muslims to overcome this *jahiliyya*, here and now, a transformation from corruption to purity, from innovation to authenticity. This can only be done though society's return to righteousness, the construction of an idealized state of purity. The way to do this is to live according to the Sunna of the Prophet and the pious forefathers (*al-salaf al-salih*). Emulating Prophetic tradition thus exemplifies a model for ethical perfection. Therefore, a distinctive habitus that pietizes everyday life is of prime concern. It comprises the major part of *daʿwa* activities and also compensates for Islamists having little access to the people.

Needless to say, this rear-facing notion of society presupposes a normative Islamic historical thinking informed by a master narrative where history serves religion and law. Accordingly, the perceived malaise and anomic situation require a specific prescription, *daʿwa*, for which a simple profession of faith is insufficient. As in Kharijite tradition, only active engagement in establishing an Islamic society is the measure of a good Muslim. Thus, based on social action in a variety of fields, Islamists encourage Muslims to set up a better society here and now through constantly contesting the political establishment. Proselytism thus becomes a major tool for spreading their ideology and a proven device with ever-expanding semantics.

DAʿWA IN THE IDEOLOGY OF JAMAʿAT-E ISLAMI AND THE MUSLIM BROTHERHOOD

As redefinition of *daʿwa* was essential for the new societal formations, both the Jamaʿat-e Islami and the Muslim Brotherhood shared similar ideas and strategies. In fact, they mutually translate and distribute the books of each other's ideologues, exchange ideas, and interact frequently. And while the financial flow is from the Arab countries to South Asia, the ideational flow is mainly the reverse.

Most of the writings of Banna, the first *murshid* of the MB, and Mawdudi, the first amir of the JI, focus on developing the qualities of the individual to handle every aspect of life in an Islamic manner. Moreover, although they decried Sufi contributions, both had some roots in Islamic mysticism and struggled to attain God's closeness in order to prepare each Muslim for proper relations with other Muslims and the creation of a unified *umma*.[17] In his *Tadhkirat Du'a al-Islam*, Mawdudi affirms that his *da'wa*, or invitation, seeks

> to immigrate to Allah and His Messenger, to demonstrate monotheism, and to announce closer bonds of faith, to end the worship of people and disseminate the worship of the Lord of mankind, to the application of sharia and Islamic sciences, to the good preparation at all levels of the jihad in the name of God, and to fight tyrants.[18]

Mawdudi reminds his readers that although Islamic *da'wa* contains political, economic, and social implications, its real success is not measured by materialistic achievements but by unflinching loyalty to Allah and the complete submission to His commands. *Da'wa*, for him, cannot succeed as long as the political establishment is hostile to it, an idea common to many Islamists. *Da'wa* is required to Islamize stray Muslims as well as non-Muslims and to establish *hakimiyyat allah* (the sovereignty of God), as enunciated by the Quran (12:40, 67), affirming that authority (*al-hukm*) belongs to God alone and those who deny it are unbelievers (Quran 5:44). Thus, paragraph 5, article 3, of the JI constitution states:

> Accept none as King, Sovereign, and Supreme Ruler, look upon none as capable of issuing orders on his own, not to think of any one as Law-Giver in [his] own right, and refuse to submit to any orders that do not conform to Allah's obedience and abide by His Law, because Allah alone is the Lord of His Universe and legitimate Sovereign of His creation.[19]

Sovereignty of God, then, cannot be achieved without applying His law. Establishing this divine system carries the responsibility of implementing sharia, the main goal of *da'wa*, so that

> by Divine Government, we mean nothing but a political system, which can replace the present one.... Should someone read our literature with open mind, he is bound to find that we do not stand for a political change only but we want to introduce that universal revolution in the individual and collective life of man which Islam calls for.[20]

Similarly, Banna, in his message entitled "To What Do We Invite Humanity?" affirms the idea of Allah's sovereignty: "It is our duty to establish Allah's sovereignty over the world, to guide all of humanity to the precepts of Islam and its teachings."[21] This can only be achieved by following the example of the forefathers, *madhhab al-salaf*.[22]

Madhhab al-salaf al-salih is again mentioned in Banna's message "Our Call/Invitation" (*Daʿwatuna*), the *locus classicus* for Islamist *daʿwa*. Here, he describes the three pillars realized through *daʿwa*, which form the path toward establishing divine government and hence empowerment. First, there is the right method to restore the principles of the Quran and Sunna as understood by the first three generations of Muslims during and after Muhammad's time. Second, this Salafi *daʿwa* must be transferred to the people. Activists guided by the faith reflect their attitudes in daily life as agents who apply God's law. Finally, there should be a resolute and trustworthy popular leadership that must be unquestionably obeyed in the quest for an all-encompassing social order based on the sharia.[23]

Like most Islamists, Banna distinguishes between "us" and "them," the "sinful people" who can be overcome by the *daʿi* alone. That *daʿi*'s reward is equal to that of a *mujahid*.[24] This is not far from Mawdudi who—like Banna—was convinced that *hakimiyyat allah* could only be achieved through a "comprehensive way of life" and an inclusive system of norms and values. Banna invented the neologism *shumuliyyat al-islam* to refer to this idea.

> We believe that Islam is an inclusive system; it is a faith and worship, a state, nationality, and religion, a spirit and deed, a holy text and a sword. . . . The Glorious Quran considers these things to be the core of Islam. [Hence, the Muslim Brothers] are a Salafiyya message, a Sunni way, a Sufi truth, a political organization, an athletic group, a cultural-educational union, an economic company, and a social idea.[25]

And if Islam is a comprehensive way of life, then Muslims are not only required to submit to God in places of worship but everywhere and at every time—in the streets, at schools, and in businesses—to reconstruct an Islamic social order. A Muslim's duty is to work for humanity, resonating Mawdudi who writes in *The Basic Principles of Understanding the Quran*:

> It [the Quran] is not a book discussing theology . . . it is a book of agitation and movement (*kitab daʿwa wa haraka*) . . . by its very revelation it shook a meek and complacent man . . . and made him confront the wayward world, struggling against evil and fighting the chiefs of idolatry and the leaders of sin and the purveyors of fallacy. This book called forth every happy spirit and every pure soul from every home and gathered them under the flag of God.[26]

Mawdudi believed that man has deviated from the path outlined in the Quran, and the way of return is through revolution, not as an actual process, but through comprehensive societal change to restore the natural order.[27] This equating of system (*nizam*) with nature (*fitra*) harkens back to what he wrote in *al-Jihad fi'l-Islam* in 1930: "In order to eradicate evil and to prevent wrong, Islam has prescribed that by systematic endeavor (*jihad*), and if necessary by war and bloodshed (*qital*), all such [un-Islamic] governments should be wiped out."[28]

The book inspired the radical Sayyid Qutb (1906–1966), who upon his return from the United States criticized the West as immoral and materialistic and the political system as barbarous.[29] Qutb postulated and eventually led the "change by hand," radicalizing Mawdudi's ideas and synthesizing a complete austere and militant path—including belief, mannerisms, and morals of the righteous predecessors not to be deviated from.[30] This was actually against the mainstream within the Muslim Brotherhood, which followed Banna's way of "good admonition"[31] and *daʿwa* as a rational and gradual process.[32] Qutb's uncompromising method, however, eventually resulted in the banning of the MB.

After Banna, the approach of the MB's leadership evolved in a different direction. In light of the membership's increasing radicalization, the second leader, Hasan al-Hudaybi (1891–1973), suggested a lenient "method of preaching toward God." His book, *Preachers, Not Judges*, published posthumously in 1977, attempted to counter the ideology of radical Islamist movements, to defend Muslims from excommunication (*takfir*), and to relieve the MB of the accusation of extremism.[33] In doing so, Hudaybi championed the least common denominator to be a Muslim: accepting the verbalization of the *shahada* as the only and unquestionable doctrinal evidence of faith. The doctrine of the need for action (*ʿamal*) in the community of the faithful, which was so crucial for the Kharijite conviction in early Islam, as well as subsequently for the Salafi position, was thereby rejected outright. Instead, he advocated the Murjiʾite principle that belief (*iman*) can only be expressed by inner faith, whereas actual acts cannot be subject to human judgment but are "postponed" (*irja'*, the term from which al-Murji'a derives) until the Day of Judgment in accordance with Quran 9:106.[34] Though the book did not elaborate on *da'wa* specifically, due to its moderate, quietist stand, *Preachers, Not Judges* had a substantial impact on the Brotherhood's *da'wa* activities and was discussed in different quarters.

Umar al-Tilmisani (1904–1986), who succeeded al-Hudaybi in 1972, advised MB student leaders to omit direct mention of the organization or the literature of its main figures (even Banna) in distributed materials or preaching sessions. Instead, when reading the letters of Banna and other MB figures, they were to present them as general advice from Islamic activists or preachers, as they would with thinkers of any era, and not as members of a particular organization.[35] Tilmisani's strategy in the 1970s clearly preferred *da'wa* over confrontation with society or accusing it of having reverted to *jahiliyya*.[36]

By the same token, the reemergence of the MB monthly periodical, *al-Da'wa*, in May 1976 was one of the most efficient tools of mobilization, developing a more coherent message than occasional speeches, brochures, posters, or books that reflect only the views of their authors. Its editorial policy in the 1970s played a major role in rebuilding group legitimacy in Egyptian society after two decades of censure and persecution. The magazine's distribution reached 100,000 copies. This continued until September 1981 when Anwar al-Sadat decided to ban all opposition and arrest nearly all of its figures, just one month before his own assassination. In the opening issue, an editorial note defined the magazine mission as "renewing *al-Da'wa*'s pact to remain the organ of an idea appealing for truth, believing in power, and calling for justice and freedom."[37] Its articles revolved around the meaning of practicing Islam in the modern age, criticizing the reform initiatives undertaken by al-Azhar and other formal organizations in the Muslim world as being incapable of creating a pious society. Generally, the main fields covered in *al-Da'wa* included historical pieces about the MB's formative years, its engagement with the political process, critique of the West, and issues about religious life and culture.[38] But the media were not enough to boost *da'wa* activities, and expansion into the public sphere would be important for winning over the masses. Sadat's alignment with neoliberal policy under his open-door policy provided an opportunity when the MB began providing basic services to overcome the disruptive effects of free-market and neoliberal reform. Hudaybi's treatise symbolized this accommodation.[39]

Tilmisani wanted to benefit from the unprecedented public freedom and open political climate that Hosni Mubarak allowed during the early years of his rule. Accordingly, the political approach of the MB overshadowed their traditional *daʿwa* and was utilized as a tool toward political goals, embodied in the slogans "Islam is the solution," during the legislative election campaigns in 1984 and 1987, and "Give your vote to Allah, give it to the Muslim Brotherhood."[40]

Tilmisani, and Mustafa Mashhur (1921–2002) after him, advocated political engagement, claiming that participation in the elections was not a substitute for *daʿwa* but rather intended to spread it into a new domain by different means. In this context, Tilmisani stressed that the MB had not entered the political arena seeking power for itself but to spread "the word of God." He stated: "When the Brotherhood talks of politics, they don't speak as political men, but as Islamic *duʿah*."[41]

During the 1990s, as jihadist groups carried out extensive terrorist attacks in Egypt, the Mubarak regime turned against the MB. The confrontation became apparent over issues such as the involvement of Egyptian troops in the 1991 Gulf War, Egyptian participation in the 1993 Madrid peace talks, and laws restricting the organization of elections for syndicates. The regime's offensive reached its peak in the mid-1990s, when hundreds of MB members—including some leaders—were arrested and tried in military courts. To survive, the MB returned to garnering grassroots support through the traditional tools of *daʿwa* activities in mosques and charitable work. On the other hand, the worsened economic situation and the "retreat of the state" opened a space for them to expand their network. With the new millennium, both the regime and the MB seemed to have reached an implicit armistice. The MB enjoyed nearly absolute freedom in the 2005 legislative election campaign and was able to exploit economic liberalization to establish financial institutions, not least through *daʿwa* activities, thereby strengthening its effect in society that eventually led to the its political takeover in the wake of the 2011 Uprising.

CHANNELS AND TOOLS OF MOBILIZATION

To attract supporters, both the MB and JI established schools, clinics, and charitable institutions, turning mosques into multipurpose social-service centers. The most important technique was a methodology for preparing *du'a*, for which Islamists eventually developed a new genre called *fiqh al-da'wa*, which will be discussed in the next section.

At his headquarters in Pathankot, Punjab, Mawdudi had envisaged the organizational structure of an Islamic society, the JI.[42] Noting that dominant Muslim leaders were highly westernized in training and outlook and therefore unlikely to carry out the "mission" sincerely, Mawdudi developed a mechanism for the selection of a limited number of committed activists capable of organizing and managing the affairs of the projected Islamic state. He focused primarily on the educated class, who would be the future leaders of the movement.[43]

Banna was similarly attentive to the educational process.[44] Though the process of training and preparing *du'a* was tedious, he sought to reach the educated through the family and at the college. The idea matured to make the *du'a* attend one week of intensive training at the Cairo headquarters and certify them before going into the field. This training was supported by a fund for the Islamic mission. In this way, ten summer delegations (from al-Azhar and from Cairo University) were organized to lead groups into the countryside, similar to the Tablighi Jama'at. By 1939, the MB could boast the opening of a special department called the Summer Team for Preaching and Guidance, as well as a two-week course for different groups. A promotion system was developed, and examinations and "appointment celebrations" for conferring the title of "Muslim Brother" were instituted. Introducing these young volunteer preachers to Egyptian society in the 1930s and 1940s was an innovation in a field long dominated by government-appointed preachers.[45] Similarly, reissuing *al-Manar* magazine in July 1939 after Rida's death encouraged the publication of other magazines such as the *Club (al-Nadi)* in Upper Egypt, and the *Good News (al-Bushra)* in the Nile delta, while touring the country attracted young people. The Technical Operations Department of the MB prepared missionaries for speeches and lectures, distributed authorized publications, and provided spiritual, mental, and physical guidance for each brother.[46]

Similarly, for targeting educated professionals, JI started to focus on building networks inside institutions of higher education. The Islami Jam'iyyat Tulaba (IJT), the student's branch of JI, avoided politics. Rather, it was conceived as a missionary movement and voluntary expression of Islamic feelings. In 1950 it launched its journal, *Azm* (Determination), followed the next year by the English-language magazine *Student's Voice*.[47] But in the 1960s IJT did begin an active political role on campuses to counter the "menace" of Prime Minister Bhutto's Pakistan People's Party's socialism. It extended its activities beyond universities to reach high schools, gaining particular momentum in the late 1970s in the wake of the Islamization drive. JI's magazines and journals focused on religious education, so that students gained familiarity with its message.[48]

JI backed its activities with academic discourses developed by the Islamic Research Academy of Karachi (1963) and the Institute of Policy Studies in Islamabad (1979), as well as by migrant institutions such as the Islamic Foundation in Leicester, UK (1973) and the Islamic Foundation of Nairobi, Kenya (1974).[49] The frame of reference, however, was a narrow "Jamaʿa" paradigm.[50] The MB's outreach in Egyptian universities, by contrast, offered young people a "solution" to problems they faced in daily life and addressed their basic human needs.[51]

Yet, given the meager success of these parties, there was no prospect of a political breakthrough. The JI has never won more than a small percentage in the provincial or national parliaments and only very recently began to establish links with future leaders drawn from a wide spectrum of society, including the civil service. The MB lived a similarly marginal political existence. The dream of an Islamic state had shattered, and its *daʿwa* efforts were disappointing. As *daʿwa* went global, with both state-sponsored institutions and nationally independent NGOs,[52] other groups proved more successful: the Ahmadiyya, which Islamists considered beyond the boundaries of Islam; the Deobandi Tablighi Jamaʿat and their Barelwi counterpart, Daʿwat-e Islami (1981),[53] which Islamists see as too easygoing; unorthodox Sufi orders; and popular "new preachers" (*al-duʿa al-judud*).[54] The missionary field became thus highly contested and the plurality of *daʿwa* became a bone of contention. It is within this context that Islamists sought to homogenize the life-worlds of Muslims by dabbling in traditional *fiqh* and its principles.

FIQH AL-DAʿWA: THE LAST RESORT?

In their quest for a new methodology of *daʿwa*,[55] and in reference to Quran 16:125, "Invite (all) to the Way of thy Lord with wisdom and beautiful preaching; and argue with them in ways that are best and most gracious," Islamists have reconceptualized and propagated Islamic values that came to be known as *adab al-daʿwa* (etiquette of Islamic proselytism), *thaqafat al-daʿiya* (culture of the preacher), or *fiqh al-daʿwa*, the law or method of Islamic proselytizing.[56] Hence, the central focus of proselytism is the *daʿi*, who must combine intellectual and social competence[57] with a good dose of persuasive ability, as anticipated by Banna calling out to "our people" (*qawmuna*).[58] In a more exclusivist form, Mashhur presented *daʿwa* ideas in his voluminous *On the Law of Daʿwa* (*Min Fiqh al-Daʿwa*), 1986. A chapter titled *Between Leadership and the Army on the Road to Mission* suggests some legal inventory in the procedure of *daʿwa*, thereby anticipating coercive power in the proselytizing field.[59] But this legal might is only supported in explanations on authentic identity and its quasi-coercive management in the narrow confines of the *jamaʿa*, since Mashhur's ideas revolve around the invitation (*daʿwa*) to martyrdom (*istishhad*). This view might be seen as a byproduct of the Nasser regime's harsh suppression of the Muslim Brotherhood.[60] Nevertheless, equating *daʿwa* with worship is intended to carry Islamic missionary efforts across the entire world. Focusing on *tarbiya* (development, training) in physical, educational, moral, and spiritual aspects, he considers jihad and *daʿwa* the pillars of *Leadership and the Army*. Thus, Mashhur's book is a battle cry, much in line with Islamist radicalism. It hegemonizes exclusivist, puritan *daʿwa* concepts that are instrumental to the creation of a distinctive Islamic identity that is under constant threat of injustice.

Islamist notions of *daʿwa* are grounded in the *ressentiment* of the disadvantaged, teaching that "the unequal distribution of mundane goods is caused by the sinfulness and illegality of the privileged, and that sooner or later God's wrath will overtake them."[61] Dr. Ali Abd al-Halim Mahmud (b. 1928), educational advisor to the MB, elaborates in his 1990 *Law of Daʿwa toward God* on how to establish a rigid Islamic system wherein proselytism is made into an individual obligation along with prayer, almsgiving, fasting, and pilgrimage. After a prolonged introduction on *fiqh al-daʿwa*, explaining its meaning, pillars, methods, results, and obligations,[62] *daʿwa* is divided into four stages with specified timelines leading ultimately to a quite narrow Islamism: (1) the acquisition of cognitive knowledge of the divine norms, lasting approximately three years; (2) the practice of this acquired knowledge in the field, requiring another two years; (3) the implementation of that knowledge, marked by action, continuous "jihad" and the essential institution of the oath of allegiance, lasting an additional three years; and (4) the final stage and ultimate goal that has no time limit—the seizure of political power and the enforcement of God's religion.

Thus, whereas the first stage is general, the second specific, and the third is concerned with jihad, the fourth and final stage possesses a normative character. Internally, it mandates that people live their lives according to what the Islamic community considers to be Islam. The treatise advocates jihad in various forms and displays a conspicuously high normative potential for disciplining society, leaving little scope for the Muslim other. This rather radical stand reflects Mahmud's sympathy for the secret apparatus and clandestine armed wing of the MB, run from 1942 to 1954. Thus, political *daʿwa* must be taken to every nook and corner of the world. Without a doubt, these points resonate with the MB's oath of allegiance.

Such legal framing seems to be stimulated by infatuated hatred for the perceived heretical tendencies of the modern state and of Western dominance, much like Mawdudi's accusations, and also displayed by the foremost ideologue of the MB in Baʿathist Syria, Saʿid Hawwa (1935–1989).[63] In *The Army of God: Its Culture and Morals*, Hawwa explains that only the *mujahidin* can succeed in defeating non-Muslims, as promised by God.[64] Knowledge of the "culture of Islam"—in combination with the development and training of Muslims and the activist understanding of *fiqh al-daʿwa*—are fundamentally necessary.[65] For its coordination, a special group is required—one that knows and understands the ideologies, workings, and strategies of Islamic movements. To acquire higher culture and morality, Hawwa recommends books written by Mawdudi, Banna, Qutb, and the Lebanese Fathi Yakan. The internalization of their ideas produces "a culture of *daʿwa*," engaging external conduct as well as internal conscience and embodied in the *mujahid*. Hawwa's resentment is thus radicalized in activist moralism, eventually accomplishing self-empowerment.

Other Islamist positions can be added, such as *The Relationship between Fiqh and Daʿwa* by the Salafi Mufid Khalid Id Ahmad Id.[66] He equates *daʿwa* to applied, practical *fiqh* and elevates it to a comprehensive status encompassing human life. Id emphasizes the role model of the *daʿi*, who must acquire reasonable knowledge of *fiqh* in order to provide qualified answers to various questions in the mission field.

The entanglement of victimhood and retributive religion is important, as it enables imagining the possibility of exchanging the authority of the repressive ruler for autonomy among his subjects and to overcome unequal distribution of goods and the illegality of the privileged strata. This imaginative retribution can be articulated in a physically visible and commonly represented legal moralism, rendering faith into the only benchmark for political action. According to Mawdudi,

> One does not become a complete Muslim by vocal profession alone. To become a complete Muslim one has to fully carry out in

> practice the instructions given by Muhammad . . . as ordained by God. For belief in God makes practical obedience to Him incumbent; and it is obedience to God which constitutes the religion of Islam.[67]

So, mere words are not enough to be a Muslim; practicing faith is the actual criterion. In such a worldview, the Prophet, the divinely ordained exemplar, is the point of reference for social and political reform and the source of continuity with the past into the present. After all, it is the Prophet who "brought about a rapprochement between spiritual and material values. It was he who harmonized Faith and Knowledge and Action."[68]

Muhammad's time is highlighted and "experienced with utmost contemporaneity. . . . Chronological distance is abolished."[69] Therefore, such interpretations maintain that *daʿwa* is an individual duty and a form of worship that can be only accomplished by internalizing Muhammad's temperament. It follows that the *sunnatization* of life-worlds is the *conditio sine qua non*. A distinctive *habitus* thus pietizing everyday life shapes the virtue of that particular community (JI and MB or any other Muslim proselytizing group), including a particular set of virtues conditioned by the etiquette of *daʿwa*, or the so-called law of preaching—*fiqh al-daʿwa*. However, since the *daʿwa* community does not have the coercive power to punish its members, the only control to be employed is moral suasion.[70]

In order to understand how soft coercion turns hard, one must look into the complex processes of how conventions turn into domesticating rules and how symbols unfold their disciplinary might. Habitualized and stabilized in rituals and embodied in institutions, such norms obtain the binding power of a justifying authority. The institutional space is supplied by the community, the *jamaʿa*, where "the whole body of believers [is] united in their common faith . . . [focusing the] attention upon the bond which fashions from a group of individuals a community of believers."[71] In other words, this space is affected by fiduciary alliances and institutionalized commemoration of rituals and symbolic actions that can create and recreate such a system of moral obligations, or deontology.[72] Speech act theory provides some insight. The public and ceremonial act of the oath of allegiance (*bayʿa*) is a case in point, as this assertive declaration of commitment calls for strategic reciprocity and moral suasion and thus establishes normative validity. The discursively established normative entanglement is located in the speech act itself, performed in and by the oath—when the utterance (locutionary act) is transformed into a promise (illocutionary act) intending an effect with the group (perlocutionary act). Accordingly, the entanglement of speech and act can be deciphered in the praxis itself. Thus, the MB requires its members to take on the following commitment:

> I pledge allegiance to God to be a loyal soldier of the Muslim Brotherhood, to show as much as possible obedience to the leaders in sorrow and in joy as long as it does not involve disobedience to God and to fight in His cause. I pay allegiance and may God be my witness.[73] [And after this oath,] the brother will . . . be reminded that as long as he is a believer, he will be determined for jihad for Allah, to work in the ranks of the *mujahidin*. We take a pledge to jihad in the way of Allah until Islam is victorious or we perish without victory but with a commitment to secrecy and obedience.[74]

Due to the accepted and customary procedure, the ceremony has a certain conventional effect. It is forcefully sincere and committed with efficacious intention. Thus, reciprocating the intentional performance, the speech act of the novice has a direct bearing on becoming a member. As such, normative structures underlie linguistic practice. Consequently, noncompliance is met with social boycott and intimidation, expulsion and *takfir*. "One who departs from the *jamaʿa* even slightly will die in ignorance," states the Ahmadiyya *bayʿa*. Eventually, the discourse can account for inflationary use of *takfir* that additionally and increasingly targets diasporic Muslims in an extraterritorial, jurisdictional manner and with a precarious potential for self-empowerment, as the notorious issue of arbitration and mediation has shown in the context of Muslim cultural enclaves.

The multilayered compression of *daʿwa* also resonates in Yusuf al-Qaradawi's *The Culture of the Preacher*.[75] His approach is comparable to that of the Indian scholar Abu'l-Hasan Ali Nadwi (d. 1999), head of Nadwat al-Ulama college in Lucknow for many decades, who called for a (mystical) purification of the soul (*tazkiyat al-nafs*). Unlike Mawdudi's politicized Islam with all its *takfir*-ist paraphernalia, Nadwi advocated a softer approach in the formation of the ideal Muslim society through flexible means, relying on "reformation" rather than "elimination" of undesirable elements in the existing society. He made extensive use of the politically quietist and nonviolent Tablighi Jamaʿat as a major vehicle in furthering this objective, which was to be accomplished, similar to Qaradawi, first and foremost through transformation of the individual.

As "spiritual leader of the global Muslim Brotherhood,"[76] and with his ostensibly peaceful *daʿwa* approach, Qaradawi was able to introduce a sort of "middle way" between violent extremism and secularism.[77] Because the traditional dichotomy of the Abode of Islam and the Abode of War no longer reflected the realities of Muslim minorities, they needed to be located in a new space to be conceptualized in the Islamic discourse: *dar al-daʿwa* (abode of preaching). In this new cartography, Muslims have the duty to spread their religion peacefully.

CONCLUSION

Islamic movements and organizations have become important reservoirs for protest and organized resistance against tyrannical regimes. Promising an Islamic solution, justice, and authenticity, these movements have particularly attracted youths in search of orientation and security in the face of social misery, alienation, and an unsecure future. Middle classes also join those ranks in their quest for security, self-respect, and moral revival. Thus, proponents of political Islam consider themselves the primary alternative power and a countervailing force in both colonial and postcolonial periods. They expand into new enterprises in the educational, socioeconomic, and political realms in order to lobby the youth early on and to practically realize Islamic norms and values. In MB and JI, as well as Salafi parlance, this is the utmost and strict practical remembrance of God. This *sunnatization* of life-worlds has contributed to the reassertion of religion in the public sphere, which explains the great appeal of Islamic movements, with their efforts toward communitarian order-making and organized self-surveillance.

Daʿwa is a proven field to expand their authority, whereby the deviations of modernity serve as a scapegoat. Banna and Mawdudi both began using *daʿwa* to stress the necessity for an Islamic alternative that applies God's law (sharia). For Banna, the aim was to restore an "Islamic order" and, eventually, establish an Islamic state. For Mawdudi it was an "Islamic movement" implementing God's sovereignty on earth in a nation state. Accordingly, the MB and JI replaced the traditional role of *daʿwa*—as peaceful invitation of non-Muslims to convert or for Muslims to improve their Islamic behavior—with a politically oriented notion of *daʿwa*. The tools for achieving these goals were media outreach, activist *daʿwa*, and the education of young Muslims. Supporting an economic system based on liberalism and creating a paradigm of brotherhood or community (*ikhwan* or *jamaʿa*) helped deepen commitment within the two organizations. Yet, these methods and tools also signify processes of segregation and enclave culture leading to marginalization and political contestation. *Fiqh al-daʿwa* was intended to endow the *jamaʿa* with a normative frame of reference and new vigor. Thus, in this sense, *daʿwa* has been employed as a means in the Islamist struggle for agency and sovereignty against political tyranny and traditional authority in the postcolonial era.

CHAPTER 5

Nothing Has Changed/ Everything Has Changed

Salafi Daʿwa in Egypt from Rashid Rida to the "Arab Spring"

RICHARD GAUVAIN

THIS CHAPTER BEGINS by situating the major contributors to the content and tenor of Egyptian Salafi *daʿwa* over the past century on a (necessarily simplified) timeline. Next, drawing on fieldwork carried out in Cairo from 2006–2009, it explores why so many Egyptians turned to Salafism in the days leading up to the Arab Spring in 2011. In particular, I focus on the *daʿwa* strategies and messages of the so-called televangelists—to date, the most popular of all Egyptian Salafi *duʿa*. In the same section, I also probe the links between the explanations ordinary Egyptians provide for wishing to engage with Salafism—often as a result of listening to the sermons of these televangelists—and the claims of Salafi scholars introduced in the first section. My argument is that the fundamental attraction of Egyptian Salafism prior to the Arab Spring is best understood in light of a cohesive and overarching *daʿwa* narrative that had already been unfolding since the time of Rashid Rida.

In the third section, I suggest that this narrative has been ruptured by events during and after the Arab Spring. This suggestion is based on interviews with a number of Salafi *duʿa* during 2016. Five years after the Arab Spring, the buoyancy and confidence that once characterized Egypt's Salafi settings seem to have vanished. For the time being, Egyptian Salafi *daʿwa* is in a state of crisis.

To conclude, I consider the apparent decline in popularity of Muhammad Hassan—a man best understood as a product of Egypt's long Salafi *daʿwa* tradition and, until recently, one of the country's most popular *duʿa* (Salafi or otherwise)—in light of this crisis.

AN EGYPTIAN SALAFI TIMELINE

The Pioneers

Organized Egyptian Salafi *daʿwa* can be traced to Rashid Rida's 1912 decision to found his Institute of Preaching and Guidance (Dar al-Daʿwa wa'l-Irshad) on the Cairene island of Ruda. This housed a college to train professional *duʿa* with the intention of preparing them to spread Islam both internally, among lapsed Muslims, and externally, among non-Muslims. In 1926, Muhammad Hamid al-Fiqi (d. 1959), who attended the Institute, founded his own society, Ansar al-Sunna al-Muhammadiyya, which kept strong ties with Saudi Arabia. Like Rida, al-Fiqi defended Wahhabi *daʿwa* against the criticisms of the wider Muslim community. Furthermore, just as Rida had recommended al-Fiqi and a handful of other students to serve in Saudi Arabia, so al-Fiqi was later able to secure work for his own colleagues and students, some of whom rose to positions of considerable importance.[1]

The main thrust of these men's Salafi *daʿwa* was to correct the "errors" that had crept into Egyptian society and beyond. According to Rida and al-Fiqi, a Muslim must prioritize God's unity (*tawhid*), avoid associationism (*shirk*), emphasize love for the Prophet and the importance of emulating his example (*sunna*), base his/her life on the Quran and Sunna, and detest unlawful innovation (*bidaʿ*). Correct belief was to be reinforced by correct practice (*manhaj*). A Salafi's ritual duties glorify God and benefit the individual and the community. For al-Fiqi and the scholars of Ansar al-Sunna, Ibn Taymiyya (d. 1328) and his student Ibn Qayyim al-Jawziyya (d. 1350) provided the first points of reference on all doctrinal matters, as well as many ritual ones.[2]

There was also a socioethical component in Ansar al-Sunna's *daʿwa*: all Muslims were instructed to unite as brothers and sisters (in the Salafi creed), uphold superior morals (particularly regarding the behavior of women), strive to improve their societies in terms of knowledge and wealth, and defend their faith against attack from hostile outsiders. Underpinning both components was the firm conviction that true, pristine Islam—as understood and practiced by the Prophet, his Companions, and the "pious ancestors" (*al-salaf al-salih*)—has been polluted by various innovations and accretions.[3]

To promote their ideas, Rida, al-Fiqi, and the Ansar al-Sunna pioneers relied primarily on print media. Rida's famous journal, *al-Manar* (the Lighthouse), was particularly influential and served as a model for his students. In the late 1920s, in Mecca, al-Fiqi established *al-Islah* (Reform), the first modern Islamic periodical in the Saudi state. Then, in 1937, back in Egypt, he began *al-Hadi al-Nabawi* (Prophetic Guidance), which, while never achieving the same success as *al-Manar*, served as the official voice of Ansar al-Sunna until its eventual closure more than thirty years later. After a brief interlude, in 1973 *al-Hadi al-Nabawi* was replaced by *al-Tawhid* (God's Unity).[4]

Unlike *al-Manar*, which promoted the cause of pan-Islam, few of Ansar al-Sunna's publications were overtly political. Nevertheless, they followed Rida in their criticism of British rule in Egypt.[5] Near the end of his life, al-Fiqi met General Naguib to congratulate him and the Free Officers on finally ridding the country of foreign rule and, in so doing, establishing the conditions for the rise of a purely Islamic society.[6] In hindsight, this meeting holds poignancy: the 1952 Revolution opened the doors to Nasser's persecution of the Islamists which, in turn, caused the spread of modern "jihadism"—a result that would have pleased neither Rida nor al-Fiqi.

Jihad and Apocalypse: The Impact of Sayyid Qutb

Ansar al-Sunna al-Muhammadiyya has exerted a profound influence over Egyptian Salafism. According to a recent study, the association has more than two hundred branches and controls more than 1,750 mosques, while every issue of *al-Tawhid* sells more than 100,000 copies.[7] Still, the Muslim Brotherhood has enjoyed the more impressive *da'wa* campaign. As a result of the fusion of ideas that took place within Salafi and Islamist settings following the Egyptian Revolution, the rudiments of Salafism permeated more deeply into Egyptian society.

The key figure in this regard is Sayyid Qutb. Originally an independent Islamist thinker, Qutb joined the Muslim Brotherhood after the Revolution in 1953 and was appointed head of its Department of Da'wa.[8] His mature vision, which crystalized in prison during the 1950s and 1960s and was forcefully expressed in his manifesto, *Ma'alim fi'l-Tariq* (Milestones on the Path), was transnational and painted a picture of the world as being polarized between good and evil. According to this text, all Muslims have a duty to perform jihad against the heretical, *jahili* forces that surround them. Qutb was executed in 1966 for his alleged part in plotting the downfall of the Nasser regime.[9]

After Anwar al-Sadat's ascension to power in 1970, Qutb's writings directly influenced the leaders of Egypt's various revolutionary movements (most notably al-Jama'a al-Islamiyya, al-Jihad, and al-Takfir wa'l-Hijra).[10] Unlike Qutb himself, some of these movements referred to themselves as Salafis. Indeed, while Ansar al-Sunna vehemently rejects his ideas, there is no question that Qutb has had a profound influence on the political approaches of a generation of Egyptian Salafis. Many of these joined the so-called "activist Salafi" movements that are typically associated with scholars such as Sayyid Qutb's brother, Muhammad Qutb, in Saudi Arabia, and Abd al-Rahman Abd al-Khaliq in Kuwait.[11]

Qutb's influence on Egyptian *da'wa* extends far beyond the political realm. Charles Hirschkind perceptively draws attention to his theory of *taswir* to describe the Quran's "visual imagination"—the way in which it renders "events, scenes, stories and sights . . . actual and immediate, pulsating with life and movement."[12] There is, he notes, something grandly cinematic to Qutb's writings. The same quality is even more apparent in the groundbreaking speech of the popular preacher Abd al-Hamid Kiskh, who also spent time in jail and whose "word as camera style" of sermonizing borrowed heavily from Qutb.[13] Kishk's sermons were the first to be captured on cassette and have profoundly influenced many of Egypt's subsequent *du'a*, the Salafi televangelists most of all.

Purists and Pietists: al-Albani and the Salafi Televangelists

Nasir al-Din al-Albani (d. 1999) was neither Egyptian nor was he known to have spent any length of time in the country, but his writings have nevertheless greatly affected the field of Egyptian Salafi *da'wa*. According to the standard biographies, he was largely self-taught.[14] Rather than dedicating himself to the Hanafi *madhhab* of his father, the young al-Albani avidly read copies of *al-Manar* in the Damascus public library. Although he later criticized many of Rida's hadith interpretations, al-Albani never truly lost his affection for his writings and zeal. Regarded by contemporary Salafis as the greatest hadith scholar of the era, al-Albani channeled his energies into *da'wa*. Few if any modern Muslim preachers have proven so effective at locating heirs to carry on their work. Like other Salafis in Egypt and elsewhere, Ansar al-Sunna came to fully endorse al-Albani's hadith scholarship, along with the scholarship of Ibn Baz, Ibn al-'Uthaymin, and other Wahhabi luminaries.[15] His theory of *da'wa* as a program of "purification and education" (*al-tasfiyya wa'l-tarbiya*), "which places creed before politics and the individual before the state," makes particular sense to the organization's leaders.[16]

The list of Egyptian Salafi scholars and *du'a* claiming to have been directly influenced by al-Albani is long. Allegedly, the closest to him of all was Abu Ishaq al-Huwayni, a hadith scholar and one of Egypt's best known Salafi "televangelists." He regularly appeared, along with Muhammad Hassan, Muhammad Hussein Ya'qub, and others, on Egypt's two main Salafi channels, *al-Nas* (the People) and *al-Rahma* (Mercy), at the time of my fieldwork between 2006 and 2013. Stylistically and rhetorically, these *du'a* are indebted to Qutb and, even more so, to Kishk.[17] Like the latter, their preaching is replete with autobiographical anecdotes, earthy humor, and phantasmagoric stories of hell and punishment. In terms of content, however, al-Albani's scholarship enjoys a uniquely privileged place in the televangelists' *da'wa*. The number of Egyptians espousing recognizably Salafi views—as influenced by al-Albani and propagated by al-Huwayni and his peers on Egypt's Salafi satellite channels—apparently reached its peak during these years.

Al-Albani's *da'wa* was characterized by its emphasis on the sphere of ritual practice, including purification and education therein. Like their *shaykh*, al-Huwayni and other followers of al-Albani attempted to remold traditional ritual practices on the grounds that Muslims who persist in performing them incorrectly will not receive the spiritual benefits to which they are entitled. From the 1980s, al-Albani-approved versions of ritual began to appear in Egyptian mosques: a characteristic finger waggling during prayer; the wearing of shoes in prayer; a modification to the formula of the *tashahhud* (instead of "Peace be upon you O Prophet," the less intimate "Peace and blessings upon the Prophet"); and so forth.

The Revolution and Its Aftermath

Following President Hosni Mubarak's forced resignation in 2011, Egypt's Salafi communities have undergone turbulent times. For present *da'wa*-related purposes, the shift of Egyptian Salafi *du'a* into politics is particularly noteworthy. For several of the more famous preachers, this move was temporary. Abu Ishaq al-Huwayni has sheepishly retreated from the political sphere;[18] Muhammad Hassan was eager to gain center stage but has been sidelined by General Abd al-Fattah al-Sisi's government.[19] After Mubarak's departure, the Salafi television channels veered quickly into politics and, with the arrival of al-Sisi in 2014, most were closed down.[20]

In the case of Hizb al-Nur, the most successful of the new Salafi parties, however, political engagement appears set to continue. Al-Nur's ability to mobilize its supporters as quickly as it did after the revolution benefited greatly from its *daʿwa* capabilities.[21] From 2013 onward, the party came under the control of Yasir al-Burhami, a preacher who until the revolution had directed Muslims away from any manner of political engagement.[22] Among several segments of Egyptian society, including many Salafis, however, there is now a profound distrust of Hizb al-Nur, and al-Burhami in particular, for the decision to support President al-Sisi (against the Muslim Brotherhood elected president Muhammad al-Morsi) and other acts of perceived hypocrisy. This distrust has had a negative effect on the popularity—and *daʿwa* potential—of the founding organization.

With al-Sisi in power, the role of Egypt's Salafi *duʿa* has come under intense scrutiny. In March 2014, the Ministry of Religious Affairs confirmed that the country's mosques operate directly under the control of the state. Eager to reimbue al-Azhar with authority, the regime dictated that all mosque imams must be graduates of this institution. In order to lawfully give a sermon, those who do not possess an Azhar-approved preaching license must obtain one. Similarly, all Friday preachers now must follow an identical sermon, provided in advance by the Ministry.[23]

Perhaps the greatest slight to Salafis (Egyptian and otherwise) took place in October 2016, when Shaykh al-Azhar Ahmad al-Tayyib declared at a conference in Chechnya that Salafis should not even be considered Sunnis. Saudi Arabian scholars, not surprisingly, reacted angrily to al-Tayyib's comment, and Egyptian responses have also been critical, though necessarily more cautious.[24] The views of a group of Cairene Salafi *duʿa* to the actions of both al-Nur and the Egyptian government are explored below.

In sum, Egyptian Salafi *daʿwa* has evolved significantly over the past century as political realities have changed considerably since the end of British rule. Externally, America and Israel replaced Britain as the main enemy, while internally, the threat of Sufism diminished. From the latter half of the twentieth century, the desire to reconcile Islam with modern (i.e., Western) science has become less often a motivating factor in discussion. Though Salafi *duʿa* once regularly referenced the works of Western scholars of religion (if only to disparage them), all such references are now absent.

The technologies and language of Salafi *daʿwa* have also evolved. The scholars of Ansar al-Sunna never stopped publishing their journal, but Qutb's ideas spread like wildfire through Egypt's colleges and working-class neighborhoods via easily digestible, pamphlet-style literature.[25] Indebted to the rhetorical style and cinematic imagination of Qutb and Kishk, the cassette sermons of Muhammad Hassan and others became popular in the 1990s. With the arrival of satellite channels, social media, and YouTube, the Egyptian public put faces to the voices of their favorite *shuyukh*. At each stage of development, it should be noted, the Egyptian Salafi *du'a* were more technologically advanced and aggressive in their proselytizing than the state-employed Azhari *shuyukh*.

Having introduced some of the key names in the development of Egyptian Salafi *da'wa*, the following section focuses on my ethnographic study of Cairo conducted between 2006 and 2009. Here, Egyptian Salafism is presented as a complex, diverse, but—from the perspective of *da'wa*—cohesive phenomenon.

DA'WA POWER: THE PUBLIC APPEAL OF THE SALAFI CALL, 2006–2009

In hindsight, 2006–2009 was a particularly good time to be conducting fieldwork in Egypt. The Islamic Revival (*sahwa*) was in full swing, and, after years in the shadow of the Muslim Brotherhood, the Salafis were eager to take center stage. The immediate success of the Salafi satellite channels, from 2006 onward, helped them to do so. Perceiving most expressions of Salafism in the country as nothing more serious than a benign alternative to the Muslim Brotherhood, Mubarak's government monitored the situation without directly interfering in the lives of most individuals.

I was left largely undisturbed to explore at least some of Cairo's Salafi landscape. In certain mosques and circles, I was able to spend considerable periods of time; in others, I was made to feel immediately unwelcome (though never in danger). Even when I knew I would not be returning, I attempted to grasp what it was about Salafism that so appealed to my interlocutors. In this section, I will attempt to explain their responses through reference to a dominant rationale, the "telling it like it really is" discourse.[26]

This *da'wa* discourse crystalized around the sermons (and sermonizing strategies) of Salafi "televangelists," such as Muhammad Hassan, Muhammad Hussein Ya'qub, and Abu Ishaq al-Huwayni. Imploring their listeners to reject the ephemeral pleasures of this world for the enduring ones of the next, these preachers churned out sermons in which they claimed to be bringing "reality" (*al-haqiqa*) to ordinary Egyptians.[27]

In my experience, the vast majority of Cairenes who visited Salafi mosque circles in the days leading up to the Arab Spring did so because they had listened to these types of sermons by these particular televangelists, their peers, and/or by those claiming to be their students. Thus introduced, the "telling it like it really is" discourse appealed to, and was employed by, students and *shuyukh* (typically aged between sixteen and fifty, in middle- and working-class environments) in mosques and other public spheres across the capital.[28]

For the remainder of this section, I wish to explore the workings of this discourse and of Salafi *daʿwa* itself in those years. I shall argue that this form of *daʿwa* succeeded among so many ordinary Cairenes, first, because it did so well at confirming the need for self-betterment; second, because it provided a particularly effective system of religious training, with attendant ritual strategies, for achieving such improvement; and third, because it wholeheartedly endorsed the abilities of its *shuyukh* to effect positive changes (using this system and its rituals) in the lives of ordinary people. Although Egypt's televangelists provide much of the immediate material and focus, my discussion of these issues regularly refers to the ideas and experiences of the pioneering *duʿa* mentioned in the previous section. These ideas and experiences provide the architectural foundations of pre–Arab Spring Egyptian Salafism.

Why did so many Cairene Muslims in pre–Arab Spring settings feel the need for spiritual (and ritual) renewal? The Salafi answer was clear: Egyptian society had been corrupted from within and without by the enemies of Islam. That is to say, much of the success of Salafi *daʿwa* in these settings lay in its apparent capacity to convince listeners that the outside world posed an *imminent* threat to their spiritual wellbeing. Those who entered Salafi circles were automatically confronted (and to some degree courted) by polemic against the enemies of Muslims. Most of the time, this polemic was not accompanied by screaming or the gnashing of teeth (although it could be) but couched in the language of *al-wala' wa'l-bara'* ("loyalty to Muslims and disavowal of non-Muslims").[29]

We may not ignore the fundamental importance of polemic to the pre–Arab Spring Salafi "telling it like it really is" discourse. Indeed, a deep resentment of colonialists, Jews, Christians, Sufis, and other self-evident enemies of Islam (the Shiʿa, the Bahaʾis, etc.) who threaten Muslim culture/values/identity is a thread running through each manifestation of

Egyptian Salafi *daʿwa*. In pre–Arab Spring Salafi preaching (and this aspect of Salafi *daʿwa* has not changed since), the figure of "the Jew" was especially grotesque and cartoonish—a symbol of Shaytan in the flesh.[30]

It was the duty of the Salafi *daʿi* to point out the threats posed by Jews (who manipulate the global media and, in vague, sinister ways, control its politics). Further, within the "telling it like it really is" discourse, the Jew served a strategic purpose. He became a foil for the *duʿa*—someone who invariably "tells it like it isn't." Unlike the equally distrusted Christian, whom most Salafi preachers in Mubarak's day knew not to criticize publicly, it was (and is) perfectly acceptable to attack Israel (and Jews) because of the ongoing conflicts between Arabs and Israelis.

Analyzing the nature of Salafi polemic among the televangelists, I was particularly struck by their reliance on "purity language." As noted, the Egyptian Salafi *duʿa* called on their listeners to exercise greater piety, honesty, and modesty in their everyday lives. The existence of a discourse in which Jews are recognized as intrinsically irreligious, deceitful, and perverse enabled the Salafis to simultaneously represent the same figure as a "condensed symbol" for both moral and physical forms of impurity.[31] Stories about Jews (and Westerners/Western women/atheists/Sufis, and so on) would be introduced into sermons lamenting the fact that the *umma* has been corrupted by lies, sexual perversion, and other filth—in short, "Judaized."

In pre–Arab Spring Salafi settings, this purity-laden message resonated as truthful for many. First-time visitors to Salafi mosques often arrived expressing feelings of fatigue and disgust. Many spoke of the need to feel purer, as if their daily lives were a source of constant defilement. Once these visitors entered the Salafis' mosque circles, they met *shuyukh* who not only diagnosed the problem ("of course you feel dirty, the world in which you live is dirty!") but also offered a solution. It should be noted that this solution was not normally phrased in terms of organized violence (i.e., jihad).[32] Rather, the solution lay in the preachers' presentation of Islam as a clear and accessible "system" (*manhaj*) with concrete boundaries that could be studied and over time mastered by diligent students. In pre–Arab Spring days, the most appealing aspect of this system was its emphasis on ritual performance as the primary means by which individual Muslims could reconstruct—and purify—their true Muslim identity.

At a technical level, the *duʿa*'s emphasis on ritual—as a specific component of *daʿwa*—was articulated via the doctrine of *tawhid al-uluhiyya*, which dictates that all forms of ritual practice are performed solely for the benefit of God.[33] The seriousness with which this doctrine was (and presumably still is) taken in Salafi ritual settings distinguishes these from other Egyptian Muslim ritual settings. In practical terms, it meant that during the timeframe of this fieldwork the Salafi preachers (particularly the televangelists) spent much of their time reminding Egyptians that it was not, after all, permissible to cheat on their fasts or to skip prayers. The same reminders were to be found repeated endlessly across Salafi *daʿwa* websites.

Before the Arab Spring, Egypt's Salafi *duʿa* also enjoyed a reputation for ritual expertise, as if they alone could be trusted to perform their acts of worship with the correct degree of technical precision. As already noted, thanks to al-Huwayni and others, many of al-Albani's ritual preferences had entered mainstream mosque ritual performances. Newcomers to Salafi circles quickly became convinced that their *shuyukh* were teaching them "real" and "authentic" Islam, shorn of the mistakes exhibited by other, non-Salafi Muslims. Unquestionably, for many of the visitors to Egypt's Salafi mosques, the act of relearning basic ritual actions was an empowering experience. Indeed, as I have noted elsewhere, the same experience allowed for the creation of a unique *habitus* within which specifically Salafi ritual identities were cultivated.[34] This emphasis on ritual performance and its mastery brought people into Salafi settings and guaranteed that, for a time at least, many stayed there.

For these reasons, in pre–Arab Spring days, Egypt's Salafi *duʿa* (particularly the televangelists) proved remarkably successful at encouraging Muslims to engage more seriously with their religion. But why, we should ask, were so many people prepared to trust the Salafi *duʿa* in the first place? The answer, I believe, is that, before the Arab Spring, Egypt's Salafi community did a very good job of presenting a unified front.[35] Within this community, the same *shuyukh* were relentlessly promoted through a wide variety of print and social media. This media emphasized, first, the solid scholarship and, second, the integrity and trustworthiness of these Egyptian Salafis.

In contrast with their competitors—the Azharis, Muslim Brothers, independent preachers (such as Amr Khaled), and so on—the Salafi *duʿa* presented themselves, and were presented by their followers, as the only ones with sufficient scholarship and training to correct the errors that had become so entrenched in Muslim and Egyptian religious tradition. Indeed, Egyptian Salafi *daʿwa* sources have traditionally dedicated much space to upholding the scholarly credentials of particular individuals.[36]

In pre–Arab Spring settings, the question of scholarly lineage (under whom has one's shaykh studied?) was of paramount importance. The weight of a scholar's reputation often differed according to locale. In these settings, however, there was a virtual consensus as to who occupied the upper echelons of the Salafi *daʿwa* hierarchy. By studying under al-Albani, Ibn Baz, and al-Uthaymin (the "big three" of modern Global Salafism), the likes of al-Huwayni, Hassan, and Hussein Yaʿqub were acknowledged, across the Egyptian Salafi landscape, as sufficiently qualified to address the nation.

The "telling it like it really is" discourse endorsed not only the scholarship but also the moral integrity of Egypt's Salafi *duʿa*. Returning to the observation that there exists—or existed—an established architecture of Egyptian Salafism, it is worth noting that the lives and personalities of these *duʿa*, as portrayed in Salafi sources, share significant similarities. All preachers, for instance, are described as being raised in pious surroundings and having spent their adulthood struggling in defense of the truth. In my experience, the same details were also repeated in the biographies of local Salafi preachers. The apparently uniform profile of the Salafi preacher bolstered the impression that Salafism itself was reassuringly uniform in nature.[37]

To summarize, before the Arab Spring, the dominant discourse of Egyptian Salafi *daʿwa* convincingly presented the outside world as corrupt and corrupting. Islam, Egypt's Salafis agreed, was under attack and its enemies—the most pernicious among whom is (and always will be) the Jew—were closing in. According to the same discourse, Salafis provided Muslims with the academic and ritual tools to protect themselves against their enemies. Representing the best of the faith, the *duʿa* were themselves recognized by this discourse as knowledgeable, pious, and courageous—ideally equipped, in short, to tell the truth.

Pre–Arab-Spring Egyptian Salafi settings were not apolitical. Although rarely engaged in politics, Salafis invariably commented—usually negatively—on the political scene. Before the Arab Spring, Egypt's *duʿa*, however, were generally careful not to mix Egyptian politics with preaching. Their appeal to ordinary Egyptians, in contrast with the Muslim Brothers or the state-sponsored scholars of al-Azhar, rested in no small degree on an ability to present themselves as untainted by involvement in Egypt's (intrinsically filthy) political system.

Quintessentially Egyptian, yet aloof from the politics of Egypt, in the 2006–2009 timeframe, al-Huwayni, Hussein Yaʿqub, Hassan, and the other televangelists who appeared on *al-Nas* and *al-Rahma* were the best known of Egypt's Salafi *du'a*. Their *da'wa*—and the "telling it like it really is" discourse itself—represented a fusion of the polemics and reformist zeal of Rida and Ansar al-Sunna, the apocalyptic imagery and rhetorical flourishes of Qutb and Kishk, and the creative and ritual-saturated scholarship of al-Albani.

REFLECTIONS ON EGYPTIAN SALAFI *DA'WA* AFTER THE REVOLUTION

The Salafi mosque settings I visited before 2011 were often busy, energetic places. They are less so now. In January 2016, during a brief visit of ten days, I returned to some of the same Cairene locations where I carried out my original fieldwork. The visit was too short to attempt an in-depth analysis of Salafi *da'wa* after the revolution. (In the current political climate, it is doubtful whether such an analysis would be possible.) I did not enter Salafi mosques or speak to people about ritual. Instead, I met with a small number of male preachers specifically to discuss the ongoing popularity—and *da'wa* potential—of Salafism in Egypt. The responses of my nine interviewees were uniformly glum. Such responses suggest that major changes have occurred across the Egyptian Salafi landscape and that, among many ordinary Egyptians (as well as some previous supporters), the Salafis—particularly the televangelists—are no longer perceived as trustworthy.

While the resulting conversations cannot be taken as representative, they do at least allow us to begin this conversation in earnest. What I found most surprising was that two of them, independently of each other, no longer claim to think of themselves as Salafis. After years of dressing in spotless *jalabiyya*s, wearing their beards long, and shaving only their mustaches, it was oddly disconcerting to encounter the same men clad in shirts and jeans with light, neatly trimmed beards. Reassuring me that they remain Muslim, they declared that they can no longer self-identify as Salafis because, in Egypt, if not necessarily elsewhere, the term itself has lost meaning and relevance.

The other respondents, although still describing themselves as Salafi, complained that their *da'wa* activities have been severely curtailed. Four admitted that they now rarely attend the mosques in which they used to practice *da'wa*. They explained that the current situation is the direct result of the social and political backlash against Salafism in postrevolutionary Egypt. Indeed, of the seven individuals who continue to self-identify as Salafi, four do not possess a license to practice *da'wa* from al-Azhar and are therefore prohibited by law from giving sermons (though they may continue to do so discreetly). Of the three who possess a preaching license, only two still give sermons in mosques.

All of my respondents—including those who no longer describe themselves as Salafi—speak of the extraordinary challenges currently facing the *da'i* in Egypt, at a time when "politics makes us hide." Their troubles began, they agree, with the ill-fated decision of the al-Nur Party to participate in the post–Arab Spring elections. Before the revolution, the same men had been highly critical of the Mubarak regime and, in the early days of the revolution, unequivocally positive regarding the potential of the political process to rectify past wrongs. While their original loyalties lay primarily with Muhammad Abd al-Maqsud and his Salafi al-Fadila (Virtue) Party, they had also spoken warmly of al-Nur and, in particular, of Yasir al-Burhami.[38]

When I reminded them of this fact, they confessed to feeling taken in. Some were angrier than others, but all described the flurry of activity that had accompanied al-Nur's entrance into the political sphere as regrettable. Poignantly, these men empathized and identified with ordinary Egyptians who, they believe, have now lost trust both in the Salafi message, and in the men who carry that message. Indeed, each agreed that, as a result of the widespread loss of faith, most Egyptians are no longer looking to Salafi *shuyukh* and organizations to solve their individual or communal problems. Worst of all, they argued, the Egyptian public is now fully aware of the rifts that divide Egyptian Salafi communities: "How can people trust the Salafis, when we do not trust each other?"[39]

Although they had little positive to say about any of Egypt's contemporary Islamists, they did not seem to oppose the mixing of religion and politics. Rather, in their view, what is of importance is that *da'wa* and politics are not mixed. By failing to separate *da'wa* from the political sphere, and by employing the skills of its preachers for political gains, al-Nur has flouted the rules of their profession. This is one of a series of betrayals of which they accuse al-Nur. Among others, they are allowing women and Christians to stand as candidates; and the decision to force the so-called "revolutionary Salafi," Hazim Abu Isma'il, out of political running.[40]

The decision to allow women and Christians to stand as political candidates goes against the grain historically for Egyptian Salafis. Until very recently, the conversation regarding a woman's right to enter politics would simply not have taken place. Salafis' traditional criticisms focused on the evils of men and women sharing the public sphere. Such an activity, it had always been felt, invariably leads to "brazenness" (*tabarruj*), a quintessentially non-Muslim (but very Western) quality.[41] It was on these grounds, for instance, that al-Fiqi criticized Egypt's 1919 Revolution, during which men and women went out into the streets to protest together.[42] Every Salafi *daʿi* mentioned here agreed on the importance of shielding women from entering the public sphere.

As for Christian men entering politics, and even representing Muslims, the idea had previously been entertained within Egyptian Muslim circles, but Salafis who wrote about political matters uniformly opposed it. Once again, al-Fiqi provides us with a historical example: when lambasting the Muslim Brotherhood for caring more for politics than religion, he specifically pointed to its hypocritical decision to support a Christian candidate, Louis Fanous, in running for the Egyptian parliament.[43] Since al-Fiqi, every Egyptian Salafi has also made it quite clear that, as a matter of religious principle, specifically the principle of *al-wala' wa'l-bara'*, Muslims are expected to keep a distance from Christians.

Hizb al-Nur's decision to allow women and Christians to join its electoral list was, for my respondents, nothing short of a betrayal of Egyptian Muslim identity. Even those individuals who no longer consider themselves Salafi agreed that for the Egyptian Salafi movement to regain momentum—and once again to attract people to its ranks—there must be a return to basic principles and practices. The onus, they emphasized, is on the *daʿi*. Anyone who has compromised his religious credentials by seeking political power is automatically disqualified.

Among those no longer deserving of the title of *duʿa* are the former darlings of Egypt's Salafi *daʿwa* scene. My interviewees were angriest with Muhammad Hassan, the man most closely associated with Salafi televangelism and once beloved by millions. Their main complaint was that by aggressively seeking political influence (and possibly riches) for himself, Hassan has forgotten his role as a *daʿi*. They point to the fact that, although Hassan has not sided with al-Nur, he was originally willing to work with al-Sisi and the military. This is not surprising, they agreed, when one remembers that, in 2011, Hassan originally supported Mubarak and only changed his position when it became clear that the former president could not win. Accusing him of political guile in these instances, they simultaneously mocked Hassan's ambitious attempt to raise money to replace America's influence on Egypt as an act of grand stupidity. On this matter, there was some debate as to whether or not the money raised went directly into the shaykh's own pockets.[44] Finally, my respondents mentioned rumors of Hassan's womanizing tendencies. While they did not think that these should be taken seriously, their very existence was proof, they reflected, of Hassan's grave mistakes as a *daʿi*.

These men are acutely aware of the need for "untainted" *duʿa* to fill the void left by Hassan and his colleagues. The names they suggested—Masʿud Anwar, Muhammad al-Zughbi, Mahmud Shaʿban, and others—seem to offer little that is new. It is interesting, however, that the same names are recognized as particularly outspoken critics of Christianity, Israel, and the West.[45] This, it seems, is the point. When describing the dilemmas now facing the Egyptian *daʿi*, my respondents agreed that it is vital once again to stand firm regarding what is, and what is not, permitted to Muslims. To their minds, in the chaos following the Arab Spring, Egyptians have lost perspective on "who we are, and who we are not." The only people to have benefitted from the Salafis' decision to enter politics, they told me, are Islam's enemies. To regain their integrity, the *duʿa* must renounce the false new dream of politics and confront these enemies.[46]

Therefore, in the views of my respondents, the Egyptian Salafi *daʿi* now has two major challenges ahead of him. First, he must save the reputation of Salafism by standing up to the representatives of al-Nur, who have sacrificed religion for political gain. Second, he must win back the trust of Egyptians by redrawing the battle lines that, until recently, clearly separated Islam's friends from its foes.

CONCLUSION

I began this chapter with a timeline of Egyptian Salafism from the perspective of *daʿwa*. The aim was to introduce what I consider having been the main ingredients of the pre–Arab Spring Salafi *daʿwa* "scene" in Egypt. The second section outlined aspects of a discourse that was widely propagated by individual Salafi *duʿa*, as well as satellite channels and social media sites in the days leading up to the Arab Spring. As a result of this discourse's appeal, an unprecedented number of people visited Cairo's Salafi mosques to take classes. Having spoken to many such mosque visitors, I was repeatedly struck by the confidence they showed in both the *shuyukh* and the public face of Salafism.

Before the Arab Spring, the success of Egyptian Salafism rested, to a large extent, on their *shuyukh*'s ability "to tell it like it is." Unswayed by political office or earthly temptations, Egypt's Salafi *du'a* were widely perceived not only as having correctly diagnosed the true nature of the malady afflicting their society but as standing ready to dispense the cure. The third section, with its focus on post–Arab Spring realities, indicates that, even among Salafis, the legitimacy of this discourse has been severely compromised.

To tie the various threads of my argument together, I conclude with a brief reflection on the life, career, and post–Arab Spring fortunes of Muhammad Hassan, the best known of Egypt's televangelists. Born of humble origins in Dakahlia in northeast Egypt in 1962, Hassan perfectly fits the profile of the modern Egyptian Salafi *da'i* before 2011. He is an Ansar al-Sunna scholar. Rising through the ranks of the Mansura branch, he was singled out for praise by Safwat Nur al-Din, leader of the organization as well as one of its most respected *du'a*.[47] Influenced both by Qutb (though guardedly) and Kishk (unreservedly), Hassan combines the former's uncompromising vision with the latter's humorous, though often fiery delivery. By studying in Saudi Arabia under Ibn Baz and al-Uthaymin and attending lectures by al-Albani in Jordan, he is—according to the criteria of Global Salafism—powerfully credentialed.[48]

Before the Arab Spring, Hassan's reach was unrivalled among Egypt's Salafi *du'a*. When Charles Hirschkind conducted research into the cassette sermon phenomenon in the 1990s, Hassan's "Death of the Apostle" was "the most popular sermon tape in Egypt."[49] When I arrived a decade later, Hassan was still the preacher most likely to be referenced by non-Salafi interviewees. He was also widely admired by many experienced Salafis for his productivity. His sermons and publications—many of which are directed specifically to Egypt's *du'a*—were to be found in mosques, bookstores, supermarkets, taxis, and minibuses, as well as hawked by street vendors across the country. Hassan not only appeared on Egypt's first Salafi satellite channel, *al-Nas*, but bought his own, *al-Rahma*, to which he invited peers such as al-Albani's student, Abu Ishaq al-Huwayni to speak.

In 2011, as protestors gathered in Tahrir Square, Hassan addressed the nation, initially to advise the Egyptian youth to stay home, then, to rise up against Hosni Mubarak's crumbling regime. He was the first high-profile Salafi to recommend joining the political arena where, intoxicated with the possibilities for change, he positioned himself as an advisor to various political entities.

As the most recognizable of Egypt's Salafis, Hassan's subsequent fall from grace has gone hand in hand with the public's overall loss of faith in Salafism. As we have seen, he now stands accused, even by erstwhile supporters, of various acts of duplicity. Concomitantly, his continuing support of Muhammad al-Morsi has provoked sustained criticism from government sources. In 2016, he was put on trial for spreading extremist ideas and "defaming religion."[50]

Before the religiopolitical rupture that took place in 2011, the appeal of Hassan's sermons lay in their fusion of many of the core ingredients of Egyptian Salafism. Nothing could have prepared him, or any other Egyptian *daʿi*, for the events that followed the Arab Spring. Hassan now finds himself without the tools to defend himself. Lacking the necessary Azhari preaching qualification, and with his books and publications on the Ministry of Religion's banned list, he has been all but silenced.[51]

Still, perhaps Hassan's situation is not quite as dire as it seems. Indeed, in being forced back to the margins of Egyptian society by al-Sisi's regime, Hassan and his peers may have been offered something of a reprieve. After all, it is only from the margins that Egypt's Salafi *duʿa* can begin, once again, to "tell it like it really is."

CHAPTER 6

Daily Piety Drills for Lay Preachers in South Asia

The Tablighi Jamaʿat and Daʿwat-e Islami

THOMAS K. GUGLER

TABLIGHI JAMAʿAT AND Daʿwat-e Islami are modern Islamic missionary movements originating in South Asia that aim for "internal" conversion—turning "nominal" Muslims into "true" Muslims. The two movements differ, however, in their self-perceptions: while the founder of the Tablighi Jamaʿat, Muhammad Ilyas (1885–1944), preferred to call his group a faith movement (*tahrik-e iman*),[1] Daʿwat-e Islami describes itself as propagating the Quran and Sunna. The Islamic projects of both movements can be described as *sunnatization*—the Islamization or remodeling of the dress, speech, appearance, and behavior of Muslims after the example set by Prophet Muhammad. The long-term goal is to create a rightly guided society. For every step taken to further sunnatize everyday routine, the assurance of receiving divine rewards is sought through the addition of pious acts or expressions. This Islamic project attracts adherents not through forced submission under particular ulama but through the relocation of responsibility to the common Muslim for calling fellow believers to behave in a way worthy of the Prophet, stressing its character as an individual obligation (*fard-e ʿayn*). Thus, lay Muslims are empowered to accept this call to perform *daʿwa*, the Quranic commandment to enjoin good and forbid evil (*al-amr biʾl-maʿruf waʾl-nahy ʿan al-munkar*).

This chapter begins with a short presentation of the Deobandi and Barelwi reformist movements from which the Tablighi Jamaʿat and Daʿwat-e Islami originally sprang. Next, a more detailed description of the Tablighis and Daʿwat-e Islami is considered, with particular attention to the seventy-two Medina rewards or piety drills that are vital for understanding the success of Daʿwat-e Islami's brand of *daʿwa*.[2] This is followed by a comparison of the two movements and a discussion of the question of charisma.

BARELWIS AND DEOBANDIS: MAJOR SOUTH ASIAN SUNNI SCHOOLS OF THOUGHT

Sunni Islam in South Asia is comprised of several schools of thought, Barelwis and Deobandis being the most popular. But these schools are not monolithic entities. Instead, each is a cluster of institutions, organizations, and movements with specific purist, political, or sectarian agendas. Hence, they differ in opinions, emphases, and approaches to Islamic piety as well as in strategies for political or apolitical mobilization. The Taliban and the Tablighis are an impressive example of two seemingly disparate movements, both tracing their origin to Deoband in North India. As an Islamist movement, the Taliban in Afghanistan opted for a top-down approach to Islamization. The comparatively[3] apolitical movement of the Tablighis advocates a bottom-up approach in what it considers "an intensification of the original Deobandi commitment to individual regeneration."[4] Both the Deobandi and Barelwi forms of religiosity include some styles that are personal, quietist, and reflective but also others that may be more direct: proselytizing, confrontational, or even openly hostile.

The seminary in Deoband was founded in 1867 by Muhammad Qasim Nanautawi (1833–1879) and Rashid Ahmad Gangohi (1829–1905) as the center for an Islamic movement that pushed for reformist (*islahi*), educational, anti-imperialist, and conservative projects conducive to creating "a community both observant of detailed religious law and, to the extent possible, committed to a spiritual life as well."[5] From its headquarters in northern India, the Deoband movement established the largest madrasa network in South Asia. Although the teachings of its founders contain some significant Sufi elements, Deobandis have become increasingly skeptical of Sufism, particularly in the second half of the twentieth century. This shift is marked by a decline in the presence of formal *tasawwuf* teachings and the disappearance of the institution of the Deobandi lodge (*khanqah*).[6] With their rational culture of purist monotheism, contemporary Deobandis stand in contrast to the revived traditionality of the Barelwis.

After 1880, a coalition of shrines and schools steadily coalesced around the person of Ahmad Raza Khan (1856–1921) from Bareilly in north India as a counterreformist movement to Deoband as well as to the other Salafi-like school of thought, the Ahl-e Hadith, to defend the indigenously traditional, custom-laden ritual practices performed at Sufi shrines. The Barelwi movement quickly began to expand its *pir*-based networks and thus became the Sunni school of thought able to mobilize the largest number of supporters in South Asia.[7] Love for the Prophet Muhammad is the chief difference between Barelwis and Deobandis. As in popular devotional Islam, Barelwis attribute special status and several exceptional features to the Prophet and also, to a lesser degree, the *awliya*, i.e., holy men, living or dead. Barelwis celebrate the Prophet's birthday (*milad al-nabi*) and consider his mediation (*wasila)* a *conditio sine qua non* for reaching Allah. The notion of Muhammadan light (*nur-e muhammadi*) claims that Muhammad existed as light even before creation and as such is present and observant. Furthermore, he possessed unique knowledge of the unknown, the hidden, and the future. Hence, the main arguments in the theological debate between believers engaging in more direct, confrontational, or hostile types of religiosity are that Deobandis consider Barelwis polytheist guru- and grave-worshippers performing a syncretic mixture of Islam and "Hindu death cults," while Barelwis consider Deobandis blasphemous infidels and enemies, who, with support from the Saudi-funded Satanists (*wahhabiyya shaitaniyya*) continuously murder and commit blasphemies against the Prophet Muhammad in order to erase Islam and Muslims from the earth.[8] For Daʿwat-e Islami, studying Khan's book on the subject is seen as a religious obligation that is repeated every year (*madani inʿamat* no. 71).

Since their inceptions over a century ago, these two Sunni reformist traditions have competed for members, resources, and authority. The Deobandi dominated due to the sheer number of their madrasas and institutions of higher education and consequently by the output of graduates and literature. The Barelwis mobilized followers through the veneration of popular saints. Soon, both schools of thought generated powerful, tradition-specific, transnational revival movements: the Tablighi Jamaʿat and Daʿwat-e Islami.[9] These two (for strategic reasons self-proclaimed "apolitical") grassroots organizations for internal *daʿwa* revolve around individual piety and self-improvement by turning sympathizers or volunteers into traveling lay preachers who learn best by teaching and encouraging others. Their key feature is the swift and cyclic deployment of temporary, nonprofessional missionaries.[10] Such preaching trips turn practitioners into a religious labor force for further mobilization. Missionary journeys are an Odyssean experience factory (both chosen and forced upon the traveler), an exodus ritual for change management, as well as an educational enterprise. They are deliberately designed to destructure daily routines, to produce solidarity and a feeling of exclusiveness that gives participants a taste of liminality and charisma, which in turn potentially affects the processes of restructuring everyday routines after the journey: leave this world to enter another.[11]

THE TABLIGHI JAMAʿAT: JOURNEY IN THE PATH OF GOD

The Tablighi movement began in 1927 in Mewat, a region around Delhi where the locals (called Mewatis or Meos) were Muslim by name but worshipped Hindu deities, celebrated Hindu festivals, and dressed like local Hindus. It is even said that few of them knew the *kalima*, the attestation of faith, and fewer still knew how to perform the regular prayers.[12] In 1924, the prominent Deobandi scholar Ashraf Ali Thanawi (1863–1943) prepared a twelve-point program for areas affected by the Hindu reversion activists of Arya Samaj.[13] He was the mentor of Muhammad Ilyas, founder of the Tablighi Jamaʿat, and his writings were used for religious instruction among Tablighis before they were replaced by the books of Muhammad Zakariya (1898–1982), the main Tablighi ideologue and nephew of Muhammad Ilyas.

Muhammad Ilyas popularized Thanawi's methods by assigning the duty of *daʿwa* to the common man and stressing collective physical movement in groups—the Jamaʿat as a moving madrasa.[14] A charismatic, Deoband-trained *ʿalim*, Muhammad Ilyas taught at the Mazahir-e Ulum School in Saharanpur, the most successful school linked to Deoband.[15] He developed a simple method that relied on motivational talks to remind nominal Muslims, who were then being targeted by a Hindu conversion (*shuddhi*) campaign, that they were indeed Muslim. For motivating Muslims to again bear testimony to the faith, there would be great reward in heaven. In this context, the act of performing itself is ideally imbued with a transformative power over the missionary: by preaching the merits of prayer, the preacher is also given renewed vigor for performing them himself. Muhammad Ilyas thus developed an effective tool for countering the Aryas, and the proselytizing campaign quickly became a powerful means to defend the community's honor.

The Tablighi doctrine is famously condensed into six fundamental points: (1) *kalima tayyiba*, precisely confess a pure faith as well as correctly understand each word's meaning; (2) *salat*, perform correct and regular ritual prayers; (3) *ʿilm o dhikr*, pursue and disseminate religious knowledge and recollection of God by repeating phrases and prayers of praise; (4) *ikram-e muslimin*, respect all Muslims; (5) *ikhlas-e niyya* sincerity of intention; and (6) *tabligh o daʿwa*, propagation and invitation, also labeled *nafr* or *tafrigh-e waqt* (making time for a missionary tour).

Largely self-financing, Tablighi volunteers travel to nearby mosques in small groups (*jamaʿat*) of five to ten people and eat and sleep there. Above all, Muhammad Ilyas considered such moving madrasas a means to educate the teachers themselves: "We have left our homes to reform ourselves, before we reform others."[16] Shared experience is vital to the cohesion of a community, and the exodus experience of a preaching journey is certainly designed to be a change-manager ritual that triggers and frames further processes of personal transformation.[17]

During a walkabout (*gasht*), teachers approach nearby Muslim households and invite the men to prayer and a religious talk at the mosque. They motivate Muslims to reaffirm the *kalima* and interactively reflect and discuss each word's meaning. Following prayer, they preach basic knowledge about Islam and deliver inspirational talks (*bayan*), after which they urge the audience to also volunteer for missionary journeys. Their modus operandi resembles a pyramid scheme in that after one *bayan* during a missionary journey ideally at least one new group of volunteers is formed to travel to another place and repeat the same procedure there. After a *khuruj*, the leader (*amir*) of the travel group files a report on the results of their preaching that includes such information as numbers of invitees, voluntary signers, troublesome households, etc.

Although such trips are a great opportunity for adventure, casting aside worldly responsibilities in the pursuit of spiritual growth, and the communal experience of brotherly love, support, and friendship, joining a *jamaʿat* is certainly not entirely a vacation: the program's time structure is intentionally kept extremely tight, and lazy lay preachers are viewed with contempt. At the end of the day, only a few hours remain for a sleep on a hard floor next to other snoring brothers who constantly correct each other when awake. The authority of the amir is stringent to the extent that participants cannot make phone calls or use the toilet without prior permission.

Nevertheless, this ritual of preaching journeys turns religious education into an event. Aligning with the megatrend of individualization, it shifts the locus of religious agency to laymen and provides experiences for the modern, adventurous individual.[18] This development, however, also meant that money became a more significant factor, as only relatively rich Muslims could afford to travel to distant countries; hence the Mewati presence in the Tablighi leadership declined along with the movement's globalization.[19]

Meanwhile, many mosques now operate permanent preaching groups with full-time members known as *muqim*. They reside periodically at the centers and observe specific responsibilities such as teaching in the madrasa. A basic missionary foray lasts three days and should ideally be undertaken once a month. Longer periods include a forty-day journey called a *chilla,* often to another country, or even a grand *chilla*, which consists of three consecutive *chillas* (120 days). A *chilla* should be done once a year and a grand *chilla* once in a lifetime. Those who have completed a grand *chilla* win special status in the internal hierarchy, with congregations organized specifically for them.

Apart from missionary journeys, Tablighis organize regular congregational meetings (*ijtima*ʿ) at mosques on Thursday evenings. Globally, there are annual, three-day mass meetings held in Raiwind near Lahore, Pakistan, and Tongi, Bangladesh.[20] This *bishwa ijtima*ʿ (world meeting), which had about five million participants in 2010, is the second-largest Islamic congregation in the world after the hajj.[21]

The most important book of the movement is a selection of annotated hadith, first published as *Tablighi Nisab* (Handbook for Proselytizing) but since 1985 circulated as *Faza'il-e A*ʿ*mal* (The Virtues of Good Deeds). It was written and compiled by the main Tablighi ideologue, Muhammad Zakariya, a nephew of Muhammad Ilyas.

After Ilyas's death in 1944, the leadership of the movement passed to his son Muhammad Yusuf (1917–1965), then to his grand-nephew Inʿam al-Hasan (1918–1995), and afterwards to a council (*shura*) including Abd al-Wahhab and Muhammad Saʿad (b. 1965), a grandson of Yusuf, who has been the predominant chief ever since. In addition to stressing proselytizing outside South Asia, Muhammad Yusuf introduced into the Tablighi canon a more aggressive tone against Christians and Jews, in particular against Israel. Later, however, Tablighi leaders became very careful not to make public arguments against the West or Christianity. Even their support for the Taliban government in Afghanistan was heavily veiled.

In proselytizing, participants seek to recreate the Prophet's society in Medina in contemporary times, thus Tablighis can be seen as a counterculture movement against Western lifestyles and secular societies. The movement is highly informal, with no membership lists or membership fees. When Tablighi missionary activities began to expand globally in the 1950s, Muslims in Pakistan and India also joined excursions to be able to visit foreign countries.[22] Tablighi travel agencies had the necessary contacts to organize foreign visas. Zia ul-Haq, the military dictator who ruled Pakistan from 1977 to 1988, approved the Tablighis freely proselytizing within the army and was the first Army Chief of Staff to attend the annual meeting in Raiwind. After 9/11, Western security agencies criticized the Tablighis for organizing trips to Pakistan for highly religious young men in the West who, once there, might eventually get in touch with more militant organizations. The German-Turkish Tablighi volunteer Murat Kurnaz, for example, was arrested by Pakistani authorities and spent five years in Guantanamo prison, although no evidence against him could be produced.[23]

BARELWI ATTITUDES TOWARD THE TABLIGHI JAMAʿAT

Barelwis came soon to oppose the activities of the Tablighis, prohibiting their preaching in their mosques and even ejecting them by force if necessary. The influential Barelwi scholar Arshad al-Qadiri (1925–2002) declared in his widely circulated publications that several Tablighi practices were un-Islamic, for example, forcing people to remain in the mosque after prayer; pressuring them to testify to the *kalima* again without reason (holding that *tabligh* [proselytizing] should be directed at non-Muslims, while *taʿlim* [instruction] is for Muslims); and causing disunity in families by sending the husbands away for missionary "hunting expeditions." He went so far as to claim that Muhammad Ilyas was a British spy sent to destroy the Muslim infrastructure and that these "tyrant Wahhabis" would systematically desecrate mosques and turn them into their private houses by boarding and lodging there. Stealing proper (Barelwi) beliefs, Tablighis would declare the systematic killing of Muslims *thawab* (reward)-generating.

> The Tablighi Jamaʿat is not the group that can be called the servants of Islam, but it is a band of parasites, plunderers of the faith, dressed in a white garb, which has emerged to make a surprise night attack on the dear most capital of Allah's Love and Marifat [knowledge].[24]

Al-Qadiri argued that by their alleged practice of *takfir* the Tablighi sword would kill millions of Muslims without shedding a single drop of blood. Furthermore, "We regard the movement as an agent of religious assassination, with the Personality of the Prophet (saw) being the prime target."[25]

Yet Barelwi youths continued to join Tablighi trips for the opportunity of traveling to other countries, thus causing Arshad al-Qadiri to make an interesting U-turn. After some years of steadily intensified speeches against the Tablighis, he decided to fight them with their own weapon, setting up a Barelwi counterorganization that was closely modeled on the Tablighi Jamʿiyat. Its intended focus was facilitating transnational piety journeys for devoutly religious young men. Together with the then leader of the Barelwi political party, the Jamiʿat-e Ulama-ye Pakistan, Shah Ahmad Nurani (1926–2003) and the Qadiri *shaykh* Pir Maruf Hussain (b. 1936), he founded the World Islamic Mission (al-Daʿwa al-Islamiyya al-ʿAlamiyya) in 1972 in Mecca but with its headquarters in Bradford, England. Although this organization never attracted sufficient funding to operate on a large scale, it still exists.

DAʿWAT-E ISLAMI: MADANI REWARDS

Far more successful was the story of Daʿwat-e Islami, which was promoted by the very same group of Barelwi ulama. On behalf of Shah Ahmad Nurani, Arshad al-Qadiri installed Muhammad Ilyas Qadiri Attar (b. 1950) in September 1981 as the leader of the organization in the Dar al-Ulum Amjadiyya in Karachi. Apart from his name, which resembles the name of the Tablighi founder, Qadiri Attar was chosen for his important connections to the Karachi business elite in Karachi, which is mostly ethnically Memon, as he himself is. He had already proven his ability to mobilize the younger generation as the Punjab President of the Barelwi student organization. The interlinked relations between the wealthy Memon mercantile class and the religious networks of Daʿwat-e Islami reaffirm the monetary-morality orders in Karachi and demonstrate the fetishization of merchant capital that, through an overt connection to charity networks, transforms merchants into holy men.[26]

> The desire for money and capital and the aspirations for religious and moral virtue hence played out at multiple levels and in various practices often in an intimate way. . . . In fact, the morality of religious discourses works in tandem with the modern spirit of

> capitalism as is evident from the participants' presentations and speeches, expressing their desire to be compatible with the ideas of modernity such as nation, economic development, and progress.... The desire to be seen as part of modernity, arising from the feeling of lagging behind the techno-scientific culture of the West, among the traditional *'ulama* goes back to the colonial period.[27]

In 2006, I had the very rare honor—which many of his disciples will never have—of personally meeting Muhammad Ilyas Attar Qadiri at his house in Karachi. His status as *murshid* (guide)—every follower of Da'wat-e Islami is requested to pledge *bay'a* (oath of allegiance) to Ilyas Attar and become his *murid* (disciple)—constitutes a highly significant, long-term difference between their membership structure and that of the Tablighis. Temporary membership is significantly more uncommon in Da'wat-e Islami, and strictness on this front serves to screen out doubters and so-called free-riders.[28] Furthermore, such stringency is enforced by *madani in'amat* (Medina rewards). Demanding rigid observance of rules and regulations enforces a level of commitment in the group. However, the degree of severity must still be sufficiently low so as not to drive away everyone but misfits and fanatics. Followers of Da'wat-e Islami are easily distinguished from other Islamic groups by their strict dress code whose most identifiable aspects are the white *shalwar-qamiz* and green turban.

The movement took Karachi by storm. Within a year, Da'wat-e Islami was holding regular weekly *ijtima'*s on Thursday nights in more than a hundred mosques in Karachi alone. Such meetings last about three hours, starting after the evening prayer with a short Quranic recitation in Arabic followed by an Urdu translation from Raza Khan's *Kanz al-Iman* (Treasure of the Faith), along with commentary. Then comes *na't* (poetic praise of the Prophet),[29] *dars* (reading) from *Faizan-e Sunnat* (see below), *bayan*, *durud* (a token of remembrance of the Prophet), and presentation of the movement's publications. Then all the doors are closed and the lights turned off for *dhikr* and *du'a* (prayer) with ritual moaning. Finally, the lights are turned on again, for *na't*, *salam*, and *halqa* (exchanging private contact information with at least four first-time participants). In some places free food is offered after the program. Participation is obligatory for followers, who should ideally spend the night in the mosque as well as bring a nonfollower along with them.

A unique aspect of these meetings is the ritual crying out of love for the Prophet, an emotional and highly impressive ritual that, due to its cultural underpinnings, limits participation to South Asians.[30] Here the systematic accumulation of mobile phone numbers is more noticeably regulated, whereas Tablighis might sometimes fail to keep in touch with visitors. Daʿwat-e Islami is also much more successful at emotional bonding, probably in part because believers with a more loving relation to their God or Prophet tend to structure their social relations around similar emotions. It may also be due to deliberate measures—similar to the "love bombing" of the Unification Church in the United States (perhaps better known as the Moonies)—such as the obligatory *madani* greeting that consists of a long and intense hug. Still, the movement clearly prohibits personal friendships (*madani inʿamat*). Apart from weekly *ijtimaʿ*, Daʿwat-e Islami organizes an annual global congregation in Multan as well as massive marches that function as Islamic pride parades.

The main publication, i.e., the most famous Barelwi version of *Faza'il-e Aʿmal,* is *Faizan-e Sunnat*, written by Muhammad Ilyas Attar. Its first edition was published in October 1988, just weeks after the deadly plane crash of Zia ul-Haq, the single most important protégé of the Tablighis in the history of Pakistan. Only after his death does the success story of Daʿwat-e Islami truly begin. Subsequent editions were modified, as several scholars criticized weak and fabricated hadith in earlier printings.

Faizan-e Sunnat is used by lay preachers to read out authorized Islamic speeches to mosque congregations after prayer. In the competition for visibility in public spaces, Daʿwat-e Islami has an edge over the Tablighis, as they have run their own television station, Madani Channel, since 2008. Watching this channel for at least seventy-two minutes a day has become a religious obligation. The highly visible green turban, called *imama*, is another luminous marker for their brand of *daʿwa* and identity. As intentional communities with the vision of little less than the total transformation of the entire world, *daʿwa* movements use such markers to express two aims: (1) to build an ark that protects those onboard (just as in Exodus where the angel of death goes from house to house killing children but sparing those whose doors are marked with blood); and (2) to constitute a lighthouse shining its beam for all and seeking to bring the world to its senses.[31]

During the first decade, the movement mostly used other mosques not necessarily associated with their organization—just as the Tablighis had done in the beginning. But in 1988, Daʿwat-e Islami's headquarters for India opened in Mumbai in an older mosque the organization had taken over. Their first center in Pakistan, the *Faizan-e Madina* in Hyderabad/Sindh, opened in 1990, and a year later the massive world headquarters and mega-mosque in Karachi was launched near the home of Muhammad Ilyas Attar. During my fieldwork, about 40,000 Muslims joined the weekly *ijtima*ʿ on Thursday evenings, but within a few years Daʿwat-e Islami had turned into a truly global mass movement for Barelwi revivalism with centers in more than a hundred countries. With financial support from the wealthy Memon community, the organization quickly dominated Karachi-based trade networks with import/export links converting from Tablighi Jamaʿat to Daʿwat-e Islami.

Processes of diversification soon created a need for new institutions. One of the first of such newly founded departments was that responsible for translating the organization's publications into different languages. Daʿwat-e Islami also built up a massive network of madrasas and institutions for higher education, which security analysts have considered "certainly militant."[32] Prior to that, Tablighis had enjoyed a significant advantage by catching madrasa students at an early age. Another new department was devoted to preaching to prison inmates. Furthermore, Daʿwat-e Islami now runs its own chain of Islamic shops, Mufti hotlines, and Dar al-Ifta offices and the organization's busy IT department has developed dozens of popular mobile apps. These apps are designed, for example, to improve Quranic recitation, provide online madrasa education, test Islamic knowledge through quizzes, stream the Madani channel, provide searchable fatwa collections, alert to prayer times with an *adhan* (call to prayer) alarm, locate the correct prayer direction, and supply Islamic ringtones. There is even the "madni torch" flashlight app.

The alternative set of Islamic rituals that Daʿwat-e Islami promotes as part of its Madani revolution revolves around two ritual practices: the missionary journey (*madani qafila*) and the rewards (*madani inʿamat*). The main slogan of the movement is: "I must strive to reform myself and the people of the whole world."

Inside Daʿwat-e Islami, male members are advised to go on an afternoon missionary round in the neighborhood once a week, a three-day missionary trip to another city once a month, a thirty-day missionary journey—preferably in another country—once a year, and to spend a year volunteering at a center once in their lifetime. Every follower must make a daily individual effort to convince other Islamic brothers to join a *qafila*. This ritual is almost identical to the Tablighi proselytizing excursion, the only difference being that Barelwis also travel to shrines.

Each follower of Daʿwat-e Islami is requested to fill out a "*madani* card" every evening after sitting alone doing *fikr-e madina* for at least twelve minutes. This is an emotional ritual of repentance in which one visualizes the Day of Judgment and reflects on one's mortality. The *madani* card lists a standard set of seventy-two pious activities for adult men that are specifically designed for gaining reward. This set also exists in several modified forms: sixty-three for Islamic sisters, ninety-two for male madrasa students, eighty-three for female madrasa students, fifty-two for prisoners in jails, and forty for children. On the *madani* card, followers calculate their daily points just as in a personal success journal. Next to each of the seventy-two items are thirty boxes for each day of the month, one of which must be marked daily with "1" or "0." Once a month, the calculated sum of spiritual points is then reported to an assigned supervisor. This *madani* point status is not to be shared with fellow Islamic brothers and sisters, since the goal is not competition but rather a race against one's former self.

This set of practices is most commonly found in the form of a small booklet, but there are also single-page forms as well as the "Madani Inamaat App" for mobile, tablet, or desktop users, which automatically calculates one's current monthly spiritual status. In the West, the mobile app--available in twenty languages for Android and iOS—has outnumbered *madani* card users. Here, for practical reasons, I speak of the *madani* "card," but this should be understood as referring to all formats.

Naturally, the time invested differs from follower to follower. To earn the reward for one of the daily pious acts, it does not necessarily have to be performed each and every day but on most days during the month. Some of these pious acts are time consuming, while most others simply remodel or reframe a practitioner's everyday routine. Examples of the latter are the inclusion of certain Islamic expressions in everyday speech or use of the imperative to behave respectfully toward Muslims. The numbers of spiritual rewards for frequent interaction and engagement among members are striking. These prove that the organization has established a program of contact to keep tabs on its members, with particular focus on recent recruits. Records are compiled of a member's phone number, address, e-mail, etc., and members are used as informants to monitor volunteers and the connected database, thus allowing the membership to run the program themselves.[33]

The *madani* card gives lay members a concrete goal to work toward, to focus on. Life becomes but a cluster of habits, and the *madani* card is a tool for self-monitoring them. At the same time, however, it is a keystone habit itself: the daily act of filling in the *madani* card spills into and starts reprogramming practically all other life routines as well.[34] This Islamic routine-evaluator creates a virtuous circle with daily positive feedback loops. At its core, the *madani* card is about creating routines that result in Islamic habit loops or the sunnatization of everyday behavior. Every habit loop consists of a cue, a routine, and a reward. The *madani* card describes the cue, mentions the routine ascribed to the Prophet Muhammad, and immediately calculates the reward promised in paradise. The feedback is daily: it gives practitioners a sense of accomplishment, and the brain begins to associate the Islamic routine with the expected reward, thus strengthening the habit loop. At the same time, this self-evaluation motivates the practitioner to become a better follower of Muhammad in his or her normal social relationships, creating communal experience as well as peer pressure.

This rational—and seemingly capitalist—way of thinking in terms of "otherworldly points" is deeply interwoven with the neoliberal discourse of highly individualized self-optimization in a *do-it-yourself* procedure. Such pious neoliberalism—the melding of Islamic piety and neoliberal development—links volunteerism, self-optimization, and management science to piety. It employs the rhetoric of individual responsibility, self-help, choice, and accountability to encourage individuals to become proactive and entrepreneurial in the interest of deepening their relation to God.[35] While Tablighis similarly seem to benefit from "a broader neoliberal turn within the Islamic revival away from state institutions toward a focus on individual autonomy, authenticity, and agency,"[36] they stress an ethics of hierarchy. Among other things, this results from the numbers of successfully completed *chillas,* which may hint at an individual's self-financing capability—to create a world of pious sociality.

Ritual theft, the copying of popular ritual practices such as missionary journeys, is not alone sufficient for understanding the success of Daʿwat-e Islami. Even more important is the additional ritual practice of *fikr-e madina* and filling out the *madani inʿamat* card. In his 1922 work *Economy and Society*, Max Weber wrote about the routinization of charisma, which is paradoxical, as charisma is by definition the exact opposite of everyday routine:[37] charisma is a force that challenges and disrupts everyday routine[38] and as a rule cannot last.[39] Hence, Weber sees only two ways for charismatic leaders to organize their succession: (1) *erbcharismatisch*, which involves the leader transferring personal charisma to his successor(s); and (2) *amtscharismatisch*, that is, creating new institutions with institutional charisma. The idea that common people strive for a permanent charismatic *habitus* could, according to Weber, only result in a strict magical ritualism (he cites the Hindu yogi as an example), which would make people practically unfit for an everyday routine, as they would have no time to properly take part in the production sector and so forth.[40] For Weber, lasting charisma was only possible for the professional religious elites. I would argue, however, that he underestimated the spirit of radical egalitarianism inherent in Islam and could not foresee the enormity of technological change and cultural transformations produced by the digital revolution. This change has resulted in a new liquidity in which the once more-visible hierarchies between professional clergy and devoted lay community are melting away. I would consider the *madani inʿamat* a tool for the masses to generate charisma autonomously, thereby independently transforming everyday routine effectively into a charismatic routine that allows employment and social engagement but also encourages entrepreneurship. The Medina rewards are associated with the transubstantive power of changing everyday routine into a quasireligious ritual, making Islam a lifestyle by "sunnatizing" aspects of everyday life.[41]

This liturgy of everyday life is a source for meaning and, as a canon of etiquette, an instrument for self-transformation and character development. Daily deeds become incentives to invest in an otherworldly account where the maximizing of salvation advantages becomes measurable. Medina rewards also provide the follower with immediate feedback at the moment one fills out one's card, thereby strengthening feelings of self-efficacy. Moreover, it serves as an effective tool for the organization to monitor its members' progress and to shape piety-related behavior patterns, thoughts, and emotions among lay preachers so that they are consistent with the norms and ethos of the organization and the translation of religious ideas into the concrete deeds of a purposeful piety of action.

CONCLUSION

In a direct comparison between the two *daʿwa* movements, it seems that the most striking difference is that the attraction of Daʿwat-e Islami results from seemingly tighter networks of social control, while solidarity among its mostly first-generation membership is still mainly dependent on its charismatic leader, Muhammad Ilyas Qadiri Attar. The individual charismas of his disciples all rely on and are the summation of the allure of his personality, so it is highly unlikely that the organization will be able to survive Attar's death unmodified. It is still unclear how his summated charisma should be passed on to the next generation of leadership. The Tablighi organization, however, has managed to exist for several generations. My personal impression—backed by the research of others[42]—is that the Tablighis did not sufficiently revise and modify their tradition to compete with the diverse array of contemporary rival movements that use Salafi symbols and arguments for identity politics. Many Muslim movements offer a more modern version of an Islamic project worthy of support and volunteering. Furthermore, in times of war the more militant and political organizations are more attractive than in periods of peace. Among Barelwis, there is no direct competition with militant movements because membership is not necessarily exclusive. It remains to be seen whether the Daʿwat-e Islami protocol of permanent self-tracking, self-control, self-surveillance, and self-optimization is destructive in the long run, a self-exploitation of the soul, so to speak.[43] The Barelwi theological technique seems more sophisticated than the Deobandi argument, since it is seductive instead of repressive, and exploits freedom rather than oppresses it.[44] The neoliberal logic attaches the emotion of freedom to transforming the subject into a lucrative project.[45]

Apart from the uncertain future of the "neoliberal project culture," there are internal frontlines too. One such frontline could be opened up from the traditional Barelwi ulama in India, some of whom have already authored fatwas calling Ilyas Qadiri Attar a secret agent of Deoband. Another even more internal frontline is the issue of Salman Taseer's murderer, Mumtaz Qadiri, the Daʿwat-e Islami member who shot the governor of the Punjab for calling the blasphemy law a "black law." Mumtaz Qadiri has since been hanged, and Barelwis are currently building a shrine in honor of "their" martyr assassin. Another Mumtaz Qadiri may one day force security agencies in Pakistan to take action against religious hate speech. Although Daʿwat-e Islami was designed to resemble the successful proselytization technique of the Tablighis, they currently have an edge over them in terms of social media usage, their TV channel, and turning volunteers into long-term members.

CHAPTER 7

Religious Propagation and Revolution among Modern Shiʿa

The Rise and Fall of the Islamic Daʿwa Party in Iraq

AMATZIA BARAM

THE TWELVER SHIʿA tradition rarely has recourse to the concept of *daʿwa*. Although never entirely overlooked by Shiʿis, propagation of the faith became an applied precept only among the activist branches of the Zaydis (the Fiver Shiʿa, mainly in Yemen) and the Ismaʿilis (the Sevener Shiʿa). From the latter, emerged a movement known as *al-daʿwa al-hadiya*—"rightly-guided religious preaching." The Twelver Shiʿa, who normally refrained from challenging the existing order, preferred to avoid this activist term, as did mainstream Sunnis, for whom it became associated with political dissent and religious sectarianism.

In modern times, Shiʿi propagation of the faith has fluctuated between the drive to expand through conversion and the need for self-preservation in a hostile Sunni environment. Sixteenth-century Iran exemplifies the former strategy in the Safavid dynasty's forced conversion of the Sunni majority so as to consolidate its rule.[1] Throughout the nineteenth century, another form of propagation was employed in the more peaceful Shiʿization of southern Iraq.[2] By the mid-twentieth century, however, as religious propagation among Sunnis became too dangerous, it was channeled almost entirely inward toward the Shiʿi community itself, which was at the same time undergoing an accelerating process of secularization.

Another aspect of modern Shiʿi proselytism is its vacillation between the opposing strategies of quietism (*quʿud*) and activism (*khuruj*). In times of great religious fervor, such as the Islamic revolution in Iran, Shiʿi propagation of the faith is highly proactive and political, seeking regime change by violent means and without regard for the dangers it might pose to the activists themselves or the community of believers. Elsewhere, such as Iraq in the same period or Pakistan in the 1980s, the goal was more to bolster the community's identity and political clout to ensure that Shiʿis received a fair share of wealth and power on the national level. And occasionally, Shiʿi religious leaders have moved between traditional Shiʿi particularism and a Shiʿi-Sunni ecumenical approach, designed to win Sunni anti-Baʿth and antisecular support.

In light of the above, it is remarkable that the first modern religious political party to be established in the Shiʿa community in Iraq chose the name Hizb al-Daʿwa al-Islamiyya (the Islamic Propagation Party). It was founded in 1957 by a group of young religious scholars under the inspiration of Muhammad Baqir al-Sadr (1935–1980), who was determined to counter the obvious decline of religious faith and the rising influence of the (atheist) Iraqi Communist Party over young Shiʿis.[3]

Following the Baʿth takeover in 1968, Hizb al-Daʿwa became a powerful organized political opposition and a major challenge to the secular regime. The party survived the execution of Sadr in 1980, as well as the eight-year Iran-Iraq conflict, but remained dormant until its reemergence following the U.S.-led invasion and the toppling of Saddam Hussein in 2003. Still, although between May 2005 and late 2016 all three prime ministers were members of Hizb al-Daʿwa, the party's practical influence markedly declined due to internal splits, rivalries, and the challenges of other political and armed Shiʿi groups.[4]

This chapter focuses on the history of Hizb al-Daʿwa, the Iraqi Shiʿi party in general, and on the teachings of its progenitor and foremost ideologue, Muhammad Baqir al-Sadr in particular. It aims to show what caused Sadr and his colleagues to depict themselves as a *daʿwa* movement in the first place; what the movement's aims were; and the extent they actually implemented religious proselytizing in their politicoreligious thought and practice from the 1950s to the demise of the Baʿth regime in 2003.

FACING THE COMMUNIST CHALLENGE

Hizb al-Daʿwa, the Shiʿi political party, was established on 12 October 1957 at the home of Muhammad Baqir al-Sadr in Najaf.[5] A leading charismatic intellectual, he, and a few colleagues, felt that religious belief was waning in young Shiʿis. Sadr's most urgent concern was the rapid spread of the Iraqi Communist Party (ICP), which drew even the sons of Shiʿi ulama and *sada* (the Prophet's descendants) into its ranks. The ICP became even more potent after the military coup of General Abd al-Karim Qasim (r. 1958–1963).[6] Sadr decided to establish a "party" (*hizb*), even though he also defined his group as a "movement" (*haraka*) and an "organization" (*tanzim*). Elaborating on the choice of the term "party," he wrote that it was because "we are the Party of God (*hizb allah*)" as we are "supporters (*ansar*) of God and of Islam." This definition seems to have served as an inspiration for Ayatollah Khomeini when, in 1982, he established Hezbollah in Lebanon. This was a daring move at the time, first because *hizb* appears in the Quran not only in the phrase *hizb allah*, the people of God (Quran 5:56; 58:22], but also in the phrase *hizb al-shaytan*, the people of Satan (Quran 58:19) so that deeply religious and traditional Shiʿi movements avoided this term; and secondly because the notion of a political party was a modern construct, adopted by the Shiʿa's archrivals, the communists and the Baʿth, with their secular and un-Islamic, if not anti-Islamic, orientations. Sadr strove to defend and justify his choice of title, arguing: "Even though the sharia does not order us to follow a certain style in spreading the word ... we have permission to choose any useful way to disseminate the meanings of Islam and ... change society." Sadr had no doubt that if the Prophet had lived in this age, he "would have chosen modern means, including the organizational formation of a modern party, to convey his Message." But why "al-Daʿwa"? On this point, Sadr offered little guidance beyond the obvious: "The title 'al-Daʿwa al-Islamiyya' is the natural name for our activity and the legal expression of our duty to call people to Islam," he explained. "The style of the call to Islam—*daʿwa*—is the way by which Islam may be brought to the largest number of people, educating them in the culture of Islam." The activists were summoning the people to Islam so the party should be called "Daʿwa."[7] Sadr made no mention of any precedents in Islam where preachers might have formed groups with the word "daʿwa" in their title.

The organizational name Hizb al-Daʿwa thus reflected the Communist concept of propaganda, which Sadr sought to counter by Islamic means, and its underlying forms of organization—a combination that yielded a rather conspicuous and seemingly contradictory effect. The new party was built on Leninist lines as a clandestine, close-knit, and highly hierarchical vanguard organization, consisting of an educated elite of "professional revolutionaries." Another source of inspiration was the revolutionary *daʿwa* of the radical Sunni ideologue Sayyid Qutb, who in his *Milestones* likewise opted for a vanguard organization.[8]

As could be expected, a secretive, radical political party led by a middle- to senior-level *mujtahid* was extremely unpopular with many clerics in Najaf. They petitioned the *marja' al-taqlid* (lit. "source of emulation," the supreme Shi'i authority of the time), Grand Ayatollah Muhsin al-Hakim (1889–1970), to instruct Sadr to forgo the new party. They argued that a cleric must be available to all members of the community equally; having his own party would prevent that. Al-Hakim accepted the request despite his close ties to the Sadrs and the fact that two of his sons, Mahdi and Muhammad Baqir, were among the party's founder-members. Sadr ostensibly relented, but in fact maintained close contact with the party and remained its spiritual leader.[9]

Almost all members of the Iraqi Hizb al-Da'wa were laymen. Many were university students in various departments, mostly the natural sciences but also dentistry and medicine. The brightest and most dedicated were taught *usul al-fiqh* (principles of jurisprudence), a subject hitherto reserved for the ulama and students of religion. Others memorized the Quran, or parts of it, and studied its exegetes. They also had to be well acquainted with Islamic philosophy and with the Prophet's life story (*sira*), as well as those of the twelve Imams.[10] Sadr intended the party to operate on two levels: a small, mostly clandestine, intellectual-professional nucleus around which was built a larger protective circle of uninitiated supporters. He may well have been aware that physicians and dentists made excellent *du'a* because communication skills were an essential part of their profession, but also because they were in regular contact with patients who depended on them and might be susceptible to the influence of such authority figures. (Before Sadr, the Christian leader of the Popular Front for the Liberation of Palestine, George Habash, had the same recruitment strategy).

Within the university precincts, *da'wa* was practiced in two major ways. One was through public meetings and celebrations on important Shi'a religious occasions such as Ashura and *Arba'in* (commemorating the death of Imam Husayn) or the birthdays of the twelve Shi'i Imams. Even more effective was the practice of having a more senior student "adopt" a first-year "freshman" in the guise of assisting the perplexed newcomer with his studies. The *da'wa* activists made no attempt to convert Sunnis, but Christians were welcomed. Additionally, Sadr had his own way of approaching lost sheep. Once or twice a week he would travel from Najaf to Baghdad to deliver a sermon at a mosque. There he practiced "targeting" (*al-istihdaf*): approaching a seemingly promising young man and applying his direct and charming style to recruit him.

Sadr conducted another kind of *daʿwa* at his Najaf madrasa: encouraging his students to seek religious knowledge and live ascetically as moral and devout Shiʿis. He wrote,

> [If a bright student] works for the material world (*liʾl-dunya*), he will become the most miserable person because he will lose out in both this material world and in the next. The material world of the student [of religion] is not a world [of any value] and [by focusing his efforts on this world] he will not gain the next world either, so let our goal be the next world![11]

The Abbasid caliphs chose luxurious lives, Sadr asserted, but this only led them to crime and sin. He brandished his disdain for the Sunni caliphs by demeaning them as against Imam Ali. Describing Ali's death at the hands of a Kharijite fanatic, Sadr explained: "Ali, who had been cursed on all the Muslim pulpits," never regretted his dedication to true Islam and to God. Turning to the experience of the greatest caliph of the Abbasid "Golden Age," he left no doubt as to who was the saint and who the villain.

> The material world of [Caliph] Harun al-Rashid was formidable [however] ... we curse [him] night and day because he immersed himself in love of the material world.... O my children, O my brothers, O my dear ones, O sons of Ali ... it was this material world, the world of Harun al-Rashid, that compelled him to imprison Musa [al-Kazim] bin Jaʿfar [the seventh Imam].[12]

Out of caution, Sadr left unmentioned the Shiʿi conviction that the caliph actually poisoned al-Kazim, and that his son poisoned the eighth Imam, a contention that the students were fully aware of.

Together with his sister, Amina al-Sadr (Bint al-Huda, 1937–1980), Sadr further reinforced their *daʿwa* by establishing libraries, expanding religious schools, and creating Committees for Preaching and Guidance (*lijan liʾl-waʿz waʾl-irshad*). In the Daʿwa Party's formative period, Sadr defined the focus of its "jihad" as "intellectual change (*al-taghyir al-fikri*) ... spreading the conscience of change in the nation and establishing and educating the agent of change [itself]." A complementary goal was to create a popular base of support for the party. The masses were to become imbued with correct Islamic values but also to function as the party's protectors and maneuvering base. In this way, they would serve as "an introduction for [the party's] leadership of the . . . [whole Islamic] nation."[13]

DAʿWA AS REVOLUTION AND MARTYRDOM

After the Baʿth takeover of Iraq in 1968, the recruitment and acculturation methods developed by the Daʿwa Party, based on the Communist model, became the means to a more radical goal. By the late 1960s, Baqir al-Sadr had begun to cite the historic example of the Imams in articulating his new activist concept of Shiʿi *daʿwa*. He declared: "We have many texts that make it clear that the Imam of [any given] time was always *ready to launch an armed struggle*, were he convinced that there were supporters and capabilities to achieve the Islamic goals that led to this armed action" (emphasis added). After Imams Ali and Husayn, the generation of devout Muslims died out, and the Islamic state sank into "deviation" (read: Sunni practice). The Imams no longer had "supportive popular bases with conscience and [readiness for] sacrifice." The Imams then turned to constructing those bases "that would prepare suitable ground for taking over the reign of government (*tasallum al-sulta*)." Even then, however, the Imams still approved of Shiʿi revolutionaries who rose up with the sword against the Umayyads. Shiʿi uprisings did in fact occur in cases where there was a "total betrayal" of Islam by the "straying [Sunni] leadership."[14] Sadr lectured his students that contrary to the prevalent perception among the Shiʿa, the Imams were not passive victims of Sunni oppression. Rather, they played a "positive" or "active" role, confronting the (Sunni) caliphs so courageously as to cause the "straying leadership" to dread the Imams.[15] Admittedly, after Imam Husayn's death the successive Imams refrained from declaring war on the Sunni caliphs. But this was only because they knew they as yet lacked the "ideological army" (*al-jaysh al-ʿaqaʾidi*) that would "believe wholly in the Imam and his omniscience (*ʾisma*)," and be entirely committed to the Shiʿi cause.[16]

By these means, Sadr eventually replaced the traditional Shiʿi approach of political passivity (*quʿud*) with political and military activism (*khuruj*). Like the Marxists, he advocated revolution rather than reform: "Our *daʿwa* to Islam must be revolutionary (*inqilabiyya*)." In a programmatic article probably written in the mid-1970s, when Khomeini was still an exile in

Najaf, Sadr argued against reform (*islah*). His communiqué opened with the greeting, "O the believing *duʿa*, the *mujahidun* for Islam, [those fighting] for returning Islam to political sovereignty. . . ." It went on to state that due to the severe deterioration of Islam under the present Arab regimes, libraries, religious committees, and new madrasas—while important in their own right—now performed only "marginal actions" and could no longer remedy the situation. What was needed, Sadr averred, was nothing short of "the total elimination of the corrupt situation and of the entire present entity (read: regime)."[17]

Clearly, Sadr's words were directed against the Baʿth regime. Probably right from the start, but certainly since the early 1970s, Sadr was preparing for a mass revolt led by the professional revolutionaries of Hizb al-Daʿwa who were ready to risk everything for their leader and the cause. The Daʿwa Party had been tolerated, and its activities remained extensive and public during the first two years of Baʿth rule, but this changed soon after. While under house arrest in Najaf from June 1979 to early April 1980, Sadr sent recorded messages to invigorate his "call." He was bound to know that this call would be his doom, and he evidently sought martyrdom.

Sadr branded the regime "bloody murderers" and "despots" who—panicking at the sound of the people's growl—arrested, tortured, and executed "tens of thousands" of Iraqis, starting with the ulama. He accused the regime of forcing the Iraqi people not to keep faith with Muhammad and Ali but to comply with "Aflaq [cofounder of the Baʿth party in Syria who later found refuge in Iraq] and other agents of the [Christian] mission and imperialism." The duty of every Muslim in Iraq, Sadr continued, was to do their utmost, including sacrificing their own life, to rid Iraq of the Baʿth "nightmare." He concluded: "I have decided on martyrdom, and this may be the last you hear from me. The gates of heaven have already opened to greet the [ascending] columns of martyrs!"[18]

Sadr's last message called unambiguously for the overthrow of the Baʿth regime.[19] He had long hoped that his death would merge with the memory of the martyrdom of Imam Husayn and spur the Shiʿi masses to revolt. Yet in May 1979, before deciding on martyrdom, Sadr had planned to escape from Najaf, though ultimately he yielded to Khomeini's order to stay.[20] From the Iranian leader's response to the execution, he seems to have expected the Baʿth regime to kill Sadr, thereby sparking a massive Iraqi Shiʿi revolt.[21] Sadr's last two messages represented a most unusual kind of *daʿwa*: a call to martyrdom.

DAʿWA ON THE SHIʿI-SUNNI DIVIDE

With the shift to an activist form of *daʿwa*, Sadr began to advocate close collaboration with Iraq's Sunnis in a common struggle against the godless Baʿth. For that purpose, he was even prepared to relegate sectarian differences to a nonissue. As we have seen, Qutb's ideas influenced the formation of Hizb al-Daʿwa. In the early 1960s, Sadr made Qutb's writings essential reading for Daʿwa Party members, a clear indication of his broad-mindedness in recognizing the importance of radical Sunni ideology. By the late 1970s, with violent confrontation in full swing, he had recognized that without the cooperation of Sunni Islamists the Shiʿi opposition had no chance of toppling the Baʿth regime.

In his last message of 1980, Sadr sounds like a true ecumenical cleric. He appeals to both the Shiʿis and the Sunnis ("[Your] Arabs and Kurds . . . [Your] Sunnis and Shiʿis . . . sons of Ali and al-Husayn and sons of Abu Bakr and Umar") and urges them to join hands in the struggle against the Baʿth regime.[22] He goes so far as to depict the first three caliphs, whom the Shiʿa generally consider to have been base usurpers, as good Muslims and just rulers. In this message, Sadr implies that the Shiʿis are ready to accept Sunni supremacy as long as the Sunnis are faithful Muslims, guarding the sharia, and implementing the rule of justice. Ali, he reasoned, fought under the command of Abu Bakr and Umar because they were just and pious.

The sincerity of this new ecumenical approach, however, was questionable. One indication of this was Sadr's negative attitude toward the Abbasid caliphate, more especially toward the shining knight of its Golden Age, Harun al-Rashid. In one of his earliest publications, *Fadak fi'l-Taʾrikh* (Fadak in History), he attacks the first two caliphs, Abu Bakr and Umar, for their inhuman and vicious treatment of Fatima, the Prophet's daughter, Ali's wife, and mother of Imams Hasan and al-Husayn.[23] Unsurprisingly, Umar in particular is severely criticized in this work for preventing the Prophet from declaring on his deathbed that Ali was his heir.[24] In Sadr's view, the Imams actively protected the whole Islamic community from "descending into the abyss of complete deviation and the total shedding of its [Islamic] principles and values."[25] In other words, had Islam been left to the Sunni caliphs, at least some of whom Sadr considered to be "straying leadership," it would have been utterly lost. Only the Imams, through their "positive" action, had saved Islam from that fate.[26]

In his February 1979 Draft Constitution for the Islamic Republic of Iran, Sadr makes no secret that the Sunnis would have to accept inferior status in the future Islamic state. According to his formulation, "The election of the president of the executive government goes to the *umma* after his candidacy is approved by the collective body of [Shiʿi] Islamic jurists *(marjaʿiyya)*. . . . The [leading] *marjaʿ* is, from the legal point of view, the general deputy of the [Vanished] Imam" therefore "the supreme representative of the state and the supreme commander of the army."[27] This is indeed the controversial doctrine of *vilayat-i faqih* (rule of the jurist), the political cornerstone of the Shiʿi Islamic revolution in Iran. Considering that only a few months later Sadr implied that the Shiʿa could accept Sunni leadership as long as they were truly Islamic, no wonder his disciples became confused.

In one of my conversations with the Shiʿi "Dr. Shammari," I asked whether he would prefer Iraq to remain united or be split into Sunni, Shiʿi, and Kurdish states. His reply was emphatic: Iraq was great in ancient pre-Islamic history and must stay united in order to be great again. It did not bother him at all when I pointed out that this was precisely Saddam's vision: to return Iraq to the glory that was ancient heathen Mesopotamia. His only caveat was that from his perspective, Iraq under Saddam was united like a donkey and its rider, the donkey being the Shiʿis and the rider the Sunnis. "All we want is to switch places," he said with a smile, in a very nonecumenical manner.[28]

ENDURING THE REGIME'S WRATH

In the course of the 1980s the Baʿth leadership occasionally discussed the option of eliminating *al-hawza al-ʿilmiyya*, the study circles of Najaf and Karbala. Eventually it was decided to allow them to exist, lest Qom win the contest for Shiʿi spiritual leadership against the holy cities of Iraq. However, the Baʿth party was adamant about "dwarfing" the *hawzas*, and the number of their students consequently dwindled. In the mid-to-late 1960s, students still numbered in the thousands, whereas by the late 1980s it was in the hundreds. The number of madrasas in Najaf also shriveled, while those of Karbala disappeared altogether.[29]

Still, in 1982 when the Iraqi Communist Party appealed to the Islamic Daʿwa Party for cooperation in the struggle against the Baʿth regime, their offer was rejected emphatically, and Hizb al-Daʿwa stuck to its original goal of fighting the ICP. The reply was quite blunt. In the first place, the Communists must become religious and believe in the "heavenly Islamic message." They must "adhere to Islamic law" and implement it fully, like the Islamic community, "under the leadership of the Prophet and the Imams." In other words, the Daʿwa Party demanded that the Iraqi Communists become born-again Muslims, and strictly Shiʿi Muslims at that. Anything less was unacceptable, even regarding a joint struggle against Saddam Hussein, "the Nimrod of our age" and "the Pharaoh of Tikrit."

With Sadr gone and the Daʿwa Party in decline, and with the imminent threat of closing the *hawza* hanging over the heads of Shiʿi clergy, in the 1980s the quietist line of *marjaʿ al-taqlid* Grand Ayatollah Abu'l-Qasim al-Khoʾi (1899–1992) won the day. The senior *mujtahidun* kept to the tradition of refraining from swearing allegiance to the ruler in the communal Friday sermon by eschewing the congregational prayer altogether. They also encouraged the people to participate in religious commemorations such as Ashura to enhance Shiʿi identity and faith. For the regime however, more disturbing was the fact that Khoʾi declined participating in the *fatiha* prayer for the dead of the Iran war. This form of passive resistance indicated his reluctance to endorse the war as a kind of jihad, as the regime demanded. In moments of truth, the Baʿth leaders had indeed to admit that they had lost the battle for Shiʿa hearts.[30]

Thus, although by 1990 the modern-style *daʿwa* initiated by Muhammad Baqir al-Sadr seemed to be failing, traditional forms of preaching and education kept the flame burning. The Najaf and Karbala clerics made every effort to protect their madrasas and to persevere even under such adverse circumstances. The Baʿth did not dare close down the shrines of the Holy Cities; on the contrary, Saddam Hussein eventually boasted about providing them massive financial support. The commemoration days and festivals, insofar as the regime acquiesced in their observation, and the madrasas, few as they were, kept the community engaged around its religious leadership. Khoʾi very reluctantly joined the Shiʿi revolt that erupted in March 1991 in the wake of the Iraqi defeat by U.S.-led coalition forces in Kuwait, even though he had initially refrained from giving it his blessing. As he feared, the revolt was crushed in rivers of Shiʿi blood. In Iraq it is widely believed that his death a year later, after being forced to denounce the revolt, was the result of poisoning by the regime's agents. But he was 93 years old and frail, and a broken heart could equally have been the cause. Despite all his efforts to protect his community, he saw in a single blow how close it was to extinction.

THE RETURN TO CONVENTIONAL SHIʿI PROSELYTISM

Passive resistance remained the order of the day throughout the 1990s under Khoʾi's successor, Grand Ayatollah Ali al-Sistani (b. 1930). The Shiʿi community was in a state of post-traumatic shock following the bloody suppression of the March 1991 revolt and had no desire for further confrontation. Nevertheless, the second half of the 1990s saw the rise of the enigmatic Ayatollah Muhammad Sadiq al-Sadr (1943–1999), Baqir al-Sadr's younger cousin from Najaf, whose conduct between Baqir al-Sadr's execution in 1980 and his own assassination in 1999—apparently at the hands of the regime—remains the subject of conflicting interpretations. His cousin's execution and the brutal 1991 suppression convinced Sadiq al-Sadr that socioreligious activism, rather than political activism, was the safest and most effective way to enhance the Shiʿi identity and Islamic devotion of his community.[31] He therefore made no effort to revive the Islamic Daʿwa Party, whose leaders were by the 1990s mostly in exile, or to create similar organizations. Instead, Sadiq al-Sadr resorted to the traditional means of preaching through the revival of the communal Friday sermon (the *khutba*) and the madrasa, by the instruction his students gave at mosques and shrines (Husayniyyat), and by sending emissaries, or "agents," to Shiʿi communities, including even the most remote villages. Abandoning his cousin's concept of *daʿwa*, Sadiq eventually returned to the proselytizing practices employed by the *mujtahid*s of the Holy Cities during the great Shiʿization drive of the nineteenth century.[32] Unlike them, however, and in actual competition rather than cooperation with the official Najaf *hawza*, his missionaries worked to deepen Shiʿi awareness and commitment to the sharia rather than to convert Sunni tribes to Shiʿism. As part of this endeavor, Sadiq al-Sadr issued a large number of fatwas, some overtly opposed to the opinions expressed by the official ulama of the *hawza*.[33]

Surprisingly, while keeping Sadiq al-Sadr at arm's length during the 1980s,[34] by the 1990s the Baʿth regime had reconsidered, and decided to reengage him, apparently to humiliate Sistani and his colleagues and in the hope of winning the charismatic young cleric to its side. Sadr concentrated his efforts mainly on the poor Shiʿi neighborhoods, such as Baghdad's largely tribal shanty town Saddam City (previously Madinat al-Thawra, or "Revolution City"), and on the Shiʿi tribes of the hinterland.[35] He and his emissaries propagated a strict form of Islam that advocated women's separation in mixed workplaces and girls' wearing the *hijab* in schools, as well as demanding the prohibition of alcohol and American films.[36] For the tribesmen, Sadr published a collection of fatwas that did not display any particular Shiʿi angle but propounded sharia solutions at the expense of tribal practices.[37] On top of this, Sadr called for preparation for the reappearance of the Expected Imam.[38] Severely criticizing the senior Shiʿi ulama for being passive and quietist, he labeled them *al-hawza al-samita* (the silent scholarly circle), while regarding himself as *al-hawza al-natiqa* (the outspoken scholar). While not calling for a revolt, just before his assassination Sadr carefully demanded the release of *hawza* students from prison.

Concomitantly, Sadr and his "agents" also referred to the social and economic ills afflicting Iraqi Shiʿi society, such as exorbitant food prices, a badly damaged infrastructure, lack of potable water, and scarcity of electrical power. Rather than accusing the regime of being at fault in the situation, Sadr blamed the West and the international embargo for the great suffering of the Iraqi people. Assigning guilt to the West, however, could easily be interpreted as an indirect attack on the regime, which refused to abide by UN Security Council resolutions, thereby prolonging the embargo. By these means, he attracted wide-spread support among the young generation in the lower classes who were eager for action and change. The urban middle class and the middle-aged, by contrast, preferred the quietist strategy of Sistani, the *marjaʿ al-taqlid*.[39] Financially supported by the regime, Sadiq al-Sadr was allowed to take over Baqir al-Sadr's madrasa and to have a say in the process of selecting foreign Shiʿi students and teachers for study in Iraq. In 1996, he founded the religious magazine *al-Huda* (the Right Guidance)[40] and a year later received permission to deliver Friday sermons in the mosques of the Shiʿi south, although he too refrained from explicitly recognizing Saddam's legitimacy.[41]

A close examination of Sadr's *khutba*s reveals that they seem highly conservative, always opening with those traditional Shiʿi formulas that could be acceptable to the Sunnis as well. But in practice many of his sermons walked a tightrope between challenging the regime and appeasing it, between an innocuous demand for return to the sharia—something the regime also favored throughout the 1990s—and a dangerous brand of eschatological theology. Sadr tried in vain to strike a balance between ecumenism and anti-Sunni barbs. However, for all his provocations, ultimately his criticism of the regime bears no comparison to that of his older martyred cousin, Muhammad Baqir al-Sadr. Sadiq never accused the regime of atheism and never called for its overthrow. On the other hand, while Sadiq al-Sadr never attacked Iran, he did challenge the authority of its spiritual leader, Ayatollah Ali Khamenei, considering himself eligible to the status of *wali amr al-muslimin* (Supreme Authority of [all] Muslims), a title hitherto reserved for Ayatollah Khomeini, and after him Khamenei. Such a claim made him *persona non grata* in Tehran.[42]

Still, Sadiq al-Sadr followed some of the modern methods of propagation used by his deceased cousin and his Daʿwa Party during the 1960s and 1970s. Like Baqir al-Sadr, he too especially appealed to the younger generation and disseminated his ideas through sermons and classes as well as through the press. The differences, though, were substantial: rather than a small, close-knit, elitist and clandestine party of professional revolutionaries, Sadiq appealed to the masses through the more conventional means of religious guidance and direction, careful to carry out his activities in the open and with the consent of the regime.

In the end, his great popularity combined with his growing audacity to bring his downfall. In February 1999, he was gunned down along with two of his sons on the outskirts of Najaf. His followers had no doubt that the Baʿth intelligence service was behind the assassination, although there were others, such as the Iranian regime, that could also have been responsible.[43] Right up to the American-led occupation and the resulting demise of Saddam Hussein and the Iraqi Baʿth party in 2003, no other religious leader had dared challenge the quietist policies of the senior Shiʿi clerics.

CONCLUSION

Hizb al-Daʿwa was a unique and groundbreaking phenomenon in Iraqi and Shiʿi history alike. The party was the creation of the young cleric and ideologue Muhammad Baqir al-Sadr, who continued to support it and fuel its vitality in the face of strong opposition from the conservative *hawza* in Najaf as long as he lived. As its name indicates, in establishing the new organization Sadr introduced two innovative concepts into the modern radical Shiʿi religious vocabulary. One was *hizb*, meaning political party; the other was *daʿwa*, in the sense of religious preaching directed mainly toward straying Shiʿi Muslims.

The concept of *daʿwa* had previously been very rarely used in Twelver Shiʿi tradition. Baqir al-Sadr introduced it as a counter to the effective propaganda of the Iraqi Communist Party, which was making deep inroads into the Shiʿi youth of the time. His model was initially based on the *daʿwa* of the Muslim Brothers in general, and, after the Baʿth's rise to power in 1968, the revolutionary *daʿwa* of Sayyid Qutb in particular. Unlike the Muslim Brothers, who preferred to define themselves as an association (*jamʿiyya*) and later as a movement (*haraka*), Baqir al-Sadr felt that creating a "Party of God" was essential to face the Communist "Party of Satan." Accordingly, his was a clandestine group of professional revolutionaries organized along Leninist lines who had the dual duty of strengthening the Shiʿi community's religious identity and preparing for an armed revolution against the Baʿth (essentially Sunni) regime. The Iraqi Hizb al-Daʿwa preceded and showed the way to Hezbollah in Lebanon as well as to a plethora of political parties established by other Shiʿi *mujtahidun* along similar lines in Iraq.

The success of Hizb al-Daʿwa in enhancing Shiʿi identity and Islamic piety in modern Iraq was the cause of its downfall. The threat it represented to the Baʿth regime led to a ferocious crackdown and the execution of its spiritual leader. Subsequently, most of its activity moved out of Iraq to Europe, Syria, and to a lesser degree Tehran. While the Iranian revolutionary government opted to countenance competing Iraqi Shiʿi resistance movements, in Iraq the Daʿwa party's elitist inclinations cleared the way for the populist-oriented organization of Sadiq al-Sadr and his son Muqtada. Personal rivalries and internal splits further prevented the Daʿwa Party from playing a decisive role in the Shiʿi-led governments elected after the 2003 invasion, despite the fact that all the prime ministers elected were members of the party.

In post-Baʿth Iraq, Muhammad Baqir al-Sadr's *daʿwa* gave way to the ongoing fiery dispute over Khomeini's controversial concept of *vilayt-i faqih* and to the new-old concept of Shiʿi Mahdism, sparked by the 2003 formation of Jaysh al-Mahdi (Army of the Awaited One) by Sadiq al-Sadr's son Muqtada. Another Mahdist militant organization from Basra, Jund al-Sama' (Soldiers of Heaven), attacked Najaf with the intention of killing all the clerics, since in their view the moment the Mahdi reveals himself there will no longer be any need for ulama.[44] Unperturbed, Grand Ayatollah Ali Sistani has continued to adhere to his nonpolitical line, interrupted by some extraordinary interventions, such as his June 2014 call for joining the military to defend Iraq against ISIS, his support for anticorruption reforms, and his general thrust to repel the efforts of Khamenei's and Qom's ulama to exert political and religious authority over the Shiʿis of Iraq and the world at large.

PART III

The Global and the Local

CHAPTER 8

Contemporary Daʿwa and the State in Southeast Asia

JULIA DAY HOWELL

THIS CHAPTER EXAMINES Islamic propagation (Indonesian: *dakwah*) in the largest Southeast Asian Muslim majority nation, Indonesia, with some comparisons to neighboring Malaysia. It focuses on the period since the 1970s, when the region was affected by particularly powerful currents of Islamic revivalism sweeping across the Muslim world. This was also a time when economic development drives initiated by the governments of both countries began to take effect and stimulate profound social changes, which created new markets for the Islamic call.

In Indonesia, newly established *daʿwa* institutions channelling funds from the Middle East as well as independent transnational *daʿwa* movement activists, many of them returned students who had studied abroad, variously complemented and competed with the religious education efforts of long-established Islamic schools and voluntary organizations such as the modernist Muhammadiyya and the traditionalist Nahdlatul Ulama. *Daʿwa* enthusiasm also stimulated the formation of new domestic but transnationally linked informal organizations and networks such as the Muslim Brotherhood-inspired *tarbiya* (education) movement. Following them, a new breed of inspired lay preachers (*duʿa*) have sought new ways to engage fellow Muslims using print but also emergent electronic media. In so doing, they have developed new *daʿwa* formats and melded *daʿwa* with business. Radio and TV appearances have made national celebrities of genial and engaging *duʿa*, while religious educators cater to the tastes, daily life patterns, and intellectual demands of new Muslim elites.

Malaysia experienced similar patterns of social change that stimulated demand for new kinds of Islamic predication, and Muslims in both countries have engaged with *daʿwa* initiatives projected into the region by the same extra-regional "providers." Nonetheless, differences in the historical legacies and the politics of ethnic pluralism have made for markedly different patterns of revival movement activity. While *daʿwa* in Malaysia has been predominantly state driven, Indonesian *daʿwa* was largely civil-society generated. This accounts for the broader scope for critical thinking in religious matters and the broader span of modes of religiosity promoted by *daʿwa* agents in Indonesia compared with Malaysia, where the state has come to define a narrowly scripturalist Islam, suppresses competing understandings of Islam, and circumscribes the free practice of minority religions.

The chapter begins with a comparison of the place of Islam in each country, as established by their respective constitutions and promoted by the states. Thereafter, the discussion will focus on Indonesia, examining the spectrum of religious thought and action promoted by *daʿwa* activists over the past several decades, from Islamist to liberal, and the variety of new institutional platforms that revival promoters have used, with special attention to innovative lay initiatives and commercial platforms.

CONSTITUTIONAL FRAMEWORKS AND SOCIETAL CONTEXTS

The founding constitutions of both Malaysia and Indonesia provided freedom of religion for their religiously and ethnically diverse populations. Nonetheless, both constitutional assemblies, after some debate, came to state the central importance of religion to their nations. Thus the constitution of Malaysia, whose indigenous Malay ethnic community made up just over half the population and which from the beginning was legally defined as Muslim, gives symbolic recognition to the centrality of the Malay religious heritage by recognizing Islam as "the religion of the Federation."[1]

In Indonesia, with a far larger population and hundreds of closely related but nonetheless diverse indigenous ethnic groups, the preamble to the constitution affirmed that the nation held to "belief in God." The founders nonetheless established a Department of Religion primarily concerned with Islamic affairs.[2] After independence, advocates for establishing Indonesia as an Islamic state were left to pursue their goal through legislative means. In the early years of the republic, Muslim parties pressing that agenda failed to achieve the majority of votes that would enable the fulfilment of their hopes. Years of authoritarian rule (first Sukarno's "Guided Democracy" from 1959 to 1966 and then Suharto's "New Order" government from 1968 to 1998), forestalled any possibility of Islamist parties putting the Islamic state issue to the vote. Then, after the turn of the century, when a freely elected parliament had once more been instated, Islamists again lacked sufficient support to amend the constitution.[3]

In Malaysia, the leading party in the country's governing coalition, the United Malay National Organization (UMNO), increasingly advanced Malay interests in terms of their legally determined Islamic identity. The defensive politics of Malay, and hence Muslim, privilege, has obliged UMNO both to compete with rival parties for Islamic credentials and to perform as an agent of Islamicization. It has done so by upgrading and expanding the national religious affairs bureau, establishing new government agencies to define and promote Islamic orthodoxy, integrate and rationalize regional (i.e., state) Islamic affairs, and establish Islamic institutions in the wider society. In this way, the Malaysian state has drawn civil society *daʿwa* agents from potentially rivalrous movements into its own bureaucratic structure. It has also provided employment in its several Islamic affairs bureaus for the large numbers of young Muslim graduates produced by the expanded education sector, forfending the discontent of unemployed Malays.[4] In short, the Malaysian state has assumed the role of primary Islamic institution builder and definer of orthodoxy. Further, since 2001, successive Prime Ministers Mahathir Mohamad and Abdullah Badawi have proclaimed that Malaysia already functions as an Islamic state and have worked to promote that perception across Malaysian society.[5]

The interventions made by the Indonesian state since the 1970s have served broadly similar goals to those of Malaysian federal governments, namely, political stabilization around a religion-infused construction of national identity and promotion of economic development through the reshaping of citizens' religious values and motivations. President Suharto, however, officially supported multiple religions as suitable choices for Indonesians, regardless of their ethnicity, in conformity with the loose concept of monotheistic religiosity that figured as the first of the Five Principles of nationhood (the *Panca Sila*). In the first two decades of his authoritarian rule, he further developed that set of heretofore vague guiding principles into an ideology of religious pluralism designed to neutralize competition from Muslim political activists.[6]

INDONESIAN STATE MANAGEMENT OF ISLAM

General Suharto came to power in 1968 in the cataclysmic aftermath of the ostensibly Communist attempted coup of 30 September 1965. To stabilize the new regime, he used a presidential decision enunciated by his predecessor Sukarno just months before the fateful coup incident to identify unambiguously the religious commitments of the entire population.[7] For the first time since independence, it was specified what kind of religion (*agama*) was to be protected under the constitution. The decision achieved this not by stating explicit criteria to determine what would count as an acceptable "religion" but rather by naming a small number of particular religions. The list included Islam and the two implicitly recognized forms of Christianity (Protestantism and Catholicism), as well as Hinduism, Buddhism, and Confucianism. Village and district heads across the country became responsible for recording the religious affiliations of citizens in their areas.

While as an administrative procedure the recording of an individual's religious identification was straightforward, for many people the choice itself was not. *Abangan* Muslims, who practiced Islamic traditions inflected with local cultures,[8] harbored apprehensions that they would have to neglect the heritage of their ancestors and be forced into regularly performing the normatively obligatory five daily prayers, a practice they were unaccustomed to. Moreover, many Muslims participated in loosely Sufi but often eclectic mystical groups whose spiritual universes encompassed beings from several religious traditions.[9] Sukarno's Presidential Decision naming the six religions congruent with the Panca Sila explicitly required citizens to leave such eclectic mystical groups and "return" to the fold of whatever "proper" religion they formally acknowledged.[10]

During the religion registration campaign, a number of Javanese *abangan* and Muslim followers of mystical groups chose to convert to Christianity (identifying as Protestant or Catholic) or to register as Hindu or Buddhist.[11] The vast majority, however, retained their Islamic identity and so experienced new incentives to regularize their religious practice in accordance with ever-more widely circulating global understandings of Islam. The program of religious affiliation registration assisted both security and economic agendas of the new regime. Development, which came with the promise of improved living standards for Indonesians who had suffered from years of economic mismanagement and instability under

Sukarno, became one of the chief incentives for the acceptance of Suharto's "New Order."[12]

A key part of the Repelita (five year) development programs was the expansion of education through state schools as well as private Islamic schools. Over the years, state funding delivered dramatic increases in levels of literacy and post-primary studies completion. Significantly, incentives were offered to the traditional Islamic schools (*pesantren*) to include general curriculum studies (math, science, and English) and to introduce graded progression equivalent to primary and lower- and upper-secondary studies. The government also funded the expansion of the Islamic tertiary education sector, enabling growing numbers of students from strict Muslim backgrounds (*santri*) to qualify for careers in the modern sector of the growing national economy.[13]

While Muslim children were increasingly becoming equipped for middle-class and elite urban employment, they were also becoming better educated in the fundamentals of their faith, as they were required to take a minimum one hour per week of religious instruction. Increased mastery of Islamic knowledge and the value placed on globally normative Islam helped shape aspirations for rightly guided piety, which the *da'wa* movement of the Suharto years catered to and further stimulated.

Muslims who had been active in Islamic parties before Sukarno's suspension of parliamentary democracy in 1959, particularly members of the banned modernist Masyumi party, hoped for new opportunities to influence the government and commit the state to enforcing Islamic law among Muslims.[14] The historic role of Muslim parties in opposing the Indonesian Communist Party seemed to provide good reason for this hope. Yet they were disappointed, as Suharto moved to control Islamic parties and limit the scope for democratic contestation generally. The government permitted the formation of an alternative Islamic modernist organization, Parmusi, but intervened in its direction and barred the participation of Masyumi leaders. Later, the four Islamic parties that had contested the election of 1971 were required to merge into a single party under a name that made no reference to Islam: the United Development Party (PPP).

In 1984, government legislation required all registered Indonesian social organizations and political parties to recognize the Panca Sila as their sole foundational principle. This caused great consternation among Islamic organizations, which were thereby obliged to feature their commitment to the New Order state before their Islamic faith.[15] The Panca

Sila remained the ideological foundation of the state, taught in all schools and made into examinable knowledge for civil servants.

CIVIL DAʿWA IN THE EARLY NEW ORDER

Although Islamic political contestation under Suharto's New Order was severely constrained, there was still considerable scope for social activism to inspire better understanding and heightened commitment to Islamic orthodoxy. In other words, *daʿwa* became possible as long as it did not challenge the regime. The government even cautiously supported it as a means of promoting morality and acceptable religious citizenship.[16] Still, the strictly controlled political environment of the New Order necessitated formation of new groupings and even institutional innovation. Notably, campus mosque-based study circles came to be some of the main vectors for *daʿwa*. Fresh currents of revivalist thought, inspired by movements in the Middle East and South Asia, were developed through the new campus *daʿwa* groups. They contested the modernist Islamic voluntary organizations represented through Masyumi (notably Muhammadiyah), as well as the traditionalist Nahdlatul Ulama, for influence over young Muslims.

Two markedly contrasting currents of religious thought came to prominence at that time. One was an Islamist revivalist current carrying the idea of "total Islam" or Islam as a complete way of life.[17] It drew chiefly on the writings of Egyptian Muslim Brotherhood founder Hasan al-Banna and Pakistani Jamaʿat-i Islami founder Abu'l-Aʿla Mawdudi.[18] Its proponents envisioned transforming all aspects of the social world, from the familial to the economic and political, into accordance with the way of life of the Prophet and his Companions in the early years of Islam. This understanding of "authentic" Islam was based on literal readings of the canonical scriptures without reference to the classical commentaries of past ulama, as signalled by the slogan "Back to the Quran and Sunna." The economically and politically weak position of so many majority Muslim societies, and the perceived corruption of their values by accelerating modernization and Western influences, could be transformed, it was thought, by implementing the correct Islam in all aspects of life. "Islam is the solution" became another catchcry of the movement.[19] A major role in the spread of "total Islam" was played by former leaders of the Masyumi Party who had come under Saudi influence.[20]

The other major stream of Indonesian Islamic revivalism was variously characterized as Renewalist, Contextualist, or Neo-Modernist (in reference to Fazlur Rahman, 1919–1988).[21] Its proponents viewed Islam's canonical texts as carriers of basic moral insights to be read and applied in light of the realities of the modern world. They saw Islam as compatible with secular legal systems in religiously plural societies, and the reformulation of Islamic law as allowable as patterns of work and family life change in modernizing societies. They also accepted local ways of practicing Islam and popular Sufism. This current of reformist thought had its origins in an emergent, progressive wing of the Modernist movement and interacted with a new cohort of progressive social activists connected to the *pesantren* and their directors (*kyai*) in the Nahdlatul Ulama organization.

THE ISLAMIST REVIVAL TREND

A key role in promoting the popularity of "total Islam" in New Order Indonesia was played by a wing of the decommissioned Masyumi party elite. Its leader, Muhammad Natsir, was a former chairman of Masyumi and also served as Vice Chairman of the Saudi-based Muslim World League. In 1967, with sponsorship from the League, he and his colleagues formed the Indonesian Council for Islamic Predication (DDII), which became the main conduit for Saudi funding for Islamist outreach in Indonesia during the Suharto era.[22] It called on Indonesian Muslims to cease performing locally derived Islamic rituals, for which purists found no proper precedent in literal readings of the Quran and Sunna, and to fully comply with Islamic law as understood by their movement.[23] Through preaching and its monthly publication, *Media Dakwah,* the organization also promoted an unprecedented cultural "Arabicization" of Indonesian Islam.[24] This was evident in their call to follow Arab Islamic dress codes (including the veiling of women), strictly segregate the sexes, and use Arabic greetings and terms of address. Such practices acted first as social markers of an exclusivist vanguard movement, but in just a decade they were already becoming mainstream. Further, whereas Masyumi had been both prodemocratic and pro-Western, DDII became increasingly anti-Western and anti-Zionist, casting Western secularism, Christianity, and Jewish "conspiracies" as threats to the Muslim world.[25] At the same time, as van Bruinessen observes, it "developed into the most persistent moral critic of the Suharto regime . . . speaking in the name of democracy as well as Islam."[26]

Early on, DDII focused its *daʿwa* efforts on university students, particularly those in secular universities, where there was considerable political ferment in the 1970s. *Media Dakwah* was widely distributed on campuses, which became major recruiting grounds for a new generation of *daʿwa* enthusiasts. With Saudi funds, large numbers of university students were sent to study at Middle Eastern universities. DDII also proselytized in the broader community, particularly among lower-class and lower-middle-class Muslims in urban areas.[27]

From the 1980s on, campus mosque-based activists propagated predominantly Islamist revival, teaching Islam as a political ideology for transforming society.[28] Students discussed the ideas of Banna and Qutb and of earlier Islamic modernists such as Muhammad Abduh, and, after the 1979 Iranian Islamic Revolution, Shiʿi authors who advocated the transformation of Muslim majority societies into Islamic states. Posters of Ayatollah Khomeini appeared in places frequented by students, and his writings were studied alongside those of Murtada Mutahhari and Ali Shariʿati, who drew on Left and Third World critiques of Western societies to construct an Islamic political philosophy.

A central role in the ideological and institutional development of campus *daʿwa* was played by students and staff of the Salman Mosque, which was attached to the prestigious Bandung Institute of Technology. It was through this mosque that DDII *daʿwa* intersected with that of the Malaysian Islamic Youth Movement (ABIM), which promoted Muslim Brotherhood Islamism. From ABIM the Indonesian *daʿwa* activists adopted a predication format called *usroh* (lit. family), small study groups directed by a senior member responsible for shaping the proper moral character of the junior members. Fifteen to twenty-five students would gather regularly in *usroh* groups to study the Quran and writings of the Muslim Brotherhood.

The linkage between DDII and ABIM was made by engineer and faculty member Imaduddin Abdul Rahim, who had taught in Malaysia in the early 1970s. He became head of the *daʿwa* section of the university students' association upon returning to Bandung and also arranged the publication of ABIM's *Panduan Usroh,* a guidebook for small-group *daʿwa*. Soon, small *usroh* study groups, linked in hierarchical networks, became widespread on the campuses of secular universities across Indonesia.[29] In addition, Imaduddin developed a more intensive predication program called Training for *Daʿwa,* which involved seven days of Islamic studies on-site with no outside contact. Highly popular, it attracted students from other universities in Bandung, as well as from Jakarta, Yogyakarta, Medan, and elsewhere in Indonesia, who carried the training model back to their universities. To facilitate ongoing cooperation among institutions with similar programs, a linkage organization, the Workshop for Campus *Daʿwa* Institutions was established in the mid-1980s. It ran joint programs and cooperated in extending their model of *daʿwa* to other universities around the country.

The Salman Mosque also initiated public outreach programs including the Family Welfare Course for mothers and the Salman Children's Education program. Its Youth Guidance Program included Islamic "mentoring" along with providing development skills and preparing high school students for university entrance exams. Participating families associated with high schools across the country patronized the program and then replicated it and other *daʿwa* training programs at their home institutions. The Salman mosque association represented, according to Rosyad, "the first on-campus Islamic organization to properly organize—in modern style—various Islamic activities for young people .. [with] a good managerial system and relatively complete facilities."[30] Many mosques in the wider community established Islamic study and social activity programs independently under the inspiration of the Salman Mosque predication programs.[31]

Other forms of Islamist *daʿwa* developed in the 1980s through the Saudi-funded, Jakarta-based Institute for Islamic and Arabic Studies (LIPIA), an initiative of the DDII. It offered Arabic language and Islamic law studies, approached predominantly from a Wahhabi puritanical and exclusivist yet politically conservative perspective (accepting rather than challenging the authority of the state). Still, its staff included teachers who had studied in Saudi Arabia during the Islamic Awakening of the early 1990s, when politically quiescent (Salafi) Wahhabism became mixed with militant Islamism imported by Muslim Brother activists escaping government crackdowns in Egypt.[32] Consequently, LIPIA also became a site for the dispersal of militant variants of Islamism, along with politically quietist Wahhabi scripturalism.

In addition, earlier in the 1980s, the politically radical but nonmilitant Hizbut Tahrir, originally based at the Bogor Agricultural Institute in West Java, was quietly proselytizing their cause of establishing a global caliphate.[33]

THE RENEWAL MOVEMENT OF CONTEXTUALIST ISLAM

Not surprisingly, the form of Islamic revivalism that the New Order government viewed as least problematic, and to which it was most ready to give support, was Contextualist Islam, particularly as developed by the Islamic Renewal Movement. Using rationalist and contextual methods, Renewalists drew basic moral principles from the Quran that they held to be as applicable in modern times to a religiously plural and democratic society such as Indonesia as they were to the form of government established in the early years of Islam by the Prophet Muhammad in Medina.

A key instigator and leading figure of the movement was Nurcholish Majdid, a young student leader with a Masyumi background. In 1970, as chairman of the Muslim University Student Association at the State Islamic Institute in Jakarta, he made a startling critique of modernist Islamic groups' obsession, as he saw it, with party politics. He argued that the reformist agenda of the modernists, who early in the century had reclaimed for laypeople the responsibility of interpreting the scriptures in light of changing times, had been neglected, being overshadowed by contestation among Islamic parties for power. In the Muslim public of the day, Majdid saw a growing interest in better understanding their faith and following its devotional practices, combined with a widespread disengagement from Islamic politics. He thus challenged his audiences to refocus away from politics and to resume the work of reinterpreting the faith's foundational texts. In so doing, he disappointed members of the Masyumi old guard who had hailed him as "the young Natsir."[34] A circle of similarly intellectually audacious students from Yogyakarta shared his concerns and over the years would help build the intellectual and social foundations for Renewalist *da'wa*.[35]

In the late 1960s, modernist-oriented intellectuals conducted a discussion group on reformist Islamic thought, especially exploring the use of rationalist approaches to the interpretation of scriptures for guiding behavior and shaping institutions under the changed circumstances of modern living. They were assisted in this by A. Mukti Ali, a professor at Yogyakarta's State Islamic Institute who had studied the rationalist exegesis of the Indian modernist Sayyid Ahmad Khan in Pakistan before earning a doctorate in Comparative Religion at McGill University in Canada. The group had broad interests in religion and theology, which they explored with Christian and other non-Muslim thinkers.[36] Ali's appointment as Minister of Religious Affairs from 1972 to 1978 signalled the importance to the Suharto regime of Muslim thinkers who could help underpin pluralist "Panca Sila" democracy. Others associated with the Yogyakarta circle who would become key figures in the Renewalist movement also found positions in Jakarta.

Nurcholish Madjid developed his approach to Islamic reform during the 1970s in dialogue with sympathetic Muslim intellectuals such as the Yogyakarta circle around Mukti Ali. On this basis, he delivered talks on campuses across the country, offering students a markedly different kind of inspiration for rightly shaping and invigorating their piety. His home university, the State Islamic Institute in Jakarta, offered significant intellectual support, particularly under Harun Nasution, who as rector from 1973–1984 championed the study of Muʿtazila rationalist exegesis.

Majdid's doctoral studies at the University of Chicago from 1978 to 1984 with the renowned South Asian modernist Fazlur Rahman also shaped his evolving approach to deriving guidance from the Quran. Particularly important for him was Rahman's concern for understanding the historical circumstances of revelation and how that might bear on the derivation of Islamic law in modern times. Majdid became a leading proponent of contextual methodologies for interpreting the scriptures. This, in turn, would undergird progressive and liberal approaches to Islam that he and other progressives elaborated over the next several decades. When disseminated through campus and public lectures, books, magazines, and Islamic studies courses, these methods and approaches appealed to the growing upper middle class and elite of Indonesian Muslim society.[37]

To carry Renewalist thought beyond university campuses and academic discussion circles, Majdid established the Paramadina Foundation in 1986. It was designed to publish the Renewalists' work, translations of foreign-language books on which they drew, and to offer short courses on Islam to the university-educated urban elite. This was done in a novel setting: office spaces in an exclusive neighborhood in South Jakarta. The offices were converted into classrooms with whiteboards and lecterns, and the courses were offered on a fee-paying basis as "packages" on specific topics such as "Introduction to the History of Islam." Over the course of a term, clients attended weekly lectures by faculty from the State Islamic Institute and other leading tertiary institutions across Jakarta. As in a university setting, the faculty presented information in prepared lectures, followed by a question and discussion period. Unlike *usroh* mentors, the lecturers at Paramadina encouraged their pupils to challenge, question, and discuss, thus fostering independent, critical thinking. Students continued discussion and debate after class.

The courses became highly popular and stimulated numerous spin-off programs offered by "graduates" residing in other cities.[38] University lecturers and professors who, through their Paramadina teaching, discovered they had a particular facility for communicating with the general public, also found opportunities for well-rewarded sideline employment giving talks on radio and TV, reaching regional and national audiences. Better-funded mosques also began offering talk-and-study series to upper-middle class and elite urbanites.

Madjid himself convened a monthly Religion Study Club held in the evening at the five-star Regent Hotel, which was similarly meant to stimulate enthusiasm for knowledge about religion (principally, but not exclusively, Islam), along with critical thinking about it. This represented a significant innovation in urban *daʿwa*, taking hybrid informative and motivational teaching about Islam into the preferred secular living spaces of urban elites. After the turn of the century, a new generation of Muslim televangelist preachers and "spiritual trainers" would also meet their better-off clientele in such glamorous hotels, as well as in major convention centers and the meeting halls of grand mosques.

Renewalist thought also gained traction in the predominantly rural *pesantren* sector, starting in the 1970s, as new cohorts of young staff—graduates from one of the tertiary-level State Islamic Institutes—began to develop new kinds of Islamic outreach to the communities surrounding their *pesantren*. By the mid-1980s, their views on the ways these traditional schools might contribute to society, and on the need for using new exegetical methods to justify and motivate such contributions, had become sufficiently influential that progressive thinkers were voted into key leadership roles in the Nahdlatul Ulama. The central figure was Abdurrahman Wahid, who served as chairman from 1984 to 1994. Wahid had joined Madjid and his modernist comrades in developing Renewalist thought, identifying key Quranic concepts to justify democracy and promote social justice. They worked to popularize these understandings among *pesantren* leaders and their teaching staffs to encourage new kinds of community engagement.

LATER NEW ORDER STATE SPONSORSHIP OF ISLAMIZATION

In the first two decades of the New Order, President Suharto, wary of challengers to his control of the state, held Islamicization firmly in check. But in the late 1980s, he began to realign his policy, instigating a series of government initiatives promoting public gestures of revivalist Islamic piety, and even supporting public Islamic institution building. Several reasons, both personal and political, have been advanced to account for this policy change. His pilgrimage to Mecca in 1991 seemed to signal a shift from his previous Javanist-occultist Islamic religiosity to some kind of globally normative piety. That shift came at a time when there was widespread criticism of the numbers of Catholics and non-Muslim Indonesian Chinese in senior government and military positions, including among Suharto's close associates. The broad diffusion of Islamist notions of Western, Christian, and Jewish conspiracies building in the 1980s, and the growing revivalist enthusiasm of that decade, including in the government quasi party GOLKAR, have also been mentioned in accounts of Suharto's change in policy toward Islamicization.[39] Thus, in its last decade, Suharto's government lifted the ban on girls wearing the veil in school; introduced the Islamic court bill (which raised them to the same level as public, military, and administrative courts); instigated a presidential decree for the Compilation of Islamic Law for the country; and built thousands of mosques.

Particularly important in gaining the support of the growing Muslim middle class was the 1990 establishment, ostensibly in response to petitioning by Muslim student activists, of the Indonesian Muslim Intellectuals Association. Directed by Bacharuddin Jusuf Habibie, then Minister of Technology and Research and close advisor to the President. The association founded the nation's first national quality Islamic newspaper, *Republika*, and the first Islamic bank, Bank Muamalat Shariah. Muslims in academia, school education, the media, and business, as well as political activists, joined it. Although it included Muslims with a broad range of Islamic orientations, Islamists, including Imaduddin, founder of the Salman Mosque *daʿwa* mentoring program, had a strong voice in the association, while the suspicious Nahdlatul Ulama leader Wahid refused to join. For those who participated, it provided career advantages, linking members in a network that included senior public servants and business people.[40]

VARIETIES OF *DAʿWA* IN THE POST-AUTHORITARIAN INDONESIAN STATE

The forced resignation of President Suharto in May 1998 and the consequent crumbling of his New Order regime, precipitated by the Asian financial crisis of the previous year, opened the way for untrammelled contestation of the 1999 elections by Islamic parties. Among them, the Justice Party (PK) sprung directly from the Islamist wing of the *da'wa* movement. It first made a modest showing, but when reformed as the Prosperous Justice Party (PKS) to contest the subsequent election in 2004, it drew sufficiently wide support to become an important political force.

The PK and PKS grew out of the campus *da'wa* movement, carrying the idea of Islam as a total way of life and using the small group (*usroh* and *halqah*) "mentoring" methods. These groups began to operate more openly and spread rapidly in the 1990s, following President Suharto's Islamic turn. Though diverse, many *usroh*s were directly or indirectly influenced by the Salman Mosque's education methods and bore a strong Muslim Brotherhood tinge. They thus came to be seen as a movement, identified by their common educational objective: *tarbiya*.[41] They likewise shared the goal of making the government the enforcer of Islamic law among its Muslim citizens. The ongoing electoral successes of the PKS, which have required appealing to a broad section of the electorate, have depended on moderating the *tarbiya* movement's target of Islamizing Indonesian society from above. The PKS has thus foregrounded its capacity, as an Islamically disciplined party, to resist corruption and to model public morality. And, like other Islamic parties with deep roots in Indonesian party politics, it has had to abandon the prospect of amending the constitution so as to require the state to enforce Islamic law on Muslims.[42]

Da'wa agents promoted a range of approaches to Islam, from radical to liberal, of such diversity as had not been seen since the 1960s. At one end of the ideological spectrum, long suppressed jihadi groups either reformed or sprang up anew, calling for radical action to combat threats to the *umma* and prepare for armed struggle to establish an Islamic state. At the other end, young progressives with Nahdlatul Ulama backgrounds formed the Liberal Islam Network (JIL) to facilitate the wider exchange of liberal approaches to Islamic knowledge that was initiated by young Muslim intellectuals on the campus of the State Islamic Studies Institute and in Paramadina Foundation in Jakarta. One of their key objectives was to reach young people through the internet to counter neo-Salafi Islam, particularly the appeals that Laskar Jihad had made so effectively through the internet to recruit fighters to battle Christians in the Moluccas and Sulawesi.[43] In addition to JIL's radio station, magazine, and community discussion forums, its website enabled young Muslim progressives to post position papers and debate the application of Islam to social issues.[44]

The kinds of *da'wa* appeals to which the vast majority of Indonesian Muslims responded, however, were calls to cultivate personal piety in some mainstream form. From the turn of the new century, commercial enterprises came to be some of the major agents of *da'wa* and providers of an increasingly broad variety of products, from fashion to halal holidays, through which people sought to display their Muslim identity and enthusiasm for correct piety.[45]

Particularly influential were the new piety improvement ministries broadcast over radio and TV. The most successful of these were promoted through companies built around a particular preacher who had become a national television celebrity. The first of these popular preachers was Abdullah Gymnastiar (Aa Gym), who achieved stardom in 2000 when he began a monthly program broadcast from Jakarta's grand Istiqlal Mosque.[46]

Gymnastiar, like Arifin Ilham and other national celebrity preachers to follow, had already developed a regional following before appearing on TV. All built their audience numbers by accepting invitations to give live sermons and inspirational talks in mosques, entertainment centers, and other large venues. Mosque committees and event organizers were obliged to offer generous honoraria to secure popular speakers for their events. The continued growth in numbers and incomes of the new Muslim middle class, and the new prestige attached to Islamic identity and Muslim piety, helped enable the generosity of mosque committees and inspire the confidence of Islamic event managers when negotiating fees.

Preaching career opportunities on TV also depended on other social changes. Crucially, in 1990 the monopoly of the national TV broadcaster began to dissolve, and numerous private operators established stations. All accepted a social responsibility to deliver Islamic programming and saw a good market in it but needed to compete for audiences. Until the turn of the century, stations had looked to presenters with some kind of conventional authority to attract audiences. Favorite choices were professors from state Islamic universities who came to be perceived as a new kind of modern credentialed ulama.

The top rating celebrity preachers of the twenty-first century, however, were entertainer-preachers.[47] Gymnastiar, again like other Muslim televangelist stars, presented himself as an ordinary layman, exceptional only in his passion for cultivating piety and talent for sharing his inspiration with ordinary people like himself. His appeal to the television networks rested on his image as a crowd pleaser, going light on scriptural references and leavening his talks with personal anecdotes and the inspirational songs he composed. Arifin Ilham used the grandeur of the mosques from which his services were televised and the large ceremonies he organized. Both preachers evoked, through dramatizations of litanies, intense emotional experiences of regret and relief springing from confidence in God's mercy.

Major twenty-first-century celebrity preachers such as Aa Gym built companies around their ministries, branding their core messages and selling under these brands not only piety improvement materials (how-to books, DVDs, and inspirational instant messaging services) but also clothing and cola. Gymnastiar's trademark linked Sufi ethical disciplines to the forms of self-cultivation advocated in American self-help books to achieve "success" in the workplace. It offered courses to both individuals and companies looking for higher productivity through better management and employee self-regulation.[48]

Such loosely Islamicized self-improvement programs have also been offered by entrepreneurial Islamic businessmen who present themselves as "trainers" and have backgrounds in business management rather than lay preaching. The most successful of these is Ary Ginanjar, who offers five-day intensive motivational programs built around his Emotional Spiritual Quotient concept in major convention centers, business meeting facilities, and now his own training complexes. In those courses, he combines the popular psychology of success, drawn from Western sources, with revivalist preaching inspiring fear of God to motivate moral discipline. He draws principally on Islam, but the training is generically "spiritual" and so notionally open to people of all faiths.[49]

Concomitantly, small, intellectually demanding and commercial Islamic studies course providers have continued into the post-Suharto period and multiplied. The Renewalist Paramadina remains an attractive study center for elite Jakartans, followed by several other commercially-run highbrow course providers who cater to well-educated Muslim urbanites alongside upmarket courses run on a fee-paying basis by mosque committees. Other providers, whether fully commercial or associated with Islamic movements, offer publicly advertised, less-demanding short courses aimed at particular market sectors or focused on a particular form of piety, such as Quran memorization. Nationally televised Quran recitation competitions have added to the prestige associated with that particular form of devotion.[50]

Commercially mediated arts also contribute to contemporary *daʿwa*. While Islamic education courses seek to enhance piety through didactic methods, novelists and short story writers use personal expression to inspire piety. The characters in their stories model the process of striving toward correct piety, detailing the trials and blessings along the way, in order to support personal efforts at religious formation. A large share of Islamic books sold in recent years have been novels, and several best sellers, such as *Laskar Pelangi* (Rainbow Warriors) and *Ayat Ayat Cinta* (Verses of Love), have been made into top-grossing films.[51] Popular Islamic short stories published in magazines have furnished concepts for soap operas.[52] In 1997, a *tarbiya* group at the University of Indonesia formed the Writing Circle Forum, which publishes short stories and novels by its members. Not to be outdone by hip Islamist youth, the *pesantren* sector has established a similar association to encourage piety-themed novel writing among teenage students.[53]

CONCLUSION

This chapter examined the contrasting stances national governments in Malaysia and Indonesia have taken toward *daʿwa* movements in their countries since the 1970s. Following the major economic and social development programs that both countries undertook, they increased support for Islamic schools and Islamic education in general, aiming to increase literacy levels and the capacity of their populations for contributing to development. But, they have invested differently in their Islamic affairs bureaucracies and taken different stances toward rival Islamic parties and movements. In Malaysia, where the interests of the dominant Malay population have come to be largely identified with Islam, and where Mahatir Muhammad's UMNO party promoted vast expansion of the Islamic bureaucracy's scope and powers, those bodies have been imbued with the authority to define Islamic orthodoxy, becoming agents of Islamic institution-building on a grand scale. In Indonesia, by contrast, President Suharto used an ideology of religious pluralism to reinforce state control so that state involvement in Islamic institution-building began later and on a modest scale. This allowed a much larger scope for civil society actors to engage in *daʿwa*. With its greater percentage of Muslims, enormous diversity among its Muslim indigenous population, and a heterogeneous array of vigorous Muslim voluntary associations, it produced diverse *daʿwa* movements, which were grafted onto established Islamic movements or emerged from them. Multiple forms of Islamist revival developed within

Indonesian civil society in some tension with the government, whereas contextualist advocates of Islamic renewal, supporters of religious pluralism, the economic rights of the poor, and progressive family and inheritance law operated freely.

After the turn of the twenty-first century, commercial TV and hybrid religious-personal development training businesses encouraged new genres of *da'wa*. In Malaysia, state TV and radio are tasked with creating intelligent programming that shows how an Islam that accords with state orthodoxy contributes to a modern, developed society. In Indonesia, private broadcasters have given airtime to entertaining laypeople alongside recognized Islamic authorities. The successful lay preachers and talk-show hosts have developed ministries and are sometimes criticized for trivializing Islamic piety, yet they do contribute to the widespread enthusiasm for becoming a better Muslim. Televangelists and trainers have developed themes not entirely welcome in Malaysia, notably the generic "spirituality" that forms a bridge between pop psychology and Islamic religiosity. Malaysia has also not seen the development of the kinds of highly autonomous "seeker spirituality" so evident in today's Indonesia.

CHAPTER 9

Islamization of Christian Lands?

Theory and Practice of Daʿwa in Europe

URIYA SHAVIT

MASSIVE LABOR MIGRATION from Muslim countries to Europe began in the late 1950s.[1] Since then the number of Europeans of Muslim faith has steadily grown. In 1990, some four percent of the European Union's population was Muslim; by 2010 the figure had risen to six percent; and by 2030 it is expected to increase to eight percent.[2] By a very modest estimate, some 6,000 Islamic houses of worship function today in England, France, and Germany alone, with hundreds more in other European countries that have smaller Muslim populations.[3]

The non-Muslim majorities first categorized European Muslims primarily on the basis of their ethnic-national identity (e.g., Turks, Pakistanis). Their transformation into a "Muslim minority" in the public mind was partly encouraged by the growth of religious sentiment and manifestations of Islam in European public spheres. The label is misleading because it singles out one aspect of a multilayered range of identifications and affiliations, as well as postulating the existence of a unified, coherent "Islam." Europe is home to a variety of attitudes on the role of Islam in public and personal life, as well as an assortment of Muslim associations that fiercely debate core Islamic concepts and have demonstrated a greater tendency to fragment than to unite. Only a minority within the European Muslim minority attempts to regulate all aspects of life based on Allah's laws and regards a religious community as the focal point of socialization.

Contemporary migration to the West has placed unprecedented theological challenges before Muslim scholars. For the first time, millions of Muslims voluntarily left their homelands and settled, mainly for economic considerations, in traditionally Christian but increasingly secular countries. Two main questions needed to be addressed: first, under what conditions, if any, is it legitimate for Muslims to make non-Muslim lands their permanent home? Second, what should be done to preserve the religious identity of Muslims living outside *dar al-islam* (the abode of Islam)?

The present chapter focuses on *daʿwa*-oriented answers to the challenge of mass migration by two ideological groups originating in the Arab world: Islamists associated with the Muslim Brotherhood movement and Salafis who adhere to the core teachings of Saudi Arabia's Wahhabi religious establishment. Both groups have engaged extensively in *daʿwa* in its two meanings: the internal sense of bringing straying Muslims back to the fold and the external one of converting non-Muslims. The first part of the chapter explores the gradual emergence of the view that a Muslim presence in the West is legitimate (and even desirable) but only if, on the one hand, Muslims unite, establish communal religious institutions, and preserve and enhance their religious identity, and on the other, engage in active conversion of non-Muslims. The second part of the chapter examines why, despite the proliferation of this *daʿwa*-centered view, it has not led to substantial proselytizing efforts among non-Muslim publics across Europe.

The analysis is based on material collected by the author in libraries, online databases, and Islamic-interest bookstores in Europe and the United States, as well as through field interviews and observations conducted at dozens of European mosques, primarily in Britain, France, Germany, and Iceland, from 2006 to 2016.

ON RESIDING IN NON-MUSLIM COUNTRIES

The four generally accepted Sunni schools of law (sing. *madhhab*) have struggled with the question of residence in non-Muslim lands since their very inception, and their rulings serve to inform contemporary theological attitudes to residence in the West. Abu Hanifa disapproved of Muslims residing in non-Muslim territory, whereas Malik strongly opposed even traveling to the lands of unbelievers for purposes of trade, since Muslims might become subject to the laws of the unbelievers. Al-Shafiʿi offered a different approach, arguing that residence among non-Muslims was permissible. Even after the establishment of an Islamic state in Medina, al-Shafiʿi noted, the Prophet allowed some Muslims to dwell in non-Muslim territories.[4] The eleventh-century Shafiʿi scholar Abu al-Hasan al-Mawardi introduced proselytizing as another justification: if a Muslim was able to practice his religion in one of the countries of the unbelievers, that country became part of the abode of Islam (*dar al-islam*), hence it was actually better to reside there because Muslims living as a minority could potentially convert non-Muslims.[5]

The issue became more acute in the period following the Spanish Reconquista. The Shafiʿi opinion remained the most lenient, invoking proselytizing as justification. Shams al-Din al-Ramli, the sixteenth-century Shafiʿi grand mufti of Egypt, relied on the aforementioned example of Muslims whom the Prophet allowed to remain in non-Muslim Mecca, arguing that Muslims living in Spanish Aragon, who could freely practice their religion, were not required to migrate to Muslim lands. Indeed, he opined, they are actually required to remain, as their residence among infidels might help propagate Islam. He asserted that the area where these Muslims resided certainly was part of *dar al-islam*, and if they left it would become *dar al-kufr* (abode of unbelief).[6] Hanafi jurists ruled likewise.[7] The Maliki opinion, articulated by North African jurists who faced the threat of Christian occupation, was generally the strictest: Muslims should not live in non-Muslim territory, primarily because they would be subject to non-Muslim laws. However, residence was permissible if a person could not leave due to physical or economic circumstances while the impediment to migration persisted.[8] Hanbalis recommended that Muslims immigrate to a Muslim land, but if they were able to practice their religion on non-Muslim territory, were safe from harm, and did not fear the loss of their religion, they might stay.[9]

In the early twentieth century, modernist apologists such as Rashid Rida revived the notion that Muslims were not required to migrate from non-Muslim lands, citing al-Mawardi's opinion about the potential for proselytizing as encouragement to remain.[10] For Rida, Islamizing the West was not merely a detached theoretical prospect but a plausible objective. His journal, *al-Manar*, dealt repeatedly with the prospect of mass Western conversion to Islam. Concerned by the extent of Christian proselytizing efforts in Muslim lands, Rida founded in Cairo in March 1912 a college, Dar al-Daʿwa wa'l-Irshad (the College for Proselytizing and Instruction), dedicated to the education of a young generation of preachers in preparation for proselytizing among Muslims and non-Muslims alike. Graduates were to be sent to infidel liberal countries or to Muslim countries where there was a danger of conversion from Islam.[11] A three-year track was to culminate in a diploma permitting students to engage in *daʿwa* in Muslim countries; completion of a six-year track was required to engage in *daʿwa* among non-Muslims.[12] But the scheme failed to materialize, and Rida concluded that financial support was as important as religious passion.[13]

INTERNAL *DAʿWA*: TEACHING WESTERN MUSLIMS THEIR RELIGION

The influx of Muslim migrants to Western lands after World War II raised concerns among Arab theologians. One of the earliest examples of their preoccupation with the new situation is Yusuf al-Qaradawi's *al-Halal wa'l-Haram fi'l-Islam* (The Lawful and the Prohibited in Islam), published in 1960. The book became one of the bestsellers of the century in the field of Islamic law, was printed in thirty editions and translated into twenty languages. Commissioned by the authorities of al-Azhar University, it was designed to clarify basic Islamic practices for Muslims living in the West.[14] Yet, although it dealt with dozens of everyday issues—from correct butchery to proper attire—*al-Halal wa'l-Haram* barely addressed the unique dilemmas that migrants face in foreign lands and did not assign them any specific tasks. These issues would emerge only later in al-Qaradawi's writing.

During the 1970s, a number of works began to stress the need for *daʿwa* activities to strengthen the religious identity of Muslims in the West, though the potential of migrants to act as missionaries was still rarely considered. Authors focused instead on the need to establish mosques, Islamic schools, and community centers, as well as creating unity among Muslims of different ethnicities and orientations to preserve the migrants' religious identity. They also urged Muslim governments and pan-Islamic organizations to take the lead in such efforts. These authors were convinced that the institutionalization of Islamic education in the West was the only way to ensure that second- and third-generation Muslims did not neglect their religious identity; that given the sociopolitical weakness of Muslim associations in the West, inter-Muslim ideological divisions were a luxury they could not afford; and that given local Muslim associations' financial fragility, they would not be able to develop adequate communal institutions without external assistance.

Such concerns permeated the Muslim World League report written by Ali ibn al-Muntasir al-Kittani. From October 1973 to January 1974, al-Kittani led a delegation that surveyed Muslim communities in twenty-eight countries in the Western hemisphere, from the United States to France and Lichtenstein to Trinidad and Tobago. His survey detailed the number of Muslims and the origins of their communities in each country; described the mosques, cultural centers, and organizations they had established; and analyzed the obstacles inhibiting them. This meticulous documentation testified to the limited institutionalization of Islamic activities in Europe at the time.

In his report, al-Kittani urged Muslim governments to assist Muslim minority communities in building schools, orphanages, mosques, hospitals, and other institutions that would function according to Islamic principles and to grant interest-free loans and financing to charitable organizations. He further envisioned local communities forming associations blind to ethnic, linguistic, and doctrinal differences, organizing at the state level to represent Muslims collectively before the authorities. Al-Kittani also suggested the teaching of Arabic and the translation and distribution of the Quran in different languages.[15]

EXTERNAL *DAʿWA*: PROSELYTIZING IN THE WEST

A new concept of migrants as potential missionaries began to surface in the 1980s. Its principal promoters were Islamist and Salafi-oriented authors. Two separate developments led them to conclude that migration should not only be tolerated but utilized in the service of the propagation of Islam. By the early 1980s, it was clear that Muslim settlement in the West was of a permanent nature. Muslim authors were concerned that some Muslims were losing their connections with their religion and becoming assimilated. The same authors were encouraged by the revitalization of religious sentiments among other elements of the Muslim migrant populations, the gradual development of Islamic communal institutions in them, and the rise in the number of Western Christians who embraced Islam.

One of the earliest examples of the new trend was Muhammad al-Ghazali's 1984 *Islam Outside Its Boundaries*, which was based on insights from several years of visits, under Saudi sponsorship, to Western countries. A student of Hasan al-Banna, al-Ghazali was expelled from the Egyptian Muslim Brotherhood in 1953 following internal power struggles. In the decades that followed, despite holding governmental and academic positions in Egypt, Saudi Arabia, and Algeria, he became one of the most prolific and acclaimed standard-bearers of al-Banna's legacy. Taking a pragmatic, religio-juristic and political approach, al-Ghazali stressed in dozens of writings the need for a revolution that would reinstate Islam as an all-encompassing guide for every aspect of life. Like other leading Arab Islamist authors of his time, his ability to freely propagate Islam as the solution to all social ills came at the cost of refraining from personal involvement in subversive political actions.[16]

Al-Ghazali was concerned with the future of Islamic identity in the West for some time. In a book published in 1979 on the future of *da'wa* at the dawn of Islam's fifteenth century, he wrote about the danger of Muslims being converted to Christianity in Australia and congratulated Saudi Arabia for its efforts to establish an Islamic center there.[17] In *Islam outside Its Boundaries*, he conceptualized the ideal identity and roles of Muslim minorities in the West. These encompass two aspects of *da'wa*: one is inward looking, emphasizing the duty of Muslims to unite and establish parallel Islamic societies; the other is outward looking, calling for proselytizing among non-Muslims.

Al-Ghazali considered the now-sizable presence of Muslims in the West an Islamic nadir that could and should be transformed into a zenith. Recollecting his visits to Muslim communities in England, Canada, and the United States on behalf of King Abd al-Aziz University, he warned that many Muslims in the West might assimilate into their host societies and consequently lose their connections with Islam. His encounters with Muslim families in the West who believed it was legitimate for their daughters to marry non-Muslims were a case in point. Al-Ghazali expressed his fear that Muslim migrants would become victims of persecution, like their brethren in the Philippines and India, and noted that in the Balkans the number of Muslims had halved in the half-century that followed the retreat of the Ottoman Empire.[18]

Islam outside Its Boundaries offered a simple formula to determine whether a Muslim migrant should return home: any Muslim whose residence abroad undermined his or his children's religious identity must return to his homeland post-haste; otherwise he would be faulted with breaking away from Islam. Al-Ghazali reminded his readers, "Loyalty [should be] to Islam, not to race. Fellowship among Muslims is the most important connection, even if places and times have created distance."[19] He likewise urged the "great block of Muslims" in Muslim lands to strengthen ties with their "brothers in belief" scattered across different places and not to consign them to their fate. Muslim schools should be established to maintain the immigrants' "relation to their heritage, traditions, and rituals *as if all that changed in their lives was their location*" [emphasis added]. The language of teaching must be Arabic, the language of the Holy Quran, and obligatory prayers must be part of any school day. Also needed were social clubs, which would bring Muslims together in a religious atmosphere of friendship and affection, increasing the prospect that Muslim men marry Muslim women instead of infidels.[20]

Moreover, al-Ghazali was confident that with suitable education and funding, Muslim migrants would not only strengthen in their faith but come to be of great service to the global spread of Islam. Though not the focus of his discourse, this idea is presented in clear, unequivocal terms. *Islam outside Its Boundaries* opens with an analysis of newspaper reports on the conversion of tens of thousands of French citizens to Islam[21] and concludes by arguing that if the Muslim nation works for that to happen, then the masses of Muslim migrants will be the vanguard of the Islamic *daʿwa*.[22] Yet growing impatient with the rigid gender regulations he had witnessed in his years in Saudi Arabia, al-Ghazali added a chapter on the "illusions of *daʿwa*," claiming that insistence on female veiling damaged the prospects of converting non-Muslims. Women, he indicated, were entitled to hold public office and even to serve as judges.[23]

In the spirit of the time, the Riyadh-based World Assembly of Muslim Youth decided to dedicate its sixth conference in January 1986 to Muslim minorities in the West. The assembly, a pan-Islamic organization established in 1972 as the young-spirited equivalent of the Muslim World League, targets Muslim youth around the world and is financed mainly by the Saudi regime. At the conference, officials and scholars repeated al-Ghazali's concerns and prospects for Muslim migrants. They cautioned against the danger of assimilation into Western societies; called on Muslim countries to assist migrants to build mosques, Islamic schools, and other institutions; but also urged the migrants themselves to spread the word of Islam in the West.

One speaker, Maniʿ Hamad al-Jahni, listed the reasons why *daʿwa* among non-Muslims was a duty. First, there was no point in waiting for Muslim societies to be fully Islamized before engaging in *daʿwa* in other societies because this was expected to be a lengthy process. Second, *daʿwa* efforts enlivened Muslim societies. Third, *daʿwa* in non-Muslim countries brought new members to Islam while also protecting those engaged in proselytizing against efforts to divert them from Islam. The lion's share of al-Jahni's lecture presented detailed ideas for proselytizing among the infidels. He called on individual Muslims and organizations to make use of contacts with non-Muslims to educate them in Islam, for example, by explaining why Muslims abstained from eating pork, avoided communal showers, and said *insha' allah*. They should also try to correct false presentations of Islam in schools and organize weekly assemblies to present the basics of the religion.[24]

Another speaker, the Egyptian Islamist journalist Muhammad Abdallah al-Samman, argued that while proselytizing outside Muslim lands was a collective duty (*fard kifaya*) hardly anyone accorded due consideration to *da'wa*. He cautioned that the erection of mosques and Islamic institutions in non-Muslim countries would promote *da'wa* only to a limited extent unless such endeavors were supported by a meticulously researched and planned strategy.[25]

These ideas were further pursued by Tunisia's mufti, Muhammad al-Shadhili al-Nayfar, in an essay he published in 1989 in the journal of the Muslim World League's Fiqh Council. Contrary to the traditional Maliki hostility to Muslim residence in non-Muslim countries, al-Nayfar allowed it on the grounds of the differences in the historical contexts. During the Reconquista, he reasoned, Spain waged war against Islam and tried to convert Muslims, while Muslims living today in non-Muslim lands enjoy religious freedom and engage in Islamic activities. Furthermore, their residence may be of merit, for if they truly manifest Islam's ideals and values, non-Muslims would be drawn to embrace the faith.[26]

CONTEMPORARY CONCEPTIONS OF *DA'WA*

By the 1990s, the potential for Islamizing the West had become a primary theme in Islamist and Salafi literature. Some even suggested that from a sharia perspective a Muslim presence in Western lands was essential. The champion of this concept to date has been Yusuf al-Qaradawi, who systemized it in a 2001 book on the religious law of Muslim minorities, as well as in a concise fatwa issued in 2006 and in several other publications. The Dublin-based European Council for Fatwa and Research, a juristic panel established in 1997 that al-Qaradawi heads, promoted his theories on migration at the initiative of the Federation of Islamic Organizations in Europe.

The core of al-Qaradawi's new systemization of the identity and duties of Western-based Muslims is the idea that Muslim residence among the infidels is legitimate, so long as they maintain their religious identity (a task requiring them to unite with fellow Muslims in their host country, regardless of ethnic or other affiliations, and establish strong religious institutions), support the interests of the Muslim nation, and spread the message of Islam. The last of these duties is by no means restricted to men of religion. Al-Qaradawi believes that Muslim migrants have gradually transformed from weak religiosity, resulting from the weak state of Islam in their countries of origin, to a religious awakening expressed in the building of mosques, Islamic schools, and Islamic institutions. He urges migrants who have reached this stage to actively engage and interact with their host societies to spread Islam's universal message.[27] Al-Qaradawi stresses that Islam has always been propagated peacefully among non-Muslims and that unlike other civilizations, including the Arab, the Islamic civilization has never been subject to the rule of ascendancy and decline and that in contemporary times it is still not losing believers.[28] These convictions are the basis on which he forms the following directive:

> Muslims in the West ought to be sincere callers to their religion. They should keep in mind that calling others to Islam is not restricted to scholars and *shuyukh*, but it goes far to encompass every committed Muslim. As we see scholars and *shuyukh* delivering sermons and lectures, writing books to defend Islam, it is no wonder we find lay Muslims practicing *daʿwa* while employing wisdom and fair exhortation.[29]

Al-Qaradawi employs a broad array of justifications to legitimize migration to infidel lands, including the need to make a living, escape political persecution, and study.[30] Yet it is proselytizing to Islam that transforms life among the infidels from a tolerated condition into a blessed mission for the entire Muslim *umma*. Al-Qaradawi goes so far as to say that considering Islam's universal mission on the one hand, and the West's leadership of the world today on the other, Muslims must have a presence in the West and spread Islam there. Indeed, were there no Muslim presence in the West, such a presence would have to be created.[31]

The Iraqi-American Taha Jabir al-Alwani is second only to al-Qaradawi in promoting the conviction that *daʿwa* legitimizes residence in the West and that it is the migrants' duty to engage in proselytizing efforts. Al-Alwani, who graduated from al-Azhar and founded the Fiqh Council of North America, regards the concept of *dar al-harb* (realm of war) as an outdated administrative term, rather than a credible sharia category. He reasons that since any country is either presently Muslim or will become Muslim in the future, the concept of a "realm of war" risks limiting the universality of Islam's message. Any place where a Muslim is able to practice his religion can be regarded as *dar al-islam*, and there he must stay, for his staying may result in the conversion of non-Muslims. Countries in which Islam has not yet spread should be regarded as *dar al-daʿwa* (realm of proselytizing). It is obligatory for Muslims to create a presence in such countries and bring them the truth of Islam.[32]

The concept of migrant as missionary has also been championed in Salafi works. While for Salafis proselytizing among the infidels has served as the almost exclusive justification for living among non-Muslims (as well as maintaining otherwise prohibited interpersonal relations with them), the absence of a clear definition as to what constitutes *daʿwa* implies that any Muslim who engages in any sort of effort to bring non-Muslims to Islam may legitimately reside permanently in the West. Abd al-Aziz Ibn Baz, Saudi Arabia's leading religious jurist from the mid-1970s until his death in 1999, issued several fatwas wherein he forbade traveling for commercial purposes, while allowing—albeit with evident disapproval and only under strict supervision—academic studies abroad "when it is a necessity." Along with studies, Ibn Baz permitted travel abroad for the purpose of *daʿwa*, a condition that potentially legitimizes any Muslim's residence abroad, so long as he participates in some activity that promotes Islam.[33] Muhammad ibn Salih al-Uthaymin, the second-ranking religious authority in Saudi Arabia in the late twentieth century, decided after deliberating at length on the dangers to which Muslims living among the infidels are exposed, that Muslims who are strong in their faith and able to exercise their religion freely, may live among the infidels, as long as they are involved in one of two activities: they must proselytize for Islam, which is a form of jihad, or study the condition of the infidels to expose their corruption.[34] Al-Uthaymin has dealt extensively with strategies for converting non-Muslims to Islam.[35] The editors of the Salafi-leaning web portal Islamweb.com, sponsored by Qatar's Ministry of Endowments and Religious Affairs, similarly argue that preserving religious identity and spreading Islam are the most important duties of Muslims in non-Muslim countries. They hold that one of the best ways to bring non-Muslims into Islam is through refraining from any form of disobedience to Allah's laws. To support this assertion, they note that "many people" have embraced Islam after establishing good relations with Muslims.[36]

Europe-based Muslim theologians and activists of Islamist and Salafi orientations, including converts to Islam, have likewise offered proselytizing as justification for residence in the West. For example, Muhammad al-Kadi al-Umrani, whose masterly 2001 PhD dissertation provides an overview of classical and contemporary religious edicts on migration, notes that in the past Muslim merchants spread Islam. To this he adds that a positive result of contemporary migration to the West is the Islamizing of a considerable number of Westerners, including intellectuals and politicians, and that some of those converts have not only become Muslims but also engage in proselytizing.[37] The German convert Pierre Vogel (a.k.a. Abu Hamza), a former boxer who acquired his Muslim education in Mecca and became a Salafi proselytizer in his homeland, asked Muslims in Germany in unequivocal terms to take part in conversion efforts.

> Who of those who sit here tried to bring his neighbor to Islam? Who wrote a translation of the Quran? Who tried to translate a book about Islam? Who created an internet website? Who distributed leaflets? Who brought with him today someone to the mosque? Who announced to friends, "Come, something will be explained in German here?" If you haven't done this, you don't belong to the *umma*.[38]

DAʿWA IN PRACTICE

The religious-legal legitimization of Muslim presence in the West as a means of converting non-Muslims has had practical implications. It encouraged private and governmental donors to fund Islamic initiatives in the West and allowed graduates of religious universities to serve as imams in European mosques.

Calls to proselytize among non-Muslims, however, have hardly been actualized, not even by associations affiliated with the theological trends that introduced them most enthusiastically. Given the volume of treatises, sermons, and religious rulings that call upon Muslims in Europe to actively bring the message of Islam to non-Muslims, this dearth of actual external missionary work in European public spheres is striking. While internal *daʿwa* among Muslims in the West has developed significantly in recent decades with the growth of Islamic communal institutions, there are no organized door-to-door missionary efforts aimed at the Christian majority and hardly any seminars or public lectures specifically targeting non-Muslims. Some mosques invite the general public to "open days," but the objective of such events is establishing good-neighborly relations; they do not involve overt proselytizing. In mosques large or small, and also in Islamic-interest bookstores, leaflets in European languages are to be found that educate in the merits of Islam, but these are rarely distributed to the general public.

Interviews I held with mosque attendees who articulated strongly critical views of the West and triumphal understandings of Islam in contemporary times indicated, to my surprise, a lack of deep engagement with the concept of the missionary migrant. I documented statements insisting on the right of every citizen to present an alternative and better way of life, as well as faith in the ultimate universal acceptance of Islam. Yet my interviewees did not regard it as their duty to actively spread Islam, nor were they aware of the rich body of scholarship that conceptualized proselytizing as the primary justification for their presence in the West. They emphasized the need for self-improvement and the importance of being active within the mosque community. The idea of actively pursuing the conversion of others seemed to them detached or far-fetched.[39]

The only group in Europe that engages in active, public proselytizing, though only to modest extent, is young Salafis. They distribute Qurans and leaflets about the truth of Islam in town squares or outside railway stations in major European cities and operate websites that impart information about Islam and relate narratives of converts. In several of my visits to Salafi mosques, I was subject to conversion attempts, something I never experienced, at least not in a direct manner, in non-Salafi mosques. These efforts were made by the young and more easily impressed activists, who seemed to be following textbook guidelines on how to turn an infidel (for example, by starting the conversation with establishing agreement on the existence of God) but never by the more experienced imams of the community.

If the concept of *daʿwa* among non-Muslims is so prolific, why have efforts employed to actualize it been so superficial? One reason is that calls to convert non-Muslims have been issued primarily by Muslim-Arabs of Islamist and Salafi orientations, two ideologies that are widespread in online Islamic operations and on the shelves of Islamic-interest bookstores in Europe but which the vast majority of Muslims in Europe—non-Arab and Arab alike—condemn, reject, or simply ignore. Media coverage of Islamist and Salafi (not to mention Salafi-Jihadi) orientations creates the impression that these are major forces within European Muslim communities, which is not the case. In Germany, it is estimated that only 0.2 percent of the Muslim population is Salafi.[40] In Birmingham, the heartland of the English Salafiyya, the imam of the local Salafi mosque told me that by his reckoning no more than two percent of the city's Muslim population identifies with this ideology.[41]

The vast majority of mosques in Europe represent ethnically based rather than pan-Islamic associations, which are established and run through the efforts of independent local associations (such as Moroccan mosques) or associations affiliated with and directed by a homeland governmental organ (which is the case with most Turkish mosques). Notions of Islamic revival and future hegemony are not entirely alien to the leadership or attendees at mosques that reject Islamism and Salafism, but such ends are not the focal point of their ideology and practice.

The appeal of the "missionary migrant" is also limited by the emergence of other conceptualizations, which allow for less provocative and more realistic, religiously grounded interpretations of Muslim life in the West. One example lies in the works of the Swiss-born Tariq Ramadan, Hasan al-Banna's grandson, who is a professor of philosophy and a prolific commentator on Muslim-Western relations. Ramadan believes that Muslims in Europe ought to remain intellectually, economically, and politically independent of religious scholars in Arab countries and Arab governments. He calls on "Western citizens of Muslim faith" to "think for themselves, develop theses appropriate for their situation, and put forward new and concrete ideas."[42] His approach to *daʿwa* is narrow in essence, as he rejects conversion attempts and limits the duty of the Muslim migrant to being "a witness of Islam's message, through his or her speech, behavior, and manner of dealing with people."[43]

Another example is the conceptualization of identity presented by Amr Khaled, the Egyptian-born television preacher who now resides in Birmingham. Khaled calls on Muslims in Europe to adopt a third way between assimilation and segregation—one that synthesizes constructive contributions to non-Muslim society with proud Islamic identity. For him, Western-based Muslims are not potential missionaries but goodwill ambassadors who must improve Islam's image in Western societies. Khaled points out that the Quran makes no reference as to whether the people of Egypt became Muslim after being saved by Prophet Yusuf. This omission, he argues, is not accidental but is meant to teach Muslims that they should never set conditions on doing good but do good for its own sake.[44]

Another reason for the lack of external *daʿwa* work is the meager means for carrying it out. Contrary to conventional wisdom, even Islamist and Salafi groups that are organizationally or at least ideologically tied to Gulf-based religious establishments do not enjoy rich coffers. European Salafi mosques I visited appeared to be modestly-funded and self-sustaining, whereas the al-Qaradawi-led European Council for Fatwa and Research receives no ongoing funding from Qatari or other donors and lacks the financial resources to even construct a state-of-the-art website in Arabic.[45] The focus on *daʿwa* by European mosque associations, whether mainstream or more radical, is therefore local and inward-looking: strengthening the religious identity of Muslims, particularly the young, rather than reaching out to non-Muslims. This focus includes, as the main spheres of activity, (1) the Friday congregational prayer, a time for religious guidance and reflection, a manifestation of the strength and cohesion of the community, and an opportunity for socializing and networking; (2) the operation of "Quran schools," where children learn basic Arabic, creed, and rituals; (3) the operation (by some mosques) of Islamic bookstores (some of them spacious, offering thousands of titles in a variety of languages); and (4) the operation of various leisure and commercial activities (including grocery stores with products that are *halal* and provide a taste of the homeland).

Finally, political concerns are also a factor: the propagators of the "missionary migrant" are aware that in social climates that have grown increasingly suspicious of migration from Muslim lands, calls to Islamize the continent can be extremely provocative. The Secretary General of the European Council, Hussein Halawa, insisted in our interviews that the Council does not seek the Islamization of Europe and does not consider proselytizing a primary objective of the Lawgiver.[46] A number of the Council's most revolutionary fatwas, however, suggest the opposite. For example, in legitimizing mortgages in Europe, the Council noted the importance of home ownership as a means to allow Muslims to present a respectable face of Islam to non-Muslims and to find the time to engage in proselytizing.[47]

CONCLUSION

Islamists and Salafis based in the Arab world are the main propagators of a concept that tasks Muslims in the West with *daʿwa* efforts directed at

Muslims and non-Muslims. The idea that a Muslim's permanent residence in the West is legitimate as a means of converting Christians to Islam is a form of apologetics. It contextualizes, in religious terms, waves of migration that were in fact motivated mainly by economic concerns. The concept of the "missionary migrant" has had some practical implications yet has rarely been actualized. Reasons for this include the limited appeal of Islamism and Salafism in general, the political sensitivity of open efforts intent on "Islamizing the West," and the desire of the vast majority of religious Muslims in the West to maintain their focus on *daʿwa* directed at Muslims.

The actual number of Europeans who have converted to Islam is not known. Because converts do not register as such, existing data is largely speculative. In my fieldwork, I came across a small number of converts (mainly in nonethnic mosques) who related how they came to recognize the truth of Islam. Their presence suggests that conversion is a real phenomenon, yet their meager proportion of mosque congregations implies that conversion is not a mass phenomenon nor are there any indications of it becoming one in the near future. Given the present scope of *daʿwa* in Europe, it is unlikely that European demographics will undergo a dramatic change in the foreseeable future.

CHAPTER 10

Daʿwa in North America

The Past, the Present, and the Future

ELYSIA GUZIK AND LARRY POSTON

A BRIEF HISTORY OF *DAʿWA* IN NORTH AMERICA

Daʿwa was not an overt objective of the earliest Muslim settlers in North America, nearly all of whom arrived as slaves from North Africa.[1] Winning converts to Islam was neither a part of their syncretistic heritage nor a practical possibility with respect to their owners or their owners' families. Voluntary immigration by Muslims to the West was not seen in any significant numbers until the late 1800s and may be divided into five distinct "waves," consisting mainly of individuals and family units fleeing insupportable economic or political situations.[2] These refugees desired nothing more than to live in peace and raise their families undisturbed, and thus attempts to proselytize the "host" populations of the U.S. and Canada—nearly all of whom were "Christian" in some sense of the word—would have created a situation in which the often desperate newcomers would be resented, shunned, and perhaps violently opposed. Therefore, Muslim immigrants maintained a low profile with respect to their neighbors and American society in general and so may be deemed "quietist" adherents of Islam.

Certainly, the overwhelming majority of Muslims living in the West today still belong in this category. An activist agenda, which would include converting non-Muslims to Islam, has never been their *raison d'être*, and while they are unapologetic about their faith when asked, they are respectful of the views of non-Muslims and appreciative of the freedom of religion that is the constitutional right of every American. If their neighbors or work colleagues inquire specifically about Islam, they are generally willing to explain the facets about which they are questioned, but they are careful not to be offensive lest they jeopardize standing in their communities.

It was not until after World War II that Muslims in North America began to discuss seriously their responsibility to spread "the gospel according to Islam." As the "melting pot" ideal that had been strongly emphasized during America's early history evolved into the "stewpot," the "salad bowl," the "cultural mosaic," and finally "multiculturalism," the necessity of keeping a low profile gradually dissipated and Muslims came to feel more "accepted" by American society at large. Fears of prejudicial treatment and deportation faded, and a steadily increasing boldness was seen on the part of more theologically oriented adherents of Islam. These "activists" understood that a Muslim living permanently in *dar al-harb* (or *dar al-kufr*)—by which is meant any geographical locale where the sharia is not in force—was an anomaly. Dr. Muzzamil Siddiqui explained this point of law as follows:

> Dar ul-Islam is the natural place of residence for Muslims. However, a Muslim is also permitted to live in Dar ul-Kufr as a temporary resident for commercial purpose, as an emissary on a diplomatic mission, or as a student or trainee for a special discipline... also as a visitor or tourist.... But in all these cases, he is a temporary resident and must return to Dar ul-Islam as soon as the task is finished.[3]

The category "emissary on a diplomatic mission" was extended to include the task of *da'wa*. As Nina Wiedl points out, "Some contemporary Muslim jurists, working from within the traditional framework of Islamic law, argue that settlement in the West is justified only insofar as it serves the larger purpose of *da'wa*."[4] If a Muslim is engaged in proselytizing non-Muslims in a non-Muslim country—even if such engagements are rare—then his/her residence in that country is justified and therefore legitimate.

Additionally, it is becoming more common for *du'a* in contemporary North America to draw upon language about "universal Islam" and the values shared across Muslim communities.[5] This tactic is especially relevant, as Muslim communities in Canada and the U.S. are experiencing unprecedented growth, largely due to continued immigration. As a way of relating to both Muslim immigrants and non-Muslims, adherents of Islam who engage in *daʿwa* in North America tend to invoke the notion of universality as opposed to divisive concepts such as the doctrine of the two abodes (i.e., *dar al-islam* and *dar al-harb*).[6] Renewed interest in Islam among Muslim immigrants has also provided an opportunity for North American-based Islamic organizations to address cultural practices brought to North America and establish community bonds along religious lines instead. Thus, for many, the main objective of *daʿwa* activity is to induce non-Muslim or nominally Muslim persons to convert to Quranic Islam. The number of such conversions has increased steadily since the 1950s, with testimonies of converts being collected, analyzed, and published in several works.[7]

EXTERNALLY/INSTITUTIONALLY ORIENTED VERSUS INTERNALLY/PERSONALLY ORIENTED MUSLIMS

Just as it is necessary to distinguish between "quietist" and "activist" Muslims in order to understand the complexities of *daʿwa* activity in North America, it is also imperative to differentiate between "external/institutional" and "internal/personal" orientations toward the Muslim faith. Larry Poston described the historical development of these orientations in his study of *daʿwa* in the United States and Europe. Traditionally, Islam reflected a predilection toward an "external/institutional missiology" in efforts to expand the religion across geographic borders and establish Islamic empires.[8] This orientation aligned well with the military model that emerged from the Muslim conquests of the seventh through eleventh centuries. However, this external/institutional orientation required modification for the modern North American context in which Christianity dominates cultural and political systems. Traditional concepts such as jihad and *daʿwa* have been, and continue to be, reinterpreted to adjust to a sociohistorical climate in which freedom of religious expression is constitutionally acknowledged as a fundamental right. Keeping such rights and freedoms in mind, *duʿa* in contemporary North America who seek to follow a more traditional external/institutional approach tend to maintain the goal of "Islamic conquest," albeit with a modified focus on educating non-Muslims about Islam through schools and media outlets rather than by applying militaristic tactics. This approach is reflected in nonprofit cultural and educational organizations such as the International Institute of Islamic Thought (IIIT) outside of Washington, D.C., whose mandate is to "help the Ummah regain its intellectual and cultural identity and re-affirm its presence as a dynamic civilization."[9]

In contrast, an internal/personal orientation is implemented by *duʿa* who emphasize individual lifestyle, actions, spirituality, and moral commitments over "creedal orthodoxy and liturgical form."[10] Within Islam, Sufism is arguably the tradition most closely aligned with this approach, as it suggests that personal connections with the divine are most appropriately fostered through individual spiritual experience and growth rather than through coercive political and militaristic strategies of proselytization and conquest. Such *duʿa* tend to take a more grassroots approach, seeking to convert individual persons instead of attempting to combat or transform an entire society. They are able to honor constitutional freedoms while focusing efforts on encouraging willing individuals to convert voluntarily to Islam after witnessing the spiritual dimensions of the religion.[11] Whereas an external/institutional orientation is informed by collectivist ideologies that perceive proselytization as a responsibility held by mosques and Muslim communities to spread Islam throughout the world, an internal/personal orientation is framed by an individualistic commitment to raise awareness through outreach activities that invite individuals to embrace Islam as their religion.

GENDER DISTINCTIONS WITH RESPECT TO *DAʿWA*

Dynamics between gender and *daʿwa* in Western Islam may be viewed from different perspectives. In North America, stereotypes circulated through mainstream media portray Muslim attitudes toward women as beyond mere patriarchy; they are instead said to border on an endemic misogyny that is allegedly found in nearly every Muslim family.[12] It is believed that Muslim women in general are forced to cover their hair, wear unflattering and bulky clothing, and expected to submit themselves completely to Muslim men. They may be punished—mentally and physically—for a variety of offenses. Consequently, it is simply assumed that the only reason a woman would ever convert to Islam would be if she were forced to do so by a Muslim husband.

Within Muslim communities, however, exegetical treatises proclaim the equality of women with men from the time of Muhammad to the present day, and contemporary studies note the appeal of Islam to contemporary women from a variety of backgrounds. Carol Anway's *Daughters of Another Path* (1996) and Karin van Nieuwkerk's *Women Embracing Islam: Gender and Conversion in the West* (2006) provide a plethora of testimonies regarding the effects of *daʿwa* on a large number of single women, including many who had considered themselves "radical feminists" prior to their conversion.

Thus, in North America a prevalent motivator for converting to Islam is the perception that the religion of Muhammad is actually complementary to Western feminism. Rather than having North American normative standards of beauty imposed on them by an oppressive patriarchal system, many Western Muslim women interpret Islamic modesty practices as a means of fostering interactions based on substance, not appearances.[13] Many American Muslim women are inspired by the history of women's contributions to the development of Islam and Islamic scholarship, going back to Khadija and other women who were among the first companions of the Prophet Muhammad.[14] In addition, many consider the veil (*hijab*) to be a material expression of faith and frame the choice to wear head and face coverings as a fundamental right to free expression—a right that echoes democratic values enshrined in the United States Constitution and Canadian Charter of Rights and Freedoms. While most North American Muslim women acknowledge that different norms and roles exist between Muslim women and men, some are inspired by the concept of "equal rights" to engage in *ijtihad*—efforts of independent reasoning and the interpretation of Islamic juridical and sacred texts—in ways that may eventually bring about a change in the general public's perception of Muslim women.[15]

With respect to the *appeal* of Islam, there is little that distinguishes women from men. Many of the women who were introduced to Islam through lectures and/or texts during their postsecondary education have reported that it was the philosophical and scholarly elements of the religion that drew them. Some claim that they were compelled by the logic of an Islamic belief system, free from confusing concepts such as the Christian Trinity.[16] Whether reading the Quran in academic classes, attending study circles (*halaqat*), or exchanging opinions and participating in debates in online forums, women from a variety of backgrounds have found the intellectual dimension of Islam appealing.

In the context of post–September 11 North America, some *muslimas* engage in outreach initiatives in order to respond to Islamophobic attitudes, stereotypes, and discrimination. With increased media coverage about Islam (which tended to connect the religion with terrorist activities and the victimization of women), Muslim women who wore clothing items such as the *hijab* or *niqab* (face veil) were particularly identifiable and continue to be targets of anti-Muslim sentiments and abuse.[17] Instances of public harassment and attacks on Muslim women in Canada and the U.S. have reportedly increased following terrorist events that were linked to Muslim extremists.[18] Statistics from the Equal Employment Opportunity Commission (EEOC) cite increased employment discrimination claims based on Muslim faith in the U.S. since 2001.[19]

Within this climate, instead of relying on a rhetoric of conversion to Islam, women's *daʿwa* efforts are often centered around presenting positive portrayals of the religion and its adherents, fostering interfaith dialogue and understanding, and drawing connections between Islam and the causes of social justice and equity. Although their missions are focused on education, advocacy, and public policy rather than *daʿwa*, nonprofit organizations such as the North American Council for Muslim Women (NACMW), Canadian Council of Muslim Women (CCMW), and Women's Islamic Initiative in Spirituality and Equality (WISE) have also been especially active since September 11 in addressing stereotypes and promoting the positive contributions of Muslim women who give back to their communities through their artwork, research, and professional service.[20] Studies on Muslim women in North America suggest a preference for demonstrating "good character" as the most significant aspect of their confession, exemplifying Islamic virtues and principles such as "being a good neighbor"—that is, being kind, compassionate, and charitable. In ethnographic interviews conducted with female converts to Islam, Anna Mansson McGinty notes that many of the participants spoke of aspiring to personally embody their faith by being a "living example [of the Prophet Muhammad] in their everyday life."[21] Furthermore, these women described how they encountered Islam not through a *daʿi* but by witnessing the actions of Muslim friends, colleagues, and residents of predominantly Muslim countries as they traveled.

Also inspirational for North American women who adopt Islam are the personal testimonies of other converts. Not only are narratives potentially persuasive, but they are also a relatively accessible and nonthreatening medium of transmitting information, emerging naturally from casual conversations.[22] Focusing on common interests and substantive issues while enabling others to do the same, women cultivate positive values by prioritizing engagement in community service over outreach activities that highlight religious differences. Journalist Myriam Francois-Cerrah comments on how Muslims she encountered as a university student influenced a change in her perspective, not through performing overt acts of *daʿwa* but "by being really nice people, really good people that you could rely on."[23] At a time of increasing global connectivity and the rise of social media, one could reasonably expect that subtler, interpersonal forms of *daʿwa* will continue to appeal to Muslim women in both Europe and North America.

Despite claims that Islam is more "woman-friendly" than it is usually given credit for being, studies have shown that the percentages of women attending mosque functions are the inverse of what is found in Christian churches. A 2011 study revealed that an average of only eighteen percent of the attendees at Friday prayers is female. Of note, however, was the following statement: "Mosques that participate in community service projects, conduct voter registration, organize open houses, and engage in interfaith activities average about 20% female attendance, compared to 16% for mosques that do not have these activities."[24] Thus, it is apparent that mosques that allow women to participate in *daʿwa* activities that contribute positively to society attract more women than mosques that either have no such activities or restrict women from participating in them.

THE EFFECTS OF ISLAMIST TERRORISM UPON *DAʿWA* EFFORTS

September 11 marked a watershed moment for Islam in the Western Hemisphere. For many Americans, the word "Muslim" became synonymous with "terrorist," and during the ensuing years a number of personalities and organizations gained reputations and followings based on their demonization of Islam's adherents. Americans in general, but in particular the followers of far-right-wing commentators were not at all disposed to receive positively any form of *daʿwa* in North America.[25]

But September 11 also functioned as a grandiose advertisement for the religion of Islam. At the "macro-level," a number of influential officials went out of their way to insist that Islam was not a "religion of the sword" and that the overwhelming majority of the world's Muslims are a peaceful people who were as horrified by al-Qaeda's actions as non-Muslim Americans were. Television documentaries and major serial publications offered extensive information regarding the histories of Muslim countries, along with their peoples' religious and cultural practices.[26] These programs and articles functioned as an indirect but nonetheless highly effective form of *daʿwa*, and the more thoughtful citizens of the U.S. and Canada became familiar with Islam in ways and to an extent that had never previously occurred.

More importantly, at the "micro-level" of North American society, neighborhoods containing a significant Muslim presence underwent an evolution in thought and attitude, as the adherents of Islam engaged in outpourings of hospitality in efforts to lay to rest the suspicions that were foisted upon them. At this level, *daʿwa* efforts became more direct, as curious persons were invited to observe or even participate in the regular *salat* prayers and *jumʿa* (Friday) services, in educational forums and the like. Muslims were compelled to answer questions—and objections—that they had previously not had to deal with, and there is evidence that they handled these questions very well indeed. Consider the following reports:

> American interest in Islam reached its pinnacle in the last quarter of 2001. The most important reason for this was the 9/11 attacks against the World Trade Center and the Pentagon. Several studies undertaken to determine the roots of terrorist ideology, as well as investigations of Islam, have enabled people to learn that Islam is a peaceful religion that enjoins tolerance, justice, mercy, and love. Islam has suddenly become a major topic of discussion all over the world. More and more world-renowned statesmen, political scientists, researchers, and thinkers consider it necessary to understand Islam correctly, and have given speeches underlining Islamic tolerance and willingness to reach agreement. Americans have approached Muslim organizations in order to find the most accurate information about Islam and Islamic history.[27]

Several narrators describe the September 11 attacks as having awakened their curiosity about Islam, which eventually led them to embrace it. In "Journey of a Lifetime: My Way to Islam," an anonymous female narrator on Islamselect.com explained that, after September 11, she wanted to examine whether Islam really was about killing and hatred. With an open mind, she searched the internet for the words "Islam" and "Quran." It so happened that her search came at a time when, at seventeen years of age, she had begun to question her Roman Catholic faith. Two years later, she moved to another city where she met Muslims at the university she was attending. They gave her books and DVDs about their faith. Joining her new friends in the mosque, she felt at home as she never had in church. That experience, she said, completed her journey to the true religion.[28]

Within two months of September 11, Nihad Awad, chair of the Council on American-Islamic Relations (CAIR), claimed that the terrorist attacks were so influential that "34,000 Americans have converted to Islam following the events of 11 September, and this is the highest rate reached in the U.S. since Islam arrived there."[29] While no evidence has ever been offered for the validity of this statistic, the claim has been widely circulated. The lack of documentation makes the number questionable, but no one questions that from the standpoint of *daʿwa* in America, September 11 did indeed have some positive effects.

CURRENT TRENDS REGARDING ISLAMIC *DAʿWA* IN NORTH AMERICA

Modern Islam has shown itself to be a capital imitator of evangelical Christianity. This is perhaps due to the enormity of the Protestant missionary efforts that inundated the Middle East in the nineteenth century and continued into the twentieth. Ahmed Deedat's Islamic Propagation Centre in Durban, South Africa, for instance, took its inspiration from the proselytizing efforts of Jehovah's Witnesses that Deedat himself experienced. This organization is representative of what an earlier study describes as "paramosque" agencies.[30] In North America, these include such groups as Musa Qutub's Islamic Information Center of America (Prospect Heights, IL), the Muslim Student Association (also known as MSA National), the Islamic Circle of North America (ICNA), the Islamic Society of North America (ISNA), and the nonorthodox Ahmadiyya.

The New York-based Islamic Circle of North America has from its inception considered *daʿwa* to be its chief purpose and function. Its work may be considered typical of current activities in North America, and one of its goals is to function as an umbrella group for all of the *daʿwa* activity on the continent.

> Dawah has always been the top priority of ICNA. This focus has kept ICNA at the forefront of dawah activities in North America for the past four decades. A few years ago ICNA initiated the WhyIslam Dawah Project. The project aims to organize the

> dawah work in North America in a professional and effective manner. Highlights of the project are [a] Toll-Free number for non-Muslims; Distribution of Islamic literature; Dawah through Masajid; Dawah by Mail; Dawah through Media; Dawah in Prisons; Campus Dawah Support; Dawah Flyers Online; Dawah through Email etc.... Recently the Chicago Chapter of ICNA also initiated an outreach effort called GainPeace through which several activities including bus advertisements, billboards, revert follow-up and presentations have been undertaken.[31]

All of the abovementioned organizations still exist and have expanded their activities. More recently established organizations include the Daʿwa Center of America (Atlanta), the Latino American Dawah Organization, the Islamic Daʿwah Center of Houston, and the Islamic Dawah Center of Plainfield (NJ), to name only a few. Each organization represents its own regional, historical, and theological interests. The Latino American Dawah Organization, established in 1997, focuses on raising awareness about Islamic heritage in Spain and Latin America and invites Latino/as to reclaim this heritage by embracing Islam through programs and free publications. The Islamic Daʿwah Center in downtown Houston (founded by basketball star Hakeem Olajuwon and opened to the public in 2002) houses prayer space, a gathering area, kitchen, offices, meeting rooms, classrooms, a museum, and a library in its 40,000-square-foot facility. It cites its mission being "to promote Islamic principles, history and culture" and its vision "to become a destination for seekers of the truth." Rather than conversion, this center is envisioned as a "peaceful place ... for prayer, for education, or for merely a little inspiration" to meet "an unfulfilled need of the Houston community to explore the rich history and cultures of Islam."[32]

Dozens of Islamic bookstores—brick and mortar as well as online locations—now specialize in "*daʿwa* materials." Among these are the Mission Dawah Shop, Dawah USA, and Just Dawah. All of these organizations have strategic programs aimed at raising the visibility of Muslims in America in a positive manner, including community outreach, "feed the hungry" programs, after-school Quran instruction, and similar "social work" activities. While all of their websites speak of a desire to introduce Americans to Islam, none speak directly of the intent to "convert" persons in the way that Christian missions seek to evangelize, make disciples, and plant churches. While it is certain that many of the Muslim leaders within these paramosque organizations desire to see conversions of Americans to Islam, the stated objectives and strategic activities are not as direct as those seen among Christian Evangelicals.

Another aspect of contemporary *daʿwa* activity is that of prison ministries. This form of outreach is currently quite controversial for two separate reasons. From the standpoint of conservative/right-wing American organizations, Muslim prison ministries are a breeding ground for establishing radical Islam and fomenting terrorism.[33] The Pew Charitable Trusts' Research Center—a far more reliable source of information—has reported by contrast that while proselytization efforts are "very common" in U.S. prisons, religious extremism is "not at all" a threat according to fifty-eight percent of prison chaplains. Contrary to claims that Islam is making tremendous inroads through the conversion of inmates, in actuality some eighty-five percent of the prison population is Christian (forty-four percent being "evangelical Protestants"), and very few of these are susceptible to proselytization.[34]

A second controversial aspect has to do with the types of Muslims who are most heavily involved in prison ministries. The Nation of Islam and the Ahmadiyya Movement—neither of which are considered acceptably "orthodox" by a majority of the world's Muslims—have placed such ministries high on their list of priorities. The Nation of Islam, under the leadership of Louis Farrakhan, remains as heterodox as the movement was under its original leader, Elijah Muhammad;[35] and the Ahmadiyya's elevation of Mirza Ghulam Ahmad (1835–1908) to the level of Islam's earlier prophets has brought about its exclusion from both the Sunni and Shiʿi divisions of Islam.[36] Consequently, conversions accomplished by either of these groups are not considered to be to "real" Islam but rather to a distorted or sectic form of the religion. With respect to the fears of "radicalization" noted above, however, in neither case would such conversions be to an "extremist" Islam in the sense in which this term is almost always used.

In keeping with these observations, current trends appear to be moving away from overt *daʿwa* activity in prisons and more toward a "pastoral caring and counseling" orientation. As noted by Harvard's *Pluralism Project*,

> Today, Muslim chaplaincy in the United States has moved away from *daʿwah* towards a focus on support and pastoral care, according to the Association of Muslim Chaplains, a professional organization begun in 2011. Many networks now exist for Muslim chaplains

> to discuss their practice, connect with others, and access useful resources. The Association of Muslim Chaplains and the Muslim Chaplain's Association are two such organizations, both open to a wide range of interpretations of the Islamic tradition while maintaining core values of respect, faith, and compassion. Today, Muslim chaplains are not necessarily imams and their ranks may include both men and women. Most chaplains will serve a Muslim community in which multiple interpretations of Islam coexist. In correctional facilities, for example, some prisoners may embrace Sunni Islam or Shiʿah Islam, while others affiliate themselves with the Nation of Islam or the Five Percenters. In recent decades, Muslim chaplains have actively sought recognition of dietary requirements within prison settings and have fought for the rights of the incarcerated to meet with representatives of their faith, to receive religious literature, and to gather regularly for prayer and weekly Jumʿah.[37]

It is then apparent that with respect to *daʿwa* activity, many Muslim prison ministries no longer aim to convert non-Muslims to Islam. This is not to say that conversions do not occur in the course of Muslim prison ministry, but providing care for those who are already Muslims is the present focus.

CYBER- OR INTERNET *DAʿWA*

In imitation of evangelical Christians' increasing use of the internet to engage in "cyber evangelism" and "cyber missions," Muslims now speak of "internet *daʿwa*."[38] For example, in response to Christianity's famous "Answering Islam" website—which functions as a resource center for Christians who seek to convert Muslims to Christianity[39]—there is now a website entitled "Answering Christianity" whose purpose is to counteract Christian evangelistic efforts aimed at Muslims.[40] Specifically, this basic HTML site (which uses highlighted text in primary colors, capital letters, and multiple question marks to emphasize points) includes "questions about Trinity that will prove Islam to be the Divine Truth from GOD!" and a list of four "very STUNNING Divine Miracles," with support from calculations of the numerical values of Quranic "Noble Verses."[41] For example, the website argues,

> The Glorious Quran has 114 Chapters. The sum of those Chapters is 6555 (1 +2 + . . . +114 = 6555). There are also 6,236 Noble Verses in the Glorious Quran. Now, IF YOU ADD EACH CHAPTER # with the number of its Verses, then you get a list of numbers. So 1 (first Chapter) +7 (# of its Verses) = 8. Do this for all Chapters.
> The sum of the odd numbers from the list = 6555.
> The sum of the even numbers from the list = 6236.
> See the XLS file for 100% confirmation.[42]

Such examples illustrate an effort to convince those who may be skeptical about Islam of the textual support for Muslims' beliefs, yet the website's unpolished appearance may diminish its credibility. The site also includes biblical citations to contest Christian beliefs about Jesus's knowledge concerning Judgment Day, points to conflicts between New Testament authors, and draws connections between Christianity and cults, slavery, and terrorism. These topics mirror the topics listed on the "Answering Islam" site. In contrast with sites that focus on interfaith dialogue and mutual understanding in working toward a peaceful world, this website reflects a more hostile approach to *daʿwa*.

Some have expressed surprise that Muslims have so quickly and seemingly uncritically adopted an indubitably "Western" innovation. As Uriya Shavit and Frederic Wiesenbach have noted,

> Muslim scholars traditionally reacted to new technologies—especially those developed in the West—with skepticism, fearing that such new innovations could bring more harm than good to Muslims. Printing machines entered the Ottoman Empire three centuries after they were first introduced in Europe. Scholars regarded them as *bidʿa*, an unlawful innovation, and it took the Napoleonic conquest of Egypt in 1798 to allow acknowledgment of their merit.[43]

Internet technology has, however, proved to be an exception. While other kinds of media often require a high degree of expertise or significant financial outlays, websites can be launched by anyone with a modicum of computer savvy. Such means may well be the future of *daʿwa* activities. As Nadia Khan observes, "Young American Muslims are often the most effective at using new media to spread Islam, sometimes in 140 characters or less."[44] Khan's observation echoes existing research on what Noorhaidi Hasan has referred to as "new *daʿwa* genres, such as cyber *daʿwa* and cellular *daʿwa*." These new genres facilitate instant information exchange across borders through mobile (e.g., SMS) and web-based applications.[45] By breaking down the obstacles to circulating information that are inherent in traditional mass media channels (e.g., hierarchies, time constraints, financial costs), online and mobile *daʿwa* can "reshape inequities"[46] in constructing religious knowledge among Muslims within and outside of North America.

CANADIAN AND AMERICAN ISLAMIC *DAʿWA*: DISTINCTIONS AND IMPLICATIONS

In describing *daʿwa* in North America, it is worth noting some important distinctions between Islam in Canada and in the United States. These countries have experienced different patterns of Muslim immigration, leading to distinctive developments in African American and African Canadian Islam, nationality-specific mosques, intrafaith divisions, Muslim student associations, and media environments.

Most Muslim immigrants to the United States[47] came to the country following the new immigration policy sponsored by then-President Lyndon Johnson in 1965, which replaced the former quota system that was biased toward persons of European origin.[48] With this new policy came Muslim university students from such countries as Pakistan, India, and Iran who established networks that facilitated future Muslim immigration under family unification policies in the 1980s and 1990s. Many Muslim immigrants viewed *daʿwa* as a responsibility in their new country, propelling propagation activities through organizations such as the Islamic Society of North America, the Islamic Circle of North America, and the Tablighi Jamaʿat.[49] Such *daʿwa* activities have been perceived as simultaneously preserving both cultural and religious heritage, shielding immigrants from negative aspects of secular American society, and spreading Islam among Americans who previously had limited awareness of the faith. But even upon attaining American citizenship, there remains a perception that Muslims and Americans are worlds apart. Visible displays of Muslim identity (e.g., wearing certain clothing items such as the *hijab*) are often interpreted as political statements in opposition to American ideals of patriotism.[50] Such an emphasis on difference has gained traction since

September 11, and many Americans—Muslim and non-Muslim alike—continue to ask, "Do Islam and Muslims belong to America? Can Muslims really be(come) Americans?"[51]

In Canada, Muslim immigration followed a similar timeline, with primarily upper- and middle-class families from Middle Eastern and South Asian countries coming in large numbers to metropolitan areas during the 1960s and 1970s. Muslims from less-privileged socioeconomic backgrounds immigrated in the 1990s, subsequent to more liberal sponsorship laws.[52] Despite official federal and provincial policies of multiculturalism and religious freedoms (e.g., the policies of the Ontario Ministry of Education and Training with respect to Antiracism and Ethno Cultural Equity, and the Canadian Charter of Rights and Freedoms), Muslims in contemporary Canada are faced with a Eurocentric education system and issues of religious accommodation when accessing public services.[53] This social context perpetuates concerns about balancing efforts to maintain an Islamic heritage with integration into Canadian society. Furthermore, it affects *daʿwa* activity by encouraging Muslims to adopt an "offensive-activist" approach over a "defensive-pacifist" one in order to transform aspects of Canadian society to reflect Islamic principles and moral codes.[54] Rather than focusing merely on retaining one's own Muslim identity, this offensive-activist approach to *daʿwa* is mainly concerned with proselytizing non-Muslims with an aim to convert them.

In addition to immigration from predominantly Muslim countries, the emergence and development of African American Islamic movements differentiates Muslim experiences in Canada from those in the United States.[55] In the U.S., the history of slavery and related socioeconomic motivators, including systemic violence and marginalization, was what drove the *daʿwa* activities of groups such as Noble Drew Ali's Moorish Science Temple, Warith Deen Muhammad's American Society of Muslims, and Elijah Muhammad's Nation of Islam.[56] These groups voiced a religious response to issues that African Americans encountered in their daily lives, from racism and poverty to self-reliance and self-development. To add relevance to their *daʿwa* work, African American Islamic groups focused their attention on inner cities and incarcerated populations.[57] Due in part to distinctive histories of slavery and race relations, these groups have had limited presence in Canada, where *daʿwa* has been conducted through organizations such as ICNA and Sound Vision that appeal to a broader North American demographic through street *daʿwa* and online media, and ISNA, which manages interfaith and community outreach initiatives.

While groups such as the Nation of Islam did not proliferate in Canada, Canadian immigration policies have fostered an environment in which ethnically affiliated mosques produce their own sets of priorities. Intra-Islamic missionary activities, such as those described in Rory Dickson's study of Tablighi Jamaʿat members at a southwestern Ontario mosque, do occur.[58] However, contemporary Canadian mosques—especially those in larger urban centers—often serve as spaces for indigenous language study and cultural maintenance. Negotiating ethnic identities within a new geopolitical context often creates intrafaith divisions and conflict.[59] These cultural divisions have implications for *daʿwa* activity in that they present norms and strategies that appear to be incompatible with one another.

In both the U.S. and Canada, organizations for Muslim students, such as the Muslim Students' Association (MSA), have played an important role in awareness and proselytization efforts. Many Muslim international students at American colleges and universities consider *daʿwa* to be a priority and thus align themselves with their campus organization for Muslim students for the purpose of effectively spreading Islam across the country.[60] Not only do they seek to resist the marginalization of Muslim students at secular, Eurocentric educational institutions, but such organizations in Canada also have mandates to perform *daʿwa*.[61] They conduct this work through a variety of activities, including hosting religious education classes; study circles; forums for interfaith discussions; Islamic awareness weeks; and partnering with large, mainstream conferences to connect with the broader community as well as their target student populations.

In addition to the aforementioned elements, the post-September 11 media environment has had a tremendous effect on the ways in which *daʿwa* activities are carried out.[62] Fear of Muslims—and Muslim converts in particular—has been fueled by network news coverage of radicalized converts such as Canadians Martin Couture-Rouleau (who drove his car into two Canadian soldiers in a shopping center parking lot in Saint-Jean-sur-Richelieu, Québec, 20 October 2014, and Michael Zehaf-Bibeau (who fatally shot Cpl. Nathan Cirillo at the Canadian National War Memorial in Ottawa, Ontario, two days later). In response to such media representations, North American Muslims who circulate information about their faith often try to balance this content by featuring revered celebrities and community members who converted to Islam (e.g., Cat Stevens and Hamza Yusuf) in their conversations, literature, and online materials in an attempt to create more positive sentiments regarding Islam.[63]

When engaging in *daʿwa*, Muslims in Canada also draw attention to the contributions Muslims have made to medicine, mathematics, architecture, arts, and sciences to help offset media coverage that associates Islam with foreign radicalization and human rights abuses (notably, the oppression of women) or domestic terrorists and sleeper cells.[64] Such contributions were showcased, for instance, in media coverage of the Aga Khan Museum, an Islamic art museum and performing arts center that opened only weeks before Michael Zehaf-Bibeau's attack on Parliament Hill in Canada's national capital in 2014.

PROGNOSIS FOR THE FUTURE OF *DAʿWA* IN NORTH AMERICA

One may describe the influence of the spiritual dimension of human existence at four distinct levels: individual, family and local community, national or tribal, and global.[65] Based on the foregoing contents of this chapter, it may be concluded that at the latter two levels (i.e., national and global) the prognosis for the future of *daʿwa* is a poor one, while Muslim missionary activity at the individual and family/local community levels will most likely be much more successful.

Generally speaking, North Americans are not highly sophisticated when it comes to selecting their sources for gathering basic information and for decision making, in particular about subjects having to do with politics and global affairs.[66] The news media—whether television-, web-, or print-based—are the chief, and in many cases the only, sources for developing convictions about populations such as the world's Muslims.[67] Consequently, as long as the media continue to focus on the actions and rhetoric of ISIS, the Taliban, al-Qaeda, Hezbollah, the Palestinian Hamas, the alleged nuclear objectives of Iran, Saudi Arabian executions for moral transgressions, the North African "Arab Spring," turmoil in Egypt, and other such phenomena, the average American's view of Islam will remain highly negative. The religion will be considered an exclusivist system characterized by arrogance, hatred, bigotry, intolerance, and fundamentalism.[68] Such characteristics are certainly unacceptable to the current generation of Western citizens who have been enculturated into a highly liberal worldview with respect to nearly every moral and ethical issue imaginable. Therefore, most invitations to convert to Islam will be met with abject disbelief and harsh resistance. The media-driven stereotypes are simply too difficult to overcome at these levels.

At the individual and family/local community levels, however, the outlook for *daʿwa* activity is much more positive. While media reporting regarding such items as ISIS atrocities lacks the "punch" that was characteristic of the September 11 attacks (mainly because of the geographical distance involved), these reports still have the ability to arouse curiosity and interest on the part of citizens in whose neighborhoods Muslims reside. According to *USA Today*, the number of mosques in America grew from 1,209 in the year 2000 to 2,106 in 2010—a growth rate of seventy-four percent in a decade.[69] These mosques have become adept at arranging special "visit days" for their neighborhoods as a means of addressing and—ideally—changing stereotypes. The internet is rife with invitations to specific mosques and instructions regarding how one should conduct oneself when making such a visit: "Etiquette of Visiting a Mosque" (Falls Church, VA);[70] "A Visit to the Mosque" (the Crescent Project);[71] "Visiting an Islamic Center" (North American Imam's Federation);[72] and "Visit a Mosque" (WhyIslam.org),[73] to name only a few.

Essentially, such a strategy represents a return to Islam's earliest days. At the beginning of his own *daʿwa*, Muhammad had very little (if any) success at the tribal/national level, much less the international level. On the contrary, his preaching aroused resentment and anger among his fellow citizens in Mecca, attitudes that eventually necessitated his *hijra* to Medina. It was rather at the individual and family levels that he won his first converts—Khadija, Abu Bakr, Ali, Zayd, and others. And it was these individuals and family members who formed the foundation of a religion that eventually became both national and international in scope.

And so still today it will be personal encounters between Muslims and non-Muslims that will be the most effective means of *daʿwa* in the contemporary world, as individuals "*invite to the Way of the Lord with wisdom and beautiful preaching*" (Quran 16:125).

CHAPTER 11

Global Islam "Made in South Asia"

The Tablighi Jamaʿat and Its Universalized Preaching Mission

DIETRICH REETZ

THE TABLIGHI JAMAʿAT (TJ) is a lay Sunni preaching movement that emerged in 1926 in North India to challenge efforts by Hindu missionaries to "reconvert" local Muslims. Since then, it has become a major force within the larger stream of normative Islamic revival among South Asian Muslims. Its pietistic agenda balances purist ambitions with spiritual practices, placing itself between Salafi and Sufi inclinations. Starting in the 1950s, it has manifested translocal and global ambitions, and today the Tablighi movement is perhaps the largest active world missionary movement of Islam. It has not only expanded within the South Asian Muslim diaspora networks, such as in the U.S. and UK, but has also managed to go entirely "native" in several Muslim communities such as the Maghreb, Central Asia, and Africa, where followers are almost entirely local Muslims.

In India, the movement's recognized founder, Muhammad Ilyas (1885–1944), prioritized strengthening faith among Muslims. Today, for many Muslims the world over, the Tablighis are a source of authentic religious knowledge and behavior based on the practice and narratives of Prophetic traditions and the founding generations of Islam, *al-salaf*. This chapter traces the trajectory of the Tablighi Jamaʿat's global mobilization where they contested the doctrine and practice of Islam in the wider "Islamic field" and developed new modes and formats for their activism in different countries.[1]

FROM *DAʿWA* TO *TABLIGH*: THE EVOLUTION OF GLOBAL PREACHING FROM SOUTH ASIA

The Tablighi Jamaʿat, "the preaching community," did not bear this name when it first emerged as an activist grassroots movement in 1925–1926. While the task of propagating religion through preaching and missionary activity was already universally recognized among Muslims, it began to assume a more structured format in the late nineteenth and early twentieth century. Preaching activity in the public sphere typified the evolution of such Muslim activism from primarily local initiatives to self-organized translocal and even global mobilization. Public preaching of Islam was understood not only as a normative Quranic duty but also as a social and cultural obligation, at times also reflecting political aspirations against the Western and Christian colonial domination by the British.[2]

Engagement with global Islam for internal political mobilization reached a staggering level with the Khilafat Movement (1918–1924), which sought to retain and revive a transnational Ottoman caliphate that Turkey was about to abolish. At the same time, Hindus and Muslims were contesting the religious space in South Asia with growing determination. It is against this background that almost all active Muslim groups of the time developed their own formats for *daʿwa*.[3]

Ilyas began actively engaging in the Mewat region in northwestern India. In the beginning, he sought primarily to confirm the faith of the Meos and prevent them from succumbing to the reconversion efforts of the Hindu reformist movement Arya Samaj.[4] He believed this was best achieved by sending out groups of Mewati Muslim students as traveling preachers to conduct *daʿwa*. In doing so, the preachers themselves would reactivate their own knowledge and practice of religion. Soon, Ilyas felt the need to provide the lay preachers with guiding literature, and the hadith collection compiled by his nephew, the Deobandi scholar Muhammad Zakariya (1898–1982), acquired a central place.[5] Originally titled *Tablighi Nisab* (Tablighi Syllabus), it was later renamed *Faza'il-e Aʿmal* (The Virtues of Good Deeds).[6] *Faza'il* remains the central text of reference among Tablighis world-wide and has been translated into numerous languages, becoming an iconic symbol of their global efforts. To make his educational message accessible for common Meos, Ilyas summarized the essence of the movement in "six essentials" (*cheh baten*) that reflected the movement's doctrine and became its trademark symbol, alongside the *jama'ats*—groups of ten to twelve traveling lay preachers—and the study of the *Faza'il-e A'mal*.

The popularity of the Tablighi concept grew rapidly both inside South Asia and soon beyond its borders. At the 1941 convention, between 20,000 and 25,000 people assembled at Nuh in Assam.[7] The ulama had at first been cautious about this outburst of public piety, but the growing appeal of the movement forced them to decide whether to support it. From 1940, students and staff of the Nadwat al-Ulama seminary in Lucknow participated openly, and in 1944, principals of a number of Islamic seminaries and academies convened to discuss what part their academies could play.[8] This cooperation would eventually grow into a global collaborative effort between religious scholars and lay preachers.[9]

In 1944, Ilyas's son, Muhammad Yusuf (b. 1917), became leader (*amir*) of the movement until his own death in 1965. Yusuf laid the foundations for the rapid geographic expansion of the movement, extending the travel itineraries of preaching groups outside South Asia. The first delegations went to England and the Hijaz in 1946, and by the early 1950s others had been sent to Burma, British Malaya, and Indonesia.[10] The third amir, Inamul Hasan (1918–1995), was credited with establishing Tablighi centers in countries such as France (1972), Belgium (1975), the UK (1978), and Spain (1992).[11]

The movement entered a new phase in the early 2000s, joining global trends in analog and digital media. Although formerly shunned by Tablighi elders, use of such media now became a structural element of the larger congregations. Followers first listened to cassettes with recorded lectures (*bayan*) and speeches that circulated in different countries of their preaching destination. That practice has since shifted to headphones. Their presence on the internet also expanded rapidly, with followers covering the missionary travels of prominent personalities on YouTube and Facebook.[12]

A GLOBAL FORMAT: CONTESTING DOCTRINES AND PRACTICES IN THE WIDER ISLAMIC FIELD

The doctrinal approach of the TJ evolved gradually, although most parameters had already been set by its founder, Ilyas. He was educated at the main Islamic seminary at Deoband in North India,[13] which followed a reformist and purist approach based on the traditional *dars-e nizami* curriculum.[14] In South Asia, their take on Sunni Islam came to be considered a separate school of thought and practice, the Deobandi *maslak*. Consistent with the Deobandi emphasis on hadith, Ilyas's main concern was the right practice of Islam so that their preaching would have a measurable impact. Tablighi preachers went from door to door, calling on people—the core meaning of *da'wa* ("call")—to attend the prayer session and sermon that their preaching party would later hold at a local mosque. Ilyas argued that Tablighis presented not a separate format but "only" the implementation of the ideal of the Prophet and his companions regarding the general preaching obligations of Muslims.[15] This approach laid the foundation for their global acceptance representing a normative approach to Islam and where the local origins of the movement from South Asia became less relevant. At the same time, it turned the Tablighi practice into a new, globalized ritual.

Tablighi preaching routine the world over included a fixed schedule of missionary tours for followers that were cumulative and would be undertaken in ascending order: three days, forty days (*chilla*), four months (grand *chilla*), and seven or twelve months. After exploring one's own area, other cities and countries were targeted for a missionary sortie (*khuruj*). Those who completed the grand *chilla* were considered members of a spiritual elite, elders, and in many countries special congregations were held for them. After returning from their travels, the Tablighi groups were expected to give a report on the local conditions and the results of their missionary efforts. Preaching groups were also expected to operate at only a subsistence level, neglecting the comfort of this world for the abundance in the hereafter.

In the course of time, the Tablighis established a more rigid system of internal self-organization, called *intizam*.[16] It was a sort of "faith bureaucracy"[17] that ran counter to the claims of its founder and successor *umara'* that the movement would rest entirely on almost spontaneous and enthusiastic self-mobilization. But this structure was also crucial for its global expansion. Centers in different parts of the world are connected through this bureaucracy, which includes consultations and advice but also instructions from headquarters, complete with visits from leadership delegations to various national chapters to check on compliance.

There is a clear distinction between chance participants and regular followers accepting the cumulative obligations. The latter made up between twenty-five and forty percent, according to various estimates, and constituted the backbone of the movement's networking. Regular congregations (*ijtima*ʿ) represent another form of participation in Tablighi activism. Aside from the Jamaʿat's annual congregations, weekly Thursday night gatherings are conducted at every center of the movement across the world, although the weekday may sometimes vary.

While leadership formerly rested with the amir of the national or local center, or of individual preaching groups, over the last fifteen years authority has decidedly shifted to a council (*shura*) format with rotating responsibility. Only *umara'* who had been installed earlier would continue in office. Wherever an amir died, as happened in the UK, or a new national chapter was organized, as in Kyrgyzstan, a council was installed. Recently, the current global amir, Mawlana Saad Kandhalawi (b. 1965), sought to reassert his authority over the *shura* system with regard to global leadership. This controversy first arose in December 2015 when efforts were made to reinvigorate the global *shura* by filling the places of members who had died.[18]

The role of the religious scholars (*ulama*) was yet another topic of debate over the long years of TJ's existence. While a growing number of Deobandi scholars made it to leadership positions, lay preachers remained relevant and important. While Mawlanas Saad in India and Tariq Jamil (b. 1953) in Pakistan were seen as important sources of knowledge, the amir of the Pakistan TJ, Haji Abdul Wahhab (b. 1923), commanded equal respect despite not being an *ʿalim* himself. In countries where the TJ had established its own madrasa at the national center, as in Pakistan, Malaysia, Indonesia, or the UK and South Africa, the impact of the ulama increased structurally, while lay preachers remained at the forefront of international *shura* activities.

The global acceptance of the Tablighis was facilitated by the flexibility of the Deoband system, which adhered to Hanafi law but accommodated other schools. The same applied to the comparatively inclusive approach of the TJ toward different doctrinal interpretations and practices of Islam, at least among Sunnis. Ilyas's six points conceptually reflected the desire to find common ground.[19] His emphasis was on the primary sources of Islam, rather than sectarian identities, and highlighted the blessings of practicing Islam over contested issues. This is why leaders called their hadith collection *faza'il* (virtues) and avoided discussing negative terms often used in mutual accusation between South Asia's different schools of thought and practice.[20]

Ilyas preferred to concentrate on the merits of certain religious practices, which, according to hadith, accrued rewards. The movement implemented this approach to the point where it became a common practice to equate various Tablighi practices with fixed amounts of reward and where regular followers constantly calculated their accumulations. This incentive-based approach became a psychological hallmark of the internal culture of the movement and of its activists' public behavior. It combined with a self-effacing attitude of inward-looking pietism and individual self-perfection, yet one that did not prevent the movement from being seen as a strong—often aggressive—collective force emphasizing in its practice the group, the *jamaʿat*, rather than the individual Muslim.[21]

Yet, aiming at least partially at doctrinal inclusion and compromise generated contestations in the global Islamic field from both Salafi and Sufi groups in different regions of the world. Critics, mostly from the South Asian Ahl-e Hadith and international Salafi groups, considered Ilyas's principles inadmissible simplifications of Islamic tenets. Contrasting his program with the assumed erudition of their scholars, they have frequently attacked Tablighi lay preachers as ill-informed and uneducated about Islam. The Ahl-e Hadith scholar Shaykh Tauseef ur Rehman and institutions such as the Jeddah Dawah Center—run by the Ahl-e Hadith in Saudi Arabia—attacked the Tablighi approach on several YouTube channels.[22]

From the other side, critics from the Sufi-oriented Barelwi movement, which supports the visitation of shrines, accused the Tablighis of being narrow-minded and strict, comparing their philosophy to Salafism.[23] Their critiques strongly resonated in regions such as Central Asia, South East Asia, and the Maghreb. Interviews with respondents in Kyrgyzstan, Malaysia, and Indonesia, as well as among Tablighi followers of Maghreb descent in France confirmed that the Tablighis were accused of subverting local practices of Islam in their drive for standardization and purification.[24] At the same time, the Barelwi preaching movement Daʿwat-e Islami (DI), founded by Muhammad Ilyas Qadri in 1981, imitated the TJ while promoting their own doctrinal profile and international appearance. Such adaptations by DI founders included the expansion of the Tablighi core program of six points to a DI list of seventy-two.[25]

The contention between Salafi and Sufi perspectives toward TJ could also be observed in their different takes on the ritual practices and rules inside the movement. While some activist respondents interviewed argued that over the years Salafi interpretations gained decisive momentum in the movement, the presence of a Sufi legacy was undeniable.[26] This combination was already clear from the six points, which display Sufi self-reflective piety. Until a few years ago, elders of the movement, acting much like Sufi *shuyukh*, initiated new followers as disciples. The reason for this closeness lay partly in the character of Deobandi reformism, which, unlike Wahhabism and other varieties of Salafism, never fully renounced Sufi influences but often selectively validated those practices and concepts that were directly mentioned in the Quran and hadith.

Although Muslims are not questioned about their origins when they join the Tablighis, respondents testified that this liberty could face real constraints in daily implementation.[27] Accepting Ahmadis, for instance, was still out of the question. But there were some frequently quoted cases of Shiʿa Muslims who had joined the Tablighis out of curiosity and who ultimately converted to Sunni Islam. There were also reports of Barelwis joining, though they still underwent some form of internal conversion. Followers of the South Asian Salafi movement Ahl-e Hadith and "modernist" Muslims who often belonged to Jamaʿat-e Islami faced the fewest problems, since their doctrines differed less from Deobandi concepts. While there are still a multitude of "ethnic" and "cultural" takes on living Islam, participating in the Tablighi movement in the end leads to an internal conversion and homogenization toward the Deobandi school of thought.

It must be emphasized here, however, that Deobandism itself is not a homogeneous phenomenon. There has been a certain polarization between more political, "radical," and more pietistic, knowledge-oriented factions. This pressure for internal conversion had its due effect on Tablighi international activities in countries where they attracted followers who had grown up with local varieties of popular Islam and were now looking for normative approaches, as in Central Asia or Southeast Asia. At the same time, their piety-driven style of self-effacing preaching attracted large numbers of Muslims from secular working environments who saw this practice as less controversial and highly compatible with a neoliberal working environment in urban areas of various countries, not only in the West but also in South Asia, Southeast Asia, and North Africa.[28]

In Pakistan, the TJ made itself particularly felt in rural and suburban communities. In comparison with India and Bangladesh, international followers visiting South Asia praised the movement in Pakistan for its high level of organization. Every district had its own center located in one of the local mosques and was represented at the annual congregation by its own delegation (*halqa*). Although the movement in Pakistan was centered in Raiwind in the Punjab, the Pashtuns were probably the most active ethnic community. In their tribal areas, the TJ centers became one of the few attractions for shared social activities. To a certain extent, the movement came to be seen as an avenue for the social advancement of Muslims from deprived regions of the country. In India, international Tablighi followers on their preaching tours particularly emphasized the historical authenticity of the movement in a multireligious setting, whereas in Bangladesh it was the spiritual experience that was praised.

As the internal organization of the TJ became more differentiated in the 1980s and 1990s, professionals, teachers, and members of the police and military had their separate formats for meeting within the movement. These efforts extended to the old and new elites such as landowners, cricket players, and entertainers, including singers and music groups. The most well-known representative of the latter category was the Pakistani Junaid Jamshed (1964–2016), a pop singer and band leader who turned to preaching as a Tablighi activist in 2004.[29] In the universities of India, Pakistan, and Bangladesh, the movement found new support among Muslim students who were particularly interested in the spatial and social mobility of its traveling preaching groups. Such travel allowed them to visit different towns, cities, and even countries and continents at low cost.

Another contested topic was the participation of women. Ilyas opened a separate avenue for them to take part while still observing Islamic propriety. The Masturat Jamaʿat (group of pious women) allowed women accompanied by male relatives or guardians to join in. In collective gatherings, such attendees would listen to the sermon from behind curtains. Though discriminatory against women, over the years such practices significantly increased the space for them within the movement. Respondents confirmed that women have begun to meet in female-only circles for group readings of Zakariya's hadith collection. This became especially common in student hostels and neighborhoods in places such as Karachi and Mumbai. The rapid increase in the number of girls receiving religious education in Deobandi madrasas in recent years, undergoing the demanding course to become an *ʿalima*, led to a significant change in the gender equation among Tablighi followers. Metcalf argues that the very form of organization necessitated shared labor during preaching tours, since men had to take care of daily chores such as cooking, washing, etc., thus challenging traditional gender roles in Muslim society.[30] Field research in Mumbai likewise showed a case of women organizing their own congregation addressed by female scholars.[31] The Tablighi approach mobilized women in Kyrgyzstan and other post-Soviet countries, not to mention the Muslim regions of Russia, as those women reconnected with the memory of female activism in Soviet times.[32]

THE LOCAL AND THE GLOBAL IN TABLIGHI ACTIVISM: SOCIAL LIFE-WORLDS BEYOND RELIGION

Since the 1970s, the movement's influence has expanded rapidly, turning it into a major factor of social and religious mobilization in India and Pakistan, as well as in the wider Muslim world and beyond. The growing impact of the TJ has attracted increasing attention to its social dimensions, political contestations, and economic impact that started in South Asia and extended across the globe. A case in point is the rise of the Taliban in Afghanistan in the mid-1990s. As both groups referred to the Deobandi doctrine, there was an assumption that they belonged to the same camp or were similar.[33] TJ functionary respondents, however, confirmed that their interaction with the Afghan Taliban was a mix of cooperation and critique, supporting the Taliban ideals of creating an Islamic state while hoping to influence their modes of implementation. As Tablighi leaders—especially in Pakistan—were in regular personal contact with Taliban leaders, including Mullah Omar, they made clear to them in private that they disagreed with many of the Taliban approaches, including the use of violence, in implementing their policies.[34]

In the aftermath of the 9/11 attacks in the U.S., Western and Russian security analysts came to believe that the TJ was instrumental in preparing the ground for radical and militant groups, to the point of providing occasions for recruitment and training. Such assumptions could not be proven, although in a number of cases known terrorists were documented to have spent at least some time with the Tablighis, notably in Pakistan, but also in Western Europe. This was the case with the former Guantanamo inmate Murat Kurnaz, a Turkish-German Muslim from Bremen.[35] While the movement consistently spoke out against violence and recommended preaching instead, respondents acknowledged that radicals and militants in their capacity as lay Muslims did occasionally drift into the movement, especially when their groups came under pressure from security forces. In hopes of "reforming" such militants, TJ elders insisted that they shun violence while on tour with the Tablighis.[36] On the other hand, the governments of India, Indonesia, and Pakistan tried to instrumentalize and manipulate the movement in the belief it would have a "pacifying" impact on the Islamist scene.

As the movement progressed from the fringes to the social mainstream, there was a growing intersection of its activities with all spheres of life, including secular education at universities or certain private school systems, as well as the wider economy. Respondents confirmed the existence of a devoted group of Tablighi regulars among bureaucrats, administrators, financial operators, and company managers, not only in the new Islamic economy but also in the mainstream. It was not unusual for participants and Tablighi activists to use preaching tours and congregations for networking and establishing economic contacts, both within their own country and internationally. Equally relevant is the local economy surrounding the congregations and local centers. Vendors of Islamic goods, clothing, and books were found in increasing numbers at events and locations such as Raiwind as well as Bhopal, Kuala Lumpur, East Java, or Dewsbury, Britain, and Bishkek, Kyrgyzstan.[37]

Although no exact statistics exist, the movement is believed to now include almost eighty million Muslims from all over the world.[38] Its headquarters in Delhi became a truly global center from which groups are dispatched all over the world for preaching as well as for reviewing compliance of preaching groups with Tablighi rules. Similar functions are being executed from the Pakistan center in Raiwind. The movement seems to be present in practically all Muslim countries, as well as in countries and regions with only a small Muslim presence, such as Japan, Hong Kong, and Latin America. Thus, the TJ became a locally influential force in the wider Islamic field beyond South Asia in South Africa, France, Britain, and the Maghreb, as well as in Malaysia, Indonesia and Kyrgyzstan.

The international branches of the Tablighi movement may be seen as filling particular social and religious niche gaps in the global market of international religious "service providers." In South Africa, the activities of the TJ reflect the comparatively comfortable social position of the Indian Muslim community. The related *madrasas* of the Tablighis operate like tuition-based private schools, with parents often arriving in expensive cars to drop their children off.[39] In contrast, school conditions were far better than those of the comparatively poor North African migrants who constituted the core of the Tablighi followers in urban Paris. In France, the movement became the second-most important Muslim organization in terms of the number of mosques it controlled—right after organizations related to the Muslim Brotherhood. At the same time, it attracted both working-class migrants of mainly North African descent in the well-known Paris neighborhood of Saint Denis and settled Muslim migrants of the second and third generation in regions such as Marseille.[40]

In Britain, the Tablighis enjoy the largest and most developed infrastructure in Western Europe, with centers and schools well attended by both educated and working-class British Muslims. The British center in Dewsbury coordinates activities of the movement Europe-wide. Tablighi activism has shaped the social culture of several parts of the city, where pubs felt forced to close down and gender segregation became a visible social norm, partly shared and partly enforced.[41] In Spain, the movement appeared to be self-conscious in an environment where privatized faith is the norm and proselytizing is largely unwelcome. It was internally divided between Pakistani migrants, primarily in Barcelona, and Muslims of North African descent elsewhere.[42]

In the U.S. and Canada, the Tablighis have operated in a similar context yet with less contestation and much more pride and confidence.[43] As several respondents confirmed, it was not considered controversial to be a religious activist in North America, as it would be in parts of Europe; it was rather a matter of pride, acknowledged by neighbors and colleagues. Tablighi and Deobandi activists run various centers, mosques, and hybrid schools with religious-cum-secular curriculums in Houston, New York, Chicago, and Toronto.[44]

In post-Soviet Kyrgyzstan, Tablighis devoted themselves to social reconstruction after the ravaging impact of the new market economy left young rural men in particular unemployed and lacking a sense of orientation.[45] In Indonesia, the movement bridged the gap between the two main contestants for Islamic revival, the more traditional and Sufi-inspired Nahdlatul Ulama (NU) and the modernist Muhammadiyya.[46]

The TJ has played different social roles in various contexts. In Gambia, followers treated it like a youth movement confronting the established system of the Sufi orders.[47] In Uganda, local groups emphasized their Salafi orientation, and thereby also a political stake in the contested Islamic field against other local Muslim actors, mainly related to the Sufi orders.[48] In the UAE, it gave a home and identity to the large number of South Asian Muslim migrant workers, and in Syria and Iraq of late, it has provided space for accommodation and rationality under circumstances of civil war and sectarian divides. It has assembled quietly in private homes in Saudi Arabia, Palestine, and Israel, providing space to voice religious and social discontent.[49]

Still, despite the plurality of local contexts, the elders of the movement in India and Pakistan have communicated a global vision wherein the world is essentially one Islamic whole in which different parts still must be awakened to the meaning of Islam and their true Muslim nature. From their global headquarters, these elders have been known to sit before world maps marked with spaces abundantly filled by Tablighi activities or direly lacking them. There they make provisions for regions that need more attention and those requiring less, where there are opportunities for expansion, and where current efforts are sufficient. In this sense, they have become actors of globalization in their own right, shaping their own world in a way that takes into consideration diverse social or cultural conditions.[50] The South African institutions have also played an important intellectual role in the global Tablighi universe. They translated into English many of the Islamic tracts that were used in Tablighi sessions and madrasas, and graduates of their schools filled teaching positions in Britain's Tablighi schools, as well as in the U.S. and Canada.

Yet, such engagement with this world remains structurally contradictory. The most active and consistent followers often have little time left to take care of worldly issues and were thus literally led out of this world. Such "over-organization," inspired by modern bureaucracy and a global management culture, has connected them with this world while at the same time has undermined that connection. The adoption of new technologies, the grudging acceptance of social media, and a continuing thirst for religious knowledge and spiritual consolation in a world that looks more difficult and complex than ever are still driving its global expansion.

CONCLUSION

As this study has shown, the TJ is not a one-dimensional preaching format but rather a plurality of engagements with religious knowledge, practice, and life-worlds of Muslims today. Moreover, it may well be argued that the Tablighi model has had a lasting effect on the wider field of Islamic *da'wa* activism. Not only has it been emulated by other movements such as Da'wat-e Islami, but its style of self-organization has also left its traces on other Muslim groups. The global expansion of the TJ and its pluralization mean that it is more difficult than ever for the leadership to control and that its future trajectory and influence still remain an open question.

Over time, its ways of world-making have become ever-more systematic. They have been marked by interventions aimed at sharing values and practices across spatial, social, and cultural divides. The Tablighis have established structures as well as practices of management and organization that—at least partly—turned the grassroots movement into a formal organization. These structural and institutional interventions have turned the Tablighis into active participants and shapers of globalization. If that process is understood not only in terms of reducing the time-space distanciation[51] across the world but also as structural and institutional intervention for shaping cross-border activity, religious as much as social, cultural, and economic, then the TJ has truly turned into an agent of globalization, a "global religious service provider" both for local citizens as well as migrant populations of Muslim descent or conversion.

PART IV

New Directions

CHAPTER 12

Neoliberal Daʿwa

The Egyptian New Preachers (al-duʿa al-judud) *and the Restructuring of Transnational Religious Preaching and Practice*

AARON ROCK-SINGER

THE EARLY YEARS of the twenty-first century saw the rise of a group of lay, educated preachers in Egypt, soon known as "the New Preachers" (*al-duʿa al-judud*). Young, well dressed, and upwardly mobile, these men turned to satellite television and the internet as they expanded beyond Egypt to the Levant, the Gulf States, North Africa, and even the United Kingdom. In their wake, they left not only legions of adoring supporters but also frustrated political elites and religious scholars, threatened by the leadership aspirations of a movement that sidestepped existing structures of political and religious authority. Yet these laymen sought to appropriate religious authority or challenge political elites as well as to foreground a previously marginal tie between preaching, piety, and economic prosperity through a mantra of "development by faith" (*al-tanmiya biʾl-iman*).

While Amr Khaled (b. 1967) is the most prominent figure within this trend, he is hardly alone, and key peers include Muʿizz Masʿud (b. 1978) and Mustafa Husni (b. 1978). All three men are products of secular education: Khaled received his B.A. from Cairo University; Masʿud studied Economics at the American University in Cairo; and Husni graduated from the Faculty of Commerce at Ayn Shams University. These men did not limit themselves to undergraduate degrees in finance-related fields, as Khaled completed his doctoral dissertation on "Islam and Co-Existence" in 2010 at the University of Wales, and Masʿud is currently enrolled in a PhD program at Cambridge University's Faculty of Divinity.[1]

This chapter, in turn, uses Khaled's television programs, periodicals, websites, and interviews with participants in his signature program,

Lifemakers (Sunaʿ al-Hayat), to explore the role of the New Preachers in the propagation of a neoliberal *daʿwa*.[2] It begins by laying out previous approaches to studying the rise of Islamic preaching informed by neoliberal economic conceptions. It then traces the roots of a neoliberal message among preachers within modern Egyptian history, with particular attention given to the increasing association of religious mobilization projects with economic productivity. The second half of the chapter turns from past to present, highlighting the rise of the New Preachers in Egypt, their vying for religious authority, and their particular projects of religious piety in comparison with Islamist, Salafi, and state competitors. At the intersection of religious proselytization and economic transformation, a distinctive *daʿwa* would reshape both preaching and individual pious practice in the contemporary Middle East.

THE ROOTS OF A NEOLIBERAL *DAʿWA*

In 1979, students at Minya University in Upper Egypt wrote to *al-Iʿtisam*, a magazine loosely affiliated with the Salafi organization Jamʿiyya Sharʿiyya, to protest an increase in the price of this periodical. These students challenged the magazine's prior claims of indifference to profit and asked accusingly whether the magazine's resort to "commercial methods" conflicted with its religious goals. In response, *al-Iʿtisam*'s editors argued that, unlike those magazines funded by state institutions, they had to cover their own costs.[3] Two years later, in an editorial note in the Muslim Brotherhood's official magazine, *al-Daʿwa*, Supreme Guide Umar al-Tilmisani explained that Islamic papers differed from other publications on a fundamental level because they reject the notion of media as a commercial enterprise (*tijara*).[4] By the early 2000s, however, the question was no longer whether religious media was a commercial enterprise—the rise of satellite television channels and internet sites with glossy advertisements left little doubt—but *how* competing preachers and religious intellectuals would define economic practice in religious terms.

What are the roots of the rise of economic productivity as a central source of religious authority and a means of pious practice? Histories and ethnographies of *daʿwa* say little about how economic considerations shape the call to Islam.[5] A partial exception to this statement is scholarship on Islamism, in which a subset of studies draws on Social Movement Theory (SMT) to emphasize the relationship between economic disappointment, mobilization, and Islamist sympathies. Most prominently, Carrie Wickham highlights the role of both mass media and local educational activities in taking advantage of the ideological opening produced by socioeconomic disappointment to communicate religious frames, while Asef Bayat argues that Islamists have successfully "built hegemony" through political pressure on the regime and through "cultural production" that communicated their distinct religious vision.[6] Yet, while this scholarship valuably casts light on the relationship between class, mobilization, and piety, it says little about the economic assumptions that underlie such calls to Islam.

In parallel, studies of Islamic economics lay out the theory of a religiously based economic system. The question of economics and Islamic thought, however, is limited to the narrowly circumscribed domain of particular financial models.[7] An exception to this broad approach is the work of Timur Kuran, which situates the rise of Islamic Economics within a particular political and cultural context, yet does not address how twentieth-century economic shifts have shaped Islamic thought more broadly.[8]

Finally, scholarship on the New Preachers notes the neoliberal economic assumptions that underlie this trend. These studies highlight the ways in which neoliberal economic shifts have facilitated both access to transnational media and new sources of funding for socioeconomic service provision, while implicitly positing a rupture between this appeal and previous forms of *daʿwa*.[9] This approach, however, tells us little about the relationship between economic shifts and Islamic thought generally or about the longer history of the rise of a neoliberal *daʿwa* specifically.

The limits of such scholarship are founded in a narrow understanding of the economic and intellectual context of spreading the call of Islam. As the debate at the beginning of this section suggests, participants in *daʿwa* have long sought to obscure the relationship between economic considerations and the production of religious thought. Histories and ethnographies of preaching have largely mirrored this approach, either focusing solely on Islamic economics or considering the role of economic shifts in the expansion of socioeconomic service provision.[10] Just as importantly, scholarship on *daʿwa* often considers state-sponsored religious education to represent a separate and intellectually distinct sphere. Consequently, such studies ignore the influence of state-sponsored visions of religio-economic change on the claims of preachers and the practices of the pious alike. Yet, preaching and education are two sides of the same coin: the transmission of models of Islamic knowledge and practice to a mass audience.[11] When we take seriously the role of state institutions as sites of Islamic transmission and as key competitors to and influences on Islamic preaching, the longer history of Islamic transmission and its relationship to changing economic winds becomes clear.

FROM LORD CROMER TO PRESIDENT NASSER

How should we understand the rise of lay preachers and their conscious decision to place neoliberal economic change as a premier form and pressing mission of *daʿwa*? How did the bounds of Islamic preaching come to encompass neoliberal economic assumptions, and should this call be understood as constituting a rupture with previous conceptions and practices of *daʿwa* in the twentieth century? This story begins not in the explicit engagement of preachers with questions of socioeconomic development *or* with the adoption of particular economic philosophies but rather with the late-nineteenth-century efforts of the Egyptian state to enter the business of mass religious education. British colonial educators sought to transform Quranic recitation schools (sing. *kuttab*) into a nationwide system with a unified curriculum. Colonial administrators believed that, as in England, correct mass socialization would prevent political uprisings, battle indolence, and increase the country's agricultural productivity.[12] These British pedagogical reforms reveal a key precursor to the emergence of an economically oriented *daʿwa*.

The question was not merely whether new forms of Islamic knowledge could be used to stimulate economic development but also whether it was possible to combine ethical cultivation with professional training. Most prominently, the Islamic Charitable Association (*al-Jamʿiyya al-Khayriyya al-Islamiyya*) began to develop a parallel educational system that would meld state-mandated subjects and "Islamic values."[13] This project, inaugurated in 1894, was aimed at those who lacked the means to study in government-run schools and began with branches in Cairo, Alexandria, Asyut, and Tanta. By 1913, it included 3,912 students.[14] Along similar lines, the Muslim Brotherhood worked during the first half of the twentieth century to develop a parallel educational infrastructure, which included thirty-one schools spanning vocational training, female education, night classes for blue collar workers, Quranic memorization, and literacy education.[15] Professional training had become an increasingly important component of state-sponsored civil education, institutionalized Islamic education, and *daʿwa*.

This bid for influence in matters usually under state control was not limited to education. Instead, the attempt to transform education into a motor of economic change, as well as the competition between state institutions and Islamist organizations to offer visions of religiously framed economic productivity, emerged from the Egyptian state's late-nineteenth-century modernization project. Alongside its goal of strengthening Egypt politically and economically in the face of European encroachment, this project sought to achieve "political order" through the creation of institutions (most notably, the army, the school, and the factory) that would produce "the modern individual . . . as an isolated, disciplined, receptive, and industrious political subject."[16] Following the Free Officers revolution in 1952, political elites and state planners alike furthered this shift as they adopted Statism, an ambitious vision of mass social and economic transformation that used technology and state access to (and seizure of) capital in attempting to remake Egyptian society. An overlooked element of the Nasserist period, however, is its religious ambitions: this leading Free Officer did not merely seek to repress particular religious groups such as the Muslim Brotherhood but to actively reshape Islamic thought and practice.[17]

Yet, while Nasser's devotion of resources to public education benefited from the deeper pockets of the Ministry of Education, such efforts did not simply produce a propaganda bonanza for the state. Instead, nationalist efforts to craft "master narratives" through religious education invariably stood in tension with "students' diverse actual experiences" stratified along lines of region, gender, class, and sect.[18] In the process, however, these students had been oriented toward a particular way of thinking: Islam was to offer not merely an abstract system of rules but a concrete basis for political, economic, and social action.[19] Economic success by the pious, in turn, would become one such measure of religious success.[20]

THE NEOLIBERAL TURN UNDER SADAT AND ITS CONSEQUENCES

The Statist tradition of political, economic, and religious control faced a new competitor in Anwar al-Sadat's neoliberal open-door economic policy of the 1970s, known as the Infitah. Based on the premise that the state's role is to create an institutional framework for the promotion of "private property rights, free markets, and free trade,"[21] Sadat emphasized private over state ownership and the potential of individual enterprise over state-sponsored structural solutions. In parallel, states across the Middle East, from Turkey to Morocco to Jordan, adopted similar economic policies.[22] Yet the challenge was not simply that neoliberal economic changes confronted preachers but that the process of spreading the call to Islam had become increasingly enmeshed within Egypt's economic order under Sadat.

Although financial concerns had long shaped efforts to engage in *daʿwa*, the increasing commercialization of Islamic media brought the consequences of broader neoliberal economic policies to the fore. Alongside the Gulf oil boom, the Infitah catalyzed the commercialization of Islamic magazines, a key site of Islamic preaching, through advertisements. Indeed, Islamic magazines from the 1970s were replete with advertisements for everything from washing machines and carpets to pasta and dessert. Instead of standing on the outer folds of these publications or deep within, advertisements coursed through the heart of the magazine, constituting inescapable components of the reading experience.[23] Neither was commercialization limited to Islamic magazines: under Sadat, the field of "commercial" religious production broadened to include not only audiocassette sermons and popular Islamic books (*islamiyyat*), but also more mundane items such as key chains, coloring books, prayer beads, and stickers.[24]

Yet, even with the increased commercialization of *daʿwa*, competing calls to Islam still did not *center* on socioeconomic development or economic productivity. This state of affairs is neatly illustrated in the converging assumptions of state and Islamist competitors in 1970s Egypt. Speaking for the Supreme Council for Islamic Affairs, a body within the Egyptian Ministry of Endowments, Muhammad Fahmi Latif sought to provide a moral high ground for those who struggled economically. To do so, he argued that the pursuit of knowledge for the sake of material gain was "bestial"; instead, knowledge should be pursued for the goal of ethical betterment.[25] Similarly, Islamists were in no hurry to draw a direct connection between economic prosperity and religious piety: in January 1978, Muslim Brother Imara Najib stressed the need for an "Islamic system" (*nizam islami*) that could achieve "social progress" (*al-taqaddum al-ijtimaʿi*) without reference to socioeconomic hierarchy."[26] How did this state of affairs shift?

Although the history of neoliberalism in Egypt under Sadat's successor Hosni Mubarak has yet to be written, the dependence of *daʿwa* on access to capital and advertisements has only expanded today, as satellite television programs hosted by leading preachers have made Islamic television into a highly lucrative industry. Hints abound as to the financial positions of the New Preachers and their competitors, even as few of them wish to disclose their incomes. An Egyptian daily paper, *Akhbar al-Barlaman*, reported that Amr Khaled received two million Egyptian pounds per program.[27] A second Egyptian paper, *Jaridat al-Masa'*, reported that the leading Salafi *shuyukh* Muhammad Hassan and Muhammad Hussein Yaʿqub each received 100,000 Egyptian pounds per month for their shows and that a modernist scholar, Khaled al-Gindi, was paid 60,000 Egyptian pounds per month.[28] Indeed, Khaled was even named as the "richest Islamic preacher" by Forbes Arabia, which estimated his 2007 income at 2.5 million dollars.[29]

That the financial success of Islamic preachers has become a boon rather than a liability reveals a changing landscape of religious contestation. This shift, far from being sudden, began in the late nineteenth century, as British colonial administrators sought to produce a politically quiescent population. The shift gathered momentum under Nasser, as religious education was utilized in the service of concrete projects of political and economic transformation, particularly his vision of Scientific Socialism. Following Sadat's 1974 neoliberal economic turn, *daʿwa* would be doubly shaped by economic considerations: not only did preachers engage the relationship between piety and economic mobility, but they modeled this vision of neoliberal piety as they sought to appeal to an upwardly mobile, middle- and upper-class audience. The following section, in turn, will explore how Amr Khaled has positioned himself vis-à-vis this transnational audience and, in doing so, sought to redefine the role of the preacher.

THE ROLE OF THE NEW *DAʿIYA*

Clad in a slick business suit or a Lacoste polo shirt rather than either the scholarly robes or broad-shouldered suits popular among Islamists, Amr Khaled consciously projects the image of a successful member of Egypt's neoliberal economic order. This presentation raises a crucial question: what is the relationship between economic success and religious authority for preachers in the contemporary Middle East? It is certainly the case that the accusation of trafficking in religion remains a serious one, directed at opponents to suggest that particular religious positions proceed not from commitment to divine intentionality but from impious, worldly desires.[30] Notwithstanding the potential pitfalls, Khaled and his ilk have made economic development the centerpiece of a project of religious reform. Their success in doing so, in turn, reflects a longer-term convergence of *daʿwa* and economic productivity and reveals the new opportunities for religious activism opened up by the increasing retrenchment of state institutions in the contemporary Middle East.

The New Preachers, however, have emerged not only out of the increasing prominence of economic development in Islamic preaching and education but also from the increasing centrality of lay preachers over the course of the twentieth century.[31] Patrick Gaffney's landmark study of preaching in Egypt, conducted between 1977 and 1991, foregrounds the specific "intermediary" role of preachers between elite discourse and local practice.[32] Gaffney posits a tripartite scheme: the preacher as a representative of "traditional authority," as an advocate of "religiously inspired modernity," and as an "apologist for Islamic fundamentalism." It is the second type that is most directly relevant to the New Preachers: respected for his (secular) professional achievement, such a preacher argues that religious authority resides in the community rather than among the scholars. This individual's role lies not in superior access to textual knowledge or divine intention but in his ability to mobilize "each believer to assume responsibility for his personal integration of the call of God in the modern world."[33] Though Gaffney says little about economic development, his second model meshes easily with the neoliberal notion that personal initiative is sufficient to produce change.

The New Preachers draw not only from a tradition of religiously inspired modernity but also from the charismatic allure of Gaffney's "Islamic Fundamentalist." Most notably, like such figures, Khaled embraces the "purported unmediated application of the Quran, carrying over its dictates and imitating the Sunna of the Prophet without passing through an intervening historical heritage."[34] Khaled, Muʿizz Masʿud, and Mustafa Husni thus draw on two traditions of preaching: while the former involves laymen leading the flock as first among equals, the latter collapses the distinction between discourse and practice by claiming unmediated access and emulation of the word of God and the Prophetic model. In both cases, direct action is central to *daʿwa*.

In this vein, Amr Khaled moves beyond both knowledge of the Islamic sciences and traditional ritual space alike to assert that the centrality of the *daʿiya* proceeds from his role as a guide to contemporary challenges. Khaled leads the way in identifying obstacles to the resurgence of the transnational *umma*, implicitly centered in the Arab world. Though it once was powerful, it now suffers from political and intellectual radicalism due to a dearth of sound models of social and political organization.[35] Accordingly Khaled's flagship television-program-turned-grassroots movement, Lifemakers (broadcast on Iqra, the first Islamic satellite channel), works to facilitate a religious, political, economic, and social renaissance (*nahda*) that will revolve around Arab and Islamic transnational unity. In turn, this unity will enable Muslims to regain their rightful place on the world stage and to conduct a "dialogue of civilizations."[36]

On an economic level, Khaled rejects capitalism, arguing that it "represents greed . . . and will fall."[37] Instead, he suggests that the "only right path . . . is Allah's system,"[38] which will produce an economic windfall. This divine system, however, is not exclusively inward looking: Khaled cites a wide range of models, among them the ancient Israelites, the Islamic hero Salah al-Din (d. 1193), and contemporary China.[39] Domestically, such a system embraces grassroots economic change, primarily through small business development, as the engine for economic self-sufficiency. While this developmental plan is not inconsistent with capitalism as an efficient economic system, Khaled rejects a "capitalism" that reflects the materialism and greed that he perceives in Western societies.[40]

The remnants of the Statist economic model are likewise incapable of satisfying the *umma*'s needs. Khaled criticizes the Egyptian government's economic planning system, particularly its inability to create jobs, to improve the everyday lives of its people, or to stimulate private economic development.[41] Such a failure in this developmental model has yielded unemployment that, at 12.2 percent in the Arab world, is nearly twice the global average.[42] He further argues that this economic failure and the resulting dearth of employment opportunities have led both to emigration from the Arab world and to the frustration of youth within the region, the latter of which will direct their anger inward in the future.[43]

Despite his unapologetic advocacy of a neoliberal vision of *daʿwa*, Khaled is deeply aware of the rupture represented by these efforts to bring economic development to forefront. Accordingly, he seeks to situate himself as a legitimate claimant to emulation of the model of the Prophet Muhammad. This process begins with his use of the term "renaissance."

And as Khaled explains, the first such renaissance occurred during the first two hundred years of Islamic history when "Arabs were masters of the world and experts in all kinds of knowledge."[44] Yet, by depicting himself as following in the footsteps of the Prophet, Khaled does more than assert religious authenticity; he also seeks to sidestep scholarly networks of religious authority. Appeal to the model of the Prophet, contested by Sunni traditionalist scholars, Salafis, and Muslim Brothers alike, enables Khaled to ask a second question that pivots on action rather than scholarly education: how can Muslim youth today live according to the prophetic model and how can a lay preacher guide them in this endeavor?

This vision of Prophetic practice, however, focuses on the spirit of reviving the *umma* rather than the particulars of early Islamic Arabia. Having witnessed the challenges faced by Egyptian Islamists as they sought to effect change within state institutions, particularly through parliamentary participation, local projects proved to hold greater promise in alleviating challenges such as unemployment, drugs, and smoking.[45] In this plan, the government's role is both limited and essential: it must ease unnecessary business regulations, facilitate economic cooperation among Arab States and promote regional free trade.[46] Put simply, private enterprise will solve the failures of a regional developmental model in which education and employment opportunities are mismatched, yielding economic frustration and social decline.[47]

As they offer a neoliberal economic vision of *daʿwa*, the New Preachers are not alone. Today, laymen and scholars from within the halls of power and outside of them, offer "religious" solutions to questions of social and economic policy, whether through the development of "Islamic economics" or a self-consciously "Islamic" self-help literature.[48] The New Preachers' use of economic success as a source of authority and development in a joint project of economic and moral reform thus reflects a greater expansion of the bounds of "religious" knowledge, as well as the new opportunities available to preachers in a time of government retrenchment and political repression.

FORMING A PIOUS FLOCK

Just as the role of the preacher has changed, so too have the positions of participants in a diverse array of piety projects. What does it mean to be pious at the intersection of neoliberal economic shifts, political quietism, and the pressing challenges of political corruption, economic decline, and social immorality? Put differently, what does a program such as Lifemakers do in practice, and what is the relationship between ethical cultivation and social change? While previous scholarship has acknowledged the broad reach of the New Preachers' *daʿwa*, it has said comparatively little about how the model of piety available to participants in this project compares with those who take part in Islamist, Salafi, and state projects.

Ethnographies of contemporary Islamic religiosity suggest a conceptually distinct realm of Islamist piety that draws on a longer history of ethical practice within Islam. Most prominently, Charles Hirschkind, Saba Mahmood, and Richard Gauvain emphasize Islamic projects of subject formation by which Egyptians in the late twentieth and early twenty-first century have oriented themselves to the divine through embodied ritual practice. While those who sympathize with the Muslim Brotherhood *also* participate in explicitly political projects, the claims of these pious Muslim men and women to their own bodies and to a renewed understanding of Islamic practice challenges state-sponsored projects by which citizens are formed and political acquiescence is secured.[49] The schema suggested by these ethnographic studies, however, oversimplifies the picture of piety in contemporary Egypt by constructing a binary contrast between Islamist and state-aligned projects.[50]

It is first necessary to note that Khaled's project does not represent a "liberal" break from his socially conservative competitors. Though he recruits men and women alike, his ambition to achieve "development by faith" carries with it a distinctly gendered vision of public and private space. On the one hand, religious reform is necessary to cleanse Islam of mistaken interpretations that justify oppression against women, whether overt violence or the denial of social, political, and economic equality.[51] Indeed, Khaled fully includes women in Lifemakers episodes and programs, and a Khaled-led delegation to engage in Muslim-Danish dialogue in Denmark at the height of the 2006 Danish cartoon crisis included both men and women.[52] On the other hand, Khaled argues that raising children should come before pursuing a career[53] and that Western emphasis on women having an "equal" role in society, including through employment, has caused women to lose their femininity.[54]

The practices of Lifemakers youth were also not wholly different from their Islamist peers. Indeed, the centrality of "development through faith" notwithstanding, these television programs and printed materials also emphasize practices of ethical cultivation that are often identified with their Muslim Brotherhood and Salafi competitors. Accordingly, in the fifth episode of this flagship program, entitled "How You Can Be Positive," Khaled instructs viewers that the domain of ethical behavior (*al-suluk al-akhlaqi*) includes one's home, school, and place of employment.[55] In a later episode, Khaled distinguished between "divine" and "practical" worship, with the latter including socioeconomic development.[56] Along similar lines, Lifemakers youth frequented mosques as part of a dawn prayer project during the month of Ramadan, with the explicit goal of preparing themselves for future endeavors outside the mosque.[57]

How do these calls for ethical cultivation shape Khaled's audience? Noha, a student at the American University in Cairo, reported that Khaled's "[s]oft, simple, yet meaningful words guided [her to] Islam instead of threatening her with the Day of Judgment or punishment in Hell." Though her choice to don the *hijab* preceded her exposure to Khaled's ideas, his programs encouraged her to "continually search for [good] deeds of all kinds, whether it means helping others or being a better Muslim."[58] Another AUC student even credits Khaled with inspiring her to wear the *hijab*.[59] Rana and Esra, two students at Cairo University, similarly report that following regular viewing of Lifemakers they began to pray more regularly.[60] A fifth student, Ola, reports that Lifemakers has motivated her to increase her level of ritual obedience—particularly prayer and fasting—by providing a template by which she can gradually increase her religiosity (*tadayyun*).[61] Yet, as Khaled reminded participants, the responsibilities of Islam include not only prayer and fasting but also success in life.[62]

The call for men and women alike to join in the cause of religiously inspired socioeconomic change, in turn, seeks to create local Islamic communities that transcend the Islamist/regime dichotomy. This does not mean drawing an absolute contrast with the Muslim Brotherhood. Indeed, like the Brotherhood, which has historically used mosques as key sites for the cultivation of a grassroots base,[63] Lifemakers local clubs use such spaces to encourage ritual practice and religious education among their members, whether through group-led initiatives to perform the early-morning prayer in Saudi Arabia,[64] or through Quranic recitation classes in Palestine.[65] Furthermore, as with their Islamist peers, ritual practice alone is insufficient. Lifemakers clubs have set up charitable organizations that move beyond the mosque. On example is the Ramadan Bag program, through which group members across Egypt distributed food packages to the poor during this holy month.[66]

Finally, like the Brotherhood, Lifemakers complements its use of mosques and establishment of clubs with student groups on university campuses. In this vein, the Lifemakers group at Alexandria University organized a clothing drive and distributed clothes among poor students at the university.[67] Along similar lines, a *Lifemakers* affiliate program, known as Guardians of the Future has offered drug addiction programs through a number of universities, including al-Fatih University in Tripoli (Libya).[68] Through providing such services, Lifemakers follows in the steps of Islamist movements and charitable organizations in Egypt and elsewhere over the past century.[69]

Yet Amr Khaled's goal is not political power. Under his guidance, branches of Lifemakers in Egypt and throughout the Arab world seek to affect local change through a variety of socioeconomic programs that position their members as pious yet depoliticized agents of development. In this vein, the Moroccan branch of the organization offers online educational programs in advertising and business development.[70] Similarly, the Cairo University website offers training for current and prospective small-business owners, guiding them in the minutia of obtaining and maintaining the relevant licenses and certifications.[71]

Though individual skill development is important, Khaled's flagship initiative also embraces larger-scale economic development. For example, students at Khartoum University organized a conference dedicated to agricultural development,[72] and their peers at the Islamic University in Gaza similarly conducted a program on organic agriculture.[73] Nor were these initiatives solely local. Lifemakers also departed from traditional models of local service provision by cooperating with three principal groups: local or multinational businesses, governments, and international nongovernmental or super-governmental organizations.

The movement's collaboration with this diverse set of actors has enabled it to expand upon the traditional set of partners in building a domestic base while enhancing its profile internationally. Two examples are illustrative. In 2005, the Gaza branch cooperated with a group of Palestinian industrial organizations to conduct a conference that taught attendees practical skills such as furniture and straw basket construction.[74] That same year, the Jordanian branch of Lifemakers worked with the Ministry of Environment to form an agricultural development program.[75]

This development focus was also not limited to local or national levels. In cooperation with the Dubai Police and the United Nations Development Program (UNDP), Lifemakers groups in Jordan, Egypt, and Palestine participated in a drug addiction program. Along similar lines, local Lifemakers partnered with the World Health Organization (WHO) to organize an antismoking campaign.[76] Developmental coordination even extended to the United Kingdom and, in August 2005, thousands of Lifemakers youth celebrated their first annual conference alongside representatives of UNDP, WHO, Dubai Police, and the British government.[77] Although *Lifemakers* has drawn on a familiar repertoire of socioeconomic service provision at local institutions, whether mosques or university campuses, their mission melds a vision of religious activism with neoliberal developmental priorities. In doing so, Khaled's followers have formed themselves as pious participants in religious change while avoiding explicit political defiance.

Indeed, Lifemakers youth appear to take the mantra of "development by faith" seriously. Muhammad, an engineer in Dubai, explains: "Faith is the main source of everything, including the development of our lives and our countries."[78] Along even more expansive lines, Noha, a Cairo University student, notes:

> Islam is not just about ... praying or fasting ... rather it is a principle to live by ... the development of faith involves not only believing in one's religion ... it includes having a positive impact on the development of society. Last but not least, I believe that if one knows religious duties very well, one automatically gets involved with the creation of a society, since religions lay down basic foundations of societies.[79]

As participants live by faith, they have embraced not only piety but also neoliberal economic development.

CONCLUSION: WHY AMR KHALED AND THE NEW PREACHERS MATTER

This chapter has shown that, while the neoliberal *daʿwa* of the New Preachers reflects unprecedented orientation of religious thought and practice toward a particular mode of grassroots development at the turn of the twenty-first century, it also emerges from a longer convergence of Islamic thought and economic practice. Although the New Preachers have embraced the connection between commerce and religious commitment, those who accuse them of trafficking in religion are likewise products of the increasing enmeshment of neoliberal economic developmental models with *daʿwa* and religious education alike.

The rise of the New Preachers also casts light on the relationship between neoliberal piety and politics in the contemporary Middle East. Transcending the false binary between the Islamism of the Muslim Brotherhood and the quietist religious vision of state-aligned preachers and scholars, Amr Khaled's neoliberal *daʿwa* melds ethical cultivation and socioeconomic development to sidestep the claims of state institutions to monopolies on religious interpretation and economic development. As the space for religious activism both within and outside the official political system has narrowed, the relevance of such an approach has only grown.

The importance of this movement lies not in its outright broad demographic reach but in its capacity to shape middle-class conceptions of piety in the Arab world and beyond. As a group, Khaled's Lifemakers represent an upwardly mobile regional middle class that, like him, is both a product and a beneficiary of the decline of Statism and the rise of neoliberalism over the past four decades. In the contested aftermath of the Arab Spring, many Islamist elites are imprisoned and their socioeconomic service programs hobbled by government restrictions. While those who support a politically quietist neoliberal religious vision are hardly alone in seeking to fill this void—prominent competitors include Salafi organizations and state institutions regionally—they promise to be one voice in the negotiation of the future of *daʿwa* and piety in the Middle East.

CHAPTER 13

The Daʿi in Contemporary Arab Television Fiction

From "The Foremost of Preachers" to "Our Master"

JAKOB SKOVGAARD-PETERSEN

HOW A *DAʿI* should look and behave is an important question in contemporary Muslim societies. It is generally agreed that *daʿwa* is a good deed, incumbent on all Muslims, but many can testify that *daʿwa* can be intrusive, or rude, or even foolish. Just as classical *fiqh* literature had to set limits to *hisba* (the duty of commanding right and forbidding wrong) to protect the believers' private lives from the intrusion of the self-righteous, *daʿwa* may be in need of guidelines.[1]

To answer the question of proper *daʿi* behavior, one may consult the expanding *daʿwa* industry: training institutes, lectures, or books on "etiquette of the preacher of Islam" (*adab al-daʿi*). This etiquette is of course idealized and normative, outlining how such preachers *ought* to behave, and written by the preachers themselves. Or, one may observe a selection of model preachers, especially those with a great following and who host their own *daʿwa* shows on television. This approach has the advantage of substituting ideals with a number of actual and up-to-date models. Several studies have taken a similar approach but have concentrated on only one specific preacher.[2]

This chapter follows a third and less common approach. In the 2000s, television preachers won such popularity and social influence that their activities were widely commented upon and regularly criticized and praised in Arab media. No longer were they anonymous missionaries but significant public figures making large sums of money and serving a rising Islam-oriented bourgeoisie.[3] Inevitably, they themselves became the objects of public scrutiny and even fictional treatment, which is itself a novel way of depicting, criticizing, and outlining the behavior of the *daʿi*. This chapter analyzes the public perception and reflection of the *daʿi*'s role in contemporary Arab TV dramas, perhaps the most influential form of cultural expression in the Arab world today. To this end, I have selected three influential fictional portraits of a *daʿi* in contemporary Egypt. I compare the three and discuss how such presentations of the *daʿi*, a religious, political, and personal role model, evolved from the late Mubarak period to al-Sisi's military takeover in 2013.

THE NEW PREACHERS, *AL-DUʿA AL-JUDUD*

In the Arab world of the 2000s, *daʿwa* became associated with television. Arab national broadcasters had adopted Islamic preaching from the very introduction of television in the late 1950s (and before that on radio), but the standard fare was the *khutba*, the sermon on Fridays and Islamic holidays. A more personal missionary style was rare, and Islamic programming was peripheral. Egyptian state television was the dominant purveyor of programs for most of the Arab World. From the 1960s to the 1990s, it produced just two real stars of *daʿwa*: the Azhari *shaykh* Muhammad Amin Mitwalli al-Shaʿrawi (1911–1998) and the physician Dr. Mustafa Mahmud (1921–2009) whose program "Science and Faith" (*al-ʿIlm waʾl-Iman*) ran for more than four hundred episodes.[4]

With the introduction of satellite TV in the 1990s, major changes in the television industry set in. Private stations emerged, some of which had many channels, and a fierce pan-Arab competition ensued.[5] Among other subjects, local and national issues gave way to topics of pan-Arab interest and Islam, evoking both controversy and passion. Channels began seeking attractive ways to present Islamic programming.[6] New formats were invented such as al-Jazeera Arabic's famous *al-Sharia waʾl-Hayat*, Sharia and Life, an Islamist take on current affairs presented by the controversial Shaykh Yusuf al-Qaradawi.[7] From the turn of the millennium, specialized Islamic channels appeared, led by the Saudi-owned channels Iqraʾ (1998), al-Majd (2003), and al-Risala (2006). Striving to become the family channel of choice in devout Arab Muslim homes, these channels could not rely on traditional Islamic programming or televised versions of Islamic literary genres. Instead, they were obliged to produce Islamized versions of well-known TV genres such as cooking and quiz programs. Some of these formats were innovative and highly popular. *Daʿwa* was a stated purpose of these new channels but also the subject of much discussion within them. While conservative, all the channels strove to reach younger audiences and in so doing promoted youthful, lay presenters.

This fresh, optimistic interpretation of Islam was countered by a second wave of more conservative, Salafi channels, based primarily in Egypt, such as al-Nas (2006) and al-Rahma (2007).[8] The cost of setting up a channel had fallen drastically, and Islamic organizations and political parties entered the fray but could hardly challenge the popularity of Iqra', and al-Risala, or the ever-growing number of Islamic subchannels from al-Majd. Ehab Galal estimates that by 2013, of 1,320 satellite TV channels in Arabic, ten percent, or some 135 channels, could be characterized as Islamic (Sunni or Shiʿa), either by self-definition or dominant content.[9]

To compete for viewers, the channels—including those defining themselves as Salafi—sought to rank their presenters and hosts as "stars" (*nujum*); the most popular were interviewed in other media and ran popular websites in their own name. Some of these preachers had no formal training in the Islamic sciences, such as the famous Amr Khalid, and preferred not to speak of Islam as dogma and law but as a divine message of love for mankind. Another famous young *daʿi,* Ahmad al-Shuqayri, tried to engage Muslim youth in communal work and positive thinking. This "modern style" was criticized by both established ulama and the new preachers of the Salafi channels such as Abu Ishaq al-Huwayni and Muhammad Hassan.[10] There was thus a great variety of opinions, as well as argumentation and preaching style—not to mention appearance. Some of the "new preachers" appeared in suit and tie or even jeans and leather jacket, while the Salafi preachers favored white gowns (sing. *jalabiyya*) and had long, untrimmed beards. Classically trained ulama appeared wearing their turbans; Muslim Brother types had trimmed beards; and a rising number of female *daʿiyyat* typically wore the *hijab* but often make-up as well.[11]

THE *DAʿI* PORTRAYED

How were these new *duʿa* portrayed in television fiction? In Arab cinema until the 1950s, ulama appeared only in minor roles; untrained preachers were not presented at all. But from the 1990s, Islamic preaching became the subject of several anti-Islamist films, which tended to depict it as a way of manipulating pious but confused young men.[12] With the proliferation of Islamic programs after 2000, and the visible and controversial appearance of the TV preachers, this was set to change. Television audiences had become familiar with the *daʿiyya*, and state cultural policies had moved from a strategy of rejecting and ignoring to cooption. As a result, the figure of the *daʿi* became the subject of special and detailed treatment. Presently the foremost genre in Arab television fiction is that of the Ramadan *musalsal*, a television serial presenting an episode daily throughout the month. The length of this dramatic genre alone ensures that details and complexities have been added to the picture.

A positive view of the *daʿi* is found in the religious *musalsalat* of Hassan Yusuf. In his youth, Yusuf was a handsome actor and a star in Egyptian films of the 1950s and 1960s, as was his wife, Shams al-Barudi. In the 1980s, the couple abandoned acting. Al-Barudi became one of the best-known "repentant actresses" who regretted her indecent roles in love films. The person who led the campaign to make such actresses repent was Mitwalli al-Shaʿrawi, Egypt's most popular TV *shaykh* and preacher.

In the early 2000s, Hassan Yusuf and Shams al-Barudi made a comeback, but now in TV drama and with Yusuf as both lead character and director. The rationale for this comeback was that film and television dramas could actually be powerful tools for *daʿwa*, provided they were morally spotless.[13] Religious drama serials had to be free of indecencies and sought to better familiarize the audience with their religion. Hitherto, religious serials had been set in earlier Muslim eras, but Hassan Yusuf managed to secure funding for three dramas, all biographies of twentieth-century Egyptian ulama who in one way or another "defended Islam" against the colonial powers and later against the forces of secularization in the Nasser and Sadat eras.

The most successful serial—and the one specifically focused on *daʿwa*—was a biography of the above-mentioned TV preacher, Mitwalli al-Shaʿrawi.[14] Entitled *Imam al-Duʿa* (The Foremost of Preachers, 2003), it is a kind of modern hagiography of Egypt's most beloved *daʿi*, and the couple's own mentor. *Imam al-Duʿa* begins with al-Shaʿrawi's birth in the Delta village of Daqadus accompanied by an omen: the local preacher, Shaykh Sabri, sees a chicken flying up and standing on the pulpit (*minbar*) at that moment. The *shaykh* takes great interest in the boy, Amin, who comes from a pious peasant family. He oversees Amin's impressive progress at the local Quranic school (*kuttab*) and later arranges Amin's marriage to his daughter Nabawiyya. We also meet a neighboring family, wealthier but also tighter-fisted than the Shaʿrawis; the son, Zaghlul, will forever be jealous of the gifted Amin, and the miserable daughter, Badriyya, stands outside the *kuttab* trying to memorize the Quranic verses being recited within. Following the events of 1919, Amin becomes a nationalist and leads the student community at the al-Azhar Institute in the district capital, Zaqaziq, where Zaghlul is also enrolled. Meanwhile, Badriyya has to work hard for her mother in cafés that are unsuitable for girls. Although sometimes clashing with his teachers, Amin excels in his studies while also engaging in national issues. At some point (in 1934), he is even imprisoned for a month.

After finishing his studies at al-Azhar (a topic not much dwelt upon), Amin is offered a teaching position in Mecca and arrives just prior to the 1952 Free Officers' revolution. He is soon engaged in defending the sacred Maqam Ibrahim within the precincts of the Great Mosque against Saudi plans to demolish it to make room for more pilgrims. Meanwhile, back in Egypt, Badriyya leaves her violent husband and with a friend opens a café. Her son Islam listens to Amin's preaching over the radio and is converted to the true faith.

From Mecca, Amin follows the nationalization of the Suez Canal and the tripartite aggression in 1956. Contrary to other Azharis, he is very critical of Nasser and his philosophy but is forced to return as a result of Egypt's boycott of Saudi Arabia. The family moves into the Hussein district in Cairo, close to the purported tomb of the Prophet's grandson but also close to al-Azhar, which is nationalized in 1961 despite Amin's protests. In episode 17, Amin has a vision in a dream of a *shaykh* who reproaches him for not utilizing his talents to the fullest in the service of religion. Invigorated, he embarks on a major media campaign against secularism. At the same time, he is directed by al-Azhar to Algeria, where he meets the Sufi *shaykh* who had appeared in his dream. The two develop a deep appreciation for each other. A critical episode occurs when Amin thanks God for the defeat of Egypt in 1967 because it also means the defeat of the secularist ideologies. He is severely criticized, but after Nasser's death in 1970 Anwar al-Sadat finds his position appealing. The victory in the 1973 war is seen as a triumph of religion: preachers had prepared and morally fortified the soldiers before they crossed the Suez Canal. Still, it is a bitter time for Amin, as it is not only the devoted soldiers who find martyrdom in the war, but soon afterward Amin's mother and his wife die, one after the other, leaving their four children to look after him.

In 1976 Sadat makes Amin al-Shaʿrawi Minister of Religious Endowments. This is not a task that Amin had wanted, but on discovering a great deal of corruption in the ministry (some of it related to his childhood rival Zaghlul), he undertakes a major shakeup. At the same time, his great skill as a TV preacher comes into full bloom. Amin is still the minister when militant Islamists abduct and kill an Azhari scholar (and former minister), Shaykh al-Dhahabi, after which he speaks to the nation about the threat of religious fanaticism. He is also still in office when Sadat makes his visit to Israel's Knesset. Initially he defends the president, but Shaʿrawi later delivers a sermon on the Jews as the perennial breakers of treaties, never to be trusted. In response, the Israelis raise a campaign against him. He is happy to end his political career and concentrate on *daʿwa*. During his last years, his preaching is specifically directed against secularism and overreliance on modern science. Several public figures take him as their spiritual mentor, and his piety becomes a model of emulation. This is also shown in the final episode, 30, which is devoted to his preparations for death.

Produced just five years after al-Shaʿrawi's passing, *Imam al-Duʿa* is restricted by historical and biographical accuracy, so major events or features of his life could not be altered. As often happens with Egyptian TV biopics, the protagonist's children sued the producer, being unhappy with particular details in al-Shaʿrawi's portrayal.[15] Indeed, the drama is laced with fictitious friends and characters, including Zaghlul and Badriyya. These two lead unstable lives and repeatedly present al-Shaʿrawi with moral dilemmas that allow him to reveal his character, as well as his method of *daʿwa*. The *shaykh* comes across as an energetic and eloquent man who knows when to press an issue and when to be patient with the people whom he wants to influence. His faith is unshakable, and he always knows how it can best be served.

THE *DAʿI* INVENTED

The Egyptian revolution of 2011, and the initial success of the Muslim Brotherhood and its political party, Freedom and Justice, as well as that of the Salafi Nur party, seemed to confirm the Islamic identification of the vast majority of the electorate. However, liberal and even secularist groups among the youth had proven a strong force during the revolution itself, believing that it was about to release new cultural expressions, not bring about further censorship. Matters came to a head with the start of Salafi attacks against anything they considered immoral, including the March 2013 Media City siege, and later a bitter clash over a new constitution.[16]

Even if a clear majority wanted to define Egypt as an Islamic state whose legislation conformed to the sharia, there were conflicting ideas about what this would entail in the cultural field. In its program, the Freedom and Justice Party ominously wrote about getting rid of the foreign "filth" that was all too common in Egyptian media and culture.[17] The narrow election victory in the summer of 2012 of an Islamist president, Muhammad Morsi, did not stimulate a new, more Islam-oriented cultural environment but tended to galvanize much of the cultural sector against it. Morsi retained as Minister of Culture Muhammad Sabir Arab of the former government, but in February 2013 the latter resigned. Morsi replaced him with Ala' Abd al-Aziz, known for his Brotherhood leanings, who in turn soon substituted several heads of cultural institutions with Islamists in a process dubbed *akhwana* ("brotherhoodization"). This was vehemently rejected by the cultural establishment and led to strikes by artists and other cultural workers who demonstrated outside the Ministry of Culture and contributed to Morsi's unpopularity in the media.[18] Massive demonstrations calling for his resignation led to his ouster by the military in early July 2013. A powerful backlash against the Muslim Brotherhood and Islamism in general set in, and later that year the organization and its party were banned.

In this atmosphere of distrust between the cultural production environment and the Morsi government, the film *al-Daʿiyya* was produced. It was screened during Ramadan right after the military takeover. Reported to be the most-talked-about drama of the year, it seems to have hit a nerve with its story of a *daʿi* who realizes how Islamic preaching can be damaging for human life and religion. Ten years after *Imam al-Duʿa*, it seemed to be the *daʿi*'s turn to be the penitent, as the country adopted a more critical approach to Islamization. That was certainly the intention of Midhat al-Adl, a physician turned playwright, who told the *New Yorker*, "I started feeling that this was a very important time for our country: we will either advance, or we will regress five hundred years. We felt this was the right time to speak."[19]

The hero of the drama is Yusuf, a young, handsome, TV preacher with a huge following. He is not a trained scholar but appears to have been selected for his telegenic qualities. In the first episodes, we see him denounce music as *haram* and stress that women are subordinate to men. Although young, he is the head of his household, which consists of his three sisters and a younger brother. Their mother has died, and their father is an incapable addict unable to provide for them but a lover of music and of popular culture. Yusuf's elder sister, Khadija, is married to his friend Hasan, who envies him his success. Hasan is a teacher but preaches for a small group of young men, one of whom is in love with Yusuf's youngest sister. Some way into the drama, Yusuf meets Nisma, a young revolutionary and violinist in the Cairo Symphony Orchestra. She lives with her mother in a neighboring house. Although initially appalled by each other's views and attitudes, they gradually fall in love. Yusuf finds himself examining the rigid convictions he has previously held and preached. He invents a new form of *daʿwa* program—more humble, reflexive, and self-critical. This program is popular with some but most unpopular with others. Among the latter is his producer, who chooses instead to promote Yusuf's brother-in-law, the weak Hasan, who even leaves his wife for the producer's attractive daughter. Even more incensed is the Salafi Shaykh Ali who has worked hard to make Yusuf an instrument in his religious and social ambitions. Yusuf breaks off collaboration with Ali but is kidnapped by Ali's Salafi gang. Eventually Shaykh Ali releases Yusuf, who is now reconciled with his father. Yusuf proposes to Nisma. The closing scene shows Yusuf at the Cairo opera listening to her in admiration. But suddenly one of the Salafis sneaks in and assassinates him. A voice-over promises another, alternative ending that omits the victory of "backwardness" (*takhalluf*). In the repeat closing sequence, we see Yusuf left unharmed, absorbing the violin cadences of his beloved Nisma.

So, with the help of art and love, a strict Salafi *daʿi* converts to a humanist *daʿi*. In this *musalsal*, *daʿwa* is not always a force for good, but socially it is highly significant: it is also a business, closely related to personal success.

THE *DAʿI* EXPOSED

The third model *daʿi* was released as a movie in January 2017 and was very well received.[20] This movie is adapted from a successful novel, published in 2012 and nominated for the Arab Booker prize in 2013.[21] The author, the well-known journalist, editor, and TV-host Ibrahim Eissa, was a staunch opponent of both President Mubarak and the Muslim Brotherhood, but not, surprisingly, of President al-Sisi and his military takeover. Eissa was prominent during the revolution and founded a TV channel in its aftermath.[22] The novel was largely written prior to the revolution in January–February 2011 but was completed after it.

Entitled *Mawlana* (Our Master), the novel is also about a TV *daʿi*. Like *al-Daʿiyya*, it is set in contemporary Egypt, where *daʿwa* is a thriving but competitive and sometimes immoral business.[23] But *Mawlana* adds a political dimension to the mix. Hatim Shinnawi is a modern, witty, charming preacher who knows what people want and is ready to give it to them, a pragmatist *daʿi* who has somehow lost his soul—at least when he is in the studio and the red light for recording is on. Like Yusuf, Hatim has a background in the popular districts of Cairo and a Sufi master who formed his character. But unlike Yusuf, Hatim is an accomplished *ʿalim*. Fascinating in its preaching and religious reflections and conversation, the novel gains added drama when the president's son (modeled after Jamal Mubarak) chooses Hatim to reconvert his wife's brother, Hasan, who has secretly converted to Christianity and adopted the name Butrus. Hatim works patiently but insistently to make the young man realize that Christianity may not be the solution to his problems and that Islam is actually quite different from what the Egyptian media and preachers have led him to believe. Here, Ibrahim Eissa exposes the business aspect of *daʿwa*: the connections between the leading political party, the intelligence directorate (*mukhabarat*), the TV owners and producers, and finally the *daʿiyya*, who enjoys the popular trust and love that all the others lack. Throughout, Eissa promotes a sometimes very specific and daring interpretation of Islam on controversial issues such as gender, non-Muslims, and even sex.

THE FICTIONAL *DUʿA* COMPARED

These are the three most popular attempts at presenting a model *daʿi* to the Egyptian audience in the form of fiction. Each claims that its preacher is the most popular of all, coming from the people and remaining in touch with them. This is typically evident in the array of audiences viewing them at home and in cafés and afterward commenting on the message. All the models consider the Egyptians a pious people but confused in their piety, especially young men, and in need of guidance. Furthermore, they all identify threats against the Egyptian people in its piety. For the al-Shaʿrawi serial, the threat comes from the West and the Westernized elites—especially under Nasser; in *al-Daʿiyya*, it comes from Salafis and other enemies of the revolution. A few themes are now selected that characterize this variety in the fictional portraits of the *daʿi*, including his attitudes to and style of *daʿwa*.

Love and Married Life

Just like real-life preachers, our three are often consulted on marital issues. This comes in the form of requests for legal rulings and advice. With real-life preachers, we would only learn about such guidance when given publicly, but here we witness both public and private counseling, and, importantly, how our *shuyukh* themselves behave in their respective marriages and love lives and can observe significant differences between them.

One major difference between *Imam al-Duʿa* and the other two serials is the virtual absence of character development in *Imam*. Although Amin al-Shaʿrawi is followed from birth, he is ever pious and ever right. Conflict and drama are inserted through extra, fictional figures who present moral dilemmas for al-Shaʿrawi to confront: his childhood friend and the neighboring family, a girl from the village, student friends who appear and reappear throughout the serial with fresh problems. The main trajectory of his life is a given of history, while the depiction of family conflicts is extremely careful. The anti-Islamist magazine *Ruz al-Yusuf* described the serial as a hagiography of al-Shaʿrawi, which no doubt was indeed the intention.

Love and family life in *Imam al-Duʿa* is therefore predictably dull. Marriage is proper, the spouses being initially shy but considerate, and we see the wife suitably wearing a *hijab* even in the bedroom. The couple have devout children who respect their father's will but develop affectionate ways of influencing his decisions. After their mother's death, they care for him for many years. The only hint at another love in his life is the poor girl Badriyya (played by Hassan Yusuf's real wife), whom he saves from the immoral casino industry and who later becomes the paragon of a devoted, fully covered *muslima*.

In *al-Daʿiyya,* family life is much more chaotic for the young preacher Yusuf, and love permeates most of the conflicts and developments. We never quite learn why Yusuf's father abandoned his children on the death of their mother—we see him doing it again when his second wife becomes pregnant—but from an early age Yusuf has been the head of five siblings living alone. Due to his success as a TV preacher, they live in a marvelous house in the well-to-do Cairo suburb of al-Maadi. Yet Yusuf's sisters, though well-bred and devout, all have their emotions and end up defying their elder brother's caring but conservative paternalism. In an early episode (8), Yusuf has a program devoted to the subject of "the woman." Here he explains that God created woman, but man must take care of her and protect her; the notion of social equality between men and women is for him a secularist ploy and alien to true Egyptian culture. Later, Yusuf revises these views, sometimes in televised sermons that bluntly state he has misunderstood the true message of Islam. When his younger brother asks him about these revisions, he explains that some Islamic texts say this and others say that, but to know the truth in the end one must consult one's heart. This, says Nisma, is "the true spirit of the religion."

In *Mawlana*, by contrast, family life is truly tormented. Hatim, the preacher who speaks with such compassion and helps so many people, has not had sex with his wife Umayma for many years, and they are fighting a continuous secret war. This stems from an incident in which their only son Umar lost consciousness in a swimming pool and Hatim disappeared from the hospital—in reality, to atone for his sins in a Sufi way by demeaning himself. Umar, now brain damaged, lives in an English nursing home, and Umayma does not allow Hatim to visit him. Later in the book, Hatim is seduced by an ostensibly pious young girl, Nashwa, who proves to be working for the secret police in an effort to exert control over him. Even if Umayma and Hatim are reconciled in the end, love is not the force that conquers everything, as it is in *al-Daʿiyya*, but mutual forgiveness despite all.

Artistic Creativity and Music

As *Imam al-Duʿa* makes clear, Shaykh al-Shaʿrawi considered the culture industries a threat to Egypt's religious identity. Accordingly, music in the serial is associated with casinos and dance. The cultural elites are seen as anti-Islamic, and the theme of "defending Islam" is recurrent. Shaykh al-Shaʿrawi succeeds in convincing actresses to abandon their profession (as happened in real life with Shams al-Barudi herself). He also manages deathbed conversions of two secular icons, namely the former president Naguib and the playwright Tawfiq al-Hakim.

While artistic creativity is not a central topic in *Mawlana*, music, drama, and art are crucial subjects in *al-Daʿiyya*. In the opening scene, Yusuf attacks them on TV as un-Islamic and stirring up passions. However, he is later moved by Nisma's violin and personality to appreciate classical music (which also cures his brother Mustafa of his psychosis) as well as poetry and drama. He even preaches that these are truly Islamic arts, just as those who practice them may also be devout Muslims. Indeed, those who preach against art and music with hate in their hearts are the real threat to Islam, and to Egypt's social stability.

Political Engagement

The three works seem to concur that *daʿwa* has political implications, but to varying degrees. The least in this respect is *al-Daʿiyya*, which is concerned with broader issues of culture war and may be seen as a warning against Salafism but does not feature politicians. Produced a year after the 2011 revolution and set during the clashes in Tahrir Square, the *musalsal* sides closely with the young revolutionaries (of whom Nisma is one) and depicts the brutality of the old regime and its security forces. There are precise references to the attack on the presidential palace in December 2012, and the Salafi siege of the Media Production City in March 2013, with the message that the Salafis are exploiting the security vacuum left in the wake of the revolution. In his new and reformed program, Yusuf deems the revolution truly Islamic and the prophet Muhammad "the greatest revolutionary" (episode 19).

As a biography of a political *shaykh*, *Imam al-Duʿa* is replete with politics. Already, as a young man, Amin al-Shaʿrawi was interested in politics and participated in nationalist events against the British. After Nasser's takeover, al-Shaʿrawi is one of the few who dare raise their voice against him. We follow him through the political upheavals of the 1960s and 1970s (but not thereafter), culminating in his stint as the Minister of Religious Endowments. Much of the politics, however, is about al-Azhar, for the major political rivalry between the regime and the Muslim Brotherhood is deliberately omitted from the drama, due to the censor or self-censorship. By contrast, when jihadist groups appear, al-Shaʿrawi is depicted as one of their main ideological opponents, which is obviously well in line with the Mubarak regime's cultural priorities. Al-Shaʿrawi's political engagement is presented as concern for the *umma* and for Egypt's threatened Islamic identity. He is depicted on the pulpit or in the studio talking about Islam as the religion of tolerance and how Western countries use their political and technological dominance to claim civilizational dominance. Politics and Islam are thus inherently connected.

In *Mawlana*, politics and Islam are also closely connected, but this is not considered a healthy condition. Rather, it is party bosses and businessmen who have discovered that they can reach the people through Islamic messages and that their status in society can prosper by their association with the icons of Islamic preaching. More than in the other works, in *Mawlana* Islam is a means to legitimacy for many social actors. Unfolding in the late Mubarak years, when Jamal Mubarak was primed to succeed his father, *Mawlana* has a concrete political setting, and some events, such as specific attacks on Copts, are mentioned. It does chronicle Egypt's political history but interprets it as stagnant and bereft of real development: the country is controlled by power, money, and secret services in a neoliberal collusion. Hatim is appalled by this situation but plays along until he finds himself out of his depth with the converted Hasan/Butrus. Hatim does not preach politics yet at the same time fails to remain aloof. Still, by Egyptian standards, he clearly has remarkably liberal ideas, for instance, on the subject of Muslim conversion to Christianity.

Daʿwa Competition

All three works present other preachers who are rivals of the hero and often respond enviously to his success. In *Imam al-Duʿa*, it is Amin's childhood neighbor Zaghlul, who also studied at the religious institute and later at al-Azhar University and who finally becomes a corrupt civil servant in the Ministry of Religious Endowments. But there are also the local village preachers, first the pleasant Shaykh Sabri and later the stern Shaykh Juda. The former is seen mentoring Amin and allowing him to develop his *daʿwa* skills at evening sessions with the local peasants. Juda cannot conceal his displeasure when (in episode 13) Amin speaks to a combined congregation of Copts and Muslims and treats the Christians as brothers.

In *Mawlana*, several other *shuyukh* appear; one of them, Shaykh Fathi, is also a TV preacher, described as having grown up in Upper Egypt under circumstances so deprived that people lose their dignity. A sulky eighteen-year-old student at al-Azhar, he is "discovered" by security officials when he speaks against joining a demonstration. As a politically loyalist *shaykh*, he is gradually promoted to become a preacher on state television. However, people back in the village know him too well to be impressed. He thunders against the new preachers who, wearing suits and ties, address youth and women on the private channels; and he holds a special grudge against Hatim, who had ridiculed a *fatwa* of his that allowed men to be alone with women if they are breastfed by them (p. 69). The scandal over this *fatwa* (based on an actual one from 2007[24]) has made it all but impossible for Shaykh Fathi to become Mufti of the Republic.

In *al-Daʿiyya,* Yusuf's brother-in-law, Hasan, is appointed his successor, mainly because the owner of the TV station, al-Khudayri, and his daughter, Mayy, want to weaken and control him. Yusuf leaves the channel for another, so his program and Hasan's compete over the airwaves as well as on billboards. Although initially more moderate than Yusuf, and much liked in the family, it is soon clear that Hasan lacks Yusuf's TV charisma. While Yusuf's new program "From My Heart to Yours" is informed by his experiences and convictions, Hasan is at a loss, unable to get his message across. At the other end of the spectrum of preachers is the Salafi Shaykh Ali, whose firebrand sermons are attended by a group of young men whom he controls.

The novel and the two *musalsalat* all employ rival preachers to contrast and illuminate the lead characters' personal and *daʿwa* capacities. Each of the rivals represents a character who is stricter and sterner than the protagonist, and their partisanship and hatred of other groups are shown to have grave potential consequences for Egypt's social cohesion. On the other hand, there are also those (Zaghlul, Fathi) who consider religion an instrument for their own social advancement. All, however, see *daʿwa* as a field with practitioners and a certain level of competition, especially media *daʿwa* in the late Mubarak era.

CONCLUSION

In Egypt of the 2000s, the sudden rise of TV preachers inspired comment, rapidly followed by fictional treatment. Shortly after becoming a TV star, the *daʿi* also became a *musalsal* hero. As we have seen, these treatments vary significantly in their attitude toward the phenomenon of the new *duʿa*. Although in principle they all support *daʿwa*, they can be critical about the way *daʿwa* has evolved financially and politically.

The trailblazer, *Imam al-Duʿa* of 2003, was an important novelty on the Egyptian cultural scene in that it was the first biopic about a contemporary *daʿi* and was even broadcast on a state channel, signaling a new compromise between the Ministry of Culture and the Islamic awakening. The *musalsal* itself is ardently antisecularist, as was Shaykh al-Shaʿrawi himself. This sometimes amounts to an Islamizing interpretation of Egypt's modern history, such that opposition to the British was manifested in religious acts, and the defeat by Israel in 1967 was the defeat of secularism. Al-Azhar is considered a bastion of Egypt's true identity, which has been threatened, but also defended and is undefeated. Hence, not the state but the ulama are the true guardians of the nation's health, and the Muslim Brotherhood is nowhere to be seen. *Daʿwa* is therefore not for everyone but is the preserve of the ulama and is their true vocation.

The pious Egyptian people are a dedicated audience who reject the culture of colonialism and the secular state. Shaykh al-Shaʿrawi is a man of the people, a brilliant *daʿi*, hence the embodiment of an organic religious bond between the Egyptians and their Islam.

Ten years and a revolution later, *Mawlana* appears, and in the summer of 2013, after a tumultuous year of Muslim Brotherhood rule and just weeks after the military takeover, Egyptians eagerly watch *al-Daʿiyya*. Now television *daʿwa* can no longer be depicted as a one-man show against the secularist current; instead, it is a marketplace and big business. Islam is no longer an identity to be defended but a field to be contested. The regime has stakes, but so does the Salafi current (the Muslim Brotherhood is again absent from *al-Daʿiyya* and not very prominent in *Mawlana*). *Daʿwa* is an industry, and the *duʿa* are created and destroyed by television bosses and producers (and in *Mawlana* by the *mukhabarat* too). *Daʿwa* can still be socially and morally beneficial and an aid to the people in their lives, but it can also be rigid, destructive, and power-serving, therefore exploitative and counter to the true message of Islam. This is what Yusuf realizes (and Hatim knows). In *al-Daʿiyya*, the message is that true Islam is about caring and loving; it is tolerant and aesthetic, but it is also ethical and emancipatory, even revolutionary.

Mawlana might concur in principle, but it is set in a more complicated and ambiguous world. Islam is no longer just a simple message that everyone instinctively understands. First of all, Egyptian society here is permeated with religion, and Muslims and Christians are manipulated by preachers or religious authorities but also by their own personal struggles. Even the *daʿi* himself, the intellectually courageous and spiritually engaged Hatim, is a struggling character haunted by doubt and reflection, prey to events beyond his full understanding. This portrayal adds new existentialist dimensions to social reflection on *daʿwa*. But it may also be one of the reasons why turning this novel into a *musalsal* has proven harder than anticipated. It would certainly be interesting to learn how the Egyptian audience might respond to such a presentation of *daʿwa*.

CHAPTER 14

From Monologue to Dialogue

Wahhabi Daʿwa and Reassessment of the "Other" after 9/11

MUHAMMAD AL-ATAWNEH

THIS CHAPTER EXAMINES the official Wahhabi discourse on the dissemination of Islam (*daʿwa*) after 9/11, with special emphasis on the doctrinal developments and changes in approaching the "Other" (Muslim and non-Muslim), in general, and on the preaching of Islam, in particular. Note that over the past four decades, and as oil prices skyrocketed, Wahhabi *daʿwa* has expanded to become globalized. Islamic centers, Muslim charities, mosques, schools, social-welfare projects, and prep schools for imams were all established to bolster this trend.

Yet, Saudi Arabia found itself in an unflattering spotlight following the events of 9/11, perhaps more so than any other country in the Middle East. The fact that fifteen of the nineteen suicide skyjackers were Saudi citizens provoked an avalanche of criticism in the West as well as in some parts of the Arab/Islamic world—even by some Saudis themselves—against Saudi religious beliefs, rulers, social customs, and education.[1] Significantly, the Saudi government, as well as the religious establishment, openly criticized the domestic religious discourse, particularly in regard to the Other, whether Muslim or not. As early as November 2001, Crown Prince, later King Abdallah (r. 2005–2015) hosted a special meeting with the state religious and legal leadership. Citing Quran 2:143, "Thus, have We made of you an *umma* justly balanced (*wasat*) . . . ,"[2] he urged those present to "accept responsibility for creating a moderate (*wasati*) religious discourse." In the same vein, at a gathering hosted at his home in Riyadh on 13 January 2003, he called upon regional leaders to promote moderation and tolerance and urged scholars and intellectuals to contribute to bringing about peace between human beings: "The scholar, the author, the thinker, the philosopher and the poet, all must strive to bring humanity together."[3] Furthermore, after his accession to the throne, King Abdallah accused some Saudi religious scholars of backing extremism when issuing edicts and aligning themselves with certain groups that have committed violence.[4]

Shaykh Abdallah al-Maniʿ, a prominent member of the Council of Senior Scholars (*majlis hayʾat kibar al-ʿulamaʾ*, CSS), followed suit in criticizing monolithic Wahhabi rhetoric and called for religious dialogue.[5] In an interview with *al-Sharq al-Awsat* newspaper, al-Maniʿ urged the Saudi authorities to initiate dialogue in Saudi Arabia, including all four schools of Law (sing. *madhhab*) within Saudi society, and among the various Islamic factions, such as the Shiʿa and the Sufis.[6] The call for dialogue also found support among some prominent nonofficial Wahhabi scholars. For example, Shaykh Aʾid al-Qarni argued that dialogue is essential in light of global and regional events.[7]

Although much of this post-9/11 criticism appears to have been lodged against extremist groups, described by Saudi officials as those who have "gone astray" (*firqa dalla*), some of it was also directed against the Saudi state religious establishment and its Wahhabi discourse. Consequently, different measures have been taken by the Saudi government, with the full cooperation of the religious establishment, aimed at undermining extremist views, promoting tolerance, and reexamining relations with other nations and cultures. For Prince Turki al-Faysal, Saudi Arabia's former Ambassador to the United States, these dramatic post-9/11 measures serve as a kind of self-examination in which "every aspect of Saudi Arabia's society and culture is being openly debated."[8]

This chapter elaborates on the post-9/11 Saudi debate, rethinking the concept of the Other and focusing on religious perceptions regarding *daʿwa*. Emphasis is placed on the question: to what extent have Wahhabi doctrines on the preaching of Islam been reformulated after the terrorist attacks in New York and Washington? I would argue that post-9/11 official Wahhabi *daʿwa* has come to acknowledge other cultures and nations, enable and promote dialogue, at the expense of its historical habit of delivering "the truth" to the ignorant Other, both Muslim and non-Muslim, by way of a monologue. Since the discussion in this chapter is entirely theoretical, those influences affecting the practical measures remain outside its scope. But first, the discussion is prefaced by a brief review of the background of modern Wahhabi *daʿwa*.

WAHHABI *DAʿWA*: BACKGROUND

The history of Wahhabi *daʿwa* may be divided into three major chronological phases, the first of which was the "domestic mission" that took place respectively under the first two Saudi states in the eighteenth and nineteenth centuries. David Commins notes that, at this stage, the Wahhabi ulama sought to "tightly control, if not prohibit altogether," travel outside the Arabian Peninsula, including to Ottoman lands, whose Muslims were described as idolaters.[9] South Asia was the only destination beyond the boundary of Najd that Wahhabi ulama considered legitimate. The Indian Ahl-i Hadith movement, which came into being in the second half of the nineteenth century, had much in common with the Wahhabis, and in times of trouble prominent scholars from Najd went there to study.[10]

The second phase of Wahhabi *daʿwa* took the form of cooperation with the Muslim Brotherhood during the 1940s and 1950s. Muslim Brother refugees who fled the oppressive regimes of Nasser and the Baʿth Party received teaching positions in the Saudi education system and were thus able to spread their views and methods among the younger Saudi generation. Ideologues such as Muhammad Qutb, brother of the radical Sayyid Qutb, helped in this way to spark the Saudi Islamic Awakening (*al-sahwa al-islamiyya*).[11]

The last and most enduring phase has been the institutionalization and globalization of *daʿwa* in the second half of the twentieth century. From the late 1970s, Saudi petrodollars helped facilitate the expansion of Wahhabi teachings into the Arab World, Africa, Asia, Western Europe, and North America. Transnational *daʿwa* activities were expressed in religious preaching, educational programs, charitable organizations, and religious patronage networks. Such activities were promoted by a new set of Islamic institutions, most important of which were the Muslim World League (MWL) established in 1962; the World Assembly of Muslim Youth (WAMY) which followed it in 1972; the General Presidency of the Directorate of Scientific Studies, Issuance of Fatwas, Propagating Islam, and [Religious] Guidance (1971–1993); the World Council of Mosques; and the Ministry of Islamic Affairs, Endowments, [Religious] Instruction and Daʿwa, which was established in 1993.[12]

Of these organizations, the Muslim World League seems to play a significant role in promoting global Wahhabi *daʿwa*. Its objectives as stated on its Website are as follows:

1. Introducing the Islamic creed, laws and lifestyle, according to the texts of the Holy Qur'an and the immaculate Sunna. . . .
2. Making every possible effort to further the message of Islam in the promotion of peace and justice; the liberation of man from worshiping deities other than Allah; establishing Muslim communities on the bases of the sublime Islamic values and the maintenance of human rights.
3. Elucidating the true Islamic tenets; refuting false allegations levelled [*sic*] against Islam; combating both the distortion of its image and deliberate misguidance that is directed against the call of the truth.
4. Developing acquaintance and cooperation between Muslim peoples and making them aware of the issues facing Muslims and their aspirations while respecting the sovereignty of their countries of residence.
5. Making efforts to address the problems facing the Muslim World and to help Muslims solve their problems and achieve their aspirations and projects.
6. Making all possible efforts to remove conflicts, divisive factors and disputes from within and between Muslim communities.
7. Striving to promote virtue and order on this Earth; to combat mischief and urge people to obey God and His Messenger, peace be upon him.[13]

In practice, the MWL undertakes a broad range of activities regarding the propagation of Islam, including publishing and media outreach, coordinating the regional activities of preachers and religious scholars, providing Arabic language instruction, and establishing Islamic centers. The primary focus of these organizations is on promoting Islamic teachings and encouraging Muslims to be more religiously observant, as well as providing interested non-Muslims and recent converts with information about Wahhabi Islam. As such, the MWL has opened offices in many Muslim-majority countries, as well as in countries with relatively large numbers of Muslims, such as France, Germany, and the United Kingdom, along with such major cities as Copenhagen, Moscow, Rome, Vienna, New York, and Washington, D.C.[14]

One of the Muslim World League's promotional strategies is to cooperate with local Islamic organizations to create an Islamic infrastructure aimed at serving the religious needs of the growing number of Muslim communities. This involves funding the construction of mosques and the operation of various Islamic centers, thus sponsoring activities designed to spread Wahhabi Islam. Such endeavors entail partnerships with other internationally recognized Muslim movements—particularly the Muslim Brotherhood—that do not necessarily share the Wahhabi worldview.[15]

The World Assembly of Muslim Youth focuses primarily on promoting solidarity in faith among the younger Muslim generation.[16] This is done through various sociocultural activities such as international soccer tournaments, summer camps, educational exchanges, and scholarship programs that enable students to study classical Islam (often in Saudi Arabia). By focusing on Muslim youth, WAMY seeks to shape the religious attitudes of future generations of Muslims. Like the MWL, WAMY has sometimes cooperated with other Muslim groups in Europe, including the Forum of European Muslim Youth and Student Organizations and a variety of groups with ties to the Muslim Brotherhood. These partnerships were designed to help spread its outreach to specific national and local Muslim communities. Between the 1970s to the 1990s, the European activities of the MWL, WAMY, and the Muslim Brotherhood became so intertwined that it was often difficult to tell them apart. Indeed, a number of senior Muslim Brotherhood figures, including Kamal el-Helbawy, the Egyptian-born founder of the Muslim Association of Britain in 1997, have served in leadership positions in both the MWL and WAMY.

DA'WA AS MONOLOGUE

For Wahhabis of all generations, genuine Islam is exemplified by the early Muslims who lived during the first three centuries after the Hijra. Wahhabis seek to follow the religious path set by these righteous forefathers (*al-salaf al-salih*) and remain devoted to their understanding of the Quran and the Sunna of the Prophet.[17] They consider being Salafi the only way for Muslims to assure membership in the exclusive "saved sect" (*al-firqa al-najiya*) mentioned in the hadith, "And this community (*umma*) will split into seventy-three sects; all of them will be in hellfire except one."[18] Muslims should thus meticulously follow the Prophet and his Companions in every thought and deed. Muhammad ibn Abd al-Wahhab stressed that God commanded people to obey Him alone and to follow the teachings of the Prophet: "As for *ijtihad*, we are imitators of the Book [Quran], the tradition, the virtuous ancestors, and the four Imams (founders of the Sunni legal schools)."[19] Salafiyya, then, is an embodiment of what the Prophet bequeathed to his *umma*, the Muslim community. Anyone who departs from it will fall into those sects doomed to hellfire.[20]

Contemporary Wahhabis have to a great extent remained faithful to the tenets of their forefathers.[21] They uphold Salafism as the spirit of their legal and theological philosophy. This adherence comes across clearly in the legal opinions (sing. *fatwa*) and writings of the highest Wahhabi religious authorities, such as those of the CSS and of the Permanent Committee for Scientific Research and Legal Opinions (CRLO).[22] One such treatise explains,

> Salafiyya is derived from the *salaf*, who were the Companions of the Prophet, and from the Imams of the first three centuries, mentioned in the hadith: "The best of the people are those who belong to my century, then those who follow them [the second century], then those who follow them [third century]. . . ." Salafis are those who follow in the footsteps of the *salaf* who, in turn, follow the Book [Quran] and the Sunna . . . and act according to them.[23]

Before 9/11, the Wahhabis often stressed the superiority of the Wahhabiyya as a Salafi movement over all other Islamic groups. As late as 1999, CSS member Salih al-Fawzan was still able to clearly state,

> To say that the Salafi [Wahhabi] movement resembles any other Islamic movement is wrong. The Salafi movement is the only one that should be followed by adopting its approach, joining it and performing jihad with it. Therefore, Muslims are not permitted to follow any other movement, since all others are straying movements.[24]

Until the end of the millennium, the Wahhabis maintained a spirit of intolerance toward other Islamic trends. Such was the case with the Shiʿa, the cultural Other par excellence. CRLO has accordingly determined, somewhat in reflection of the Shiʿi concept of impurity (*najasa*), that eating their food, intermarrying with them, or even shaking their hands is forbidden.[25] Abdallah ibn Jibrin (a former member of the CSS) went further by referring to the Shiʿa as *rafida* (a pejorative label that denotes their rejection of the first three Caliphs) whose killing is not a sin.[26] The mainstream Twelver Shiʿa were further denounced for their claims regarding the distortion of the Quran by the third Caliph Uthman ibn Affan (r. 644–656), the negation of the authentic Sunni hadith corpus, and the incorporation of new sources based on the twelve Imams.[27]

The Wahhabis were similarly intolerant of other monotheists. In a legal opinion published by CRLO, the scholars reject the public "call for unification of religions" (i.e., Islam, Judaism, and Christianity),[28] which aimed at the promotion of tolerance among the peoples of the monotheistic religions by means of joint religious activities such as the establishment of multifaith prayer centers, especially in universities and airports; the publication of the Quran, the Bible, and the New Testament bound in one volume; and the encouragement of joint conferences and symposia in both the East and the West.[29] This fatwa considers these measures in blatant contradiction to the hallowed principle that Islam abrogates all previous religions. Calling for the unification of these three monotheistic faiths might be construed as a de facto admission that they are equal and permission for people to adopt whichever one they wish. This would involve the denial of Islam as the purest of all the religions—the Quran being the only true book and the Prophet Muhammad the seal of all the prophets. Their stance was based on Quran 3:85, "If any one desires a religion other than Islam (submission to Allah), never will it be accepted of him; and in the hereafter he will be in the ranks of those who have lost (all spiritual good)," as well as Ibn Taymiyya, who opined,

> Churches and synagogues are not God's houses, but rather Allah's houses are the mosques. They [churches and synagogues] are houses of infidelity (*kufr*), even though God's name is mentioned in them. Houses are evaluated according to the creed of their people. People who reject God's last Prophet ... are disbelievers, hence their houses are designated for the worship practiced by disbelievers.[30]

Muslims, according to Wahhabi ulama at the time, are totally forbidden from publishing the Hebrew Bible and the New Testament, let alone binding them together with the Quran.[31] CRLO considered all meetings with Jewish and Christian groups to be an acknowledgment of the validity of their religious beliefs and practices, thus potentially dangerous and liable to "enable them [Jews and Christians] to achieve ... their aims, breaking the bonds of Islam."[32] This statement was based on Quran 5:49: "And follow not their vain desires, but beware of them lest they beguile thee from any of that [teaching] which Allah hath sent down to thee."[33] Nonetheless, the Wahhabi scholars noted that calling non-Muslims in general, and the People of the Book in particular, to Islam is not only permitted but incumbent on all Muslims, as long as it is done in accordance with the rules of Islam.

In the wake of 9/11, however, official Wahhabi Islam seems to have increasingly abandoned this exclusivist approach and reconsidered its relations with other cultures, Muslim and non-Muslim alike. That is, the senior Wahhabi ulama who form part of the religious establishment have sought to counter extremism within the Saudi Kingdom, especially in regard to ideological groups that depict others as infidels (*kuffar*) or polytheists (*mushrikun*). Numerous campaigns were launched by the Saudi government and religious leadership toward this end.[34] The various national and interfaith dialogues launched since then indicate a new official Wahhabi approach to the Other. Even the MWL and WAMY are expected to play important roles in this new mission. Thus, a historical shift seems to be taking place in Wahhabi *daʿwa*, from a one-sided call to Islam to a mutual, interfaith encounter, a shift from monologue to dialogue.

THE NATIONAL DIALOGUES

After 9/11, and especially following the terror attacks perpetrated by al-Qaeda inside the Kingdom from 2003 to 2005,[35] the Saudi government and the official Wahhabi establishment recognized the need to open lines of communication with the Other, both Muslim religious minorities within Saudi Arabia (including Shiʿites and Sufis) and non-Muslims. With this objective, the King Abdulaziz Center for National Dialogue (Markaz al-Malik ʿAbd al-ʿAziz liʾl-Hiwar al-Watani, KACND) was established on 23 July 2003. It seeks to promote dialogue among various religious, ideological, and cultural segments of Saudi society, as clearly indicated in the objectives of the Center published on its website. The first objective reads: "to consolidate national unity within the framework of the Islamic faith and to deepen it further through comprehensive national dialogue." The seventh objective elaborates the notion of dialogue from yet another angle by targeting organizations and individuals outside the Kingdom.[36] All in all, the objectives and goals of KACND signify a new trend in Saudi rhetoric, one that acknowledges other cultures and religions by calling them to dialogue (*hiwar*).[37] In fact, to date, the call to dialogue has generated a succession of national conferences, during which Saudis from diverse religious backgrounds and political orientations have come together and held frank discussions on sensitive issues, e.g., religious differences/tolerance, educational issues, and the Islam/global interface.[38]

Of particular relevance to this chapter is the fifth national conference, 13–16 December 2005 in Abha, capital of the Asir region, an event that marked an expansion of the Saudi public sphere. The conference was entitled, "We and the Others: A National Vision for Dealing with World Cultures." Note that the "we" in the title denoted "Saudi citizens, regardless of their religions, opinions, and orientations," while "the Others" referred in general terms to "all other human societies, their religions and civilizations."[39] The conference followed thirteen preparatory meetings, convened under the auspices of KACND, with more than 700 Saudi participants, including male and female scholars, intellectuals, authors, and cultural figures from various groups within Saudi society. Among other things, this conference, devoted to religious tolerance and cultural pluralism, affirmed the following:

> The conveners affirmed that Saudis, in all their rainbow of colors, are part of the international human society and are working alongside other civilized societies in actualizing the noble values [shared by all of] humanity and cooperating with other societies in caring and spreading prosperity on Earth. Saudis have based their culture on the noble values of Islam and the true Arab customs, which both stand for the respect of the other and his beliefs and for disciplined and balanced openness towards his culture and intellect. They also believe that internal diversity in jurisprudence, intellect, culture and society is a universal law.[40]

One significant outcome of the fifth conference was the creation of a National Vision comprised of five sections. The preamble presents the guiding principles and values for dealing with other cultures and nations as follows:

1. The unity of the Human Race, wherein all humans are united in a fellowship going back to the father of Mankind, Adam. . . .
2. Human dignity, reserved for all the children of Adam, whether male or female . . . to protect dignity, blood, honor, wealth, lineage, and the freedom of human consciousness.

3. Moral values, represented by justice, kindness, fidelity, mercy, and tolerance, along with the rejection of betrayal, injustice, and transgression.
4. Uniting interests and deterring evil, but not at the expense of others.
5. Knowing, communicating, and cooperating with the other for the sake of truth and to benefit Humanity.[41]

The adoption of the principles and values of human equality, justice, civil rights, and freedom of religion for all people indicates a new phase in Wahhabi rhetoric regarding the Other and whose tone differs significantly from the period leading up to 9/11. Cognizant of the shift, the authors of the National Vision have suggested a redefinition of certain fundamental Islamic principles such as loyalty (*al-wala'*), disavowal (*al-bara'*), jihad, *daʿwa*, and intercultural communication (*mukhataba*). According to this new perception, "loyalty" should be a bond of love and support that Saudis exchange with Muslims throughout the world, regardless of their religio-legal orientations. "Disavowal," on the other hand, means avoiding all that contradicts Islam, i.e., cooperation is permitted with others in pursuance of global human interests, except in cases of conflict with Islam.[42] As for jihad, the envisioned definition is "making efforts to command good and forbid evil" (*al-amr bi'l-maʿruf wa'l-nahi ʿan al-munkar*). Thus, going to war is considered to be an exceptional case, allowed only in case of defense. Offensive jihad has no place in Islam, according to the authors of the 2005 National Vision, therefore relations between Muslims and non-Muslims should be peaceful.[43]

The Wahhabi official religious establishment is directly involved in this endeavor to moderate religious discourse regarding the Other. For instance, Grand Mufti Abd al-Aziz Al al-Shaykh was nominated Chairman of the Prince Sultan ibn Abd al-Aziz Chair for Contemporary Islamic Studies at King Saud University, established in 2008.[44] The stated aim of this new center is to enhance *wasatiyya* ("Islamic moderation," "the Muslim median way") by supporting study and research that affirms the tolerance and moderation of Islam, counters extremism, and instills pluralistic values in the younger generation.[45] The staff includes distinguished Saudi and foreign scholars and provides financial support for academic studies.[46]

Since its establishment, the chair has published several books on the relations between Islam and other cultures, among them *al-Tasamuh wa'l-ʿUdwaniyya bayna al-Islam wa'l-Gharb* (Tolerance and Hostility between Islam and the West), by the Saudi religious scholar Salih al-Hasin, who has held many prominent positions, including membership in the CSS; *Huquq al-Insan fi al-Yahudiyya wa'l-Masihiyya wa'l-Islam Muqaranatan bi'l-Qanun al-Dawli* (Human Rights in Judaism, Christianity, and Islam in Comparison with International Law) by Khalid al-Shanibar, faculty member at King Saud University; and, most importantly, *al-Hurriyya al-Diniyya bayna al-Muslimin wa-Ahl al-Kitab* (Religious Freedom between Muslims and People of the Book [Jews and Christians]), by Khalid al-Qasim, executive director of the chair.[47] Furthermore, in March 2009, the chair initiated the Project for the Encyclopedia of Research on the Middle Way with a budget of 12 million riyals (approx. $3.2 million U.S.).[48] Among the topics included are *da'wa* and intercultural relations. According to al-Qasim, the project's director, emphasis was to be placed on the Islamic legal and theological principles of *wasatiyya* and on ways of approaching the Other. He stressed that this Encyclopedia would correct prior misconceptions and biases regarding these issues in Islam.[49]

The work of the above academic chair, which is undertaken under the supervision of Shaykh Abd al-Aziz Al al-Shaykh, indeed indicates a fundamental shift in the Saudi-Wahhabi rhetoric regarding "the saved sect." It shows that Wahhabis are now endeavoring to redefine their religious and theological philosophy on tolerance and intercultural relations. The concept of *wasatiyya* is being gradually placed at the core of current Wahhabi reflection as part of a transformation from exclusivism to accommodation. There is, as yet, no precise and comprehensive definition of Wahhabi *wasatiyya*, and it is still too early to determine any outcomes of this trend. Yet the direction was set in al-Qasim's 2009 book, wherein he reinterprets the famous verse, Quran 2:256, "Let there be no compulsion in religion," to mean that Islam guarantees religious freedom.[50]

INTERFAITH DIALOGUE

With all its difficulties, the national dialogue represents a potential break from the traditional monolithic Wahhabi discourse of exclusivism. For the first time, the official Wahhabi establishment acknowledges the existence of internal religious and cultural diversity within Saudi society itself. In the same vein, one also observes changes in the Wahhabi position and a novel openness toward other religions and cultures outside Saudi Arabia. That is, the Wahhabis now profess to acknowledge non-Muslim religions and even nonmonotheistic religions such as Hinduism and Buddhism. They seem to be on the way toward shattering their self-made exclusion and approaching the outside world. "Dialogue" has become a key term in twenty-first-century Wahhabi discourse on the Other, Otherness, and tolerance, both within the Kingdom and without. In an opening speech at a conference entitled, "The International Islamic Conference for Dialogue," organized by the Muslim World League, 4–6 June 2008 in Mecca, Grand Mufti and Chairman of the Constituent Council of the MWL, Abd al-Aziz Al al-Shaykh, stated,

> Dialogue between people is one of life's necessities and a means for connection, coexistence, and exchanging interests within any nation. Indeed, there is diversity among people in their habits and morals. They are different in their languages, colors, habits, and minds, and this is a universal truth.... The diversity between people in their thoughts and beliefs is an issue that the Holy Qur'an affirms. Allah (S.W.) says: "And if your Lord had willed, He could have made Mankind one community; but they will not cease to differ" [Quran 11:118]. The importance of dialogue in Islam is shown through valuing it and calling for it, in order to uplift people and nations, especially the call to Allah (S.W.). Allah (S.W.) says: "Invite to the way of your Lord with wisdom and good instruction and argue with them in a way that is best" [Quran 16:125]. To be engaged in dialogue is human nature, and Allah (S.W.) says: "But man has ever been, most of anything, [prone to] dispute" [Quran 18:54].[51]

Abdallah ibn Abd al-Muhsin al-Turki, Secretary General of the MWL, added in the same vein,

> Dialogue is a means that derives both its legitimacy and its significance from the legitimacy and importance of the goals it strives to achieve. Dialogue is both an authentic Qur'anic methodology and a prophetic practice. It is a principle that is instilled in the mind of the Islamic Nation (Ummah) and has characterized the relations between Muslims and others since the dawn of Islam and throughout its long history and profound heritage. It is also based on both the magnanimity of Islam and the essence of Divine Law (Shariʿah), from which Muslims derive their methodology.[52]

On this and similar occasions, the Wahhabi leadership has begun to encourage dialogue among nations with diverse cultures and religions. The objectives and goals of such interfaith dialogue, as outlined in the new vision statement of the MWL, include the following:

1. To introduce Islam, its principles, humane tenets and heritage, and the great civilization it possesses that enables it to effectively contribute to guiding the march of human civilization.
2. To refute allegations leveled against Islam and rectify the distorted images of Islam, its states and organizations in religious, academic and media circles.
3. To contribute to confronting challenges and to offer solutions to problems that face humankind, as a result of their abandoning religion and departing from its principles and values, an act that led to the suffering of mankind from injustice, vice, terrorism, violations of human rights, and pollution of the environment that God Almighty has bestowed on them.
4. To support and defend just causes pertaining to human-rights violations and to form international public opinion that supports such causes and helps achieve their legitimate demands.
5. To expose those promoting the clash of civilizations [Samuel Huntington] and end-of-history theories [Francis Fukuyama]. To reject claims that Islam is an enemy of contemporary civilization, thereby inculcating Islamophobia in the minds of people, imposing dominance of the world, and disseminating a single culture.
6. To acquaint ourselves with people of other faiths and their cultures and together to establish common principles that achieve peaceful coexistence and security of human society worldwide. To cooperate with each other in spreading ethical values, truth, benevolence, and peace, and to challenge hegemony, exploitation, injustice, moral deviation, family breakdown, and other evils that threaten societies.
7. To solve problems and disputes that may occur between Muslims and others in countries and communities, whether as majorities or minorities. To secure an atmosphere suitable for national and social coexistence.
8. To achieve understanding with humane cultures and civilizations, as well as to urge Muslims to join multicivilization [*sic*]

arrangements of mankind and use this understanding to achieve and maintain world peace.

9. To interact and communicate with the followers of Islamic schools of thought, in order to achieve the unity of the Muslim *Umma* and to lessen fanaticism and antagonism.[53]

In practice, both the Saudi government and the Wahhabi religious establishment have sponsored several international conferences, meetings, and seminars for dialogue in Saudi Arabia and abroad over the past decade. Participation in these meetings was initially confined only to adherents of monotheistic faiths. According to King Abdallah, "The idea is to ask representatives of all monotheistic religions to sit together ... as we all believe in the same God."[54] But dialogue was soon expanded to include nonmonotheistic participants. In this regard, Prince Turki al-Faysal noted: "In these times, we must all learn to speak in God's language, that is, one of love and respect for people of all faiths, races and nationalities."[55]

In June 2004, the Saudi government hosted the first International Islamic Conference on Dialogue in Mecca, followed by a long series of conferences and workshops that took place all over the world: New York, Madrid, Vienna, Almaty (Kazakhstan), Buenos Aires, Tokyo, Colombo (Sri Lanka), Taipei, and most recently Hong Kong.[56] A large number of participants (including scholars, researchers, preachers, religious leaders, representatives of public relations agencies, and other institutions concerned with dialogue between human cultures and civilizations) participated in these conferences. A quick glimpse at the final statements and declarations indicates that dialogue has been used as the fundamental apparatus for communication between the various religions and cultures. For example, the summation from the international conference in Mecca, also known as the Mecca Declaration, addressed "all governments, organizations and peoples, irrespective of their religions and cultures," urging them to undertake the following:

1. Foster understanding between them and us [Muslims] that we believe in God as the Creator, worship Him alone, and seek the guidance He revealed to His prophets and messengers.
2. Challenge injustice, tyranny, despotism and hegemony, and to help each other in ending wars, conflicts, and international problems. To work together to promote a culture of tolerance and dialogue, and to support institutions promoting dialogue. To use dialogue as

a means for achieving understanding, cooperation and world peace. To desist from wasting human resources and to stop the exploitation of individuals' talents for the productions [*sic*] of weapons of mass destruction that threaten the future of the Earth.

3. Cooperate with each other for the promotion of moral values and the building of international ethical arrangements that resist the attack of moral deviation, combat extra-marital relationships, and provide solutions for the dangers surrounding the family in a manner that secures the right of all to live within happy families.
4. Work together as inhabitants of the Earth, according to the wish of God, who sanctioned our Forefather, Adam, and his progeny to reform the Earth and halt aggression, for the right of the coming generations to live in an environment devoid of all types of pollution. To minimize the dangers of environmental damage by means of common actions that seek to lessen the consequences of pollution and to guide industrial, technological advancement.
5. Cooperate with the world community in eliminating corruption and unhappiness, which need to be remedied through the mercy of God, which is the essence of the message sent to the Prophet Mohammad (pbuh). "We sent thee not but as a mercy for all creatures" (The Holy Quran, 21:107).[57]

Finally, the conference recommended establishing an international center for the interaction of civilizations.[58] Accordingly, a center for interfaith dialogue was inaugurated on 26 November 2012 in Vienna under the name King Abdullah bin Abdulaziz International Centre for Interreligious and Intercultural Dialogue (KAICIID). The major objective of this center, as presented on the homepage of its website, is

> to foster dialogue among people of different faiths and cultures that bridges animosities, reduces fear, and instills mutual respect. Intercultural and interreligious dialogue helps build communities' resistance against prejudice, strengthens social cohesion, supports conflict prevention and transformation and can serve to preserve peace.[59]

Two more conferences were held in 2008 in Madrid and at the UN headquarters in New York, at which the Saudi delegates expressed their commitment to international human rights, cultural pluralism, and freedom for all nations.[60] In the closing remarks given at a press conference, the Saudi Foreign Minister, Prince Saud al-Faysal, stressed the commitment of Saudi Arabia to the aforementioned goals and principles, as they appear in the UN Charter. The UN Assembly acknowledged the Saudi initiative, calling for the broadening of intercultural dialogue and global support for religious tolerance.[61]

Of particular interest for the purposes of this volume are the Wahhabi attempts to theorize and conceptualize dialogue vis-à-vis their concept of *daʿwa*. Much has been written on this issue under the auspices of the MWL, thus indicating the symbiotic connection between *daʿwa* and dialogue. In the article "Dialogue and Its Objectives in the Qurʾan and Sunna," for example, Secretary General Saʿd ibn Ali al-Shahrani asserted,

> Civilized dialogue with the West is considered an application of the principle of Verbal Jihad. . . . Dialogue falls under the Jihad by tongue, which is a great field and a suitable situation from which Muslims can benefit in order to accomplish one of the duties of our religion, which is the Call (*daʿwah*) to Allah (S.W.) with wisdom, good advice and reasoning in the best manner. The Call and Invitation to Islam and expounding the good and the virtues of this religion are the highest and the most sublime of the objectives of dialogue.[62]

According to al-Shahrani, *daʿwa* must therefore be conducted as a dialogue in which one side cannot ignore the Other. As such, a statement such as "We are always right and the Other is always wrong" merely obstructs the path of dialogue—in addition to being unrealistic in many cases. Al-Shahrani found support for his view in the Quran, which, for him, "puts interlocutors on the same level, whatever their convictions." Thus, "in dialogue, the truth does not belong to any one party; both parties are involved in the journey to find it together."[63] In this context, he quotes Quran 34:24, in which the Prophet addresses the idolaters: "Say, 'Who provides for you from the heavens and the earth?' Say, 'Allah.' Indeed, we or you are either upon guidance or in clear error." For al-Shahrani, then, *daʿwa* is ultimately synonymous with dialogue. Both, he stresses, "should be impartial, magnanimous, flexible, lenient, and open, without compromising the convictions or retracting the constants, but to argue in the best manner."[64]

Wahhabi openness toward other cultures and communities has significantly expanded to include nonmonotheistic religions and cultures. This was apparent in the conference held in Hong Kong, 18–19 November 2015, under the title, "Dialogue and Peaceful Coexistence." It was attended by a large number of participants consisting of scholars, researchers, leaders, and members of different religions and cultures from Hong Kong and East Asia. According to the organizers, the conference discussed four major themes: religious and cultural dialogue; cultural diversity in Hong Kong; human values in multicultural societies; and religion and the culture of peaceful coexistence.[65] For MWL Secretary General Dr. Abdallah al-Turki, such conferences aim "at achieving the global peace and noble values for which the World is longing, in a world where values are declining."[66]

The final message, written and published by the conference participants relates to the importance of dialogue, while stressing universal principles and values related to tolerance. It calls for the development of better appreciation between the peoples of the world, peaceful coexistence, and for the promotion of noble, universal human values, as follows:

1. All men are equal in human dignity; divine honor includes everyone. [God] has endowed [human beings] with minds and the ability to procreate and inhabit the Earth. All this has come to happen according to God's design as brought by the divine messages.
2. Humanity's different religions, cultures and races are ordained by Allah. They are one of His signs.... "And of His signs is the creation of the heavens and the Earth, and the diversity of your languages and your colors. Indeed, in that are signs for those of knowledge" [Quran 30:22].
3. Communities' religious and cultural diversity call for the establishment of a fair partnership within a social contract approved by everyone. This accord must be best used to get the maximum of the diversity of visions for the sake of enriching civil and cultural life, and to achieve national development.... "O Mankind, indeed, We have created you from male and female and made you peoples and tribes that you may know one another. Indeed, the most noble of you in the sight of Allah is the most righteous of you" [Quran 49:13].
4. Ethnic or cultural superiority must be rejected outright, and unjust images of racial discrimination must be denounced.... "O mankind, fear your Lord, who created you from one soul and created from it its mate and dispersed from both of them many men and women" [Quran 4:1].

5. The divine messages' basic tenets have been revealed to promote peace and compassion among all people. And they are keen on providing human civilization with moral and spiritual values, and take advantage of its achievement. They have been sent down also to preserve the environment, and protect the Earth from pollution and hazards.[67]

CONCLUSION

The events of 9/11 and the subsequent criticism of Wahhabi Islam as "the cradle of violent extremists," triggered a Saudi-Wahhabi self-examination on fundamental issues that included *daʿwa* doctrines. Prominent Wahhabis have come to recognize the problematic nature of the traditional doctrine of the "saved sect" and of *al-wala' wa'l-bara'*. An internal process was set in motion to reconfigure the relevant religious and ideological concepts. It became necessary to address negative images of Islam, in general, and of Wahhabi Islam in particular. Accordingly, the Saudi government, with the full support and cooperation of the official Wahhabi religious establishment, initiated a number of programs to encourage both internal and external dialogue to promote universal values in regard to tolerance and pluralism and to improve international communication.

This transformative process is manifested on both the theoretical and the practical levels. Significantly, for more than a decade, Wahhabi scholars have been reinterpreting and redefining key doctrinal concepts, including *daʿwa* and interfaith dialogue. These new interpretations represent a fundamental shift in the Wahhabi perceptions of the Other and of the scope of *daʿwa*. This is evident in the new attitude toward other religions, particularly Christianity and Judaism, as well as toward Shiʿa, Sufis, and other minority groups in Saudi Arabia. In the wake of 9/11, the Wahhabis became ready to meet and enact dialogue with peoples of other religions and cultures, as illustrated by the national and international interfaith/intercultural conferences sponsored by the Saudi government and conducted by MWL and KAIICID with unprecedented openness.

This process of self-examination has caused Wahhabism to relinquish its self-imposed, puritanical isolation as the "saved sect," moving from "exclusivism" to accommodation of the Other and turning *daʿwa* from one-sided monologue into a more attentive mutual dialogue.

CHAPTER 15

Jihadi Soft Power

The Changing Importance of Daʿwa in Salafi-Jihadi Discourse since the Arab Uprisings

ADAM HOFFMAN

ISLAMIC REVIVALIST MOVEMENTS share the same basic goal of implementing God's rule on earth, yet they diverge on the question of the best methods for achieving this objective and on how to promote an Islamic society or even an Islamic state. In modern times, the strategy of *daʿwa* has usually been associated with "mainstream" Islamist movements such as the Muslim Brotherhood, while more radical movements have rejected it in favor of more immediate action: violent combat (jihad) or leaving mainstream Muslim society (*hijra*).[1] Such has been particularly the case with the violent Salafi-Jihadi trend, which advocates fighting "infidels" and "apostates" as the only answer to the dire predicament of contemporary Islam. Still, the new opportunities that arose during the dramatic events of the Arab uprisings prompted some of its leading organizations and ideologues to reconsider nonviolent preaching and proselytizing, or *daʿwa*. This chapter dwells on the civic aspects of the Salafi-Jihadi trend by examining the recent change in the importance of *daʿwa* in the discourse and practice of Salafi-Jihadist organizations.

The Jihadis' recent resort to methods of preaching can be understood on two levels. On one hand, it is part of a larger trend toward an increasing use of *daʿwa* by a variety of Islamist actors, ranging from the Muslim Brotherhood and "quietist" Salafis to traditional religious establishments, including Saudi-sponsored international Wahhabi institutions.[2] On the other hand, it can be seen as a result of the dramatic developments inspired by the Arab Uprisings on Islamic politics, most notably the emergence of Salafi political parties,[3] the radicalization of the Muslim Brotherhood in

Egypt,[4] and the political integration and later electoral success of al-Nahda Islamist party in Tunisia.[5] In the process, preaching Islam has gained more legitimacy in the eyes of Salafi-Jihadists, who came to regard it as an effective additional strategy for drawing people closer to their ideals.

In analyzing the recent Salafi-Jihadi *daʿwa*, I draw on Joseph S. Nye's concept of "soft power." The term refers to an actor's ability to attract others by the legitimacy of its policy, rather than by relying on coercion alone.[6] While the term is usually used in the context of the foreign policies and public diplomacy campaigns of states, it may also help us discern the Salafi-Jihadists' strategies in their attempt to attract others to their values and political community.

The chapter begins with a brief description of Salafi-Jihadism, focusing on its core characteristics and relation to the wider Salafi movement. It then proceeds to discuss the initial critique of *daʿwa* among Salafi-Jihadists and traces the changes that have taken place in their position. The final part analyzes the contemporary use of *daʿwa* by al-Qaeda's organization in Syria, Jabhat al-Nusra, and the Islamic State in Syria and Iraq (ISIS), which split from al-Qaeda and, at least for a time, seemed to have superseded it. ISIS's territorial project was finally defeated in March 2019, though the organization still exists, while al-Nusra became defunct in July 2016, when it formally rebranded as Jabhat Fatah al-Sham. The discussion is based on a variety of Salafi-Jihadi media products (including videos, *anashid*,[7] and images) and textual primary sources.

THE PRIMACY OF JIHAD AND CRITIQUE OF *DAʿWA*

As its name implies, Salafi-Jihadism is part of the broader Salafi trend.[8] Salafis derive their name from the pious forefathers of Islam (*al-salaf al-salih*), whose exemplary understanding and implementation of the Quran and Sunna of the Prophet Muhammad they seek to emulate in all aspects of life. This implies belief in the absolute Oneness of Allah (*tawhid*), while any straying from it is considered to be associating partners to Him (*shirk*) and unlawful innovation (*bidʿa*). Salafi-Jihadists share these tenets, but unlike mainstream Salafis, who are usually quietist,[9] for them, jihad, in the sense of violent action,[10] is a central tenet of the correct creed (*ʿaqida*) and a necessary tool for realizing *tawhid* and defending the purity of the faith. The Palestinian-Jordanian Abu Muhammad al-Maqdisi (b. 1959), a leading ideologue of the trend, depicts it as "a current which unites the call to *tawhid* in all its aspects with jihad for that purpose at the same time."[11] Salafi-Jihadis thus seek to change the existing political order by waging holy war against Islam's perceived enemies. Additionally, they further argue that in the current circumstances jihad has become an individual duty (*fard ʿayn*) incumbent on every Muslim. As Osama bin Laden declared, "the peak of this religion [Islam] is jihad."[12] Thus, being a Salafi-Jihadi means following the example of the Prophet as closely as possible and emphasizing the militant aspect of his life as known from the Quran and the Sunna.

The centrality of jihad in Salafi-Jihadi discourse eclipses more peaceful concepts and strategies, most notably that of *daʿwa*—the "invitation" or "call" to Islam—a theme that is repeatedly mentioned in the Quran and illustrated in the example of the Prophet. The Quran extols the person who calls others to embrace Islam, "And who is better in speech than one who invites to Allah and does righteousness and says, 'Indeed, I am of the Muslims,'" (Quran 41:33) and instructs Muslims to propagate the religion, "Call to the way of your Lord with wisdom and good preaching" (Quran 16:125). Several hadith likewise highlight the importance of preaching Islam and the rewards for those who undertake it.

In modern times, *daʿwa* has come to denote a gradual, nonviolent approach to the Islamization of society. This development is primarily associated with the work and legacy of Hasan al-Banna (1906–1949), founder and first leader of the Society of the Muslim Brothers. Banna transformed *daʿwa* into the motor of Islamic politics and collective action. Under his leadership, it became synonymous with the Muslim Brotherhood's mission and with the Islamic movement itself.[13] On the official website of the movement, he is accordingly described as "a great Muslim and teacher of *Daʿwa*."[14] Mustafa Mashhur (1921–2002), the fifth General Guide and editor of its official journal, *al-Daʿwa*, further maintained that through it "progress is made. Each step leads to a higher level of success. There will be the Muslim individual, the Muslim home, the Muslim society, so that the extensive Islamic groundwork is set for the establishment of an Islamic government, which will combine with others like it to form an Islamic caliphate across the Muslim world."[15] *Daʿwa* is thus positioned at the heart of the Muslim Brotherhood's political approach of "evolution, not revolution," in which gradual Islamic action and nonviolent preaching form the best method for combatting secularization and the oppression of the modern state. It includes not only verbal preaching and propagation but also the provision of social services, community outreach, sports events, and religious education in schools and universities.

The internal relationship between *daʿwa* and jihad is illustrated in the trajectory of Hamas, the Palestinian Islamist movement. *Daʿwa* institutions established by Sheikh Ahmed Yassin (1937–2004) in the 1970s in the Gaza Strip focused on education, religious preaching, and welfare, before it turned, at the beginning of the first intifada in 1987, to an armed jihad against Israel.[16]

In the Salafi-Jihadi camp, by contrast, *daʿwa* was usually considered to be of secondary importance. Influential ideologues such as al-Maqdisi were aware of the need to perform it alongside jihad, in the belief that "any jihad that discards *daʿwa* will quickly become nothing more than isolated attacks that do not bring about true change."[17] Many others, however, including his erstwhile disciple Abu Musʿab al-Zarqawi (1966–2006), leader of al-Qaeda in Iraq and the forefather of the Islamic State (IS), have rejected it outright as a strategy associated with pragmatism, democracy, and collaboration with secular forces within the existing political order. In the anti-Hamas video *The Disguise of the Religion*, for example, the leaders of a mass rally who pledge to stay true to the path of the Muslim Brotherhood's *daʿwa* and wage jihad in the path of God are condemned for following "the path of the Ikhwani [Muslim Brotherhood] *daʿwa* rather than the path of Allah." Other scenes then show them meeting with prominent Shiʿi figures, namely Iran's supreme leader Ayatollah Khamenei (b. 1939) and Hezbollah's leader Hasan Nasrallah (b. 1960).[18] Hamas's *daʿwa* is thus associated with the Muslim Brotherhood and presented as the betrayal of Islam and collaboration with the hated Shiʿites.

In the same vein, al-Qaeda singled out the Muslim Brotherhood and other Middle Eastern *daʿwa* movements as the primary target of its polemic, while downplaying their historical achievements for the Islamic cause. From its perspective, the Muslim Brothers were disappointing because by working within the political system they sought to integrate with a corrupt, heretical order. The ideological basis for this anti-Brotherhood polemic was Ayman al-Zawahiri's essay, *al-Hisad al-Murr* (The Bitter Harvest), which gained a place of honor in al-Qaeda's canonic library.[19]

Salafi-Jihadists thus maintain that jihad, rather than nonviolent and gradual *daʿwa*, must take precedence over all other methods in view of the current dire state of the *umma* in which "apostate" regimes oppress Islam and fight the *mujahidin*. Muhammad Abd al-Salam Faraj (1954–1982),[20] the radical ideologue of the Egyptian jihad group that assassinated President Sadat, had already articulated this argument in his 1979 manifesto, *The Neglected Duty*.

> Some of them say that the right road to the establishment of an (Islamic) State is *daʿwa* only, and the creation of a broad base.... But then, how can *daʿwa* be widely successful when all means of communication today are under the control of the pagan and wicked [State] and [under the control] of those who are at war with God's religion?[21]

At the beginning of the twenty-first century, Anwar al-Awlaki (1971–2011), a Yemeni-American who was one of the leaders of al-Qaeda in the Arabian Peninsula (AQAP) and a key propagandist for the organization in English, explicitly argued, "Jihad today is *fard ʿayn* (an individual obligation). It therefore supersedes *daʿwa* in importance since *daʿwa* is a recommended act or at most a collective duty (*fard kifayah*). *So anything that supports jihad should take precedence over things that support daʿwa*" (emphasis mine). For Awlaki, "The best thing for *daʿwa* is the sword."[22]

Still, the centrality of armed jihad to Salafi-Jihadists notwithstanding, Omar Ashour has recently argued, [In] "the late 1990s and throughout the 2000s several armed Islamist movements, factions and groups underwent remarkable behavioral and ideological transformations towards abandoning and delegitimizing political violence as well as *adopting nonviolent activism as a method of socio-political change*" (my emphasis).[23] For this tendency, which he defines as post-jihadism, jihad must be understood as a means to an end rather than an end in itself. According to "post-jihadists" such as Sayyid Imam al-Sharif, former al-Qaeda ideologue and leader of the Egyptian al-Jihad group, "jihad is not the only legitimate option to confront an illegitimate reality." The willingness to engage in self-criticism and ideological revision is an interesting phenomenon, although it remains marginal to the wider Salafi-Jihadi trend.

AL-QAEDA: NEW OPPORTUNITIES, SHIFTING METHODS

Their initial attitude notwithstanding, recent years have witnessed a palpable increase in the importance of *daʿwa* in the discourse and practice of Salafi-Jihadi groups. The Arab Uprisings of 2011 in particular created new opportunities for freer operation across the Middle East and North Africa. The events that became known as the Arab Spring were ignited by peaceful, mostly secular protesters, but the security vacuum that resulted from the regional instability and the removal of the mechanisms of state repression in many countries created new openings for jihadist activity. For many Salafi-Jihadists, the popular protests against the Arab regimes were thus a blessed development. Bin Laden defined the fall of the Arab dictators as a "great historical event,"[24] while others were enthusiastic to watch the fall of the despised Arab dictators in Tunisia, Egypt and Syria, Yemen and Libya.[25] Bin Laden urged Muslims to make the most of the "great and rare historic opportunity" that presented itself in the region after the fall of the Arab dictators.[26]

It was in these circumstances that the top leadership of al-Qaeda began to stress the importance of *daʿwa* for jihadi groups. Zawahiri (b. 1951), who took over the leadership of al-Qaeda after Bin Laden's death in May 2011, highlighted the importance of preaching and propaganda in an official document titled *General Guidelines for Jihad*. Zawahiri claimed,

> It is not a hidden secret that our work in this stage has two aspects: The first is military and the second propagational. . . . As far as the propagational work is concerned, it aims to create awareness in the *Umma* regarding the threat posed by the Crusader onslaught, clarify the true meaning of Tawheed in the sense that the rule and sovereignty belongs to Allah alone, and stress upon the importance of brotherhood based on Islam and the unity of all Muslims [*sic*] lands.[27]

Zawahiri's emphasis on propaganda and the importance of creating "awareness in the *Umma*" is based on his decades-long experience in the jihadist movement, first against the local regime in Egypt in the 1960s–1980s ("the near enemy") and later in the global jihadi movement, within the leadership of al-Qaeda ("the far enemy").[28] Despite repeated attempts to overthrow the government and establish an Islamic political system, Zawahiri admitted, "The goal of establishing an Islamic government in Egypt is yet to be achieved."[29] He attributed the failure to the elitist nature of the jihadist movement, which regarded itself as a vanguard responsible for creating an Islamic society, and to its inability to instill correct Islamic awareness among large parts of society. Zawahiri now argued, "The jihad movement must come closer to the masses," and warned, "It must be extremely careful not to get isolated from its people or engage the government in the battle of the elite [the jihadist movement] against the authorities."[30]

To close the gap between the jihadists and the Islamic *umma*, i.e., Muslim society, and to come "closer to the masses," Zawahiri began to call for a readopting of *da'wa*, without neglecting violent struggle. While, "There is no solution without jihad,"[31] he urged the jihadists to also engage in *da'wa* in its broadest sense: "The jihad movement must dedicate one of its wings to work with the masses, preach, provide services for the Muslim people, and share their concerns through all available avenues for charity and educational work. We must not leave a single area unoccupied. We must win the people's confidence, respect, and affection."[32] Only by helping the people could the jihadist movement hope to Islamize society and harness it in its battle against the Arab regimes.

Zawahiri thus called upon his radical followers to popularize the jihadist message outside the ranks of the *mujahidin*, as well as within them, by means of *da'wa*.

> Focus on spreading awareness amongst the general public so as to mobilize it. Similarly, focus on spreading a greater level of awareness and understanding amongst the mujahid vanguard [in order] to create an organized, united, ideological, and aware jihadi force that strongly believes in the Islamic faith, adheres to its rulings, shows humbleness to the believers, and deals with the disbelievers with firmness. At the same time, full effort should be put in immediately to ensure that people with scholarly and propagational abilities come forth from within the ranks of the mujahideen so that our message and ideology may be preserved and the call to Jihad may be spread amongst Muslims.[33]

DA'WA IN JABHAT AL-NUSRA AND THE ISLAMIC STATE (ISIS)

Public and scholarly attention to Salafi-Jihadists in the past two decades has by the nature of things focused on their spectacular acts of terrorism, including suicide attacks and mass killings. The extreme brutality of ISIS, with its filmed beheadings, genocide, and sex slavery, have only reinforced the perception that Salafi-Jihadists are engaged exclusively in violence and the glorification of killing and martyrdom. Of course, these have always been and still remain the core characteristics of this trend. Its combat against the "Crusader" West and "straying" Muslims is based on the concept of *al-wala' wa'l-bara'* (loyalty toward other Muslims and enmity toward non-Muslims).[34] Still, the path charted by Zawahiri marked a significant shift in the prevalent Salafi-Jihadi discourse from an almost exclusive focus on violent jihad to a broader conception of the movement's mission, a shift that has gone largely unnoticed by Western scholars and analysts.[35] Yet, by fulfilling one of the most fundamental socioreligious obligations of the believer, Salafi-Jihadists aspire to demonstrate that their action encompasses all spheres of Islamic life—not only the battlefield of jihad but also the mosque, the street, and the marketplace—the public sphere of *da'wa*. Thereby they have also sought to break their elitist image as a revolutionary vanguard and connect directly to the Muslim masses.

Jabhat al-Nusra, al-Qaeda's Syrian affiliate, and ISIS were the two most prominent Salafi-Jihadist organizations active in recent years. Although the two groups differed significantly in the contents and scope of their *da'wa* activities, both became increasingly engaged in religious and social outreach and publicized their activities in images and videos posted on social media. Not unlike the Muslim Brotherhood, which they generally despised, their *da'wa* included public preaching, distributing religious literature, and holding Quran recitation competitions, as well as conducting public services, holding youth games, distributing sweets to children, and providing food to the poor.

Jabhat al-Nusra represented the more gradual approach to promoting Islam among the two groups. This does not mean, however, that the content of its *da'wa* message was in any way divorced from that of violent jihad. In this vein, one preacher of the organization clarified to his audience, "Both revolution and jihad will continue until Allah is worshipped alone around the globe and the banners of *tawhid* are raised in the land of Allah completely."[36] Thus, rather than replacing jihad, Jabhat al-Nusra's *da'wa* actually served as a method to popularize it among the masses. Its employment was designed to present a nonmilitant face for the group and accordingly help spread its message to a broader audience—beyond the ranks of the *mujahidin*.

Jabhat al-Nusra's *da'wa* videos portrayed its men as preachers who in public gatherings gently call the people to Islam and teach them about their religion. Unlike the recorded wills of "martyrs" (sing. *shahid*), which feature those who intend to carry out suicide attacks in an explosive vest, carrying a Quran, and wearing a determined and defiant expression,[37] the preachers in al-Nusra's videos wear traditional gowns (sing. *jalabiyya*) and smile at the audience. Each video opens and concludes with a religious chant (*nashid*), which sets the tone for the *daʿwa* event it depicts. Professionally edited and featuring the logo of al-Nusra's Preaching and Guidance Office, the videos are generally shot in public locations and seem to depict scenes of everyday life: city streets, roads, and countryside. These settings help portray the organization's *daʿwa* activities as public events that directly connect to the everyday lives of the people.

A video produced by the Preaching and Guidance Office in the Sahil (Syria's coastal region) may serve to illustrate the organization's approach.[38] It starts with an al-Nusra member declaring, "We begin with his [the Prophet Muhammad's] saying: 'convey from me even a [single] verse,'" followed by two other members repeating the sentence while distributing fliers to passing motorists. Then comes a hadith attributed to the Prophet to the same effect, written on the screen in Arabic and English and read aloud in Arabic. Afterward, scenes show members of the organization hanging posters on billboards in the streets, arranging games for youths, and distributing sweets to children. While these scenes are depicted, a *nashid* recites Quran 16:125: "Invite to the way of your Lord with wisdom and good instruction and argue with them in a way that is best."

In addition to inviting people to Islam, al-Nusra's *daʿwa* efforts also aimed to guide and inform the masses about the correct understanding and practice of Islam. In another video, a member of the Preaching and Guidance Office announces the opening of a new initiative: the Campaign for Support of the Shariʿa. The purpose of the campaign, as he explains, is "to inform people about the religion of Allah" so that people "will know what is permitted (*halal*) and what is forbidden (*haram*)." After this statement, the video shows al-Nusra's men handing out pamphlets and preaching to a crowd on the street and in the mosque.[39]

As with the Muslim Brotherhood, this peaceful approach to the preaching of Islam is complemented by the provision of public services. Another *daʿwa* video of Jabhat al Nusra, which starts with a *nashid* about "the convoy of goodness," shows its men distributing tanks of cooking gas to the poor and baking bread at a local bakery. Between these scenes, the video shows civilians thanking al-Nusra for its efforts.[40] The distribution of food and other necessities to the needy falls under the Islamic obligation of almsgiving, but by publicizing it as a community work it becomes part of the *daʿwa*.

In war-torn Syria, many parts of the country have lacked any semblance of normal life. The Syrian regime was either unable to provide public services, or intentionally denied them to cities controlled by rebels.[41] In such a reality, any organization that provided food and other necessities of life fulfilled a critical function. By acting as a humanitarian organization and not just as a jihadi force, Jabhat al-Nusra connected directly to the grassroots and provided much-needed aid in a dysfunctional state, thereby following the example set by the Muslim Brothers from their very beginning.

Of course, Jabhat al-Nusra's civil activities also provided it with ample opportunity to present its ideology to the broader public, defined the ethical boundaries of its community, and divided the world between "believers" and "infidels." In a video that features one of al-Nusra's *daʿwa* forums in Aleppo, the preacher tells the crowd of young girls, boys and adult men,

> We have two groups: a group with faith in Allah and his Messenger, and a group which apostates the Messenger of God. . . . Now there is a war between the two groups: one fights for Allah, and the other fights for Satan and *taghut* [tyrant, the Salafi-Jihadist designation for secular Arab regimes]. Who are you with? Now, to the heart of the matter: O you who have believed, do not take the Jews and the Christians as allies. They are [in fact] allies of one another [Quran 5:51]. We are believers, and they are infidels.[42]

While Jabhat al-Nusra endeavored to capitalize on its civilian activities to harness public support for its jihadi goals, the Islamic State was much more focused on jihad and fighting. Along with the numerous videos and images regularly produced by the organization, this was also clearly presented in its famous *nashid* "Saleel al-Sawareem" (Clashing of the Swords), which declares that "the path of fighting is the path of life."[43] Still, *daʿwa* as a nonviolent method became noticeable even in the publications of this notoriously brutal organization. One video that illustrates its approach opens with a *nashid* and an official Islamic State minibus named "the *daʿwa* convoy" driving to a theme park crowded with children in the Iraqi city of Mosul. Once there, an ISIS militant addresses the crowd of men and children: "There are many issues that the Muslims are asking [themselves]. [One of them is] why did the Islamic *umma* lose its way? Allah's answer is: You have forsaken jihad in the path of Allah. You have forsaken jihad in the path of Allah." Following him, two children and a teenager address the crowd, referring to them as "soldiers of the swords of jihad."[44] The message is clear, jihad is Islam and Islam is jihad, and the *daʿwa* targeted at children and youth serves as a tool to propagate jihad.

The message of the centrality of jihad is reinforced by the appearance of Islamic State personnel in the video. In contrast to Jabhat al-Nusra's videos, the men and children are dressed as *mujahidin*, armed and wearing combat vests. This "*daʿwa* event" is thus ultimately also jihadi in nature but seeks to instill the values of jihad and fighting by using a softer approach to propagate these messages in comparison with full-on armed jihad, which is usually prioritized in ISIS videos and publications.

Such *daʿwa* events may be construed as instances of nonviolent activist method of sociopolitical change. However, unlike the "post-jihadism" trend discussed by Ashour, Islamic State's *daʿwa* events were taken *in addition to*, not instead of, violent activism and were meant to legitimize and support it. They constituted a supplementary method of indoctrination to jihad by nonviolent means.

This relatively softer approach is displayed in full in a video of a *daʿwa* forum in the city of al-Raqqa, ISIS's capital in Syria, published during the month of Ramadan. In it, ISIS militants are smiling and playing games such as musical chairs with the children and teenagers in the crowd. At the center of the event is the *daʿwa* performed by the militants: one of them rhetorically asks the gathered crowd, "What is the most important duty of every Muslim, indeed of every human being who acknowledges that duty?" to which he answers, "This is *tawhid*." Another recites in proper intonation the Quranic verse, "So let those fight in the cause of Allah who sell the life of this world for the Hereafter. And he who fights in the cause of Allah and is killed or achieves victory—We will bestow upon him a great reward" (Quran 4:74). A third militant addresses the crowd with the words: "O *umma* of Islam, the *umma* of Muhammad, the *umma* of jihad and *tawhid*. This is the month of Ramadan, the month of conquests. Rise up and adhere [to your religion]. There is no god but Allah"—highlighting the importance of complete adherence to Allah alone in the holy month of Ramadan.[45]

Although both ISIS and Jabhat al-Nusra thus engaged in and publicize their *daʿwa* activities, there was still an important difference between the two organizations. While all of al-Nusra's videos took place in civilian settings, such as the mosque, the street, and the marketplace, ISIS's relevant videos often took place among its fighters on the frontlines of jihad. One such ISIS video that presents a "*daʿwa* tour" actually seems to focus more on boosting the morale of the fighters than preaching Islam to the masses in the city. The militant *daʿi* is shown citing Quranic verses that mention jihad and fighting.[46]

The nonmilitant aspects of ISIS's *daʿwa* were more visible in photos posted on social media, which were directed to a global Muslim audience. One such set of photos shows a religious studies class in Fallujah, Iraq,[47] while in another a "photographed report" of "*daʿwa* for Allah" presents Islamic State militants handing out fliers to people on the road and studying together in a mosque.[48] These photos demonstrated to prospective supporters that the organization is engaged in preaching Islam, as well as in fighting its enemies.

THE FUNCTIONS OF SALAFI-JIHADI *DAʿWA*

The endeavors of Jabhat al-Nusra and the Islamic State in the field of *daʿwa* and community outreach reflect an increasing awareness of the importance to their long-term survival of winning the "hearts and minds" of the population in the areas where they operate. In line with Joseph S. Nye's conceptualization, Salafi-Jihadi *daʿwa* could therefore be conceptualized as "jihadi soft power." In contrast to "hard power," which refers to coercive measures such as military force and economic sanctions (or in the case of extremist organizations, physical punishments and public executions), soft power "co-opts people rather than coerces them." It consists of "the ability to attract, and attraction often leads to acquiescence." Its resources are those "that produce such attraction," which include "an attractive culture, ideology, and institutions."[49]

By implementing a basic obligation of Islam, propagation of the faith, Salafi-Jihadists frame their actions as religiously legitimate and therefore desirable in an Islamic cultural context. This strategy has proven effective in post–"Arab Spring" Libya and Tunisia, where analysts have noted that *daʿwa* activities provided leverage for groups such as Ansar al-Sharia to gain wide popularity and support.[50] Salafi-Jihadists are hardly alone in using soft power to expand their influence, as recent research has shown with transnational religious actors such as U.S. evangelicals and Shiʿa networks in Iran and Iraq.[51]

Yet, while both Jabhat al-Nusra and the Islamic State used *daʿwa* as a soft power mechanism, they did so in different ways. This is clearly evident in their conduct in the Syrian civil war. Al-Nusra's political approach, which some observers have termed "jihadist lite,"[52] was gradual and sought to integrate the organization within the local communities rather than confront or coerce them. By preaching Islam with kind words and providing aid and public services, the organization sought to position itself as the defender of the Syrian people against the regime in order to gain popular support. An extensive report on al-Nusra by the Institute for the Study of War confirms this point.

> This approach is a direct outgrowth of its [al-Nusra's] adherence to Zawahiri's methodology for a *daʿwa*-based jihad, in which gaining the acceptance of local populations is prioritized over taking direct control by jihadist forces. An important indicator of the effectiveness of Jabhat al-Nusra's strategy is that Shariah courts with Jabhat al-Nusra participation generally enjoy local acceptance.[53]

Thus, on the basis of Zawahiri's emphasis on popular support for the jihadist movement, *daʿwa* served Jabhat al-Nusra by expanding its influence in Syria and paving the way for jihadist governance.

In the case of the Islamic State, the use of *daʿwa* was primarily motivated by the desire for religious legitimacy to back its claims for Islamic statehood and the caliphate. The organization presented itself as the only home for (Sunni) Muslims worldwide and as the sole legitimate political structure of true Islam. Its first spokesman, Abu Muhammad al-Adnani, killed in late August 2016, claimed in one of his speeches, "There is no place on the face of the earth where the Sharia of Allah is implemented and the rule is entirely for Allah except for the lands of the Islamic State."[54] According to this logic, Islamic institutions, most notably Islamic courts and Islamic morality police (*hisba*), were set up in ISIS territories. In its capital of Raqqa, in Mosul, and elsewhere, patrol cars regularly inspected the marketplaces and enforced the rules of propriety and modesty, while offenders and "traitors" were severely punished with execution or amputation.[55]

The public practice of *daʿwa* was thus part of the overall effort to demonstrate the Islamic character of ISIS's governance. This point is illustrated in one of its more popular *anashid*, which stresses the organization's adherence to the sharia. The song states that in the territories under the organization's control, "There are callers (*duʿa*) for pure guidance, defiant. By the law of God they have arisen and triumphed."[56] According to this narrative, beyond the borders of the Islamic State, Islam is being oppressed and the callers to the religion are persecuted, but the Islamic State implements true Islam and allows the practice of *daʿwa*. In this way, *daʿwa* events were marketed as part of the piety of the Islamic State and provided as further proof of its religious legitimacy.

CONCLUSION

By its very nature, Salafi-Jihadi discourse has prioritized jihad as the superior strategy in the struggle against the near and far enemies facing the *umma*. Accordingly, *daʿwa* is associated with the much-criticized Muslim Brotherhood and its nonviolent political strategies. In recent years, however, there has been a palpable shift in the importance jihadists have attached to the preaching of Islam. This is largely a result of the new political opportunities presenting themselves in the Middle East and North Africa in the wake of the events of the Arab Spring. Although the importance of popular support to jihadist activity and its long-term political projects was not entirely absent before that (as demonstrated in the writings of Ayman al-Zawahiri), the regional upheavals gave Islamist and jihadist movements the operational freedom to openly preach their message and call others to their cause. Consequently, as this chapter has shown, even the al-Qaeda affiliate Jabhat al-Nusra and, to a lesser extent, the ultraradical ISIS engaged in the practice of *daʿwa*.

The rising importance of *daʿwa* for Salafi-Jihadists points to their growing recognition of the limitations of exclusive reliance on violence in advancing their goals and the need for incorporating the community within their political projects. Meir Hatina has argued that al-Qaeda's ongoing polemics against the Muslim Brotherhood reflect the inferiority of jihadism vis-à-vis the communal, *daʿwa*-based approach of the Brotherhood.[57] The embrace of *daʿwa*, in one way or another, by the most prominent contemporary Salafi-Jihadi organizations demonstrates its enduring power to create popular support. While much has been said of the rise of jihadism since the onset of the Arab Uprisings of 2011, a process that has sometimes been described as a shift "from Arab Spring to Islamic Winter," this chapter has shown that one of the long-term effects of these momentous events was the adoption of *daʿwa* among some of even the most militant Salafi-Jihadists.

A more accurate description of this particular effect of the "Arab Spring" on Islamist politics would therefore be the regional rise of both jihad and *daʿwa* as complementary strategies within the Salafi-Jihadi trend. This development somewhat blurs the existing typologies of Islamist movements that pose as communal/political movements, such as the Muslim Brotherhood and its satellites, versus militant/radical organizations such as al-Qaeda and ISIS. While by no means erasing the differences between these two forms of Islamism, the recent adoption of nonviolent *da'wa* by Salafi-Jihadists alongside their sanctification of armed jihad seems to remind us that in Islam, preaching the faith and struggling in the path of God have never been mutually exclusive.

Notes

INTRODUCTION

1. Yasin Dutton, "Conversion to Islam: The Quranic Paradigm," in *Religious Conversion: Contemporary Practices and Controversies,* eds. Christopher Lamb and M. Darol Bryant (London: Cassell, 1999), 151–65.
2. Egdunas Racius, "The Multiple Nature of the Islamic Daʿwa" (PhD diss., University of Helsinki, 2004).
3. See Moshe Sharon, *Revolt: The Social and Military Aspects of the ʿAbbasid Revolution* (Jerusalem: Hebrew University, 1990); Heinz Halm, *The Fatimids and Their Traditions of Learning* (London: I. B. Tauris, 1997).
4. See especially, Richard Eaton, "Approaches to the Study of Conversion to Islam in India," in *Approaches to Islam in Religious Studies,* ed. Richard C. Martin (Tucson: University of Arizona Press, 1985), 107–23.
5. Linda Gale Jones, *The Power of Oratory in the Medieval Muslim World* (Cambridge, UK: Cambridge University Press, 2012); Jonathan P. Berkey, *Popular Preaching and Religious Authority in the Medieval Islamic Near East* (Seattle: University of Washington Press, 2001).
6. David Commins, *The Wahhabi Mission and Saudi Arabia* (London: I. B. Tauris, 2006).
7. Itzchak Weismann, "Modernity from Within: Islamic Fundamentalism and Sufism," *Der Islam* 86 (2011):142–70.
8. For an overview, see Peter Mandaville, *Global Political Islam* (London: Routledge, 2007).
9. See the classic studies: Thomas W. Arnold, *The Preaching of Islam: A History of the Propagation of the Muslim Faith*, 2nd ed. (London: Constable, 1913); Nehemia Levtzion, ed., *Conversion to Islam* (New York: Holmes and Meier, 1979).
10. See, e.g., The Islamic Foundation, ed., *Christian Mission and Islamic Daʿwa: Proceedings of the Chambesy Dialogue Consultation* (Leicester: The Islamic Foundation, 1982).

11. Racius, *Multiple Nature.*
12. Henning Wrogemann, *Missionarischer Islam und gesellschaftlicher Dialog* (Frankfurt a. M.: Lembeck, 2006).
13. Larry Poston, *Islamic Daʿwah in the West: Muslim Missionary Activity and the Dynamics of Conversion to Islam* (New York and Oxford: Oxford University Press, 1992).
14. Nina Wiedl, *Daʿwa: Der Ruf zum Islam in Europa* (Berlin: Hans Schiler, 2008).
15. Matthew J. Kuiper, *Da'wa and Other Religions: Indian Muslims and the Modern Resurgence of Global Islamic Activism* (London: Routledge, 2018).
16. Dale F. Eickelman and James Piscatori, *Muslim Politics* (Princeton: Princeton University Press, 1996), 35–36.
17. Carrie R. Wickham, *Mobilizing Islam: Religion, Activism, and Political Change in Egypt* (New York: Columbia University Press, 2002).
18. Richard Gauvain, *Salafi Ritual Purity: In the Presence of God* (New York: Routledge, 2012).
19. Janine A. Clark, *Islam, Charity, and Activism: Middle-Class Networks and Social Welfare in Egypt, Jordan, and Yemen* (Bloomington: Indiana University Press, 2004).
20. Saba Mahmood, *Politics of Piety: The Islamic Revival and the Feminist Subject* (Princeton: Princeton University Press, 2005).
21. Charles Hirschkind, *The Ethical Soundscape: Cassette Sermons and Islamic Counterpublics* (New York: Columbia University Press, 2006).
22. Chanfi Ahmed, *Preaching Islamic Revival in East Africa* (Newcastle upon Tyne: Cambridge Scholars Publishing, 2018).
23. Florian Harms, *Cyberdaʿwah: Islamische Mission im Internet: Voraussetzungen, Analyse und Vergleich von daʿwa-Sites im World Wide Web* (Aachen: Shaker, 2007); Johanna Pink and Mathias Bruckner, eds., *Muslimische Internetnutzung in globaler und lokaler Perspektive* (Würzburg: Ergon, 2009).
24. Reinhard Schulze, *Islamischer Internationalismus im 20. Jahrhundert: Untersuchungen zur Geschichte der Islamischen Weltliga* (Leiden: Brill, 1990).
25. This holds true both for the classic study of Richard P. Mitchell, *The Society of the Muslim Brothers* (New York: Oxford University Press, 1969), and the most comprehensive recent study by Carrie R. Wickham, *The Muslim Brotherhood: Evolution of an Islamist Movement* (Princeton: Princeton University Press, 2013). But see Itzchak Weismann, "Framing a Modern Umma: The Muslim Brothers' Evolving Project of Daʿwa," *Sociology of Islam* 3, 3–4 (2015):146–69. For the European scene, see Lorenzo Vidino, *The New Muslim Brotherhood in the West* (New York: Columbia University Press, 2010).
26. Seyyed Vali Reza Nasr, *The Vanguard of the Islamic Revolution: The Jamaʿat-i Islami of Pakistan* (Berkeley: University of California Press, 1994); Irfan Ahmad, *Islamism and Democracy in India: The Transformation*

of Jamaat-e-Islami (Princeton: Princeton University Press, 2009). But see in this case, Christian W. Troll, "Two Conceptions of Daʿwa in India: Jamaʿat-i Islami and Tablighi Jamaʿat," *Archives de Sciences Sociales des Religions* 87 (1994):115–33.

27. Muhammad Khalid Masud, ed., *Travellers in Faith: Studies of the Tablighi Jamaʿat as a Transnational Islamic Movement for Faith Renewal* (Leiden: Brill, 2000); Yoginder Sikand, *The Origins and Development of the Tablighi-Jamaʿat (1920–2000): A Cross-Country Comparative Study* (New Delhi: Orient Longman, 2002).
28. Thomas K. Gugler, *Mission Medina: Daʿwat-e Islami und Tabligi Gamaʿat* (Würzburg: Ergon, 2011). See also his contribution to this volume.
29. Husam Tammam, "Yusuf al-Qaradawi and the Muslim Brothers: The Nature of a Special Relationship," in *The Global Mufti: The Phenomenon of Yusuf al-Qaradawi,* eds. Bettina Gräf and Jakob Skovgaard-Petersen (New York: Columbia University Press, 2009), 55–83; Mohammed Moussa, *Politics of the Islamic Tradition: The Thought of Muhammad al-Ghazali* (Abingdon: Routledge, 2016).
30. Seyyed Vali Reza Nasr, *Mawdudi and the Making of Islamic Revivalism* (New York: Oxford University Press, 1996); Jan-Peter Hartung, *A System of Life: Mawdudi and the Ideologisation of Islam* (London: Hurst, 2013).
31. Jaquelene Brinton, "Preaching and the Epistemological Reinforcement of *Ulama* Authority: The Sermons of Muhammad Mitwalli Shaʿrawi," *Intellectual Discourse* 19, no. 1 (2011):97–121; Gilles Kepel, *The Prophet and Pharaoh: Muslim Extremism in Egypt* (London: Al Saqi Books, 1985), ch. 6; Aaron Rock-Singer, "Amr Khaled: From Daʿwa to Political and Religious Leadership," *British Journal of Middle Eastern Studies* 37, no. 1 (2010):15–37, and his chapter in this volume; See also, Patrick D. Gaffney, *The Prophet's Pulpit: Islamic Preaching in Contemporary Egypt* (Berkeley: University of California Press, 1994); and Shosh Ben-Ari, "The Rating of Allah: Renaissance of Preaching in the Age of Globalization," in *Islamic Myths and Memories: Mediators of Globalization,* eds. Itzchak Weismann, Mark Sedgwick, and Ulrika Mårtensson (Farnham Surrey: Ashgate, 2014), 185–207.
32. Hanspeter Mattes, *Die innere und äußere Mission Libyens* (Mainz: Grünwald, 1986); Wilfried Buchta, *Die iranische Schia und die islamische Einheit 1979–1996* (Hamburg: Orient Institut, 1997).
33. Jamal Malik, *Colonization of Islam: Dissolution of Traditional Institutions in Pakistan* (New Delhi: Manohar, 1996); Jamal Malik, "Islamic Mission and Call: The Case of the International Islamic University, Islamabad," *Islam and Christian-Muslim Relations* 9, no. 1 (1998):31–45; Seyyed Vali Reza Nasr, *Islamic Leviathan: Islam and the Making of State Power* (New York: Oxford University Press, 2001); and Farish Noor, *The Malaysian Islamic Party, 1951–2013: Islamism in a Mottled Nation* (Amsterdam: Amsterdam University Press, 2014).

CHAPTER 1

1. For *da'wa* focused on non-Muslims versus *da'wa* focused on the *umma*, see Egdunas Racius, *The Multiple Nature of the Islamic Da'wa* (PhD diss., University of Helsinki, 2004), parts 3 and 4.
2. Dale F. Eickelman and James Piscatori, *Muslim Politics* (Princeton: Princeton University Press, 1996), 35–36; Saba Mahmood, *Politics of Piety: The Islamic Revival and the Feminist Subject* (Princeton: Princeton University Press, 2005), 57–64.
3. Charles Hirschkind, *The Ethical Soundscape: Cassette Sermons and Islamic Counterpublics* (New York: Columbia University Press, 2006), 108–15.
4. Jamal al-Din al-Afghani and Muhammad Abduh mention *da'wa* in their seminal journal when referring to the Mahdiyya movement in the Sudan. See their *al-'Urwa al-Wuthqa* (Beirut: Dar al-Kitab al-'Arabi, 1980), 219–20; Abd al-Rahman al-Kawakibi likewise refers to it once in his *Umm al-Qura*, in the sense of propagating Islam among Westerners. See his *Umm al-Qura* (Beirut: Dar al-Ra'id al-'Arabi, 1982), 106.
5. Muhammad Rashid Rida, *Tafsir al-Qur'an al-Shahir bi-Tafsir al-Manar* (Cairo: al-Manar, 1911), 4, 26ff.
6. Albert H. Hourani, *Arabic Thought in the Liberal Age, 1798–1939* (Oxford: Oxford University Press, 1962), 227.
7. Richard P. Mitchell, *The Society of the Muslim Brothers* (New York: Oxford University Press, 1969), 5; Brynjar Lia, *The Society of the Muslim Brothers in Egypt: The Rise of an Islamic Mass Movement, 1928–1942* (Reading, UK: Ithaca Press, 1998), 29.
8. Henri Lauzière, *The Making of Salafism: Islamic Reform in the Twentieth Century* (New York: Columbia University Press, 2015), 70–84.
9. Itzchak Weismann, "Framing a Modern Umma: The Muslim Brothers' Evolving Project of Da'wa," *Sociology of Islam* 3, 3–4 (2015):146–69.
10. Hasan al-Banna, *Mudhakkirat al-Da'wa wa'l-Da'iya* (Cairo: Dar al-Nashr wa'l-Tawzi' al-Islamiyya, 1986).
11. Hasan al-Banna, "Da'watuna," *Majmu'at Rasa'il* (Cairo: al-Maktaba al-Tawfiqiyya, n.d.), 9–31.
12. Ibid., "Risalat al-Mu'tamar al-Khamis," 184.
13. Ibid., "Ila ayyi Shay Adu' al-Nas," 33–62.
14. See Israel Gershoni and James P. Jankowski, *Redefining the Egyptian Nation, 1930–1945* (Cambridge: Cambridge University Press, 1995).
15. Hasan al-Banna, "Da'watuna fi Tawr Jadid," *Majmu'at Rasa'il* (Cairo: al-Maktaba al-Tawfiqiyya, n.d.), 125–45.
16. Alusi, for instance, mentions *da'wa* only occasionally in his *History of Najd*, usually in verb form rather than as a noun. In an imaginary dispute between two scholars, an Iraqi and a Najdi (read Wahhabi), he refers to the concept of *tawhid* as propagated (*da'a*) by Ibn Abd al-Wahhab, while in the shaykh's biography he mentions his call and the indignation of the people

of Arabia. See Mahmud Shukri al-Alusi, *Ta'rikh najd* (Cairo: Maktabat Madbuli, n.d.), 86, 108.

17. Lauzière, *The Making of Salafism*, 88–89.
18. Muhammad Hamid al-Fiqi, *Athar al-Da'wa al-Wahhabiyya fi'l-Islah al-Dini wa'l-'Umrani fi Jazirat al-'Arab wa-Ghayriha* (n.p., AH 1354 [1935]).
19. Ahmad Muhammad al-Tahir, *Jama'at Ansar al-Sunna al-Muhammadiyya: Nash'atuha, Ahdafuha, Manhajuha, Juhuduha* (Cairo: Jama'at Ansar al-Sunna al-Muhammadiyya—al-Markaz al-'Amm, 2006), 61–72.
20. Ibid., 1–2.
21. Ibid., 15.
22. Ibid., 17–19.
23. Ibid., 24, 31.
24. Gilles Kepel, *The Prophet and Pharaoh: Muslim Extremism in Egypt* (London: Al Saqi Books, 1985), 52–59.
25. On these institutions see, Michael Farquhar, "Saudi Petrodollars, Spiritual Capital, and the Islamic University of Medina: A Wahhabi Missionary Project in Transnational Perspective," *International Journal of Middle East Studies* 47, no. 4 (2015):701–21; Reinhard Schulze, *Islamischer Internationalismus im 20. Jahrhundert: Untersuchungen zur Geschichte der Islamischen Weltliga* (Leiden: Brill, 1990).
26. On Ghazali, see Mohammed Moussa, *Politics of the Islamic Tradition: The Thought of Muhammad al-Ghazali* (Abingdon: Routledge, 2016), 13–21.
27. On Qaradawi, see Bettina Gräf and Jakob Skovgaard-Petersen, eds., *Global Mufti: The Phenomenon of Yusuf al-Qaradawi* (New York: Columbia University Press, 2009).
28. Muhammad al-Ghazali, *Fi mawqib al-da'wa*, 2nd ed. (Cairo: Dar al-Kitab al-'Arabi, 1957).
29. Ibid., 3–4.
30. Muhammad al-Ghazali, *Ma'a Allah: Dirasat fi'l-Da'wa wa'l-Du'a* (Cairo: Dar al-Kutub al-Haditha, 1965).
31. The initiative to teach *da'wa* as an academic field at al-Azhar probably came from Mahmud Shaltut, its reformist rector from 1958 to 1963, who as early as 1933 had published a book on the subject, basically arguing that spreading Islam by force was forbidden. See Mahmud Shaltut, *al Da'wa al-Muhamadiyya wa'l-Qital fi'l-Islam* (Cairo: al-Matba'a al-Salafiyya, 1933).
32. Ghazali *Ma'a Allah*, 6–8.
33. Ibid., 12–13. The term "signposts" may indicate Ghazali's criticism of Qutb's turn to jihad in his famous manifesto that bears that name.
34. Ibid., 18, 28–34.
35. T. W. Arnold, *The Preaching of Islam: A History of the Propagation of the Muslim Faith*, 2nd ed. (London: Constable, 1913).
36. Ghazali, *Ma'a Allah*, 87–88.

37. Ibid., 149–69, 233–72, 341ff. Other systematic expositions of *da'wa* by ulama associated with the Muslim Brotherhood include the Iraqi Abd al-Karim Zaydan, *Usul al-Da'wa* (n.p., 1976), and the Syrian Muhammad Abu al-Fath al-Bayanuni, *al-Madkhal ila 'Ilm al-Da'wa: Dirasa Minhajiyya Shamila li-Ta'rikh al-Da'wa wa-Usuliha wa-Manahijiha wa-Asalibiha wa-Wasa'iliha wa-Mushkilatiha fi Daw' al-Naql wa'l-'Aql* (Beirut: Mu'assasat al-Risala, 1991).
38. Yusuf al-Qaradawi, *Thaqafat al-Da'iya*, 2nd ed. (Beirut: Mua'ssasat al-Risala, 1979). The seminal work in this genre is al-Bahi al-Khuli, *Tadhkirat al-Du'a* (Cairo: Dar al-Kitab al-'Arabi, 1952). Khuli, a close associate of Banna, was appointed to teach *da'wa* at al-Azhar after 1954, and Qaradawi was among his students. Like Banna, however, he graduated from the teachers' seminary in Cairo (Dar al-'Ulum) and therefore was not an *'alim*. See Yusuf al-Qaradawi, "Athar Ustadhuna al-Bahi al-Khuli," accessed 27 May 2016, www.qaradawi.net/new/Articles-3427.
39. Qaradawi, *Thaqafat al-Da'iya*, 5–9.
40. Ibid., 21, 57, 73, 97. On the Muslim Brothers' concept of *nizam Islami*, see Mitchell, *Society of the Muslim Brothers*, 234–36.
41. Qaradawi, *Thaqafat al-Da'iya*, 106–7, 123–27, 130–37, 140–46.
42. See Farquhar, "The Islamic University of Medina."
43. See Schulze, *Islamischer Internationalismus*, 181ff.
44. I am indebted to Prof. Reinhard Schulze for both of these references.
45. Kepel, *The Prophet and Pharaoh*, 103–24.
46. Hasan Isma'il al-Hudaybi, *Du'a: La Quda: Abhath fi'l-'Aqida al-Islamiyya wa-Manhaj al-Da'wa ila Allah* (Cairo: Dar al-Tiba'a wa'l-Nashr al-Islamiyya, 1977).
47. Weismann, "Framing a Modern Umma," 156–60. See also Carrie Rosefsky Wickham, *Mobilizing Islam: Religion, Activism, and Political Change in Egypt* (New York: Columbia University Press, 2002), 139–43.
48. Mustafa Mashhur, "Khamsun 'Aman 'ala al-Tariq," in *Min Fiqh al-Da'wa,* ed. Mustafa Mashhur (Cairo: Dar al-Tawzi' wa'l-Nashr al-Islamiyya, 1995), 1:93–94.
49. Ibid., 12.
50. Ibid., 99–117.
51. Fathi Yakan, *Mushkilat al-Da'wa wa'l-Da'iya* (Beirut: Mu'assast al-Risala, 1987), 18.
52. Fathi Yakan, *Kayfa Nadu' ila al-Islam,* 3rd ed. (Beirut: Mu'assast al-Risala, 1977), 21–26.
53. Sa'id Hawwa, *Ijaza Tukhassisu al-Du'a* (Cairo: Dar al-Salam, 1987).
54. 'Abd al-'Aziz Ibn Baz et al., *Fatawa 'Ulama al-Balad al-Haram* (Cairo: Dar Ibn Haytham, 2004), 522–31.
55. Stéphane Lacroix, *The Islamic Awakening: The Politics of Religious Dissent in Contemporary Saudi Arabia* (Cambridge, MA: Harvard University Press, 2011), 53–56.

56. Muhammad Qutb, *Kayfa Naduʿ al-Nas?* (Cairo: Dar al-Shuruq, 2001).
57. Ibid., 6–8. On the doctrinal debate over *irja'*, which accepts as Muslim whoever professes the faith without regard to his deeds, see Daniel Lav, *Radical Islam and the Revival of Medieval Theology* (Cambridge: Cambridge University Press, 2012).
58. Apparently in critical reference to al-Qaeda, which purports to embody the *solid base* of Islam.
59. Qutb, ibid., 13–16, 21–24.
60. Asaf Maliach, "Abdullah Azzam, al-Qaeda, and Hamas: Concepts of Jihad and Istishhad," *Military and Strategic Affairs* 2, no. 2 (2010):79–80.
61. Joas Wagemakers, *A Quietist Jihadi: The Ideology and Influence of Abu Muhammad al-Maqdisi* (Cambridge: Cambridge University Press, 2012), 29–50.
62. Abdallah ʿAzzam, *Kalimat min Khat al-Nar al-Awwal* (n.p, n.d.).
63. The full title of the book is Abu Muhammad al-Maqdisi, *Millat Ibrahim wa-Daʿwat al-Anbiya' wa'l-Mursalin wa-Asalib al-Tugha fi Tamiyʿha wa-Sarf al-Duʿa ʿAnha* (n.p, n.d.).
64. His main reference is Quran 60:4, in which Abraham says, "We disavow you and what you worship. Between us and you there is eternal enmity and hatred until you believe in God alone."
65. See, Lutfi Wa'il, *Zahirat al-Duʿa al-Judud: Tahlil Ijtimaʿi: al-Daʿwa, al-Tharwa, al-Shuhra* (Cairo: al-Hay'a al-Misriyya al-ʿAmma li'l-Kitab, 2005).
66. ʿAsim al-Ghazzi, *Hiwarati maʿa ʿAmru Khalid* (Cairo: Arij li'l-Nashr, 2004), 1, 13.
67. On the concept of objectification, see Eickelman and Piscatori, *Muslim Politics*, 37–45.
68. See Jaquelene Brinton, "Preaching and the Epistemological Reinforcement of *Ulama* Authority: The Sermons of Muhammad Mitwalli Shaʿrawi," *Intellectual Discourse* 19, no. 1 (2011):97–121.
69. Hirschkind, *The Ethical Soundscape*, 153–56, traced this kind of preaching to Sayyid Qutb's *al-Taswir al-Fanni fi'l-Qur'an*, written in the 1940s in his preradical phase. Hirschkind translates it as "the cinematographic imagination." On Amr Khaled, see Aaron Rock-Singer, "Amr Khaled: From Daʿwa to Political and Religious Leadership," *British Journal of Middle Eastern Studies* 37, no. 1 (2010):15–37, and his chapter in this volume.
70. Muhammad Mutawali al-Shaʿrawi, *Usul al-Daʿwa* (Cairo: al-Matbaʿa al-Tawfiqiyya, n.d.).
71. Ibid., 157–68.
72. Ibid., 172–74.
73. Ibid., 181–85.
74. Amr Khaled, "The Episodes of the Series Daʿwa li-Taʿayush," accessed 11 December 2016, http://www.assabile.com/amr-khaled-141/series/daawa-litaayush-116.

75. Faruqi's European counterpart as pioneer of Western *daʿwa*, Khurram Murad, belonged to Jamaʿat-i Islami and served as director of the Islamic Foundation in Leicester from 1978 to 1986. See his *Daʿwa among Non-Muslims in the West* (Leicester: The Islamic Foundation, 1986). For an analysis see, Larry Poston, *Islamic Daʿwah in the West: Muslim Missionary Activity and the Dynamics of Conversion to Islam* (New York and Oxford: Oxford University Press, 1992), 81–90; Nina Wiedl, *Daʿwa: Der Ruf zum Islam in Europa* (Berlin: Hans Schiler, 2008), 110–33.
76. John L. Esposito and John O. Voll, *Makers of Contemporary Islam* (New York: Oxford University Press, 2001), 23–24.
77. Wiedl, *Daʿwa*, 173–81; Frank Peter, "Tariq Ramadan," in *Islamic Movements in Europe: Public Religion and Islamophobia in the Modern World*, eds. Frank Peter and Rafael Ortega (London: I. B. Tauris, 2014), 274–77.
78. Ismail Raji al-Faruqi, *Islam and Other Faiths*, ed. Ataullah Siddiqui (Leicester: The Islamic Foundation, 1998), part 3.
79. Ibid., 305–14.
80. Ibid., 338–43.
81. Tariq Ramadan, "Daʿwa in the West," accessed 28 March 2014, http://www.tariqramadan.com/spip.php?article72.
82. Tariq Ramadan, *Western Muslims and the Future of Islam* (New York: Oxford University Press, 2004), 72–75.
83. Jamal al-Banna, *Istratijiyyat al-Daʿwa al-Islamiyya fi'l-Qarn 21* [sic] *Kama Tuqaddimuha Daʿwa al-Ihya' al-Islami* (Cairo: Dar al-Fikr al-Islami, 2000).
84. Ibid., 5–8.
85. Ibid., 15–18.
86. Ibid., 23.

CHAPTER 2

1. Hilal Ahmed, "Muzaffarnagar 2013: Meanings of Violence," *Economic and Political Weekly* 48, no. 40 (2013):10–13.
2. The Indian government banned this organization on two occasions, in 1948 and in 1993, though the Supreme Court revoked both decisions. See Irfan Ahmad, *Islamism and Democracy in India: The Transformation of Jamaat-e-Islami* (Princeton: Princeton University Press, 2009, and New Delhi: Permanent Black, 2010).
3. Naik runs a well-funded NGO, the Islamic Research Foundation (IRF), which publishes his books, distributes CDs of his lectures, and manages his website.
4. Wahiduddin Khan's critique of Mawdudi and Jamaʿat-e Islami's political interpretation of *din* (religion) underlines the contested aspects of postcolonial *daʿwa* discourse. See Maulana Wahiduddin Khan, *The Political Interpretation of Islam* (Noida: Goodword Books, 2015).

5. Farzana Shaikh, *Community and Consensus in Islam: Muslim Representation in Colonial India, 1860–1947* (Cambridge: Cambridge University Press, 1991), 49–53.
6. Ziya-ul-Hasan Faruqi, *The Deoband School and the Demand for Pakistan* (Calcutta: Asia Publishing House, 1963), 113–19.
7. Muhammad Qasim Zaman, *The Ulama in Contemporary Islam: Custodian of Change* (Princeton and Oxford: Princeton University Press, 2007), ch. 1. See also Barbara Metcalf, *Husain Ahmad Madani: The Jihad for Islam and India's Freedom* (Oxford: Oneworld Publications, 2008).
8. Christian W. Troll, "Two Conceptions of Da'wa in India: Jama'at-i Islami and Tablighi Jama'at," *Archives de sciences sociales des religions* 87 (1994):115–33.
9. Laura Dudley Jenkins, "Legal Limits on Religious Conversion in India," *Law and Contemporary Problems, Galanter-Influenced Scholars* 71, no. 2 (2008):109–27.
10. Other minority religions (Buddhism, Jainism, and Sikhism) are constitutionally recognized as offshoots of the Hindu religion.
11. Rev. Stanislaus v. State of Madhya Pradesh and Ors, on 17 January 1977, AIR 908, 1977 SCR (2) 611.
12. Criticizing this judgment, Faizan Mustafa argues that the "right to propagate one's idea is inherent in the concept of freedom of speech and expression. Hence propagation should also be seen as an expression of freedom of speech." See *Freedom of Religion in India: Contemporary Challenges*, 4th AAE Memorial Lecture full text Freedom of Religion in India—Contemporary Challenges, accessed 19 November 2019, https://csss-isla.com/wp-content/uploads/2019/08/Prof.-Faizan-Mustafas-4th-AAE-Memorial-Lecture.pdf.
13. The classification of India's past into the three exclusive phases of ancient, medieval, and modern was not entirely understood in terms of a universally accepted categorization of time. Instead, these phases were always separated to discern the dominance of a particular religion in different moments of Indian history. Thus, Hindu-ancient, Muslim-medieval, and Christian-modern are established as legitimate categories. For an evolution of the theories of conversion to Islam, see Richard M. Eaton, "Approaches to the Study of Conversion to Islam in India," in *Approaches to Islam in Religious Studies*, ed. Richard C. Martin (Tucson: University of Arizona Press, 1985), 107–23.
14. *Report of the National Commission for Religious and Linguistic Minorities* (Delhi: Ministry of Minority Affairs, 2007), 139.
15. The Constitutional validity of this Order has already been challenged and the Supreme Court will have to decide this issue.
16. Still, this religion-based restriction is only for the SC category. Muslim and Christian communities can be included in the ST and OBC (Other Backward Classes) lists.

17. Except for the Meenakshipuram case (where 200 Hindu lower-caste families embraced Islam publicly in January 1981) no other incident of conversion to Islam has come up in the public sphere, yet stories of forced conversion by Muslim rulers dominate the political discourse. For an ethnographic analysis of this case, see Mohammed Kalam, "Religious Conversions in Tamil Nadu: Can These be Viewed as Protest Movements?" *Indian Anthropologist* 20 (1990):39–48.
18. *Report of the National Commission for Religious and Linguistic Minorities*, 169.
19. See T. N. Madan, "Religion of India: Plurality and Pluralism," in *Religious Pluralism in South Asia and Europe,* eds. Jamal Malik and Helmut Reifeld (New Delhi: Oxford University Press, 2004), 43–73; see also the chapter by Malik in this volume.
20. Abu'l-A'la Mawdudi, *A Historic Address at Madras*, trans. Mohammad Siddiqui Naveed (Delhi: Markazi Maktaba Islami, 2009), 32.
21. Muhammad Yusuf led the Tablighi Jamaʿat in the crucial years of the postpartition period, especially in the 1960s, when a new phase of Muslim politics began. See Hilal Ahmed, *Muslim Political Discourse in Postcolonial India: Monuments, Memory, Contestation* (Delhi: Routledge, 2014), 126–39.
22. Mufti Muhammad Rawshan Shah Kasimi, *Malfuzat wa-Iqtibasat Mawlana Muhammad Yusuf* (Delhi: Rashid Publications, n.d.), 19.
23. Ibid., 20.
24. Barbara Metcalf, "Living Hadith in Tablighi Jamaʿat," *Journal of Asian Studies* 52 (1993):603–5.
25. Kasimi, *Malfuzat wa-Iqtibasat*, 46.
26. See Muhammad Khalid Masud, "Ideology and Legitimacy," in *Travellers in Faith: Studies of the Tablighi Jamaʿat as a Transnational Islamic Movement for Faith Renewal,* ed. Muhammad Khalid Masud (Leiden: Brill, 2000), 79–120. For a critical discussion of the principles of the Tablighi Jamaʿat, see Yoginder Sikand, *The Origin and Development of the Tablighi Jamaʿat (1920–2000): A Cross-Country Comparative Study* (Delhi: Oriental Longman, 2002), 65–75.
27. In this regard, Tablighi Jamaʿat's initial work in the Mewat region south of Delhi is a good example. The Jamaʿat focused on the reconversion of Muslims into what it called "true Islam" (in reaction to the Hindu *shuddhi* [purification] movement) and did not campaign for the direct conversion of non-Muslims. See Yoginder Sikand, "Arya Shuddhi and Muslim Tabligh: Muslim Reactions to Arya Samaj Proselytization (1923–30)," in *Religious Conversion in India: Modes, Motivations, Meanings,* eds. Rowena Robinson and Sathianathan Clarke (Delhi: Oxford University Press, 2003), 98–117.
28. See Ahmad, *Islamism and Democracy*, 207–9; also, Jamal Malik, *Islam in South Asia: A Short History* (Leiden: Brill, 2008), 403–35.

29. Abul Lais Islahi Nadwi, *Bharat ka Nawnirman awr Hum* (Rebuilding India and Our Role), trans. Afzal Husain (Delhi: Markazi Maktaba Islami, 2014), 31–32.
30. Abu'l-A'la Mawdudi, "Foreword," *Quran Majid* (New Delhi: Maktaba al-Hasanat, 1970), ii.
31. Writ Petition 227 of 1985, accessed 19 November 2019, https://archive.org/stream/CalcuttaQuranPetitionSitaramGoel/Calcutta%20Quran%20Petition%20%28Sitaram%20Goel%29_djvu.txt.
32. Arshad Madani and Muhammad Sulaiman, *Preface to the Quran Sharif: Anuwad and Vyakhya* (Delhi: Jami'at-e Ulama-e Hind, 1992), ii–v.
33. JIH's emphasis on Hindi should be seen in the political context in which Urdu turns out to be a minority (read: Muslim) language. See Paul Brass, *Language, Religion and Politics in North India* (Cambridge: Cambridge University Press 1974), 182–217.
34. Maulana Wahiduddin Khan, "Conversion: An Intellectual Transformation," *Alrisala*, accessed 19 November 2019, https://ia800806.us.archive.org/12/items/mwk-eng-book/Convertion-An-Intellectual-Transformation.pdf.
35. Ibid. Maulana Wahiduddin Khan, *Three Stages of Da'wah Work*, accessed 2 March 2017, http://alquranmission.org/Da'wahDesc.aspx?id=4.
36. Ibid.
37. Ibid.
38. Syed Abul Hasan Ali Nadwi, *Inviting to the Way of Allah* (London: Ta-Ha Publishers and UK Islamic Society, 1992), 9.
39. Ibid., 17.
40. Syed Abul Hasan Ali Nadwi, *Live to Lead: A Call to Indian Muslims* (Lucknow: Islamic Research and Publications, 1980), 4.
41. Jan-Peter Hartung, *Viele Wege und ein Ziel. Leben und Wirken von Sayyid Abû l-Hasan 'Alî al-Hasanî Nadwî, 1914–1999* (Würzburg: Ergon, 2004). Jamal Malik, "Canons, Charismas and Identities in Modern Islam," in *Charisma and Canon: The Formation of Religious Identity in South Asia: Festschrift for Professor Heinrich von Stietencron*, eds. V. Dalmia et al. (Delhi: Oxford University Press, 2001), 381–85. Ahmed, *Muslim Political Discourse*, 259–62.
42. Syed Abul Hasan 'Ali Nadwi, *Karwan-e Zindagi* (Lucknow: Maktaba-e Islam, 2003), 154–62.
43. Syed Abul Hasan Ali Nadwi, *Muslims in India*, trans. Mohammad Asif Kidwai (Lucknow: Academy of Islamic Research and Publication, 1976), 5.
44. Syed Abul Hasan Ali Nadwi, *Hindustani Musalman Aik Drishti Main (An Overview of Indian Muslims)* (Lucknow: Academy of Islamic Research and Publication, 2014); Syed Abdul Hasan Ali Nadwi, *Try to Understand the Problems and Sentiments of Indian Muslims: A Pre-requisite for Peaceful Co-existence* (Lucknow: All India Solidarity Forum. n.d.).

45. Hilal Ahmed, "Naik, Zakir," *Oxford Islamic Studies Online*, accessed 10 November 2016, http://www.oxfordislamicstudies.com/article/opr/t343/e0183.
46. Ibid.
47. Ibid.
48. Ibid.
49. Ibid.
50. Zakir Naik, *The Foregone Conclusion: The Second Letter to India*, accessed 28 November 2016, http://indiatoday.intoday.in/story/zakir-naik-open-letter-to-india-facing-the-foregone-conclusion/1/819726.html.

CHAPTER 3

1. See Roel Meijer, ed., *Global Salafism: Islam's New Religious Movement* (London: Hurst, 2009), Introduction.
2. *Jihad al-talab* refers to a preemptive war against non-Muslim countries in order to expand the abode of Islam (*dar al-islam*).
3. Based on the hadith: "The best people are those of my generation [*qarni*], then those who come after them, then those who come after them." *Sahih al-Bukhari* (Damascus and Beirut: Dar ibn Kathir, 1423/2002), hadith no. 6429.
4. See, e.g., Abu Ameena Bilal Philips, *The Fundamentals of Tawheed*, 2nd ed. (Riyadh: International Islamic Publishing House, 2005), 17–42.
5. See also Itzchak Weismann "A Perverted Balance: Modern Salafism between Reform and Jihad," *Die Welt des Islams* 57 (2017), 33–66.
6. Quintan Wiktorowicz, "Anatomy of the Salafi Movement," *Studies in Conflict and Terrorism* 29 (2006):207–39. However, Salafis may also be divided on specific creedal issues, such as what constitutes faith, sin, and apostasy. See Joas Wagemakers, "Salafistische Strömungen und ihre Sicht auf al-wala' wa-l-bara' (Loyalität und Lossagung)," in *Salafismus: Auf der Suche nach dem wahren Islam,* eds. Behnam T. Said and Hazim Fouad (Freiburg im Breisgau: Herder, 2014), 56; and Justyna Nedza, "Salafismus—Überlegungen zur Schärfung einer Analysekategorie," ibid., 90–95.
7. The chapter is partly based on the results of a qualitative content analysis of over a hundred recorded lectures and Salafi publications on *da'wa* conducted between 2011 and 2013 during my PhD studies at Ben-Gurion University of the Negev.
8. *Manhaj* (method) refers to the Salafi method of approaching and understanding the scriptures, implementing their beliefs, practicing *da'wa*, and general interaction in daily life.
9. Paul E. Walker, "Da'wah: Qur'anic Concepts," in *The Oxford Encyclopedia of the Modern Islamic World,* ed. John Esposito (New York: Oxford University Press, 1995), 1:343–46.
10. 'Abd al-'Aziz ibn 'Abdallah ibn Baz, *Majmu' Fatawa wa-Maqalat Mutanawwi'a*, comp. Muhammad ibn Sa'd al-Shuway'ir (Riyadh: Dar al-Qasim,

1420/1999–2000), 2:341; Muhammad ibn Salih al-Uthaymin, *Zad al-Daʿiya ila Allah*, 3rd ed. (Riyadh: Dar al-Watan, 1413/1992–1993).

11. Ibn al-Uthaymin, "For Whom Is It Obligatory to Call to Allah?" in Muhammad bin ʿAbdul-ʿAziz al-Musnad, comp., *Fatawa Islamiyah: Islamic Verdicts* (Riyadh: Darussalam, 2002), 8:32; Ibn Baz, "Warn People against Deviants," in al-Musnad, *Fatawa Islamiyah: Islamic Verdicts*, 8:53; Abu Muhammad ʿAsim al-Maqdisi, *Millat Ibrahim (The Religion of Ibrahim) and the Calling of the Prophets and Messengers and the Methods of the Transgressing Rulers in Dissolving It and Turning the Callers Away from It*, 2nd ed. (Online: At-Tibyan, n.d.), accessed 16 November, 2019, www.kalamullah.com/Books/MillatIbraheem.pdf; Pierre Vogel, "Die Reaktionen der Mushrikun auf die Dawah zur Zeit des Propheten Muhammed Teil 1/2," accessed 16 November 2019, www.youtube.com/watch?v=Mfs5hzq09fg.
12. Ibn Baz, "The Character of the Caller to Islam," in al-Musnad, *Fatawa Islamiyah: Islamic Verdicts*, 8:46; Pierre Vogel, "Dawa-Kurs 1 (Einführung) Pierre Vogel," accessed 23 April 2015, www.youtube.com/watch?v=9wU26e1D5hc; ʿAbdul ʿAdhim Abu ʿAbdir-Rahman, "Die Milde in der Dawa," accessed 16 November 2019, http://www.salaf.de/verschiedenes/mp3/AA%20Diverse/Die%20Milde%20in%20der%20Dawa.MP3.
13. Paris Dawah, "L'importance de la dawah (partie 1)," accessed 16 November 2019, www.paris-dawah.fr/dawah-2/article-6- limportance-de-la-dawah/; al-ʿUthaymin, "The Many Islamic Groups and Their Differences," in al-Musnad, *Fatawa Islamiyah: Islamic Verdicts*, 8:52.
14. ʿAbd al-ʿAziz ibn ʿAbd Allah ibn Baz, *al-Daʿwa ila Allah wa-Akhlaq al-Duʿa* (Online: IslamHouse, 2006), accessed 16 November 2019, www.islamhouse.com/ar/books/1886 (all subsequent references to this work will be to the electronic version). Ibn Baz, *Majmuʿ Fatawa*, 2:341; al-ʿUthaymin, *Zad al-Daʿiya*; al-ʿUthaymin, "Taʿaddud al-Jamaʿat wa-Ikhtilafiha," in *Fatawa Islamiyya*, comp. Muhammad bin ʿAbd al-ʿAziz al-Musnad (Riyadh: Dar al-Watan, 1415/1994–95) 4:278.
15. Ibn Baz, "La Maniʿ min Tadhir al-Nas min Ahl al-Dalal," in al-Musnad, *Fatawa Islamiyya*, 4:279.
16. Ibn Baz, *al-Daʿwa*, 10.
17. Abdul Azeez ibn Baaz and Muhammad ibn Saalih al-Uthaymeen, *Muslim Minorities* (Hounslow: Message of Islam, 1998), 7.
18. Ibid., 14; ʿAbdul ʿAdhim Abu ʿAbdir-Rahman, "Dawaübung," accessed 3 July 2010, www.way-to-allah.com/unterrichte- predigten/abduladhim.html.
19. Ibn Baz, *al-Daʿwa*, 10.
20. Interview with *Daʿiyat* A, B, C, and E, 10 May 2009, al-Nur Mosque, Berlin. Interviewees requested anonymity.
21. ʿAbd al-ʿAziz ibn ʿAbd Allah ibn Baz, "Mudayaqa Duʿat al-Batil li-Ahl al-ʿIlm wa'l-Khayr," accessed 16 November 2019, https://binbaz.org.sa/fatwas/1075/.

22. Ibn Baz, *al-Daʿwa*, 8.
23. Habibiflo Dawah Produktion, "Abu Abdullah—Benefizveranstaltung vom 21.4.2013 Hamburg," accessed 28 October 2015, www.youtube.com/watch?v=uSbDObhb9Q4. Belkaid moved to Leicester, UK, some six years ago.
24. Ibn Baz, *al-Daʿwa*, 10.
25. Muhammad Nasir al-Din al-Albani, *Hadhihi Daʿwatuna* (Algeria: Dar al-Mahaja, 1434/2013), 20.
26. Albrecht Noth, *The Early Arabic Historical Tradition: A Source-Critical Study* (Princeton: Darwin Press, 1994), 146–67.
27. Walker, "Daʿwah," 345; Egdunas Racius, *The Multiple Nature of the Islamic Daʿwa*. PhD diss., University of Helsinki, 2004), 37.
28. Ibid., 150.
29. See Mohamed-Ali Adraoui, "Purist Salafism in France," *ISIM Review* 21 (2008):12; Sadek Hamid, "The Development of British Salafism," ibid., 10; Nina Wiedl, *The Making of a German Salafiyya: The Emergence, Development and Missionary Work of Salafi Movements in Germany* (Aarhus: CIR, 2012), 18.
30. Ibn Baz, *al-Daʿwa*; al-Islam Suʾal wa-Jawab, "Ayhuma ʿUla: Daʿwa Ghayr al-Muslimin liʾl-Islam am Daʿwa al-Muslimin Ghayr al-Multazimin liʾl-Iltizam?" accessed 16 November 2019, http://islamqa.info/ar/186813.

    Al-Islam Suʾal wa-Jawab (Islam Q & A) is a popular, multilingual fatwa website supervised by the Saudi-based Salafi scholar Muhammad Salih al-Munajjid (b. 1960), a former student of Ibn Baz and Ibn al-ʿUthaymin. The website was banned in Saudi Arabia because it issues independent fatwas.
31. Ibn Baz, *al-Daʿwa*, 2 (citing Quran 51:56 as textual evidence).
32. Vogel, "Dawa-Kurs 1."
33. Abu Muhammad ʿAsim al-Maqdisi, *Millat Ibrahim wa-Daʿwat al-Anbiyaʾ wa-l-Mursalin* (Online: Minbar al-Tawhid wa-l-Jihad, 1984) esp. 26, accessed 22 April 2015, www.tawhed.ws/r?i=iti4u3zp. All subsequent references to this work refer to the Arabic edition.
34. International Dawah, "Abu Ubayda und M. Islam über Kundgebungen, Teil 1, 2," accessed 14 September 2015, www.youtube.com/watch?v=ZfcYjeze6sA&feature=related.
35. Al-Sulami seems to diverge from al-Maqdisi, for whom disavowing polytheists does not imply prohibiting *daʿwa* toward non-Muslims "with wisdom and beautiful preaching." Muslims must disavow polytheists "in their hearts" but should not show open hostility toward those who are interested in Islam and who do not show enmity toward the religion of Allah (al-Maqdisi, *Millat Ibrahim*, 26).
36. al-Ghuraba Media, "Antwort auf das Lies Projekt von Shaykh Abu Sufyan As Sulami," accessed 30 April 2014, www.youtube.com/watch?v=O1rJTvYkYGA; Carmen Becker and Nina Wiedl, "Populäre Prediger im deutschen Salafismus," in *Salafismus in Deutschland. Ursprünge und*

Gefahren einer islamisch-fundamentalistischen Bewegung, ed. Thorsten Gerald Schneiders (Bielefeld: transcript, 2014), 204.

37. Anwar al-Awlaki, "Was Islam Spread by The Sword—Al Shaheed, Imam Anwar Al Awlaki (R. H.)," accessed 24 April 2015, www.youtube.com/watch?v=xitkIrUvyZ8.
38. Ibn Baz, *al-Da'wa*, 11.
39. al-'Uthaymin, *Zad al-Da'iya*, 9; Ibn Baz, *al-Da'wa*, 6, 8, 15.
40. Al-Islam Su'al wa-Jawab, "Al-Da'wa ila al-Islam," accessed 16 November 2019, https://islamqa.info/ar/12376; Ibn Baz, *al-Da'wa*, 6; Paris Dawah, "L'importance."
41. Ibn Baz, *al-Da'wa*, 6; al-Islam Su'al wa-Jawab, "al-Da'wa."
42. Ibn Baz, *al-Da'wa,* 15; al-Islam Su'al wa-Jawab, "al-Khuruj li-'l-Da'wa," accessed 16 November 2019, https://islamqa.info/ar/41687.
43. al-Albani, *Hadhihi Da'watuna*, 5; al-Islam Su'al wa-Jawab, "Ayhuma 'Ula," and "al-Da'wa."
44. al-Maqdisi, *Millat Ibrahim*, 32.
45. Ibn Baz, *al-Da'wa*, 6.
46. al-'Uthaymin, "Ala Man Tajib al-Da'wa ila Allah," in al-Musnad, *Fatawa Islamiyya*, 4:266–67; al-'Uthaymin, *Zad al-Da'iya*, 4; al-Islam Su'al wa-Jawab, "Ayhuma 'Ula."
47. Ibn Baz, *al-Da'wa*, 8.
48. *Taghut* (lit., someone who oversteps boundaries) commonly refers in Salafi-Jihadi publications to a tyrant who demands obedience ("worship") to himself instead of only to Allah.
49. Both quotes: Abu Muhammad 'Asim al-Maqdisi, edited transcript of an interview with *al-Nida* magazine (1999), included in the introduction to *This Is Our 'Aqidah*, 2nd ed. (Online: At-Tibyan, n.d.), 19, accessed 16 November 2019, https://archive.org/details/ThisIsOuraqidah-AbiMuhammadAl-maqdisi.
50. al-Maqdisi, *Millat Ibrahim,* 6.
51. Ibn Jibrin, "Hukm al-Khuruj li-l-Da'wa Idha Rafada al-Ahl", in al-Musnad, *Fatawa Islamiyya*, 4:275.
52. Ibn Baz, *al-Da'wa,* 7.
53. Ibn Baz, "Al-Turuq al-Najiha li-l-Da'wa ila Allah Subhanahu," in al-Musnad, *Fatawa Islamiyya*, 4:268.
54. Pierre Vogel, "Pierre Vogel—Dawa Kurs 5 (Friede, Freude, Eierkuchen)," accessed 15 November 2019, https://www.youtube.com/watch?v=mH090764MRs.
55. Neil bin Radhan, "Tafsir al-Imran (HausImrans) (mp3)," accessed 15 September 2010, http://durus.de/unterrichte/tafsir/3aalimran/index.php. Bin Radhan is a German Salafi imam and *da'i* who grew up and studied Islam in Saudi Arabia.
56. Nina Wiedl, *Zeitgenössische Rufe zum Islam. Salafitische Da'wa in Deutschland, 2002–2011* (Baden-Baden: Nomos, 2017), 246–48;

MillatuIbrahimUK, "Is Millatu Ibrahim a Group?" accessed 1 November 2012, www.youtube.com/watch?v=Mh5aPwuhvM&feature=related.

57. Abu Muhammed al-Maqdese [*sic*], "An Advise [*sic*] for the American Muslims," accessed 10 July 2010, http://tawhed.net/r.php?i=1206101a; see also Wiedl, *Zeitgenössische Rufe zum Islam*, 247.
58. Abu Hamza al-Masri, "1/3 Das korrekte Dawah Verständnis—Shaikh Abu Hamza al Masri," accessed 29 September 2015, www.youtube.com/watch?v=kzhA2OySV_s.
59. Khaled Abou el-Fadl, "Islamic Law and Muslim Minorities: The Juristic Discourse on Muslim Minorities from the Second/Eighth to the Eleventh/Seventeenth Century," *Islamic Law and Society* 22, no. 2 (1994):150.
60. Muhammad ibn Salih al-ʿUthaymin, *Majmuʿ Fatawa wa Rasaʾil*, comp. Fahd ibn Nasir al-Sulayman (Riyadh: Dar al-Watan, 1413/1992–1993), 3:25–30; Die Wahre Religion, "Wir hoffen, dass ihr anhand von Beispielen erklären könnt, was mit der Aussage gemeint ist: Die Kuffar als enge Freunde oder Beschützer zu nehmen ist haram," accessed 15 January 2010, www.diewahrereligion.de.
61. Compare al-Lajna al-Daʾima, "Shurut al-Daʿwa al-Najiha wa-l-Kutub Aladhi Tatahaddathu ʿan Dhalika," in al-Musnad, *Fatawa Islamiyya*, 4:268f; Ibn Baz, *al-Daʿwa*, 8; Abu Dujana in Die Wahre Religion, "Das vollständige Interview mit dem DWR-Team (ZDF)—Abu Dujana & Ibrahim Abou-Nagie (1/4)," accessed 4 November 2010, www.youtube.com/watch?v=wIt71PnfJw4&NR=1; Paris Dawah, "Qui peut faire dawah?" accessed 16 November 2019, www.paris-dawah.fr/news/qui-peut-faire-la-dawah/. References to Quranic verses and hadith in this section are taken from the works cited.
62. Ibn Baz, *al-Daʿwa*, 15; Paris Dawah, "Les qualités d'un prédicateur," accessed 16 November 2019, www.paris-dawah.fr/news/article-9-les-qualites-dun-predicateur/; Vogel, "Dawa-Kurs 1."
63. Paris Dawah, "La sincérité (partie 1)," accessed 16 November 2019, www.paris-dawah.fr/news/la-dawah-est-une-science-la-sincerite-partie-1/.
64. Compare Ibn Baz, *al-Daʿwa*, 16; al-Lajna al-Daʾima, "Shurut al-Daʿwa," 268f; Paris Dawah, "Les qualités"; Abu ʿAbdir-Rahman, "Die Milde."
65. al-Islam Suʾal wa-Jawab, "La Tatruk Daʿwa Ghayr al-Muslim Khashiya Shatmihi al-Din," accessed 16 November 2019, http://islamqa.info/ar/77579; Abu ʿAbdir-Rahman, "Dawaübung."
66. Ibn Baaz and al-ʿUthaymeen, *Muslim Minorities*, 20; Abu ʿAbdir-Rahman, "Die Milde."
67. Ibn Baz, *al-Daʿwa*, 10. Similarly, Abu Sufiyan al-Sulami in al-Ghuraba Media, "Antwort;" al-Maqdisi, *Millat Ibrahim*, 26.
68. Paris Dawah, "Les qualités."
69. Pierre Vogel, "Pierre Vogel—Tipps zur Verbesserung der Dawa (Dawa-Kurs 2)," accessed 16 November 2019, https://www.youtube.com/watch?v=LjN5dvDQexE.

70. Abu ʿAbdir-Rahman, "Dawaübung."
71. al-ʿUthaymin, "Ala Man Tajib al-Daʿwa?" 267; Vogel, "Dawa-Kurs 1"; Die Wahre Religion, "Islamische Daʿwah Pflicht," accessed 29 December 2009, www.diewahrereligion.de.
72. Paris Dawah, "Qui peut faire dawah?"
73. Ibn Baz, "Khudh ʿIlmihi wa-Daʿ ʿAmalihi," in al-Musnad, *Fatawa Islamiyya*, 4:275.
74. Ibn Baz, "Baka'uk Fadl min Allah," in al-Musnad, *Fatawa Islamiyya*, 4:285.
75. Al-Islam Su'al wa-Jawab, "Hukm al-Jihad wa-Anwaʿihi," accessed 16 November 2019, https://islamqa.info/ar/20214; Ibn Baz, "Aʿzam al-Jihad," in al-Musnad, *Fatawa Islamiyya*, 4:261f.
76. Racius, *Multiple Nature*, 51.
77. ʿAbd al-ʿAziz ibn ʿAbd Allah ibn Baz, *Majmuʿ Fatawa wa Maqalat Mutanawwiʿa*, comp. Muhammad ibn Saʿd al-Shuwayʿir (Online: imambinbaz.org, n.d.), 18:116, accessed 16 November 2019, https://binbaz.org.sa/books/pdf/17852.
78. Ibid., 27:52 (Online edition by imambinbaz.org), accessed 16 November 2019, https://binbaz.org.sa/books/pdf/17856; see *Ibn Taymiyya on Public and Private Law in Islam or Public Policy in Islamic Jurisprudence*, trans. Omar A. Farrukh (Beirut: Khayats, 1966), 135–36.
79. Noth, *Early Arabic*, 146–49.
80. This principle is based, inter alia, on the Prophet's order to the Muslim armies: "Whenever you meet your polytheist enemies, invite them [first] to adopt Islam." See Majid Khadduri, *War and Peace in the Law of Islam* (Clark, NJ: The Lawbook Exchange, 2007), 96–98; Majid Khadduri, *The Islamic Law of Nations: Shaybani's Siyar* (Baltimore: Johns Hopkins University Press, 1966), 76; Rudolph Peters, *Jihad in Classical and Modern Islam* (Princeton, NJ: Markus Wiener, 1996), 4.
81. Ibn Baz, *Majmuʿ Fatawa* (online edition, imambinbaz.org), 18:120–21.
82. Jonathan Birt, "Wahhabism in the United Kingdom: Manifestations and Reactions," in *Transnational Connections and the Arab Gulf*, ed. Madawi al-Rasheed (Abingdon: Routledge, 2004), 170.
83. Ibn Baz, *Majmuʿ Fatawa* (online edition, imambinbaz.org), 27:52.
84. Peters, *Jihad*, 2.
85. Ibn Baz, *Majmuʿ Fatawa* (online edition, imambinbaz.org), 18:132, 136–37.
86. Compare Behnam T. Said, "Salafismus und politische Gewalt unter deutscher Perspektive," in *Salafismus*, eds. Behnam T. Said and Hazim Fouad (Freiburg im Breisgau: Herder, 2014), 209, and Abu Khadeejah Abdul-Wahid, "Are We in a Period Similar to the Prophet in Makkah as It Relates to Fighting Jihad?" accessed 16 November 2019, www.abukhadeejah.com/are-we-in-a-period-similar-to-the-prophet-in-makkah-as-it-relates-to-fighting-jihad/.
87. The truce concluded by the Prophet with the Meccans that allowed Muslims to perform the hajj to Mecca and enabled people from each side to join the other.

88. Vogel, "Verbreite die Botschaft."
89. Pierre Vogel, "Einführung in die Methodik der Koran Interpretation (Teil 2/3)," 2009, accessed 20 November 2010, www.ezpmuslimportal.de/index.php?option=com_hwdvideoshare&task=viewvideo&Itemid=1&video_id=816&lang=de.
90. Vogel, "Tipps zur Verbesserung der Dawa."
91. al-ʿAwlaki in "Was Islam Spread by the Sword?"
92. See also Hoffman's chapter in this volume.
93. al-Masri, "1/3 Das korrekte Dawah Verständnis."
94. MillatuIbrahimUK, "Is Millatu Ibrahim a Group?"
95. al-Maqdese [*sic*], "An Advise."
96. Said, "Politische Gewalt," 212–14.
97. "Abu Usama Al-Gharib: Is It Not Time to Rise up?" with English subtitles, accessed 24 April 2015, www.youtube.com/watch?v=rfslcRj_yUk.

CHAPTER 4

1. Eran Lerman, "Mawdudi's Concept of Islam," *Middle Eastern Studies* 17 (1981):492.
2. Henning Wrogemann, *Missionarischer Islam und gesellschaftlicher Dialog* (Frankfurt am Main: Lembeck 2006); Egdunas Racius, "The Multiple Nature of the Islamic Daʿwa" (PhD diss., University of Helsinki, 2004).
3. Patrick D. Gaffney, *The Prophet's Pulpit Islamic Preaching in Contemporary Egypt* (Berkeley: University of California Press, 1994), 33.
4. David Commins, *The Wahhabi Mission and Saudi Arabia* (London: I. B. Tauris, 2006), 130ff.
5. In fact, especially since the 1970s, there has been a boom in *daʿwa* publications, suggesting that it was reinvented, as it were. See Ismail R. al-Faruqi, "On the Nature of Islamic Daʿwah," *International Review of Mission* 65/260 (1976):391–409; Torsten Janson, "Daʿwa: Islamic Missiology in Discourse and History," *Swedish Missiological Themes* 89 (2001):355–415.
6. On Ahmadi proselytism see, Simon Ross Valentine, *Islam and the Ahmadiyya Jamaʿat: History, Belief, Practice* (New York: Columbia University Press, 2008); Gerdine Jonker, *Missionizing Europe: The Ahmadiyya Quest to Modernize Islam* (Leiden: Brill, 2015).
7. See Yoginder Sikand, *The Origins and Development of the Tablighi Jamaʿat, (1920–2000): A Cross-Country Comparative Study* (New Delhi: Orient Longman, 2002), and Gugler's and Reetz's chapters in this volume.
8. Muhammad Rashid Rida, *al-Manar wa'l-Azhar* (Cairo: Dar al-Manar, 2007), 259; Davis A. Kerr, "Islamic Daʿwa and Christian Mission: Towards a Comparative Analysis," *International Review of Mission* 89/353 (2000):155; Albert H. Hourani, *Arabic Thought in the Liberal Age, 1798–1939* (New York: Oxford University Press, 1962), 227.
9. Jamal Malik, *Islamische Gelehrtenkultur in Nordindien: Entwicklungsgeschichte und Tendenzen am Beispiel von Lucknow* (Leiden: Brill, 1997), 356, 453–55.

10. Sayyid Abu'l-A'la Mawdudi, *al-Jihad fi'l-Islam* (Lahore: Idara Tarjuman al-Qur'an, 2006).
11. Michael Cook, *Commanding Right and Forbidding Wrong in Islamic Thought* (Cambridge: Cambridge University Press, 2001), 515–16.
12. Al-Sayyid Muhammad Husayn Fadlallah, *Uslub al-Da'wa fi'l-Qur'an* (Beirut: Dar al-Malak, 1994), 33.
13. E.g., Bassam al-'Amush, a professor of sharia and former MB leader in Jordan, *Fiqh al-Da'wa* (Amman: Dar al-Nafis, 2005), 13.
14. E.g., Jama'a Amin 'Abd al-'Aziz, *al-Da'wa: Qawa'id wa-'Usul* (Alexandria: Dar al-Da'wa, 1999), 22–25.
15. E.g., 'Abd al-'Aziz 'Abdallah Ibn Baz, *al-Da'wa ila Allah wa-Akhlaq al-Du'a* (Riyadh: Office of Scientific Research and Ifta Administration, 2002), 16–17.
16. Jamal Malik, *Colonialization of Islam: Dissolution of Traditional Institutions in Pakistan* (New Delhi: Manohar, 1996), ch. 1.
17. Larry Poston, *Islamic Da'wah in the West* (New York: Oxford University Press, 1992), 77–78.
18. Abu'l-A'la al-Mawdudi, *Tadhkirat Du'a al-Islam* (Damascus and Beirut: al-Maktab al-Islami, 1983), 50.
19. Jama'at-e Islami Pakistan, *The Creed*, article 3, accessed 4 October 2019, http://jamaat.org/en/dastoorOrManshoor_detail.php?article_id=56.
20. Jama'at-e Islami Pakistan, *Dawah*, accessed 4 October 2019, http://jamaat.org/en/jamaatOrDawat.php?cat_id=12.
21. Hasan al-Banna, *Majmu'at Rasa'il* (Cairo: Iqra' Foundation, 2011), 32; See also Weismann's chapter in this volume.
22. Ulrika Mårtensson, "'Islamic Order': Semeiotics and Pragmatism in the Muslim Brotherhood?" *Journal of Islamic Research* 9 (2015):43.
23. Banna, *Majmu'at Rasa'il*, 29.
24. Mårtensson, "Islamic Order," 45.
25. Khalil al-Anani, "The Power of the Jama'a: The Role of Hasan al-Banna in Constructing the Muslim Brotherhood's Collective Identity," *Sociology of Islam* 1 (2013):50; Banna, *Majmu'at Rasa'il*, 136–37.
26. Cited in Lerman, "Mawdudi's Concept," 498f.
27. Jan-Peter Hartung, *A System of Life: Mawdudi and the Ideologisation of Islam* (London: Oxford University Press 2013), 166–67.
28. Sayyid Abu'l-A'la Mawdudi, *al-Jihad fi'l-Islam* (Lahore: Idara Tarjuman al-Qur'an, 2006), 156. For an analysis, see Jamal Malik, "Sayyid Abu al-A'la al-Mawdudi, al-Jihad fi al-Islam (1930)," in *Geschichte des politischen Denkens. Das 20. Jahrhundert,* ed. Manfred Brocker (Frankfurt am Main: Suhrkamp, 2018), 217–32.
29. Hartung, *A System of Life*, 210–13.
30. The word *manhaj* seems to be a neologism meaning clear path. Quran 5:48 uses *minhaj* together with *shir'a* (from which sharia is derived): "To each of you We prescribed a law and a method."
31. Cook, *Commanding Right*, 523.

32. Charles Tripp, "Sayyid Qutb: The Political Vision," in *Pioneers of Islamic Revival,* ed. Ali Rahnema (London: Zed Books, 2005), 172.
33. Hasan Isma'il al-Hudaybi, *Du'a, La Quda: Abhath fi'l-'Aqida al-Islamiyya wa-Manhaj al-Da'wa ila Allah* (Cairo: Dar al-Tiba'a wa'l-Nashr al-Islamiyya, 1977). For an analysis, see Barbara H. E. Zollner, *The Muslim Brotherhood: Hasan al-Hudaybi and Ideology* (Abingdon: Routledge, 2009).
34. Zollner, 71; On the debates over *irja',* see Daniel Lav, *Radical Islam and the Revival of Medieval Theology* (Cambridge: Cambridge University Press, 2012).
35. Abdullah al-Arian, *Answering the Call: Popular Islamic Activism in Sadat's Egypt* (New York: Oxford University Press, 2014), 115, 117, 159.
36. Lorenzo Vidino, *The New Muslim Brotherhood in the West* (New York: Columbia University Press, 2010), 49.
37. Al-Arian, *Answering the Call,* 183.
38. Gilles Kepel, *The Prophet and Pharaoh: Muslim Extremism in Egypt* (London: Al-Saqi Books, 1985), ch. 4.
39. Peter Mandaville, *Global Political Islam* (London: Routledge, 2007), 99.
40. Carrie Rosefsky Wickham, *The Muslim Brotherhood: Evolution of an Islamist Movement* (Princeton, NJ: Princeton University Press, 2013), 46–47.
41. Ibid., 48.
42. Khurshid Ahmad and Zafar Ishaq Ansari, "Mawlana Sayyid Abul A'la Mawdudi: An Introduction to His Vision of Islam and Islamic Revival," in *Islamic Perspectives: Studies in Honour of Mawlana Sayyid Abul A'la Mawdudi,* eds. Khurshid Ahmad and Zafar Ishaq Ansari (London: The Islamic Foundation, 1979), 363–83.
43. Khalid B. Sayeed, "The Jama'at-i-Islami Movement in Pakistan," *Pacific Affairs* 30 (1957):62–63.
44. See his messages to the youth and to students in *Majmu'at Rasa'il,* 334–56.
45. Brynjar Lia, *The Society of the Muslim Brothers in Egypt: The Rise of an Islamic Mass Movement, 1928–1942* (Reading, UK: Ithaca Press, 1998), 106–7, 163–66.
46. Richard P. Mitchell, *The Society of the Muslim Brothers* (New York: Oxford University Press, 1969), 171–72.
47. John L. Esposito and John O. Voll, *Makers of Contemporary Islam* (New York: Oxford University Press, 2001), 42.
48. Seyyed Vali Reza Nasr, *The Vanguard of the Islamic Revolution: the Jama'at-i Islami of Pakistan* (Berkeley: University of California Press, 1994), 64–65, 73–75; Humeira Iqtidar, *Secularizing Islamists? Jama'at-e-Islami and Jama'at-ud-Da'wa in Urban Pakistan* (Chicago: University of Chicago Press, 2011), 73–77.
49. Nasr, *Vanguard of the Islamic Revolution,* 24, 62.
50. Compare al-Anani, 53ff.
51. Carrie Rosefsky Wickham, "Interests, Ideas, and the Islamic Outreach in Egypt," in *Islamic Activism: A Social Movement Theory Approach,*

ed. Quintan Wiktorowicz (Bloomington: Indiana University Press 2004), 243–44.

52. See Reinhard Schulze, *Islamischer Internationalismus im 20. Jahrhundert: Untersuchungen zur Geschichte der Islamischen Weltliga* (Leiden: Brill, 1990), 279–91.

53. On Daʿwat-e Islami, see Thomas K. Gugler, *Mission Medina: Daʿwat-e Islami und Tabligi Gamaʿat* (Würzburg: Ergon, 2011).

54. See, for example, Florian Harms, "Der Prophet ruft aus dem Cyberspace. Formen islamischer Mission im Internet," in *Von Chatraum bis Cyberjihad: Muslimische Internetnutzung in globaler und lokaler Perspektive,* eds. Johanna Pink and Mathias Bruckner (Würzburg: Ergon, 2009), 169–212.

55. Ahmad Ahmad Ghalwash, *Al-Daʿwa al-Islamiyya: Usuluha wa-Wasaʾiluha* (Cairo: al-Risala Foundation, 1978), 57, 271–372.

56. For more on *fiqh al-daʿwa* see Jamal Malik, "Fiqh al-Daʿwa: The Emerging Standardization of Islamic Proselytism," *Die Welt des Islams* 58 (2018):206–43.

57. ʿAbdallah al-Khatir, "Al-Daʿwa ila Allah: Tawajihat wa-Dawabit," *al-Bayan Magazine* 7 (2008):19, 22–27; Ghalwash, *Al-Daʿwa al-Islamiyya*, 459–70; Muhammad al-Ghazali, *Maʿa Allah: Dirasat fiʾl-Daʿwa waʾl-Duʿa* (Cairo: Nahdat Misr, 2005), 149–68.

58. Banna, *Majmuʿat Rasaʾil,* 12, 16, 32.

59. Mustafa Mashhur, "Bayna al-Qiyada waʾl-Jundiyya ʿala Tariq al-Daʿwa," in *Min Fiqh al-Daʿwa,* ed. Mustafa Mashhur (Cairo: Dar al-Tawziʿ waʾl-Nashr al-Islamiyya, 1986).

60. Itzchak Weismann, "Framing a Modern Umma: The Muslim Brothers' Evolving Project of Daʿwa," *Sociology of Islam* 3, nos. 3–4 (2015): 156–60.

61. Max Weber, *The Sociology of Religion* (Boston: Beacon, 1993), 110.

62. ʿAli ʿAbd al-Halim Mahmud, *Fiqh al-Daʿwa ila Allah* (Cairo: Dar al-Wafaʾ liʾl-Tibaʿa waʾl-Nashr waʾl-Tawziʿ, 1990), 312.

63. On him see, Itzchak Weismann, "Saʿid Hawwa and Islamic Revivalism in Baʿthist Syria," *Studia Islamica* 85 (1997):131–54.

64. Saʿid Hawwa, *Jund Allah: Thaqafatan wa-Akhlaqan* (Cairo: Maktabat Wahbah, 1990, original prob. 1973), 4.

65. Ibid., 59 60, 72f, 179 82.

66. Mufid Khalid ʿId Ahmad ʿId, *al-ʿAlaqa bayna al-Fiqh waʾl-Daʿwa* (Beirut: Dar Ibn Hazm liʾl-Tibaʿa waʾl-Nashr waʾl-Tawziʿ, 1995).

67. Abuʾl-Aʿla al-Mawdudi, *Towards Understanding Islam* (U. K. I. M. Daʿwa Centre, 1960), 74.

68. Ibid., 43.

69. Emmanuel Sivan, "The Enclave Culture," in *Fundamentalisms Comprehended,* eds. Martin E. Marty and R. Scott Appleby (Chicago: University of Chicago Press, 1995), 11–68; the citation is p. 38.

70. Ibid., 7, 18.

71. L. Gardet, "Djamaʿa," *The Encyclopedia of Islam*, New Edition (Leiden: Brill, 1992), 2:411.
72. See also C. Snouck Hurgronje, *Verspreide Geschriften* (Bonn: Kurt Schroeder, 1923–1927), 2:314f.
73. Compare Mitchell, *Muslim Brothers*, 169.
74. http://goldandguns.wordpress.com/2012/11/27/mapping-the-muslim-brotherhood/, accessed 22 March 2013.
75. Yusuf al-Qaradawi, *Thaqafat al-Daʿiya* (2nd ed. Cairo: Maktabat al-Risala, 1979).
76. Vidino, *New Muslim Brotherhood*, 4.
77. Husam Tammam, "Yusuf al-Qaradawi and the Muslim Brothers: The Nature of a Special Relationship," in *The Global Mufti: The Phenomenon of Yusuf al-Qaradawi*, eds. Bettina Gräf and Jakob Skovgaard-Petersen (London: Hurst, 2009), 69.

CHAPTER 5

1. For the story of Rida, al-Fiqi, and the Wahhabis, see Henri Lauzière, *The Making of Salafism: Islamic Reform in the Twentieth Century* (New York: Columbia University Press, 2015), ch. 2.
2. See also the chapters by Weismann and Wiedl in this volume.
3. Bernard Haykel, "On the Nature of Salafi Thought and Action," in *Global Salafism: Islam's New Religious Movement*, ed. Roel Meijer (London: Hurst, 2009), 33–51.
4. Ahmad al-Tahir, *Jamaʿat Ansar al-Sunna al-Muhammadiyya: Nasha'tuha-Ahdafuha-Manhajuha-Juhuduha* (Cairo: al-Markaz al-ʿAmm, 2006), 273–328.
5. Umar Ryad, "Islamic Reformism and Great Britain: Rashid Rida's Image as Reflected in the Journal al-Manar in Cairo," *Islam and Christian-Muslim Relations* 21 (2010):263–85.
6. ʿAdl al-Sayyid, ed., *al-Hakimiyya wa'l-Siyasa al-Sharʿiyya: ʿInda Shuyyukh Jamaʿat Ansar al-Sunna al-Muhammadiyya* (Cairo: Dar al-Ibana, 2009), 119–22.
7. Samuel Tadros, *Mapping Egyptian Islamism* (Washington, D.C.: Hudson Institute, 2014), 15.
8. See Adnan A. Musallam, *From Secularism to Jihad: Sayyid Qutb and the Foundations of Radical Islamism* (Westport, CT: Praeger, 2005).
9. See Ahmad Moussalli, *Radical Islamic Fundamentalism: The Ideological and Political Discourse of Sayyid Qutb* (Beirut: American University of Beirut, 1992); Charles Tripp, "Sayyid Qutb: The Political Vision," in *Pioneers of Islamic Revival*, ed. Ali Rahnema (London: Zed Books, 1994), 154–83.
10. See Gilles Kepel, *Muslim Extremism in Egypt: The Prophet and Pharaoh* (London: University of California Press, 1986).
11. On Muhammad Qutb, see Madawi al-Rasheed, *Contesting the Saudi State: Islamic Voices from a New Generation* (Cambridge: Cambridge University

Press, 2007), 66–67. On ʿAbd al-Khaliq, see Carine Lahoud, "Koweït: salafisms et rapports au pouvoir," in *Qu'est-ce que le Salafisme?* ed. Bernard Rougier (Paris: Presses Universitaires de France, 2008), 126–29.

12. Sayyid Qutb, *al-Taswir al-Fanni fi'l-Qur'an*, 36, cited in Sayed Khatib, *The Political Thought of Sayyid Qutb* (New York: Routledge, 2006), 87.
13. Charles Hirschkind, *The Ethical Soundscape: Cassette Sermons and Islamic Counterspheres* (New York: Columbia University Press, 2006), 154–67.
14. On al-Albani's life and works, see e.g., Muhammad al-Shaybani, *Hayat al-Albani wa-Atharuhu wa-Thana' al-ʿUlama' ʿalayhi* (n.p.: Maktabat al-Sirrawi, 1986).
15. Al-Albani is reported to have met al-Fiqi and published in the association journal, *Al-Tawhid*. See al-Shaybani, *Hayat al-Albani*, 64–65; al-Tahir, *Jamaʿat Ansar al-Sunna al-Muhammadiyya*, 321. He also gave lectures in Ansar al-Sunna centers and, notably, in the group's headquarters in ʿAbdin. See mention of al-Albani in ʿAbdin on al-Huwayni's website, http://alheweny.me/pages/page/about, accessed 6 December 2019.
16. Stéphane Lacroix, "Between Revolution and Apoliticism: Nasir al-Din al-Albani and his Impact on the Shaping of Contemporary Salafism," in *Global Salafism*, ed. Roel Meijer, 70.
17. Kishk's influence is explicitly applauded by al-Huwayni, who refers to an early encounter with Kishk both to highlight al-Albani's superiority (over Kishk) and as the reason he dedicated himself to scholarship, as well as by Hassan and Yaʿqub.
18. See Ahmad ʿUrfa, "Abu Ishaq al-Huwayni li-Haraka Salafiyya: Iʿtazaltu hatta La Yuqalu ʿani Kha'in wa-ʿAmil," accessed 8 October 2019, http://www.youm7.com/story/2015/10/30/2416302/بالصور-أبو-إسحاق-الحوينى-لحركة-سلفية-اعتزلت-حتى-لا-يقال-عنى-#.
19. Hassan is not permitted to preach and was even accused of spreading extremist ideas. For more on this *daʿi*, see the conclusion.
20. *Al-Rahma* continues but in watered-down form, see Tadros, *Mapping Egyptian Islamism*, 102–3.
21. Pre-Arab Spring, al-Daʿwa al-Salafiyya's main school of preaching, al-Furqan Institute, was famously productive. Its journal, *Sawt al-Daʿwa*, and website, *AnaSalafy.com*, had also broadcasted the organization's brand and message to great effect. On the Salafis' shift into politics, with mention of the various *daʿwa* networks, see Khalil al-Anani and Maszlee Malik, "Pious Way to Politics: The Rise of Political Salafism in Post-Mubarak Egypt," *Digest of Middle East Studies* 22 (2013):57–73.
22. Stéphane Lacroix, "Egypt's Pragmatic Salafis: The Politics of Hizb al-Nour," *Carnegie Endowment for International Peace*, accessed 9 October 2019, http://carnegieendowment.org/2016/11/01/egypt-s-pragmatic-salafis-politics-of-hizb-al-nour-pub-64902.
23. See George Fahmi, "The Egyptian State and the Religious Sphere," *Carnegie Middle East Center,* 18 September 2014, accessed 26 December 2016,

http://carnegie-mec.org/2014/09/18/egyptian-state-and-religious-sphere-pub-56619.

24. See Ahmad ʿAbd al-Tawab, "Baʿd Taʿrifahu, Ahl al-Sunna wa'l-Jamaʿa 'Thawra Salafiyya' ʿala Shaykh al-Azhar," accessed 26 December 2016, http://www.elyomnew.com/news/inside/2016/09/03/58598.
25. Kepel, *Muslim Extremism*, 202.
26. The following quote, from a female student in Madinat al-Nasr (March 2009), is typical: "We are surrounded by deception. We are lied to by our government, our media, and our traditional authorities. The only ones who tell us the truth are the Salafi *shuyukh*. They tell it like it really is."
27. For representative examples of their preaching, see "Haqiqat al-Tawhid," https://m.youtube.com/watch?v=ECtlDkUl8ks (Hassan); "Haqiqat al-Dunya," https://m.youtube.com/watch?v=HssoP2RPaGY (Hussein Yaʿqub); "Haqiqat al-Shiʿa," https://m.youtube.com/watch?v=GfLDYCVouhc (al-Huwayni), accessed 26 December 2016.
28. A minority of upper-class Egyptians were attracted to the same discourse (also as a result of listening to sermons by these televangelists). For pro-Salafi attitudes among groups of upper-class Egyptian women, see Richard Gauvain, *Salafi Ritual Purity: In the Presence of God* (New York: Routledge, 2012), ch. 5.
29. On this concept, see Joas Wagemakers, "Framing the 'Threat to Islam': *al-Wala' wa-l-Bara'* in Salafi Discourse," *Arab Studies Quarterly* 30, no. 4 (2008):1–22.
30. Well before the creation of Israel, Rashid Rida drew attention to the threats posed by that "most miserable people," the Jews. For Qutb, who incorporated *The Protocols of Zion* into his polemic, the Jew represents Islam's nemesis—crude and animalistic, yet sufficiently wily to penetrate the defenses of the world's richest governments, see Esther Webman, "The Jew as a Metaphor for Evil in Arab Public Discourse," *Journal of the Middle East and Africa*, 6 (2015):275–92. The same language was a regular feature of Salafi televangelism.
31. Gauvain, *Salafi Ritual Purity*, 247.
32. Ibid., 160–72.
33. See, e.g., Muhammad Hassan, *Khawatir ʿala Tariq al-Daʿwa* (Mansura: Maktabat al-Fiyad li'l-Tijara wa'l-Tawziʿ, 2006), 90. On this concept, see Haykel, "Nature of Salafi Thought," 39, n. 14.
34. Gauvain, *Salafi Ritual Purity*, 153ff.
35. As noted, the pre–Arab-spring Egyptian Salafi landscape contained numerous, often acrimonious divisions. Ordinary Egyptians were largely unaware of these divisions, however, because at that moment Egyptian Salafi *daʿwa*—not Egyptian Salafism—had crystalized into the ethical movement described here. That is to say, regardless of personal political opinions and loyalties, virtually all Salafi *duʿa* painted the same harmonious picture of

current realities by emphasizing the importance of ethical improvement through sustained study and diligent worship.

36. Ansar al-Sunna venerated its leading scholars, all of whom are referred to as *du'a*, in print; it now also does so through its social media. When Salafism reached a much wider Egyptian audience through the *da'wa* efforts of the televangelists, social media sites including these men's impressive curricula vitae quickly appeared. As a general rule, a certificate of learning (*ijaza*) was not needed in the Salafi circles in which I spent time.
37. Seemingly all well-known Egyptian Salafis were born and raised in rural villages, among pious folk, and memorized the Quran at a precociously young age. More important than his birthplace are the *da'i*'s "conversion" and "struggle" narratives. The biographies of all Egyptian Salafi *du'a* invariably contain both a "eureka" moment (al-Fiqi reading Ibn Taymiyya) and stories of heroism (Qutb, Kishk, al-Huwayni in prison cells).
38. On al-Fadila Party, see Tadros, *Mapping Egyptian Islamism*, 55, 62.
39. A number of spats between high-profile Salafi *du'a* have attracted public attention. At the time of writing, for instance, Muhammad 'Abd al-Maqsud's criticisms (in 2015) of Muhammad Hassan have received nearly 700,000 views. See https://www.youtube.com/watch?v=0MbhQJ5iDjM, accessed 26 December 2016.
40. Tadros, *Mapping Egyptian Islamism*, 60–61.
41. For the definitive Salafi work on *tabarruj*, written by a female Ansar al-Sunna scholar, Ni'mat Sidqi, see Ellen McLarney, *Soft Force: Women in Egypt's Islamic Awakening* (Princeton, NJ: Princeton University Press, 2015), ch. 3.
42. See, e.g., http://www.ahlalhadeeth.com/vb/showthread.php?t=57148, accessed 26 December 2016.
43. See, e.g., http://alrased.net/main/articles.aspx?selected_article_no=6412. accessed 26 December 2016.
44. On Hassan's plans for fund-raising, see *Ahram Online*, http://english.ahram.org.eg/NewsContent/3/0/34561/Business/0/Prominent-Egyptian-Salafist-promises-to-replace-US.aspx, accessed 26 December 2016.
45. See, e.g., https://www.youtube.com/watch?v=FHffKAHnLjg (Anwar); https://www.youtube.com/watch?v=WBJh08zrEfQ&feature=related (al Zughbi); https://www.youtube.com/watch?v=sCKHsZAetWs (Sha'ban), both accessed 26 December 2016.
46. Paradoxically, this same point was also made by the self-declared ex-Salafis who now wear Western clothes.
47. See, e.g., http://www.fanzar.net/vb/showthread.php?t=25479; for Hassan's equally fond recollection of Nur al-Din, see https://www.youtube.com/watch?v=nhHUnoI1arw, accessed 26 December 2016.
48. This is not to suggest that, before the Arab Spring, Hassan went without criticism in Egypt. See Gauvain, *Salafi Ritual Purity*, 291.

49. Hirschkind, *The Ethical Soundscape*, 169.
50. For the original charges against Hassan, and later news of his exoneration, see Ahmad al-Jaʿfari, "Al-Hukm ʿala Muhammad Hassan li-Ittihamihi bi-Izdiraʾ al-Adyan wa-Nashr Afkar Mutattarifa," *al-Yawm al-Sabaʿ*, 13 March 2016; Kamil Kamil, "Taʿarraf ʿala Radd fiʾl Muhammad Hassan baʿd Baraʾatihi min ʿIzdiraʾ al-Adyan," *al-Yawm al-Sabaʿ*, 30 October 2016.
51. Hassan's base of support in his home governorate of Dakahlia likely remains strong, and he claims to continue to deliver "reality" to the Egyptian people. See his recent interview on *al-Rahma* on "The Reality of Daʿish": https://m.youtube.com/watch?v=avY4KgOLHBU, accessed 26 December 2016.

CHAPTER 6

1. M. Anwarul Haq, *The Faith Movement of Mawlana Muhammad Ilyas* (London: Allen and Unwin, 1972).
2. These are available online in a number of Asian and European languages: Ameer-e-Ahl-e-Sunnat, "72 Madani Inamaat," accessed 1 February 2017, https://www.dawateislami.net/bookslibrary/131.
3. Dale F. Eickelman and James Piscatori, *Muslim Politics* (Princeton: Princeton University Press, 2004), 51, 152.
4. Barbara D. Metcalf, "'Traditionalist' Islamic Activism: Deoband, Tablighis, and Talibs," in *Islamic Contestations: Essays on Muslims in India and Pakistan,* ed. Barbara D. Metcalf, (New Delhi: Oxford University Press, 2004), 265–84.
5. Barbara D. Metcalf, *Islamic Revival in British India: Deoband, 1860–1900* (New Delhi: Oxford University Press, 2005 [1982]), 87.
6. Ron Geaves, "The Contested Milieu of Deoband: 'Salafis' or 'Sufis'?" in *Sufis and Salafis in the Contemporary Age,* ed. Lloyd Ridgeon (London: Bloomsbury, 2015), 203.
7. Usha Sanyal, *Devotional Islam and Politics in British India: Ahmad Riza Khan Barelwi and His Movement, 1870–1920* (New Delhi: Oxford University Press, 1996).
8. Imam Ahmad Raza, *Husam al-Haramain* (Stockport, UK: Raza Academy Publication, 2005 [1906]), 32–50, 71.
9. Thomas K. Gugler, *Mission Medina: Daʿwat-e Islami und Tabligi Gamaʿat* (Würzburg: Ergon, 2011).
10. Thomas K. Gugler, "Muslim Youths on Tablighi Journeys," *Asien* 126 (2013):76–78. Roger Peterson, Gordon Aeschliman, and R. Wayne Sneed, *Maximum Impact Short-Term Mission: The God-Commanded Repetitive Deployment of Swift, Temporary Non-Professional Missionaries* (Minneapolis: Stempress, 2008). Mufti Inam Haq Qasmi, *Injunctions Pertaining to the Traveller* (New Delhi: Adam, 2003).
11. Neil J. Smelser, *The Odyssey Experience: Physical, Social, Psychological, and Spiritual Journeys* (Berkeley: University of California Press, 2009), 12.

12. Yoginder Sikand, *The Origins and Development of the Tablighi-Jamaʿat, 1920–2000*, (New Delhi: Orient Longman, 2002), 112–29.
13. Maulana Ashraf Ali Thanwi. *Islamic Renaissance: Muslim Revival and Awakening* (Delhi: Adam, 1997).
14. Muhammad Khalid Masud, ed., *Travellers in Faith: Studies of the Tablighi Jamaʿat as a Transnational Islamic Movement for Faith Renewal* (Leiden: Brill, 2000), lv–lvi.
15. On the Saharanpur-based networks of Ilyas see, Jan-Peter Hartung, *Viele Wege und ein Ziel: Leben und Wirken von Sayyid Abu l-Hasan ʿAli al-Hasani Nadwi, 1914–1999* (Würzburg: Ergon, 2004), 81–87, 322–29, 506–7.
16. Barbara D. Metcalf, "Remaking Ourselves: Islamic Self-Fashioning in a Global Movement of Spiritual Renewal," in *Accounting for Fundamentalisms: The Dynamic Character of Movements,* eds. Martin E. Marty and R. Scott Appleby (Chicago: University of Chicago Press, 1994), 711.
17. Smelser, *The Odyssey Experience*, 1–27.
18. Gerhard Schulze, *Die Erlebnisgesellschaft: Kultursoziologie der Gegenwart* (Frankfurt am Main: Campus, 1992), 54.
19. Sikand, *Origins and Development*, 158.
20. The first Bangladeshi Tablighi meeting was in Chittagong in 1954, the second in Narayanganj in 1958. Since 1966, it has taken place annually in Tongi.
21. Eirini Lemos, "What Is the Festival of Bishwa Ijtema?" *Telegraph*, 7 January 2016, accessed 16 December 2016, http://www.telegraph.co.uk/news/worldnews/asia/bangladesh/12088120/What-is-the-festival-of-Bishwa-Ijtema-and-where-is-it-held.html.
22. For missionary journeys, the sending entity takes charge of preparations, i.e., organizing visas, round-trip tickets, financial support, logistical concerns such as airport drop-offs and pick-ups, housing, food, and ground transportation, on-site field orientation and instruction, and handling local political or governmental requirements.
23. Murat Kurnaz, *Fünf Jahre meines Lebens: Ein Bericht aus Guantanamo* (Berlin: Rowohlt, 2007).
24. Arshad al-Qadri, *Tableeghi Jamaat* (Mumbai: Sunni Youth Federation, 2000), 106–7.
25. Ibid., 89.
26. Noman Baig, "God and Greed: Money and Meditation in Karachi's Marketplace" (PhD diss., University of Texas, 2014), 70.
27. Ibid., 44, 65.
28. See Rodney Stark, "Why Religious Movements Succeed or Fail: A Revised General Model," *Journal of Contemporary Religion* 11, no. 2 (1996):137–38.
29. See Patrick Eisenlohr, "Naʿt: Media Contexts and Transnational Dimensions of a Devotional Practice," in *Islam in South Asia in Practice,*

ed. Barbara D. Metcalf (Princeton, NJ: Princeton University Press, 2009), 101–12.

30. Hence, Daʿwat-e Islami has practically no presence in North Africa or Turkey. It recruits mostly Muslims of South Asian origin, with the exception of China, where Daʿwat-e Islami seems to be ahead of Tablighi Jamaʿat, something the movement also claims for South America.
31. Timothy Miller, "Intentional Communities: The Evolution of Enacted Utopianism," in *Revisionism and Diversification in New Religious Movements,* ed. Eileen Barker (Surrey, UK: Ashgate, 2013), 213–15.
32. International Crisis Group, *Pakistan: Karachi's Madrasas and Violent Extremism* (Brussels: ICG, 2007), 11.
33. See Douglas Atkin, *The Culting of Brands: Turn Your Customers into True Believers* (New York: Portfolio, 2004), 67–69.
34. Charles Duhigg, *The Power of Habit: Why We Do What We Do and How to Change* (New York: Random House, 2013), xiv.
35. Mona Atia, "'A Way to Paradise': Pious Neoliberalism, Islam, and Faith-Based Development," *Annals of the Association of American Geographers* 102 (2012):808, 822.
36. Arsalan Khan, "Islam and Pious Sociality: The Ethics of Hierarchy in the Tablighi Jamaat in Pakistan," *Social Analysis* 60, no. 4 (2016):110.
37. Max Weber, *Wirtschaft und Gesellschaft* (Tübingen: Mohr, 1922), 141.
38. Peter L. Berger, *The Many Altars of Modernity: Toward a Paradigm for Religion in a Pluralist Age* (Berlin: De Gruyter, 2014), 7.
39. Weber, *Wirtschaft und Gesellschaft*, 787.
40. Ibid., 304–7.
41. Thomas K. Gugler, "Sunna, Sunnaisierung und imitatio Muhammadi: Die Islamisierung der Individualsphäre als Programm der Tablighi Jamaʿat und Daʿwat-e Islami," in *Die Sunna leben: Zur Dynamik islamischer Religionspraxis in Deutschland,* eds. Paula Schrode and Udo Simon (Würzburg: Ergon, 2012), 228. See also, Jamal Malik, "The Luminous Nurani: Charisma and Political Mobilization among the Barelwis in Pakistan," *Social Analysis* 28 (1990):38–50.
42. See Sikand, *Origins and Development*, 251.
43. Byung-Chul Han, *Psychopolitik. Neoliberalismus und die neuen Machttechniken* (Frankfurt am Main: S. Fischer, 2014), 84f.
44. Ibid., 27.
45. Ibid., 9.

CHAPTER 7

1. See Moojan Momen, *An Introduction to Shiʿi Islam: The History and Doctrines of Twelver Shiʿism* (New Haven, CT: Yale University Press, 1985), 107–9.
2. Yitzhak Nakash, *The Shiʿis of Iraq* (Princeton, NJ: Princeton University Press, 1994), ch. 1.

3. On Muhammad Baqir al-Sadr and his teachings, see Chibli Mallat, *The Renewal of Islamic Law: Muhammad Baqir al-Sadr, Najaf and the Shiʿi International* (Cambridge: Cambridge University Press, 1993); T. M. Aziz, "The Role of Muhammad Baqir al-Sadr in Shiʿi Political Activism in Iraq from 1958 to 1980," *International Journal of Middle East Studies* 25 (1993):207–22.
4. For a general description of the party now, see Florian Bernhardt, *Hizb ad-Daʿwa al-Islamiyya: Selbstverständnis, Strategien und Ziele einer irakisch-islamistischen Partei zwischen Kontinuität und Wandel, 1957–2003* (Würzburg: Ergon, 2012); Rodger Shanahan, "Shiʿa Political Development in Iraq: The Case of the Islamic Daʿwa Party," *Third World Quarterly* 25 (2004):943–54.
5. *Hizb al-Daʿwa al-Islamiyya: Taʿrif Mujaz bi-Taʾsisihiwa-Masiratihi wa-Ahdafihi* [The Islamic Daʿwa Party: A Short Introduction on Its Foundation, Course, and Objectives] (Najaf: n.p., 2003), 2. An earlier political Shiʿi party, al-Nahda (Renaissance), was founded in the 1920s, but its activity was intermittent, and it died out in the early 1930s. Its goal was to protect Shiʿi political interests rather than bring about a religious revival, as was later the case with the Daʿwa Party. See Hanna Batatu, *The Old Social Classes and the Revolutionary Movements of Iraq* (Princeton, NJ: Princeton University Press, 1978), 185, 327–31.
6. Batatu, *Old Social Classes*, 764ff.
7. Muhammad Baqir al-Sadr, "Hawla al-Ism wa'l-Shikl al-Tanzimi li-Hizb al-Daʿwa al-Islamiyya" (On the Name and Organizational Form of the Daʿwa Party), in *Min Fikr al-Daʿwa al-Islamiyya: al-Shahid al-Rabiʿ al-Imam al-Sadr*, ed. Muhammad Baqir al-Sadr (Tehran: Hizb al-Daʿwa al-Islamiyya al-Iʿlam al-Markazi, 1980), 9–11.
8. Sayyid Qutb, *Maʿalim fi'l-Tariq* (numerous editions).
9. Amatzia Baram, "From Radicalism to Radical Pragmatism: The Shiʿite Fundamentalist Opposition Movements of Iraq," in *Islamic Fundamentalism and the Gulf War*, ed. James Piscatori (Chicago: American Academy of Arts and Sciences, 1991), 28–51.
10. Amatzia Baram, "Two Roads to Revolutionary Shiʿi Fundamentalism in Iraq," in *Accounting for Fundamentalism: The Dynamic Character of Movements*, eds. Martin E. Marty and R. Scott Appleby (Chicago: University of Chicago Press and American Academy of Arts and Sciences, 1994), 539.
11. Muhammad Baqir al-Sadr, *Muqaddimat fi'l-Tafsir al-Mawduʿi li'l-Qur'an* [Introductions to the Objective Interpretation of the Quran] (Beirut: Dar al-Taʿaruf li'l-Matbuʿat, 1980), 218.
12. Ibid., 216–17.
13. al-Sadr, "Hawla al-Ism," 31.
14. ʿAbdallah al-Fayyad, *Ta'rikh al-Imamiyya wa-Aslafihim min al-Shiʿa* [The History of the Imami Shiʿa and Their Forebears] (Baghdad: Matbaʿat

As'ad and Baghdad University, 1970), 24–26; al-Sadr, *Muqaddimat fi'l-Tafsir*, 25–26.

15. Muhammad Baqir al-Sadr, *Ikhtarna Laka* [We Chose for You] (Beirut: Dar al-Ta'aruf li'l-Matbu'at, 1975), 67.
16. Ibid., 68–69; See also al-Fayyad, *Ta'rikh al-Imamiyya*, 25–26.
17. al-Sadr, "Hawla al-Ism," 35–38.
18. A. Najaf, *al-Shahed al-Shahid* (Tehran: n.p., early 1980s), 131–32, 142–43.
19. Amatzia Baram, *Saddam Husayn and Islam, 1968–2003: Ba'thi Iraq from Secularism to Faith* (Washington, D.C.: Woodrow Wilson Center and Johns Hopkins University Press, 2014), 135–38; *al-Da'wa Chronicle* (London) 3 (July 1980), 2.
20. *Al-Da'wa Chronicle* 3 (July 1980), 4.
21. For details, see Amatzia Baram, "The Impact of Khomeini's Revolution on the Radical Shi'i Movement of Iraq," in *The Iranian Revolution and the Muslim World,* ed. David Menashri (Boulder, CO: Westview, 1990), 131–54, esp. 141–44.
22. Najaf, *al-Shahed al-Shahid*, 135–38; See also *al-Da'wa Chronicle* 3 (July 1980), 2.
23. See Rachel Kantz-Feder, "Fatima's Revolutionary Image in Fadak fi al-Ta'rikh (1955): The Inception of Muhammad Baqir al-Sadr's Activism," *British Journal of Middle Eastern Studies* 41 (2014):79–96.
24. See *Hadith al-Dar* in al-Fayyad, *Ta'rikh al-Imamiyya*, 19–21.
25. al-Sadr, *Ikhtarna Laka*, 62.
26. Ibid., 62–63, 66–67.
27. Muhammad Baqir al-Sadr, *Lamha Fiqhiyyah Tamhidiyya 'an Mashru' Dustur al-Jumhuriyyah al-Islamiyya fi Iran* [A Preliminary Legal Observation on the Draft of the Constitution of the Islamic Republic of Iran], (Beirut: Dar al-Nahar li'l-Matbu'at, Silsilat al-Islam Yaqudu al-Hayat, no. 1, 1979), 19–20.
28. Interviews with "Dr. Shammari," London, Sept. 1990. In 2003, "Dr. Shammari" became a very prominent member of the Shi'i leadership in Baghdad.
29. Abbas Kazim, "The Hawza under Siege: A Study in the Ba'th Party Archive," IIBSU Occasional Paper 1 (Boston: Boston University Institute for Iraqi Studies), June 2013; Muhammad Baqir al-Hakim, *al-Hawza al-'Ilmiyya* (Najaf: Matba'at al-Zaytun, 2005).
30. Kazim, "The Hawza under Siege."
31. Amatzia Baram, "Sadr the Father, Sadr the Son, the 'Revolution in Shi'ism' and the Struggle for Power in the *Hawzah* of Najaf," in *Iraq between Occupations: Perspectives from 1920 to the Present,* eds. Amatzia Baram, Achim Rohde, and Ronen Zeidel (New York: Palgrave Macmillan, 2010), 143–58.
32. See Selim Deringil, "Shi'ism in Hamidian Iraq: A Study of Ottoman Counter-Propaganda," *Die Welt des Islams* 30 (1990):50.

33. In one of his fatwas, Sadiq al-Sadr allowed smoking during the Ramadan fast. This most exceptional ruling clashed head-on with the fatwas of the more senior *mujtahidun*. See Patrick Cockburn, *Muqtada al-Sadr and the Battle for the Future of Iraq* (New York: Scribner, 2008), 99.
34. Kazim, "The Hawza under Siege," 26–27.
35. International Crisis Group, *Iraq's Muqtada al-Sadr: Spoiler or Stabiliser?* Report no. 55, 11 July 2006.
36. Baram, *Saddam Husayn and Islam*, 271–72.
37. Muhammad Sadiq al-Sadr, *Fiqh al-ʿAshaʾir: Hiwar Fatawa maʿa Marjaʿ al-Muslimin Zaʿim al-Hawza al-ʿIlmiyya Samahat Ayat Allah al-ʿUzma al-Sayyid Muhammad al-Sadr* (Beirut: Dar al-Najwa), 1997.
38. Cockburn, *Muqtada al-Sadr*, 78–94, 91–93.
39. International Crisis Group, *Iraq's Muqtada al-Sadr*.
40. Cockburn, *Muqtada al-Sadr*, 89–93.
41. Ismaʿil al-Waʾili, ed., *Dustur [Muhammad Sadiq] al-Sadr* [al-Sadr's Constitution] (Najaf: Muʾassasat Baqiyyat Allah li-Nashr al-ʿUlum al-Islamiyya, Maktabat dar al-Mujtaba, 2004/1434), 267
42. International Crisis Group, *Iraq's Muqtada al-Sadr*, 4.
43. One of Saddam Hussein's generals, with reliable sources in the domestic security organizations, informed me that his contacts had sworn to him that the regime had not been involved. He asked that his name not be mentioned. Interviewed in June 2011.
44. Read more, for example, at LiveLeak.com, "Iraqi TV Airs Video Showing Leader of Jund al-Samaa (Army of Heaven)," accessed 7 July 2016, http://www.liveleak.com/view?i=555ca47d45#bG9zrma8Ro3vaIA1.99; Mike Few, "The Untold Story of the Battle against the 'Soldiers of Heaven' (updated)," *Small Wars Journal*, accessed 7 July 2016, http://smallwarsjournal.com/blog/the-untold-story-of-the-battle-against-the-%E2%80%98soldiers-of-heaven%E2%80%99-updated.

CHAPTER 8

1. Gordon Means, *Political Islam in Southeast Asia* (Boulder, CO: Lynne Rienner, 2009), 5.
2. Bernard J. Boland, *The Struggle of Islam in Modern Indonesia* (The Hague: Martinus Nijhoff, 1971), 106–7.
3. Luthfi Assyaukanie, *Islam and the Secular State in Indonesia* (Singapore: Institute of Southeast Asian Studies, 2009), 184–90; Bernhard Platzdasch, *Islamism in Indonesia: Politics in the Emerging Democracy* (Singapore: Institute of Southeast Asian Studies, 2009), 264–320.
4. See, e.g., Joseph Chinyong Liow, *Piety and Politics: Islamism in Contemporary Malaysia* (New York: Oxford University Press, 2009); Seyyed Vali Reza Nasr, *The Islamic Leviathan: Islam and the Making of State Power* (New York: Oxford University Press, 2001).

5. Kamaruzzaman Bustamam-Ahmad, "Contemporary Islamic Thought in Indonesian and Malay World: Islam Liberal, Islam Hadhari, and Islam Progresif," *Journal of Indonesian Islam* 5 (2011):112; Liow, *Piety and Politics*, 192.
6. See Robert Hefner, *Civil Islam: Muslims and Democratization in Indonesia* (Princeton, NJ: Princeton University Press, 2000), 121.
7. Presidential Decision no. 1, 1965.
8. Clifford Geertz, *The Religion of Java* (New York: Free Press, 1960), 11–120.
9. On the mystical groups (*golongan kebatinan*) see M. C. Ricklefs, *Islamisation and Its Opponents in Java: A Political, Social, Cultural and Religious History, c. 1930 to the Present* (Singapore: NUS Press, 2012), 43–54, 116–32.
10. Julia Day Howell, "Modernity and the Borderlands of Islamic Spirituality in Indonesia's New Sufi Networks," in *Sufism and the "Modern" in Islam*, eds. Martin van Bruinessen and Julia Day Howell (London: I. B. Tauris, 2007), 217–41.
11. Hefner, *Civil Islam*, 106–8.
12. Means, *Political Islam*, 98–99.
13. Robert Hefner, "Print Islam: Mass Media and Ideological Rivalries among Indonesian Muslims," *Indonesia* 64 (1997):77–103.
14. On the Masyumi, see Deliar Noer, *The Modernist Muslim Movement in Indonesia, 1900–1942* (Singapore: Oxford University Press, 1973); Platzdasch, *Islamism in Indonesia*, 30–99.
15. Martin van Bruinessen, "Genealogies of Islamic Radicalism in Post-Suharto Indonesia," *Southeast Asia Research* 10 (2002):117–54; Greg Fealy "Islamisation and Politics in Southeast Asia: The Contrasting Cases of Malaysia and Indonesia," in *Islam in World Politics*, eds. Nelly Lahoud and Anthony Johns (London: Routledge, 2005), 152–69.
16. Robert Hefner, "Islam, State and Civil Society: ICMI and the Struggle for the Indonesian Middle Class," *Indonesia* 56 (1993):1–35; M. Bambang Pranowo, "Islam and Party Politics in Rural Java," *Studia Islamika* 1, no. 2 (1984):1–19.
17. Elizabeth F Collins, "Islam Is the Solution: Dakwah and Democracy in Indonesia," *Kultur* 3, no. 1 (2003):156.
18. See Malik's chapter in this volume.
19. Noorhaidi Hasan, "The Making of Public Islam: Piety, Agency, and Commodification on the Landscape of the Indonesia Public Sphere," *Contemporary Islam* 3 (2009):233; Rifki Rosyad, *A Quest for True Islam: A Study of the Islamic Resurgence Movement among the Youth of Bandung* (Canberra: ANU E-Press, 2006), 40.
20. Noorhaidi Hasan, "The Salafi Movement in Indonesia: Transnational Dynamics and Local Development," *Comparative Studies of South Asia, Africa and the Middle East* 27, no. 1 (2007):87–89.
21. Noorhaidi Hasan, "Islamist Party, Electoral Politics and Daʿwah Mobilization among Youth: The Prosperous Justice Party (PKS) in Indonesia," *Journal of Indonesian Islam* 6 (2012): 17–47.

22. van Bruinessen, "Genealogies of Islamic Radicalism," 122.
23. William Liddle, "Media Dakwah Scripturalism: One Form of Political Thought and Action in New Order Indonesia," in *Toward a New Paradigm: Recent Developments in Indonesian Islamic Thought,* ed. Mark Woodward, Program for Southeast Asian Studies Monograph Series (Tempe: Arizona State University, 1996), 323–56.
24. Hasan, "The Making of Public Islam," 229–50.
25. Elizabeth Collins, "Islam Is the Solution," 151; Robert Hefner, *Civil Islam,* 103–7.
26. Martin van Bruinessen, "Liberal and Progressive Voices in Indonesian Islam," in *Reformist Voices of Islam,* ed. Shireen Hunter (London: Routledge, 2008), 189.
27. Ibid.
28. Collins, "Islam Is the Solution," 156–57.
29. van Bruinessen, "Genealogies of Islamic Radicalism," 126.
30. Rosyad, "A Quest for True Islam," 33–36.
31. Ali Said Demanik, *Fenomena Partai Kesejahtera: Transformasi 20 Tahun Gerakan Tarbiyyah di Indonesia* (Jakarta: Teraju, 2002).
32. See Stéphane Lacroix, *The Islamic Awakening: The Politics of Religious Dissent in Contemporary Saudi Arabia* (Cambridge, MA: Harvard University Press, 2011).
33. Greg Fealy, "Hizbut Tahrir in Indonesia: Seeking a 'Total' Muslim Identity," in *Islam and Political Violence,* eds. Shahram Akbarzadeh and Fethi Mansouri (London: I. B. Tauris, 2007), 151–64.
34. On Majdid, see Greg Barton, "Neo-Modernism: A Vital Synthesis of Traditionalist and Modernist Islamic Thought in Indonesia," *Studia Islamika* 2, no. 3 (2014):9–13; Peter Burns, *Revelation and Revolution: Natsir and the Panca Sila*, South-East Asian Monograph Series, no. 9 (Townsville, AU: Committee of South-East Asian Studies, James Cook University of North Queensland, 1981).
35. van Bruinessen, "Liberal and Progressive Voices," 191–92.
36. Greg Barton, *Abdurrahman Wahid: Muslim Democrat, Indonesian President* (Sydney: University of New South Wales Press, 2002); and van Bruinessen, "Liberal and Progressive Voices."
37. Hefner, *Civil Islam*, 116–19.
38. Julia Day Howell, "Modernity and the Borderlands," 217–41.
39. Robert Hefner, "Islam, State and Civil Society," 1–35.
40. Martin van Bruinessen, "Islamic State or State Islam? Fifty Years of State-Islam Relations in Indonesia," in *Indonesien am Ende des 20. Jahrhunderts,* ed. Ingrid Wessel (Hamburg: Abera, 1996), 19–34; Hefner, "Islam, State and Civil Society," 125, 128–38.
41. Van Bruinessen, "Genealogies of Islamic Radicalism," 31; Demanik, *Fenomena Partai Kesejahtera.*

42. Nadirsyah Hosen, "Religion and the Indonesian Constitution: A Recent Debate," *Journal of Southeast Asian Studies* 36, no. 3 (2005):419–40.
43. On this organization, see Noorhaidi Hasan, *Laskar Jihad: Islam, Militancy, and the Quest for Identity in Post–New Order Indonesia* (Ithaca, NY: Cornell University Press, 2006).
44. Interviews at JIL's Jakarta office, 2006. See also Assyaukanie, *Islam and the Secular State*, 201–2.
45. Greg Fealy, "Consuming Islam," in *Expressing Islam: Religious Life and Politics in Indonesia,* eds. Greg Fealy and Sally White (Singapore: ISEAS Press, 2008), 15–39; Hasan, "The Making of Public Islam," 230–31, 238.
46. James Hoesterey, *Rebranding Islam: Piety, Prosperity, and a Self-Help Guru* (Stanford, CA: Stanford University Press, 2015); Julia Day Howell, "Modulations of Active Piety: Professors and Televangelists as Promoters of Indonesian 'Sufisme,'" in *Expressing Islam*, eds. Fealy and White, 40–62.
47. James Hoesterey, "Prophetic Cosmopolitanism: Islam, Pop Psychology, and Civil Virtue in Indonesia," *City and Society* 24 (2012):44–48; Howell, "Modulations of Active Piety," 67–70. For the parallel trend of the New Preachers in the Middle East, see Aaron Rock-Singer's chapter in this volume.
48. Julia Day Howell, "'Calling' and 'Training': Role Innovation and Religious De-differentiation in Commercialized Indonesian Islam," *Journal of Contemporary Religion* 28 (2013):407–12; see also Daromir Rudnyckyj, "Spiritual Economies: Islam and Neoliberalism in Indonesia," *Cultural Anthropology* 24, no. 1 (2009): 110, 118.
49. Ibid., 120–22.
50. Anna Gade, *Perfection Makes Practice: Learning, Emotion, and the Recited Qur'an in Indonesia* (Honolulu: University of Hawaii Press, 2004), 228–33.
51. Akh Muzakki, "The Islamic Publication Industry in Modern Indonesia: Intellectual Transmission, Ideology, and the Profit Motive" (PhD diss., University of Queensland, 2009), 122–25.
52. Saja Hariyadi, "Islamic Popular Culture and the New Identities of Urban Muslim Young People in Indonesia: The Case of the Islamic Films and Islamic Self-Help Books" (PhD diss., University of Western Australia, 2013), 79–107.
53. Monika Arnez, "*Dakwah* by the Pen: Reading Helvy Tiana Rosa's *Bukavu*," *Indonesia and the Malay World* 37, no. 107 (2009):51.

CHAPTER 9

1. Jorgen S. Nielsen, *Muslims in Western Europe*, 3rd ed. (Edinburgh: Edinburgh University Press, 2004), 1–59.
2. Pew Research Center, "5 Facts about the Muslim Population in Europe," 19 July 2016, accessed 15 December 2016, http://www.pewresearch.org/fact-tank/2016/07/19/5-facts-about-the-muslim-population-in-europe.

3. Soeren Kern, "Muslims Converting Empty European Churches into Mosques," Gatestone Institute, 16 January 2012, accessed 20 October 2016, https://www.gatestoneinstitute.org/2761/converting-churches-into-mosques.
4. Khaled Abou el-Fadl, "Islamic Law and Muslim Minorities: The Juristic Discourse on Muslim Minorities from the Second/Eighth to the Eleventh/Seventeenth Centuries," *Islamic Law and Society* 1, 2 (1994):146–47. On al-Shafi'i's attitude, see also Sami A. Aldeeb Abu-Sahlieh, "The Islamic Conception of Migration," *International Migration Review* 30, no. 1 (1996):43.
5. Abou el-Fadl, "Islamic Law and Muslim Minorities," 150.
6. Ibid., 159–60; Alan J. Verskin, *Oppressed in the Land? Fatwas on Muslims Living under Non-Muslim Rule from the Middle Ages to the Present* (Princeton, NJ: Markus Wiener, 2013), 31–33.
7. Abou el-Fadl, "Islamic Law and Muslim Minorities," 161.
8. Ibid., 153–7; Verskin, *Oppressed in the Land?*, 21–30; Sarah David-Secors, "Muslims in Norman Sicily: The Evidence of Imam al-Mazari's Fatwas," *Mediterranean Studies* 16 (2007):51–59; Jocelyne N. Hendrickson, "The Islamic Obligation to Emigrate: al-Wansharisi's Asna al-Matajir Reconsidered" (PhD diss., Emory University, 2009), 56–70, 136–76.
9. Abou el-Fadl, "Islamic Law and Muslim Minorities," 157; Salim b. 'Abd al-Ghani al-Rafi'i, *Ahkam al-Ahwal al-Shakhsiyya li'l-Muslimin fi'l-Gharb* (Beirut: Dar Ibn Hazm, 2002), 58–60; For Ibn Taymiyya's opinion on the matter, see Khalid bin 'Ali bin Muhammad al-'Anbari, *The Impact of Man-Made Laws in Determining the Judgment of an Abode as Being One of Disbelief or Islam* (Amman: Jamiah Media, 2007, originally published in Arabic in 2004), 64–66.
10. Umar Ryad, "A Prelude to Fiqh al-Aqalliyat: Rashid Rida's Fatwas to Muslims under non-Muslim Rule," in *In-Between Spaces: Christian and Muslim Minorities in Transition in Europe and the Middle East,* eds. Christiane Timmerman et al. (London: Peter Lang, 2009), 241–44.
11. Rashid Rida, "Jama'at al-Da'wa wa'l-Irshad," *al-Manar* 14, no. 2 (1 March 1911): 114–20.
12. Charles C. Adams, *Islam and Modernism in Egypt: A Study of the Modern Reform Movement Inaugurated by Muhammad 'Abduh* (New York: Russel and Russel, 1968; first published 1933 by Oxford University Press [Oxford]), 196–98.
13. Rashid Rida, "Al-Islam fi Inkaltra," *al-Manar* 18, 14 (14 February 1915): 73–79.
14. Yusuf al-Qaradawi, *al-Halal wa'l-Haram fi'l-Islam* (Cairo: Matkabat Wahba, 2004, originally published in 1960), 9–11.
15. 'Ali ibn al-Muntasir al-Kittani, *al-Muslimun fi Urubba wa-Amrika* (Beirut: Dar al-Kutub al-'Ilmiyya, 2005), 296–308.
16. See also Weismann's chapter in this volume.
17. Muhammad al-Ghazali, *al-Da'wa al-Islamiyya fi'l-Qarn al-Hali* (Cairo: Dar al-Shuruq, 2000), 82.

18. Muhammad al-Ghazali, *Mustaqbal al-Islam Kharij Ardihi: Kayfa Nufakkiru Fihi?* (Cairo: Dar al-Shuruq, 1997, first published 1984), 54.
19. Ibid., 70.
20. Ibid., 78–79.
21. Ibid., 5–11.
22. Ibid., 78.
23. Ibid., 27–29.
24. Mani' Hamad al-Jahni, "al-Islam li-Ghayr al-Muslimin: Barnamaj Muqtara li'l-Da'wa bayna al-Aqalliyyat al-Muslima," in *al-Aqalliyyat al-Muslima fi'l-'Alam* (Riyadh: al-Nadwa al-'Alamiyya li'l-Shabab al-Islami, 1986), 165–77.
25. Muhammad 'Abdallah al-Samman, "Istratijiyyat al-Da'wa al-Islamiyya fi Duwal Ghayr Islamiyya," in *al-Aqalliyyat al-Muslima*, 181–93.
26. Muhammad al-Shadhili al-Nayfar, "al-Tajannus bi-Jinsiyya Ghayr Islamiyya," *Majallat al-Majma' al-Fiqhi al-Islami* 2, no. 4 (1989):177–252.
27. Yusuf al-Qaradawi, *Fi Fiqh al-Aqalliyyat al-Muslima* (Cairo: Dar al-Shuruq, 2006, originally published in 2001 at the invitation of Rabitat al-'Alam al-Islami), 20–22.
28. Yusuf al-Qaradawi, *Ta'rikhna al-Muftara 'Alayhi* (Cairo: Dar al-Shuruq, 2008, first published 2005), 200–205.
29. Yusuf al-Qaradawi, "Duties of Muslims Living in the West," 7 May 2006, originally posted on Islamonline.net, accessed 10 January 2007.
30. al-Qaradawi, *Fiqh al-Aqalliyyat*, 17.
31. Ibid., 33.
32. Taha Jabir al-'Alwani, *Fi Fiqh al-Aqalliyyat al-Muslima* (Cairo: Nahdat Misr, 2000), 16–18,36–51; al-'Alwani, "al-Hukm al-Shar'i fi-Musharakat al-Muslimin fi'l-Haya al-Siyasiyya al-Amrikiyya," *al-Sharq al-Awsat*, 13 November 1999, 16; al-'Alwani, "Madhkahl ila Fiqh al-Aqalliyyat," *al-Majallah al-'Ilmiya* 4–5 (June 2004):84–85.
33. 'Abd al-'Aziz ibn Baz, "Kayfa Nuharib al-Ghazw al-Thaqafi al-Gharbi wa'l-Sharqi," Binbaz (n.d.), http://www.binbaz.org.sa/mat/8164; ibn Baz, "Hukm al-Safar Kharij al-Duwal al-Islamiyya," Binbaz (n.d.), http://www.binbaz.org.sa/index.php?pg=mat&type=fatawa&id=58; "Hukm al Safar ila al-Kharij li'l-Dirasa wa-Ghayriha," Binbaz (n.d.), http://www.binbaz.org.sa/index.php?pg=mat&type=fatawa&id=1719; "al-Safar ila al-Kharij" (n.d.), http://www.binbza.org.sa.\ index\php?pg=mat&type=fatawa&id=41 (all accessed 31 December 2016).
34. Muhammad ibn Salih al-'Uthaymin, "al-Iqama fi Bilad al-Kuffar," in *Fatawa al-Balad al-Haram* (Cairo: Dar al-Tawfiqiyya, n.d.), 189–91.
35. Muhammad ibn Salih al-'Uthaymin, "Inviting to Allah in Communities Where There Are Muslim Minorities," in *Muslim Minorities: Fatawa Regarding Muslims Living as Minorities,* eds. 'Abd al-'Aziz ibn 'Abdallah ibn Baz and Muhammad b. Salih al-'Uthaymin (London: Message of Islam, 1998), 43–59.

36. "Muslim Minorities in non-Muslim Countries," Islamweb.net, 20 July 2004, accessed 20 October 2019, https://islamweb.net/en/fatwa/88291/muslim-minorities-in-non-muslim-countries.
37. Muhammad al-Kadi al-ʿUmrani, *Fiqh al-Usra al-Muslimah fi'l-Muhajar* (Beirut: Dar al-Kutub al-ʿIlmiyah, 2001), 29–127.
38. Quoted in Uriya Shavit, *The New Imagined Community* (Brighton: Sussex Academic Press, 2009), 168. On Vogel, see also Wiedl's chapter in this volume.
39. Shavit, *The New Imagined Community*, 152–85.
40. Bundesamt für Verfassungsschutz (Federal Office for the Protection of the Constitution), accessed 5 February 2016, https://www.verfassungsschutz.de/de/arbeitsfelder/af-islamismus-und-islamistischer-terrorismus/was-ist-islamismus/salafistische-bestrebungen. On the meager number of Salafis in Germany, see also Nina Wiedl, *The Making of a German Salafiyya The Emergence, Development and Missionary Work of Salafi Movements in Germany* (Aarhus: Centre for Study in Islamism and Radicalisation, 2012), 9.
41. Interview with Abu Khadija, Salafi Mosque, Birmingham, 10 October 2015.
42. Tariq Ramadan, *Western Muslims and the Future of Islam* (New York: Oxford University Press, 2004), 6.
43. Ibid., 81; Ramadan, "Europeanization of Islam or Islamization of Europe?" in *Islam, Europe's Second Religion,* ed. Shireen T. Hunter (Westport, CT: Praeger, 2002), 213.
44. For an official English translation of the text see, http://amrkhaled.net/articles/articles542.html. For a translation into German, see Amr Khaled, *Integration im Islam: Über die Rolle der Muslime in Europa* (Karlsruhe: Andalusia, 2005). For an audio version of the original sermon in Arabic see, http://amrkhaled.net/sound_libaray/multimedia172.html.
45. I observed its limited funding during my visit to the Council's headquarters in February 2013. For a lament on the implications of its limited resources, see ʿAbd al-Majid al-Najjar, *Fiqh al-Muwatana li'l-Muslimin fi Urubba* (Beirut: al-Majlis al-'Urubbi li'l-Ifta' wa'l-Buhuth, 2009), 69–70.
46. My interview with Hussein Halawa at the Islamic Cultural Center of Ireland, 13–14 February 2012.
47. For the full text of the fatwa, see Imam Muhammad Imam, "Fatwa Tujizu Shira' al-Manazil bi-Qard Ribbawi li'l-Muslimin fi Ghayr Bilad al-Islam," *al-Sharq al-Awsat*, 3 October 1999, 25; Yusuf al-Qaradawi, "Shira' Buyut al-Sukna fi'l-Gharb ʿan Tariq al-Bunuk," in *Fi Fiqh al-Aqalliyyat al-Muslima*, 174–79. An English translation is *Fatwas of European Council for Fatwa and Research*, trans. Anas Usama al-Tikriti and Shakir Nasif al-ʿUbaydi (Cairo: Islamic INC, 2002), 160–68.

CHAPTER 10

1. Denise A. Spellberg, *Thomas Jefferson's Qur'an: Islam and the Founders* (New York: Vintage, 2013).

2. Yvonne Haddad and Adair Lummis, *Islamic Values in the United States: A Comparative Study* (New York: Oxford University Press, 1987), 13–14.
3. Muzzamil Siddiqui, "Muslims in a Non-Muslim Society," *Islamic Horizons* May–June (1986):22.
4. Nina Wiedl, "*Daʿwa* and the Islamist Revival in the West," *Current Trends in Islamist Ideology* 9 (2009):122–23.
5. Anna Mansson McGinty, *Becoming Muslim: Western Women's Conversions to Islam* (New York: Palgrave Macmillan, 2006), 19.
6. Ibid.
7. See testimonies included in, Amin Ahsan Islahi, *Call to Islam and How the Holy Prophets Preached* (1982); Jeffrey Lang, *Struggling to Surrender* (1994); Badar Azimabadi, *Islam: The Final Choice* (1995); Carol Anway, *Daughters of Another Path* (1996); Muzaffar Haleem, *The Sun is Rising in the West: Journeys to Islam* (1999); and Iqbal Unus, *Muslim American Life: Reflections and Perspectives* (2014).
8. Larry Poston, *Islamic Daʿwah in the West: Muslim Missionary Activity and the Dynamics of Conversion to Islam* (New York: Oxford University Press, 1992), 51. The use of the term "missiology" arises from the Islamic analog to what Christianity calls its "Great Commission," as seen in Matthew 28:19–20: "Go and make disciples in all the nations. . . ." The Muslim equivalent of this missiological imperative is found in Quran 2:143: "Thus have We made of you an *umma* justly balanced, that you might be witnesses over the nations."
9. Poston, *Daʿwah*, 54–55.
10. Ibid., 57.
11. Ibid., 62–63.
12. See, for instance, Ida Lichter, "Misogyny in the Muslim World: Bound by Culture or Religion?" *Huffington Post*, 25 May 2011, accessed 13 December 2016, http://www.huffingtonpost.com/ida-lichter-md/misogyny-bound-by-culture_b_803942.html.
13. Wiedl, "*Daʿwa*," 123.
14. Yvonne Haddad, Jane Smith, and Kathleen Moore, *Muslim Women in America: The Challenge of Islamic Identity Today* (New York: Oxford University Press, 2006), 42.
15. Ibid., 18–19.
16. Ibid., 47.
17. Press Association, "Study Shows 'Demonisation' of Muslims," *Guardian*, 14 November 2007, accessed 30 December 2016, http://www.theguardian.com/media/2007/nov/14/pressandpublishing.religion.
18. See, e.g., U. Jamil, "Discrimination Experienced by Muslims in Ontario," *Diversity Magazine* 9, no. 3 (2012), accessed 22 October 2019, http://www.ohrc.on.ca/en/creed-freedom-religion-and-human-rights-special-issue-diversity-magazine-volume-93-summer-2012/discrimination-experienced

-muslims-ontario; S. Nasser, "Paris Attacks Backlash 'Nothing New,' Canadian Muslims Say, But Public Also Supportive," *CBC News*, 24 November 2015, accessed 30 December 2016, http://www.cbc.ca/news/canada/toronto/paris-attacks-backlash-nothing-new-canadian-muslims-say-but-public-also-supportive-1.3331724; National Council of Canadian Muslims, *ODIHR Hate Crime Report*, Ottawa, 2014, accessed 17 December 2016, http://www.nccm.ca/wp-content/uploads/2014/11/Hate-Crime-Report-2013-National-Council-of-Canadian-Muslims.pdf; Spence, D. "Why Online Islamophobia Is Difficult to Stop," *CBC News*, 1 November 2014, accessed 30 December 2016, http://www.cbc.ca/news/why-online-islamophobia-is-difficult-to-stop-1.2810242.

Despite these accounts, it is worth noting that a 2011 report by the U.S. Department of Justice stated that more Muslim-American men (46%) than women (39%) reported experiencing hostile acts after 9/11; see U.S. Department of Justice. "Confronting Discrimination in the Post-9/11 Era: Challenges and Opportunities Ten Years Later," 19 October 2011, accessed 30 December 2016, http://www.justice.gov/sites/default/files/crt/legacy/2012/04/16/post911summit_report_2012-04.pdf.

19. "What You Should Know about the EEOC and Religious and National Origin Discrimination Involving the Muslim, Sikh, Arab, Middle Eastern, and South Asian Communities," U.S. Equal Employment Opportunity Commission, accessed 30 December 2016, http://www.eeoc.gov/eeoc/newsroom/wysk/religion_national_origin_9-11.cfm.
20. NACMW describes some of their post-September 11 education and advocacy efforts on their website: http://pluralism.org/profile/north-american-council-for-muslim-women/ (accessed 30 December 2016).
21. McGinty, *Becoming Muslim*, 19.
22. Haddad et al., *Muslim Women*, 41–42.
23. Myriam Francois-Cerrah, *My Journey to Islam*, 8 October 2012, accessed 30 December 2016, http://www.youtube.com/watch?v=-JlkisV72os.
24. Sarah Sayeed, Aisha al-Adawiya, and Ihsan Bagby, "Women and the American Mosque," *The American Mosque 2011* (Plainfield, IN: Islamic Society of North America, 2013).
25. See Robert Steinback, "The Anti-Muslim Inner Circle," *Intelligence Report Southern Poverty Law Center*, 17 June 2011, accessed 30 December 2016, http://www.splcenter.org/fighting-hate/intelligence-report/2011/anti-muslim-inner-circle.
26. Evelyn Alsultany, "Arabs and Muslims in the Media after 9/11: Representational Strategies for a 'Postrace' Era," *American Quarterly* 65 (March 2013):161–69.
27. Harun Yahya, "The Rapid Spread of Islam in America," The Rise of Islam.com, accessed 17 December 2016, http://www.riseofislam.com/islam_in_america_02.html.

28. Uriya Shavit and Frederic Wiesenbach, "Muslim Strategies to Convert Western Christians," *Middle East Quarterly* 16, no. 2 (2009):3–14.
29. See, for instance, Salwa Muttaqi, "34,000 Americans Converted to Islam," Tell Me about Islam, accessed 17 December 2016, http://tellmeaboutislam.com/34000-american-entered-islam.html.
30. Poston, *Daʿwah*, 93ff.
31. "Outreach," Islamic Circle of North America, http://www.icna.org/outreach/ (accessed 17 December 2016).
32. "History," Islamic Daʿwah Center, accessed 30 December 2016, islamic-dawahcenter.org/about-us/.
33. See, for instance, James K. Dooghan, *Muslim Prison Ministry: Hindering the Spread of the Radical, Militant, Violent and Irreconcilable Wing of Islam* (Fort Leavenworth, KS: U.S. Army Command and General Staff College, 2006).
34. "Religion in Prisons: A 50-State Survey of Prison Chaplains," Pew Research Center, 22 March 2012, accessed 23 October 2019, http://www.pewforum.org/2012/03/22/prison-chaplains-exec/.
35. See, e.g., C. Eric Lincoln, *The Black Muslims in America* (Grand Rapids, MI: Eerdmans, 1994); and Aminah Beverly McCloud, *African American Islam* (New York: Routledge, 1994).
36. Mirza Tahir Ahmad, *Invitation to Ahmadiyyat* (Sydney, AU: Law Book Company of Australasia, 1980); and Muhammad Ali, *The Founder of the Ahmadiyya Movement: A Short Study* (London: Forgotten Books, 2012).
37. "Muslim Chaplaincy in the U.S.," the Pluralism Project (Cambridge, MA: Harvard University, n.d.), accessed 30 December 2016, http://pluralism.org/religions/islam/issues-for-muslims-in-america/muslim-chaplaincy-in-the-u-s/.
38. John Edmiston, "Internet Evangelism and Cybermissions: Their Impact upon How We Will Do Missions in the 21st Century," accessed 30 December 2016, http://cybermissions.org/articles/21stC_missions.pdf.
39. "Answering Islam," accessed 30 December 2016, http://www.answering-islam.org/.
40. "Answering Christianity," accessed 30 December 2016, http://www.answering-christianity.com/ac.htm.
41. Ibid.
42. Ibid.
43. Shavit and Wiesenbach, "Strategies," 3–4.
44. Nadia Khan, "American Muslims in the Age of New Media," in *The Oxford Handbook of American Islam,* eds. Yvonne Haddad and Jane Smith (New York: Oxford University Press, 2014), 381.
45. Noorhaidi Hasan, "The Making of Public Islam: Piety, Agency, and Commodification on the Landscape of the Indonesia Public Sphere," *Contemporary Islam* 3 (2009):230.

46. Vit Sisler, "The Internet and the Construction of Islamic Knowledge in Europe," *Masaryk University Journal of Law and Technology*, 1 (2007):205–18.
47. For a detailed historical overview of Muslim immigration to the United States, see the chapters by Randa B. Serhan and Sylviane A. Diouf in *Oxford Handbook*, eds. Haddad and Smith, 15–28, 29–46.
48. Haddad et al., *Muslim Women*, 6.
49. On the Tablighi Jamaʿat see Gugler's and Ahmad's chapters in this volume.
50. Christoph Schumann, "A Muslim 'Diaspora' in the United States?" *Muslim World* 97 (2007):11–32.
51. Mukahit Bilici, *Finding Mecca in America: How Islam Is Becoming an American Religion* (Chicago: University of Chicago Press, 2012), 2.
52. Sheila McDonough and Homa Hoodfar, "Muslims in Canada: From Ethnic Groups to Religious Community," in *Religion and Ethnicity in Canada*, eds. Paul Bramadat and David Seljak (Toronto: Toronto University Press, 2009). See also Regula B. Qureshi, "Transcending Space: Recitation and Community among South Asian Muslims in Canada," in *Making Muslim Space in North America and Europe*, ed. Barbara Metcalf (Berkeley: University of California Press, 1996), 46.
53. Roshan A. Jahangeer, *Towards an Inclusive Secularism and a Transformative Model of Community Engagement in Québec* (Toronto: Tesselate Institute, 2014), accessed 30 December 2016, http://www.tessellateinstitute.com/newsite/publications/towards-an-inclusive-secularism-and-a-transformative-model-of-community-engagement-in-quebec/. See also Jasmin Zine, "Redefining Resistance: Towards an Islamic Subculture in Schools," *Race Ethnicity and Education* 3 (2000):293.
54. Larry Poston, "The Future of Daʿwah in North America," in *Muslims and Islamization in North America: Problems and Prospects*, ed. Amber Haque (Kuala Lumpur: A. S. Noordeen, 1999).
55. For a more detailed overview, see Carolyn Moxley Rouse, "African American Islam," in *Oxford Handbook*, eds. Haddad and Smith, 87–99.
56. McCloud, *African American Islam*.
57. Kathleen Moore, "Muslim Women in the United States," in *Oxford Handbook*, eds. Haddad and Smith, 187–207.
58. Rory Dickson, "The Tablighi Jamaʿat in Southwestern Ontario: Making Muslim Identities and Networks in Canadian Urban Spaces," *Contemporary Islam* 3, no. 2 (2009):99–112.
59. Nadeen Memon, "From Mosques to Madrassas: Civic Engagement and the Pedagogy of Islamic Schools," in *Islam in the Hinterlands: Exploring Muslim Cultural Politics in Canada*, ed. Jasmin Zine (Vancouver: University of British Columbia Press, 2012), 185–207.
60. Haddad et al., *Muslim Women*, 44.
61. Zine, "Redefining Resistance," 293–316.

62. Pre- and post-September 11 rhetoric about Muslims in the U.S. has been documented elsewhere, e.g., Charles Kimball, "The War on Terror and Its Effect on American Muslims," in *Oxford Handbook*, eds. Haddad and Smith, 490–506; Peter Gottschalk, "Islamophobia and Anti-Muslim Sentiment in the United States," in *Oxford Handbook*, eds. Haddad and Smith, 507–20; and Ahmadullah Siddiqi's chapter in *Muslims and Islamization*, ed. Haque, 203–30.
63. Khan, "American Muslims in the Age of New Media," 376–88.
64. Yasmin Jiwani, "Colluding Hegemonies: Constructing the Muslim Other Post 11 September," in *Islam in the Hinterlands*, ed. Zine, 115–36.
65. Ronald L. Johnstone, *Religion in Society: A Sociology of Religion*, 8th ed. (New York: Routledge, 2006), ch. 3.
66. See Ilya Somin, *Democracy and Political Ignorance: Why Smaller Government Is Smarter* (Palo Alto, CA: Stanford University Press, 2013).
67. Maxwell McCombs, *Setting the Agenda: Mass Media and Public Opinion*, 2nd ed. (Cambridge, UK: Polity Press, 2014).
68. A 2015 poll revealed that fifty-five percent of Americans hold an "unfavorable" view of Islam and Muslims. See Mona Chalabi, "How Anti-Muslim Are Americans? Data Points to Extent of Islamophobia," *Guardian*, 8 December 2015, accessed 24 October 2019, https://www.theguardian.com/us-news/2015/dec/08/muslims-us-islam-islamophobia-data-polls. For comparative purposes, see "How Americans Feel about Religious Groups," Pew Research Center, 16 July 2014, accessed 24 October 2019, http://www.pewforum.org/2014/07/16/how-americans-feel-about-religious-groups/.
69. Cathy Lynn Grossman, "Number of U.S. Mosques Up 74% since 2000," *USA Today*, 29 February 2012.
70. Dar Al-Hijrah Islamic Center, "Etiquette of Visiting a Mosque (Masjid)," accessed 30 December 2016, http://hijrah.org/media/etiquette-of-visiting-a-mosque-masjid/.
71. Fouad Masri, "A Visit to the Mosque," accessed 30 December 2016, http://www.crescentproject.org/files/podcasts/MosqueVisit.pdf.
72. North American Imam's Federation, "Visiting an Islamic Center," accessed 30 December 2016, http://imamsofamerica.weebly.com/visiting-a-mosque.html.
73. Why Islam, "Visit a Mosque," accessed 30 December 2016, http://www.whyislam.org/services/visit-a-mosque/.

CHAPTER 11

1. "The Islamic field" is a term derived and modified from Pierre Bourdieu, "Genesis and Structure of the Religious Field," *Comparative Social Research* 13 (1991):9–10.
2. For the role of preaching in South Asian Islam in the late colonial period, see Sana Haroon, "The Rise of Deobandi Islam in the North-West Frontier

Province and Its Implications in Colonial India and Pakistan, 1914–1996," *Journal of the Royal Asiatic Society* 18 (2008):47–70.

3. For different preaching formats at the time, see Dietrich Reetz, *Islam in the Public Sphere: Religious Groups in India, 1900–1947* (New Delhi: Oxford University Press, 2006), 56ff, tab. 2.1; Jamal Malik, *Islam in South Asia: A Short History* (Leiden: Brill, 2008), ch. 12.
4. See Shail Mayaram, *Resisting Regimes: Myth, Memory, and the Shaping of a Muslim Identity* (Delhi: Oxford University Press, 1997).
5. Muhammad Khalid Masud, *Travellers in Faith: Studies of the Tablighi Jamaʿat as a Transnational Islamic Movement for Faith Renewal* (Leiden: Brill, 2000), 4.
6. Muhammad Zakariya, *Tablighi Nisab* (Delhi: n.p., 1940); numerous editions, later under the title: *Fazaʾil-e Aʿmal*. English edition: Muhammad Zakariya with Ihtishamul Ḥasan Kandhalawi and ʿAshiq Ilahi, *Fazaʾil-e-Aʿmaal* (New Delhi: Idara Ishaat-E-Diniyat, 1994).
7. Abul Hasan ʿAli Nadwi, *Hazrat Mawlana Muhammad Ilyas awr Unki Dini Daʿwat* [Mawlana Muhammad Ilyas and His Religious Mission] (Lucknow: Tanvir, 1964 [1946]); Muhammad Asif Kidwai, trans., *Life and Mission of Maulana Mohammad Ilyas* (Lucknow: Academy of Islamic Research and Publications, 1979), 142.
8. M. Anwarul Haq, *The Faith Movement of Mawlana Muhammad Ilyas* (London: Allen and Unwin, 1972), 95. On the Nadwa, see Jamal Malik, *Islamische Gelehrtenkultur in Nordindien: Entwicklungsgeschichte und Tendenzen am Beispiel von Lucknow* (Leiden: Brill, 1997); Jan-Peter Hartung, *Viele Wege und ein Ziel: Leben und Wirken von Sayyid Abu l-Hasan ʿAli al-Hasani Nadwi (1914–1999)* (Würzburg: Ergon, 2004).
9. Nadwi, *Life and Mission*, 22.
10. Farish Noor, *Islam on the Move: The Tablighi Jamaʿat in Southeast Asia* (Amsterdam: Amsterdam University Press, 2012).
11. Masud, *Travellers in Faith*, 20.
12. See Muslim Speakers, "Tablighi Jamaat Amazing Effort," accessed 2 September 2011, https://www.youtube.com/watch?v=KaJdwA8cdQI; "Shahid Afridi Official," accessed 15 June 2018, https://www.facebook.com/ShahidAfridiOfficial10/.
13. On this institution, see Barbara Daly Metcalf, *Islamic Revival in British India: Deoband, 1860–1900* (Princeton, NJ: Princeton University Press, 1982).
14. Malik, *Gelehrtenkultur*, 129–56, 522–29.
15. See Gugler, this volume, as well as Ehteshamul Hasan and Ashique Elahi, *The Teachings of Tabligh* (Delhi: Idara Ishaat-E-Diniyat, 1989), 15–19.
16. Interviews with TJ functionaries from their Raiwind Center in Lahore, Pakistan, October 2002. For their organizational features, see also the detailed description in the biography of the second amir, Muhammad Yusuf, by Muhammad Sayyid Sani Hasani, *Sawanih Hazrat Mawlana*

Muhammad Yusuf Kandhalawi [Biography of Muhammad Yusuf Kandhalawi] (Lucknow: Maktaba Dar al-ʿUlum Nadwat al-ʿUlama', 1982).

17. Dietrich Reetz, "The 'Faith Bureaucracy' of the *Tablighi Jamaʿat*: An Insight into Their System of Self-Organisation (*Intizam*)," in *Colonialism, Modernity, and Religious Identities: Religious Reform Movements in South Asia,* ed. Gwilym Beckerlegge (Delhi: Oxford University Press, 2008), 98–124.
18. The conflict over control of the global movement pitched Mawlana Saad in Delhi against both the Raiwind center in Pakistan and local followers of Mawlana Zubair, an earlier TJ leader and relative who had died in 2014. It led to violent clashes between the two factions in Delhi and in the UK. See Sajid Iqbal, "A House Divided," accessed 15 June 2018, https://www.dawn.com/news/1391624/a-house-divided.
19. Iftikhar Husain Faridi, *Irshadat wa Maktubat-e Hazrat Mawlana Shah Muhammad Ilyas Dihlawi* (Lahore: Makki Dar al-Kutub, 1997), 114–16; Yoginder Sikand, *The Origins and Development of the Tablighi Jamaʿat, 1920–2000: A Cross-Country Comparative Study* (New Delhi: Orient Longman, 2002).
20. Muhammad Ilyas and Sayyid Abu al-Hasan ʿAli Nadwi, *Makatib, Hazrat Mawlana Shah Muhammad Ilyas* (Karachi: Dar al-Ishaʿat, 1982 [1952]), 142.
21. On Tablighi activism as a form of cultural and social critique, see Barbara Daly Metcalf, "Living Hadith in the Tablighi Jamaʿat," *Journal of Asian Studies* 52 (1993):584–608.
22. See the website of the Jeddah Dawah Center, http://www.jdci.org, and its video channel NoorTV on YouTube, http://www.youtube.com/user/NNoorTV. See also https://www.youtube.com/watch?v=13y88mfH1zg for a direct reference of the channel to the center. There is a six-part YouTube lecture series, arguing against the Tablighi Hadith collection, by Shaykh Toseefur Rehman, "Fazail e Amaal ki Haqiqat," uploaded in 2008, https://www.youtube.com/watch?v=qHKYLA4vOnI. There is a similar and more recent twelve-part series by another Ahl-e Hadith scholar, Sheikh Meraj Rabbani, on the Ahl-e Hadith video channel TawheedAurShirk, uploaded in 2013, https://www.youtube.com/watch?v=g81EYOETm04, all accessed 10 August 2016.
23. See Usha Sanyal, *Devotional Islam and Politics in British India: Ahmad Riza Khan Barelwi and His movement, 1870–1920* (Delhi: Oxford University Press, 1996).
24. Interviews with respondents in Kyrgyzstan, 2012; Indonesia and Malaysia, 2005, 2009, 2010; and France, 2008.
25. See Thomas K. Gugler, *Mission Medina: Daʿwat-e Islami und Tabligi Jamaʿat* (Würzburg: Ergon, 2011). For the DI critique of their competitor, TJ, see Arshad al-Qadiri, *Tablighi Jamaʿat: Haqaʾiq wa Maʿlumat* (Lahore: Maktaba Nabawiya, n.d. [1969]).

26. See Yoginder Sikand, "Reformist Sufism of the Tablighi Jamaʿat: The Case of the Meos of Mewat, India," in *Sufism and the "Modern" in Islam,* eds. Martin van Bruinessen and Julia Day Howell (London: I. B. Tauris, 2007), 129–48.
27. Interviews with Tablighi respondents in Pakistan and India in 2002; Malaysia, Indonesia, and South Africa in 2005; Britain in 2006.
28. See Humeira Iqtidar, "How Long Is Life? Neoliberalism and Islamic Piety," *Critical Inquiry* 43 (2017): 790–812.
29. "The Enigma That Was Junaid Jamshed," *Express Tribune*, 7 December 2016, accessed 1 December 2017, http://tribune.com.pk/story/1256459/profile-enigma-junaid-jamshed/.
30. Barbara Daly Metcalf, "Tablighi Jamaʿat and Women" in *Travellers in Faith*, ed. Masud, 44–58. See also Mareike Jule Winkelmann, *From Behind the Curtain: A Study of a Girls' Madrasa in India* (Amsterdam: Amsterdam University Press, 2005), and Arsalan Khan, "Pious Masculinity, Ethical Reflexivity, and Moral Order in an Islamic Piety Movement in Pakistan," *Anthropological Quarterly* 91 (2018):53–77.
31. Darakshan Khan, "Shaping This World and the Next: Tablighi Women and the Discourse of Perfection" (paper, International Workshop on the Tablighi Jamaʿat: Studies of a Transnational Islamic Revivalist Movement, Oxford Center for Islamic Studies, 2012). For women's participation in Bangladesh, see Maimuna Huq, "The Politics of Belief: Women's Islamic Activism in Bangladesh" (PhD diss., Columbia University, 2006).
32. Mukaram Toktogulova, "The Localization of the Transnational Tablighi Jamaʿat in Kyrgyzstan: Structures, Concepts, Practices, Metaphors," Crossroads Asia Working Paper Series 17 (2014).
33. See Barbara Metcalf, "'Traditionalist' Islamic Activism: Deoband, Tablighis, and Talibs," in *Islamic Contestations: Essays on Muslims in India and Pakistan,* ed. Barbara Metcalf (New Delhi: Oxford University Press, 2004), 265–84.
34. Interviews with respondents from the inner Tablighi administrative system, Lahore, October 2002.
35. See Agnes Steinbauer, "Der Mann aus dem Drahtkäfig," *Süddeutsche Zeitung*, 19 May 2011, http://www.sueddeutsche.de/politik/murat-kurnaz-buch-der-mann-aus-dem-drahtkaefig-1.886592, and "Tablighi Jamaat. An Indirect Line to Terrorism," *Security Weekly*, 23 January 2008, https://www.stratfor.com/weekly/tablighi_jamaat_indirect_line_terrorism (both accessed 6 January 2017).
36. Informed Tablighi respondents with administrative background also confirmed this practice for the early preindependence stage of the Tablighis (Lahore 2002).
37. Field observations in Pakistan and India in 2002; Malaysia and Indonesia in 2005; Britain in 2006; and Kyrgyzstan in 2012.

38. Structured analysis by this author based on respondent interviews calculated that since in South Asia alone the participation rate in the annual congregations ranges from two to three million each, this suggests a mobilization potential of up to forty to sixty million followers in South Asia, based on the assumption there could be up to seven to eight times more followers than participants at congregations. As the congregations of Southeast Asia, Western Europe, North America, and the Maghreb, as well as West and South Africa draw lesser numbers of around five hundred thousand to one million each, it is fair to assume that their mobilization potential could reach another twenty to forty million Muslims. The smaller congregations of Muslims in Russia, Central Asia, and the Mashriq are not considered.
39. Private observation. See Goolem Vahed, "Contesting 'Orthodoxy': The Tablighi-Sunni Conflict among South African Muslims in the 1970s and 1980s," *Journal of Muslim Minority Affairs* 23, no. 2 (2003):313–34.
40. Field studies in France in March 2008; cf. Dietrich Reetz, "Laïcité and Piety: The Tablighi Jamaʿat in France," in *Islamic Movements of Europe: Public Religion and Islamophobia in the Modern World,* eds. Frank Peter and Rafael Ortega (London: I. B. Tauris, 2014), 195–98.
41. Field studies in Britain in November 2006, March 2010. See Bulbul Siddiqi, *Becoming "Good Muslim": The Tablighi Jamaat in the UK and Bangladesh* (Singapore: Springer Singapore, 2018); Zacharias P. Pieri, *Tablighi Jamaat and the Quest for the London Mega Mosque: Continuity and Change* (London: Palgrave Macmillan, 2015); Riyaz Timol, "Religious Travel and Tablighi Jamaʿat: Modalities of Expansion in Britain and Beyond," in *Muslims in the UK and Europe (I),* ed. Yasir Suleiman (Cambridge: Center of Islamic Studies, University of Cambridge, May 2015), 194–206.
42. Field studies in Spain in May 2008. See Sol Tarres, "The Tablighi Jamaʿat in Spain," in *Islamic Movements of Europe,* eds. Peter and Ortega, 191–94; Guillermo Martín-Sáiz, "Islam and the Tablighi Jamaʿat in Spain: Ghosts of the Past, Limits of Representation, and New Developments," in *Secularisms in a Postsecular Age? Religiosities and Subjectivities in Comparative Perspective,* eds. José Mapril et al. (Cham, CH: Springer International, 2017), 67–85.
43. For North America and Britain, see Barbara Daly Metcalf, *Making Muslim Space in North America and Europe* (Berkeley: University of California Press, 1996), 110ff.
44. Field research, May and June 2010.
45. Field study, Kyrgyzstan in October 2012.
46. Field studies, Malaysia, Indonesia and Singapore, October 2005, September 2009, and October 2010. See Noor, *Islam on the Move,* and Julia Howell's chapter, this volume.
47. Marloes Janson, *Islam, Youth, and Modernity in the Gambia* (Cambridge, UK: Cambridge University Press, 2013).

48. Sallie Simba Kayunga, *Islamic Fundamentalism in Uganda: A Case of the Tabligh Youth Movement* (Kampala: Center for Basic Research, 1993).
49. In the academic literature, the movement's influence in those countries is only mentioned in passing. Activities in Saudi Arabia were confirmed to me by a Saudi academic scholar in January 2017. See also the internet blog of a Saudi Tablighi activist quoting home visits, AHMADTRINI's weblog, 17 January 2015, accessed 1 February 2017, https://ahmadtrini.wordpress.com/2015/01/17/fatwa-from-arab-and-non-arab-scholars-regarding-jamah-dawah-and-tableegh-ar-en/.
50. Respondents in South Africa (2005), the U.S. (2010), and the UK (2006). Interviews with Tablighi activists from the leadership circle of the Pakistan headquarters in Lahore, October 2002.
51. Anthony Giddens, *The Consequences of Modernity* (Cambridge, UK: Polity, 1990), 64.

CHAPTER 12

1. For information on Khaled, see Amr Khaled, "Amr Khaled CV," Amrkhaled.net. Amr Khaled, n.d., accessed 8 Dec. 2015. For Mas'ud, see "Moez Masoud," Faculty of Divinity Cambridge University, n.d., accessed 8 December 2015.
2. This study is based on fifty episodes of Khaled's hit program Lifemakers (aired between 2005 and 2006), sixteen issues of his magazine of the same name, and interviews with participants in local Lifemakers branches. All interviews conducted as part of this research took place between December 2006 and January 2008. The interviews with Amr Khalid's supporters asked a series of questions that focused on the reasons why these youth participated in Khaled's initiatives and where they saw Khaled and the Lifemakers program in twenty years.
3. "Barid al-I'tisam," *al-I'tisam*, September 1979/Shawwal 1399, 43.
4. "Akhi al-Qari," *al-Da'wa*, July 1981/Ramadan 1401, 3.
5. For Egyptian examples, see Richard P. Mitchell, *The Society of the Muslim Brothers* (New York: Oxford University Press, 1993); Brynjar Lia, *The Society of the Muslim Brothers in Egypt: The Rise of an Islamic Mass Movement* (Reading, UK: Ithaca Press, 1998). Also see, Charles Hirschkind, *The Ethical Soundscape: Cassette Sermons and Islamic Counterpublics* (New York: Columbia University Press, 2006). For Arabic-language literature on Egypt specifically, see Rif'at Sayyid Ahmad, *al-Harakat al-Islamiyya fi Misr wa-Iran* (Cairo: Sayna' li'l-Nashr, 1989), and Wa'il 'Uthman, *Asrar al-Haraka al-Islamiyya fi Misr, 1968–1975* (Cairo: al-Shirka al-Misriyya li'l-Tiba'a, n.d).
6. Carrie Rosefsky Wickham, *Mobilizing Islam: Religion, Activism, and Political Change in Egypt* (New York: Columbia University Press, 2002), 119–49; Asef Bayat, *Making Islam Democratic: Social Movements and the Post-Islamist Turn* (Stanford: Stanford University Press, 2007), 35. These

SMT scholars built on the work of political scientists who initially argued that Islamism represented a response to "exogenous structural strains" such as rapid socioeconomic transformation, rural-urban migration paired with insufficient infrastructure, increasingly expensive basic commodities, and political disappointment. For discussion of this historiographical point, see Quintan Wiktorowicz, *Islamic Activism: A Social Movement Theory Approach* (Bloomington: Indiana University Press, 2004), 6.

7. For overviews of the theory of Islamic finance, see Maha-Hanaan Balala, *Islamic Finance and Law: Theory and Practice in a Globalized World* (London: I. B. Tauris, 2011); and Mahmoud A. El-Gamal, *Islamic Finance: Law, Economics, and Practice* (New York: Cambridge University Press, 2006).
8. Timur Kuran, *Islam and Mammon: The Economic Predicaments of Islamism* (Princeton: Princeton University Press, 2004), esp. 82–102.
9. Yasmin Moll, "Islamic Televangelism: Religion, Media and Visuality in Contemporary Egypt," *Arab Media and Society* 10 (2010):1–27; Yasmin Moll, "Building the New Egypt: Islamic Televangelists, Revolutionary Ethics and 'Productive' Citizenship," Fieldsights-Hot Spots Cultural Anthropology Online, 23 May 2013, http://www.culanth.org/fieldsights/231-building-the-new-egypt-islamic-televangelists-revolutionary-ethics-and-productive-citizenship. See also Mona Atia, *Building a House in Heaven: Pious Neoliberalism and Islamic Charity in Egypt* (Minneapolis: University of Minnesota Press, 2013), esp. 135–58; Samuel Lee Harris, "Development through Faith: The Maʿadi Life Makers and the Islamic Entrepreneurial Subject" (Master's thesis, Georgetown University, 2008).
10. In the former case, Mitchell, *Muslim Brothers*, 272–82, highlights the centrality of Islamic economics but says little about how economic processes shaped preaching more broadly; in the latter case, Hirschkind, *The Ethical Soundscape*, 128, notes the ways in which neoliberal economic shifts stimulated the expansion of socioeconomic service provision in mosques and community centers but says little about how economic questions came to pervade discourses of *daʿwa*.
11. Studies of Islamic education in Egypt adhere to a similar division. See, for example, Gregory Starrett, *Putting Islam to Work: Education, Politics, and Religious Transformation in Egypt* (Berkeley: University of California Press, 1998).
12. Starrett, *Putting Islam to Work*, 30, 45.
13. Founded in 1892 by Cairene notables in response to a call by the Egyptian Khedive Abbas II, the Islamic Charitable Society sought to compensate for the limited reach of state-controlled education. Though less well known than the Islamist and Salafi organizations that arose in the early twentieth century—most notably, the Jamʿiyya Sharʿiyya, Ansar al-Sunna al-Muhammadiyya, and the Muslim Brotherhood—this organization was the first to engage actively in developing alternative educational

institutions framed by an Islamic ethical project. See Ahmad Shalabi Hilmi and ʿAbd al-ʿAzim Muhammad Ibrahim Ramadan, *Fusul min Taʾrikh Harakat al-Islah al-Ijtimaʿi fi Misr: Dirasa ʿan Dawr al-Jamʿiyya al-Khayriyya al-Islamiyya* (Cairo: al-Hayʾa al-Misriyya al-ʿAmma liʾl-Kuttab, 1988), 42–4, 108–11.

14. Ibid., 151.
15. Muhammad ʿAbd al-ʿAziz Dawud, *al-Jamʿiyyat al-Islamiyya fi Misr wa-Dawruha fi Nashr al-Daʿwa al-Islamiyya* (Cairo: al-Zahra liʾl-Iʿlam al-ʿArabi, 1992), 267–68.
16. Timothy Mitchell, *Colonising Egypt* (Berkeley: University of California Press, 1991), xi.
17. For a study of al-Azhar's ulama during the second half of the twentieth century, see Malika Zeghal, *Gardiens de l'Islam: les oulémas d'al-Azhar dans l'Egypte contemporaine* (Paris, Presses de Sciences Po, 1996). For a brief discussion of the politics of religious education under Nasser, see Gregory Starrett, *Putting Islam to Work*, 77–80.
18. Eleanor Abdella Doumato and Gregory Starrett, "Textbook Islam, Nation Building, and the Question of Violence," in *Teaching Islam: Textbooks and Religion in the Middle East,* eds. Eleanor Abdella Doumato and Gregory Starrett (Boulder, CO: Lynne Rienner, 2007), 24.
19. Starrett, *Putting Islam to Work*, 62, 77–86.
20. Yet there were still holdouts among Islamic organizations that consciously refused to meld religious knowledge and socioeconomic development. Most notably, al-Jamʿiyya al-Sharʿiyya focused on training imams in the Quran and Sunna and gave little thought to projects of religiously framed economic guidance. See Muhammad ʿAli Masʿud, *al-Jamʿiyya al-Sharʿiyya li-Taʿawun al-ʿAmilin biʾl-Kitab waʾl-Sunna al-Muhammadiyya ʿAqidatan wa Minhajan wa Sulukan* (Cairo: al-Jamʿiyya al-Sharʿiyya, 1982), 28.
21. David Harvey defines neoliberalism as a "a theory of political economic practices that proposes that human well-being can best be advanced by liberating individual entrepreneurial freedoms and skills within an institutional framework characterized by strong private property rights, free markets, and free trade. The role of the state is to create and preserve an institutional framework appropriate to such practices." David Harvey, *A Brief History of Neoliberalism* (New York: Oxford University Press, 2005), 2.
22. Timothy Mitchell, "Dreamland: The Neoliberalism of Your Desires," *Middle East Report* 210 (Spring 1999):28–33; Karen Pfeifer, "How Tunisia, Morocco, Jordan and Even Egypt Became IMF 'Success Stories' in the 1990s," *Middle East Report* 210 (1999):23–27. See also Wickham, *Mobilizing Islam*, 41–62. On the overlap between Islamic charity and neoliberalism in Egypt more broadly, see Atia, *Building a House*, 135–65.

    The limited role of advertisements prior to this point was often involuntary. Advertisements for the cinema, alcohol, cigarettes, smoking, women's clothing, and even razor blades were unacceptable to Islamic publications. See Shuʿayb ʿAbd al-Munʿim Ghubashi, *Sihafat al-Ikhwan al-Muslimin: Dirasa fiʾl-Nashʾa waʾl-Madmun min 1933 ila 1952* (Cairo: Dar al-Tawziʿ waʾl-Nashr al-Islamiyya, 2000), 47.

23. For example, advertisements for household furniture appeared regularly in the Muslim Brotherhood's mouthpiece. See, *al-Daʿwa*, August 1976/ Shaʿban 1396, 51.
24. Gregory Starrett, "The Political Economy of Religious Commodities in Cairo," *American Anthropologist* 97 (1995):53.
25. Muhammad Fahmi Latif, "al-Islam waʾl-Tarbiya waʾl-Taʿlim," *Minbar al-Islam*, April 1977/Jumada al-Ula 1397, 101.
26. ʿImara Najib, "Nazra Islamiyya fi Mushkilat al-Taʿlim," *al-Daʿwa*, January 1978/Safar 1397, 28.
27. "Akhbar al-Barlaman Tanfarid bi-Nashr Asʿar al-Mashayikh waʾl-Duʿa Nujum al-Fadaʾiyyat fi Ramadan," *Akhbar al-Barlaman*, 22 September 2007, 10.
28. "Bursat al-Duʿa Tashtaghil fi Ramadan," *Jaridat al-Masaʾ*, 21 September 2007. Based on September 2007 exchange rates, 100,000 Egyptian pounds were equivalent to US$17,886, while 60,000 Egyptian pounds was equivalent to US$10,730.
29. "Amr Khaled Richest Islamic Preacher: Forbes," *al-Arabiyya*, 9 December 2008, accessed 14 December 2015, https://www.alarabiya.net/articles /2008/02/28/46255.html.
30. For example, see a 2013 episode of the Egyptian comedian Tawfiq ʿUkasha, in which he describes Khaled as not merely a Muslim Brotherhood preacher (an unsubstantiated yet long-running allegation) but also a "trafficker in religion" (*tajir din*). See Tawfiq ʿUkasha, "Yakshif Haqiqat ʿAmr Khalid Daʿiya Ikhwani wa Tajir Din," accessed 9 December 2013, https:// www.youtube.com/watch?v=WIyjF4mKX2k. As the debate in *al-Iʿtisam* suggests, such accusations of trafficking in religion first emerged in full force during the 1970s.
31. Armando Salvatore, "Social Differentiation, Moral Authority, and Public Islam in Egypt: The Path of Mustafa Mahmud," *Anthropology Today* 16, no. 2 (April 2000):12–15; Hatsuki Aishima and Armando Salvatore, "Doubt, Faith and Knowledge: The Reconfiguration of the Intellectual Field in Post-Nasserist Cairo," *Journal of the Royal Anthropological Institute* 15 (2009):41–56.
32. While the location of the *daʿiya* differs from that of the *khatib* or the *waʿiz* described by Gaffney—the former works outside traditional ritual spaces whereas the latter almost exclusively inhabits the mosque—the essential mediatory function does not.
33. Patrick Gaffney, *The Prophet's Pulpit: Islamic Preaching in Contemporary Egypt* (Berkeley: University of California Press, 1994), esp. 194–250, quotation on 237.

34. Ibid., 238–39.
35. ʿAmr Khalid, "Sunaʿ al-Hayat . . . wa Shababuha . . . wa Qaʾiduha . . . tahta al-Mikruskub," *Sunaʿ al-Hayat* (February 2005), 4–6.
36. ʿAmr Khalid, "Halmi: al-Tiknolojiyya waʾl-Sinaʿa," *Sunaʿ al-Hayat* 49 min, RAM, accessed 14 December 2015, http://amrkhaled.net/ar/library/program/7326.
37. ʿAmr Khalid, "al-Muhafaza ʿala Mawaridina," *Sunaʿ al-Hayat*, 48 min., RAM, accessed 14 December 2015, https://www.youtube.com/watch?v=afeSzYEzlMI.
38. Ibid.
39. ʿAmr Khalid, "Majal al-Sinaʿa al-Saghira," *Sunaʿ al-Hayat*, 56 min., RAM, accessed 14 December 2015, http://www.shobiklobik.com/islam/amrkhaled.asp?cat=13.
40. ʿAmr Khalid, "Ihlam bi-Baladak baʿda ʿIshrin Sana," *Sunaʿ al-Hayat* (Part 2), 56 min., RAM, accessed 14 December 2015, https://www.youtube.com/watch?v=p5YWkIu7hoI.
41. ʿAmr Khalid, "al-Duktur ʿAli al-Din Hilali fi Hiwar Khass li-Shabab Sunaʿ al-Hayat," *Sunaʿ al-Hayat* (March 2005), 8–11.
42. ʿAmr Khalid, "Mushkilat al-Bitala," *Sunaʿ al-Hayat*, 52 min., RAM, accessed 14 December 2015, http://www.shobiklobik.com/islam/amrkhaled.asp?cat=13.
43. ʿAmr Khalid, "Majal al-Sihha" *Sunaʿ al-Hayat* (Part 3), 58 min., RAM, accessed 14 December 2015, http://www.shobiklobik.com/islam/amrkhaled.asp?cat=13.
44. ʿAmr Khalid, "Muqaddama," *Sunaʿ al-Hayat* (Part 3), 61 min., RAM, accessed 14 December 2015, https://www.youtube.com/watch?v=R1WmPqfMjSc.
45. ʿAmr Khalid, "Sunaʿ al-Hayat . . . wa Shababuha," 4–6.
46. ʿAmr Khalid, "al-Shaykh ʿAbd al-Fattam al-Bazm [. . .] Mufti Dimashq: Sunaʿ al-Hayat Akhrajat biʾl-Daʿwa min Qawalibiha al-Muhanata, *Sunaʿ al-Hayat* (April 2005), 9–10.
47. ʿAmr Khalid, "Mushkilat al-Bitala."
48. For an analysis of self-help literature and its relation to the formation of pious subjects, see Jeffrey T. Kenney, "Selling Success, Nurturing the Self: Self-Help Literature, Capitalist Values, and the Sacralization of Subjective Life in Egypt," *International Journal of Middle East Studies* 47, no. 4 (2015):663–80.
49. The "secular" project of subject building, as Talal Asad notes, seeks to lay claim to broad swaths of society, including those historically seen as "religious." See Talal Asad, *Formation of the Secular: Christianity, Islam and Modernity* (Stanford: Stanford University Press, 2003), 199. For Hirschkind's and Mahmood's views of the bounds of the Islamist project of subject formation, see Hirschkind, *The Ethical Soundscape*, esp. 117–18

and 137–38; Saba Mahmood, *Politics of Piety: The Islamic Revival and the Feminist Subject* (Princeton and Oxford: Princeton University Press, 2005), esp. 113–17. See also Richard Gauvain, *Salafi Ritual Purity: In the Presence of God* (New York: Routledge, 2013), 189.

50. For a longer discussion of this critique, see Aaron Rock-Singer, "Prayer and the Islamic Revival: A Timely Challenge," *International Journal of Middle East Studies* 48, no. 2 (2016):293–312.
51. ʿAmr Khalid, "Rafʿ al-Zulm ʿan al-Marʾa," *Sunaʿ al-Hayat*, 57 min., RAM, accessed 14 December 2015, http://amrkhaled.net/ar/library/program/7326.
52. Ibid.
53. ʿAmr Khalid, "al-Duktura Zaynab ʿAbd al-ʿAziz Turatib al-Awlawiyyat fi Hayat al-Marʾa," *Sunaʿ al-Hayat* (August 2005), 16–18. This approach has considerable precedent within the Muslim Brotherhood.
54. Khalid, "Rafʿ al-Zulm."
55. ʿAmr Khalid, "Kayfa Takun Ijabiyyan," *Sunaʿ al-Hayat*, 61 min., RAM, accessed 28 December 2015, https://www.youtube.com/watch?v=K5DTYdMJK2I.
56. ʿAmr Khalid, "Mashruʿ al-Kumbyutir," *Sunaʿ al-Hayat*, 49 min., RAM, accessed 14 December 2015, https://www.youtube.com/watch?v=3_v6sU1cnj8.
57. ʿAmr Khalid, "al-Istiqsa,'" *Sunaʿ al-Hayat*, 56 min., RAM, accessed 14 December 2015, https://www.youtube.com/watch?v=gBsS6HFfIoA.
58. Electronic communication, 5 January 2007.
59. Electronic communication, 2 February 2007.
60. Rana and Esra, personal interview, 27 December 2007.
61. Ola, personal interview, 22 December 2007.
62. ʿAmr Khalid, "Thamar Sunaʿ al-Hayat," *Sunaʿ al-Hayat*, 65 min., RAM, accessed 14 December 2015, https://www.youtube.com/watch?v=lS_wBahtKVo.
63. See Wickham, *Mobilizing Islam*, 97–98.
64. ʿAmr Khalid, "Shabab Sunaʿ al-Hayat fi-l-Saʿudiyya," *Sunaʿ al-Hayat* (July 2005), 28–31.
65. ʿAmr Khalid, "Akhbar Sunaʿ al-Hayat," (February 2005), 16–17.
66. ʿAmr Khalid, "Mushkilat al-Bitala."
67. ʿAmr Khalid, "Akhbar Sunaʿ al-Hayat," ibid.
68. ʿAmr Khalid, "Akhbar Sunaʿ al-Hayat," (December 2005), 33–34.
69. For more on the emergence of Islamic charitable associations in twentieth-century Egypt, see ʿAbd al-Ghaffar Shukr, ed., *al-Jamʿiyyat al-Ahliyya al-Islamiyya fi Misr* (Cairo: Dar al-Amin liʾl-Nashr waʾl-Tawziʿ, 2002).
70. "Madha Yaqraʾ al-Misriyyun fi-Shahr Ramadan," *al-Karama al-Misriyya*, 1 October 2007, 16.
71. Student Association of the University of Cairo, *Mawqaʿ Kull al-Taliba*, accessed 15 December 2007, http://www.alltalaba.com/tegara.php.

72. ʿAmr Khalid, "Akhbar Sunaʿ al-Hayat," (May 2005), 21–26.
73. ʿAmr Khalid, "Akhbar Sunaʿ al-Hayat," (October 2005), 48–52.
74. ʿAmr Khalid, "Akhbar Sunaʿ al-Hayat," (July 2005), 32–33.
75. ʿAmr Khalid, "Taqrir: Tuyur al-Mustaqbal fi Urdun," *Sunaʿ al-Hayat* (December 2005), 37–39.
76. ʿAmr Khalid, "Akhbar Sunaʿ al-Hayat," (December 2005), 33–34.
77. ʿAmr Khalid, "'Better Future' Conference," *Working for a Better Future*, accessed 8 January 2007, www.betterfutureconference.com.
78. Muhammad, electronic communication, 1 January 2007.
79. Noha, electronic communication, 5 January 2007.

CHAPTER 13

1. Michael Cook, *Commanding Right and Forbidding Wrong in Islamic Thought* (Cambridge: Cambridge University Press, 2000), 479–86.
2. Lindsay Wise, "Amr Khaled: Broadcasting the Nahda," *Transnational Broadcasting Studies* 13 (2004), accessed 28 September 2016, www.*tbsjournal.com*/Archives/Fall04/wiseamrkhaled.html; Yasmin Moll, "Islamic Televangelism: Religion, Media and Visuality in Contemporary Egypt," *Arab Media and Society* 10 (2010):1–26.
3. Patrick Haenni, *L'islam de marché: l'autre revolution conservatrice* (Paris: Le Seuil, 2005), 33–38.
4. On Mustafa Mahmud see, Stephan Conermann, *Mustafa Mahmud (geb. 1921) und der modifizierte islamische Diskurs im modernen Ägypten* (Berlin: Schwarz, 1996).
5. Naomi Sakr, *Arab Television Today* (London: I. B. Tauris, 2007); Lila Abu-Lughod, *Dramas of Nationhood: The Politics of Television in Egypt* (Cairo: American University in Cairo Press, 2005), 163–91.
6. Jakob Skovgaard-Petersen, "New Media in the Muslim World," in *The Oxford Encyclopedia of Islam and Politics* (New York: Oxford University Press, 2014), 2, 183–88.
7. On this program, see Ehab Galal, "Yusuf al-Qaradawi and the New Islamic TV," in *The Global Mufti: The Phenomenon of Yusuf al-Qaradawi*, eds. Bettina Gräf and Jakob Skovgaard-Petersen (New York: Columbia University Press, 2009), 149–80; Jakob Skovgaard-Petersen, "The Global Mufti," in *Globalization and the Muslim World*, eds. Birgit Schaebler and Leif Stenberg (Syracuse: Syracuse University Press, 2004), 153–65.
8. On the new types of programming and the rise of the Salafi channels, see Khaled Hroub, ed., *Religious Broadcasting in the Middle East* (London: Hurst, 2012).
9. Ehab Galal, ed., *Arab TV-Audiences: Negotiating Religion and Identity* (Frankfurt am Main: Peter Lang, 2014), 9–10.
10. On these figures, see Stéphane Lacroix, *Sheikhs and Politicians: Inside the New Egyptian Salafism* (Brookings Doha Center, 2012).

11. Saba Mahmood, *Politics of Piety: The Islamic Revival and the Feminist Subject* (Princeton, NJ: Princeton University Press, 2005).
12. Walter Armbrust, "Islamists in Egyptian Cinema," *American Anthropologist* 104 (2002):922–31.
13. Karin van Nieuwkerk, "Of Morals, Missions and the Market: New Religiosity and 'Art with a Mission' in Egypt," in *Muslim Rap, Halal Soaps, and Revolutionary Theatre: Artistic Developments in the Muslim World,* ed. Karin van Nieuwkerk (Austin: University of Texas Press, 2011), 177–205.
14. For a biography of al-Sha'rawi and an analysis of his preaching, see Jaquelene Brinton, "Preaching and the Epistemological Reinforcement of *Ulama* Authority: The Sermons of Muhammad Mitwalli Sha'rawi," *Intellectual Discourse* 19, no. 1 (2011):97–121.
15. *Al-Ahram Weekly*, 5 December 2002.
16. Clark Lombardi and Nathan Brown, "Islam in Egypt's New Constitution," *Foreign Policy*, 13 December 2012, accessed 28 September 2016, http://foreignpolicy.com/2012/12/13/islam-in-egypts-new-constitution/.
17. Freedom and Justice Party, "Barnamaj Hizb al-Hurriya wa'l-'Adala," *al-Masri al-Yaum,* 5 April 2011.
18. Safa Azab, "Hal Yumkin 'Akhwanat' al-Fann fi Misr ma' ba'd al-Thawra?" *al-Sharq al-Awsat*, 30 Apr il 2013.
19. Leslie Chang, "Egypt's Soap Opera Islamists," *New Yorker*, 22 July 2013.
20. https://www.youm7.com/story/2017/1/5/-298فيلم-مولانا-لـ-عمرو-سعد-يحقق
3041739/ألف-جنيه-فى-, accessed 10 January 2017.
21. MLYNXQUALEY, "Looking at the Longlist: Fiery Journalist Ibrahim Eissa Recognized for 'Mowlana,'" ArabLit: Arabic Literature and Translation, 8 January 2013, accessed 1 November 2019, http://arablit.org/2013/01/08/looking-at-the-longlist/; "Eissa's 'Mowlana' to Become TV Series," *Ahram Online*, 29 July 2012, http://english.ahram.org.eg/NewsContent/5/35/48968/Arts—Culture/Stage—Street/Eissas-Mowlana-to-become-TV-series.aspx.
22. On Eissa and the revolutionary transition, see Tourya Guaaybess, "Broadcasting and Businessmen in Egypt: Revolution is Business," in *Arab Media Moguls,* eds. Donatella della Ratta, Naomi Sakr, and Jakob Skovgaard-Petersen (London: I. B. Tauris, 2015), 165–86.
23. Ibrahim 'Isa, *Mawlana* (Doha: Dar Bloomsbury, 2012).
24. BBC News, "Breastfeeding Fatwa Causes Stir," 22 May 2007, accessed 12 December 2016, http://news.bbc.co.uk/2/hi/6681511.stm.

CHAPTER 14

1. For example, in the U.S., Senator John McCain said that Saudi Arabia had satisfied extremists at home by allowing them "to have the megaphone" and even by financing some such groups. Similarly, Senator Joseph Lieberman explained that the Saudis were trying to "ride the back of this tiger" (al-Qaeda). Senator Joseph Biden, on the other hand, accused the Saudis of "having to essentially buy off their extreme groups in order to maintain

themselves." The late Laurent Murawiec went even farther by describing Saudi Arabia as the "kernel of evil," arguing that Saudis "are active at every level of the terror chain, from planners to financiers, from cadre to foot soldier, from ideologist to cheerleader." See respectively, "Senators Jump on Anti-Saudi Bandwagon," *Middle East Economic Survey* 44, 29 October 2001; E. Sciolino and N. MacFarquhar, "Naming of Hijackers as Saudis May Further Erode Ties to U.S.," *New York Times*, 25 October 2001; and the *Washington Post*, 6 August 2002.

2. English translations of Quranic verses are taken from Abdullah Yusuf Ali, *The Holy Qur'an* (Brentwood, MD: Amana, 1989). Other English translations are by the author.
3. *Al-Sharq al-Awsat*, 15 November 2001.
4. *Al-Sharq al-Awsat*, 23 March 2006.
5. *Al-Sharq al-Awsat*, 30 March 2006.
6. Ibid.
7. Ibid.
8. Prince Turki al-Faisal, "We're Trying Hard to Change," *USA Today*, 4 June 2006. http://usatoday30.usatoday.com/news/opinion/editorials/2006-06-04-opposing-view_x.htm.
9. David Commins, *The Wahhabi Mission and Saudi Arabia* (London: I. B. Tauris, 2006), 130.
10. On Ahl-i Hadith, see Barbara Daly Metcalf, *Islamic Revival in British India: Deoband, 1860–1900* (Princeton, NJ: Princeton University Press, 1982), 268–96; Martin Riexinger, *Sana'ullah Amritsari (1868–1948) und die Ahl-i Hadis im Punjab unter britischen Herrschaft* (Würzburg: Ergon, 2004); Claudia Preckel, "Islamische Bildungsnetzwerke und Gelehrtenkultur im Indien des 19. Jahrhunderts: Muhammad Siddiq Hasan Han (st. 1890) und die Entstehung der Ahl-e hadit-Bewegung in Bhopal" (PhD diss., Bochum University, 2005).
11. Stéphane Lacroix, *The Islamic Awakening: The Politics of Religious Dissent in Contemporary Saudi Arabia* (Cambridge, MA: Harvard University Press, 2011), 37–51.
12. Ayman al-Yassini, *Religion and State in the Kingdom of Saudi Arabia* (Boulder, CO: Westview, 1985), 68; and Weismann's chapter in this volume.
13. Muslim World League, "Objectives and Methods of MWL," http://en.themwl.org/content/objectives-methods-mwl, accessed 13 December 2016. See also, Reinhard Schulze, *Islamischer Internationalismus im 20. Jahrhundert: Untersuchungen zur Geschichte der Islamischen Weltliga* (Leiden: Brill, 1990), pt. 2.
14. Joseph Liu, "Muslim World League and World Assembly of Muslim Youth," Pew Forum, 15 September 2010, http://www.pewforum.org/2010/09/15/muslim-networks-and-movements-in-western-europe-muslim-world-league-and-world-assembly-of-muslim-youth/.
15. Ibid.

16. World Assembly of Muslim Youth, "al-Nadwa al-ʿAlamiyya liʾl-Shabab al-Islami," accessed 4 January 2017, http://www.wamy.org/.
17. ʿAbd al-Rahman ibn Qasim, *al-Durar al-Saniyya fi al-Ajwiba al-Najdiyya* (Riyadh: Dar al-Iftaʾ, 1965), 7:48; Hrair Dekmejian, "The Rise of Political Islamism in Saudi Arabia," *Middle East Journal* 48 (1994):635–38. On the Salafi trend in the contemporary Islamic world, see Roel Meijer, ed., *Global Salafism: Islam's New Religious Movement* (London: Hurst, 2009); Itzchak Weismann, "A Perverted Balance: Modern Salafism between Reform and Jihad," *Die Welt des Islam* 57 (2017), 33–66. See also the chapters by Wiedl and Gauvain in this volume.
18. Abu ʿIsa Muhammad al-Tirmidhi, *al-Jamiʿ al-Kabir* (Beirut: Dar al-Gharb al-Islami, 1996), 6:381, hadith no. 2641.
19. Muhammad ibn ʿAbd al-Wahhab, *Muʾallafat al-Shaykh al-Imam Muhammad Ibn ʿAbd al-Wahhab* (Riyadh: Imam Muhammad ibn Saʿud Islamic University, 1977), 1:225–27.
20. For a further account on classical Wahhabi "exclusivism," see Elisabeth Sirriyeh, "Wahhabis, Unbelievers and the Problem of Exclusivism," *Bulletin of the British Society for Middle Eastern Studies* 16, no. 2 (1989):123–32.
21. Ahmad al-Dawish, *Fatawa al-Lajna al-Daʾima liʾl-Buhuth al-ʿIlmiyya waʾl-Iftaʾ waʾl-Daʿwa waʾl-Irshad* (Riyadh: Maktabat al-ʿAbikan, 2000), 2:165–66.
22. In Saudi Arabia, the CSS and the CRLO constitute the only two official institutions for issuing fatwas. Led by the Grand Mufti, these institutions sit atop the "religious pyramid," providing the ultimate statements on sharia. They serve to complement each other, so while the CSS issues official *fatawa* on major public issues, the CRLO is responsible for conducting research, administering private *iftaʾ*, and providing administrative support for the CSS. See Muhammad Al-Atawneh, *Wahhabi Islam Facing the Challenges of Modernity: Dar al-Ifta in Modern Saudi Arabia* (Leiden: E. J. Brill, 2010), 17–34.
23. Ahmad al-Dawish, *Fatawa al-Lajna al-Daʾima*, 2:165, fatwa no. 1361. Further relevant CRLO *fatawa* can be found in ibid., 2:143–81, 12:241–42.
24. ʿAdil al-Faridan, *al-Muntaqa min Fatawa Fadilat al-Shaykh Salih b. Fawzan b. ʿAbd Allah al-Fawzan* (Beirut: Muʾassasat al-Risala, 1999), 1:361, fatwa no. 209. See also the interview with Ibn Baz regarding this issue in *al-Muslimun* 28 (July 1996). Notably, the Wahhabi perception of Salafism was rejected by many modern movements and scholars. Among the most prominent was the attack of the Syrian scholar; Weismann "A Perverted Balance," 33–66. See also al-Buti, who argued that Salafism is no more than a "blessed historical period" that is not essentially different from any other in Muslim history. See Muhammad Saʿid al-Buti, *al-Salafiyya: Marhala Zamaniyya Mubaraka La Madhhab Islami* (Damascus: Dar al-Fikr, 1988), 132–44.

25. Mamoun Fandy, *Saudi Arabia and the Politics of Dissent* (New York: St. Martin's, 1999), 200; al-Dawish, *Fatawa al-Lajna al-Da'ima*, 2:263–69.
26. *Al-Jazeera al-ʿArabiyya*, no.11, December 1991. See also Stéphane Lacroix, "Between Islamists and Liberals: Saudi Arabia's New Islamo-Liberal Reformist Trend," *Middle East Journal* 58 (2004):345–65.
27. al-Dawish, *Fatawa al-Lajna al-Da'ima,* 2:269, fatwa no. 11461.
28. Ibid., 12:274–97, fatwas nos. 19402 and 17300; and 2:77, fatwa no. 6364; "Unification of Religions," accessed 13 December 2016, http://en.islamway.net/article/8452/unification-of-religions.
29. Ibid., fatwa no.19402, 12:274–84.
30. Cited in al-Dawish, *Fatawa al-Lajna al-Da'ima,* 12:282.
31. Ibid., 12:81, fatwa no. 19402.
32. Ibid., 283.
33. Ibid.
34. See Muhammad Al-Atawneh, "Wahhabi Self-Examination Post-September 11th: Rethinking 'Other,' 'Otherness' and Tolerance," *Journal of Middle Eastern Studies* 47, no. 2 (2011):255–71.
35. Thomas Hegghammer, *Jihad in Saudi Arabia: Violence and Pan-Islamism since 1979* (Cambridge: Cambridge University Press, 2010).
36. See KACND's website: http://www.kacnd.org/eng/center_goals.asp, accessed December 2015.
37. Ibid.
38. For a detailed description and assessment of the various meetings, see Mark C. Thompson, *Saudi Arabia and the Path to Political Change: National Dialogue and Civil Society* (London: I. B. Tauris, 2014).
39. For more on this conference, see "al-Liqa' al-Watani al-Khamis," accessed 13 December 2016, https://www.kacnd.org/Meetings/details/5.
40. *Al-Sharq al-Awsat,* 16 December 2005, and the center's website: http://www.kacnd.org/ fifth_national_meeting.asp, accessed December 2015.
41. *Al-Sharq al-Awsat,* 16 December 2005. Also, http://www.kacnd.org/fifth_national_meeting.asp, accessed December 2015.
42. http://www.kacnd.org/fifth_national_meeting.asp, accessed December 2015.
43. Ibid.
44. *Al-Riyadh,* 3 April 2008.
45. King Saud University website, accessed December 2015, http://ksu.edu.sa/sites/ksuarabic/mngmnt/rectoranddeputies/Udb/islamicchair/Pages/goals.aspx. See also ʿ*Ukaz*, 12 December 2009.
46. *Al-Sharq al-Awsat*, 2 January 2008. Also http://ksu.edu.sa/sites/ksuarabic/mngmnt/rectoranddeputies/udb/islamicchair/Pages/workfr.aspx, accessed December 2015.
47. ʿ*Ukaz*, 12 December 2009.
48. http://www.islamfeqh.com/News/NewsItem.aspx?NewsItemID=1089, accessed December 2015.

49. *Al-Riyadh*, 18 March 2009.
50. Khalid al-Qasim, *al-Hurriyya al-Diniyya bayna al-Muslimin wa-Ahl al-Kitab* (Riyadh: Kursi al-Amir Sultan li'l-Dirasat al-Islamiyya al-Muʿasira, 2009); *ʿUkaz*, 12 December 2009; *al-Riyadh*, 27 December 2009; *al-Watan*, 27 December 2009.
51. Muslim World League, "The International Islamic Conference for Dialogue: Makkah al-Mukarramah," accessed 4 January 2017, http://en.themwl.org/content/international-islamic-conference-dialogue, 21–24.
52. Ibid., 41.
53. Muslim World League, "The International Islamic Conference for Dialogue," 631–32.
54. King Abdallah's call has been reported by Saudi and international media. See, for example, "Saudi Arabia's King Abdullah," accessed 13 December 2016, http://worldnews.about.com/od/saudiarabia/qt/abdullahfaith.htm.
55. al-Faisal, "We're Trying Hard to Change."
56. *Al-Hayat*, 8 June 2004.
57. Muslim World League, "The International Islamic Conference for Dialogue," 639–40.
58. *ʿAyn al-Yaqin*, 17 June 2008.
59. KAICIID, "About Us," accessed 13 December 2016, http://www.kaiciid.org/about-us.
60. *Al-Hayat*, 7 June 2008 and 8 November 2008; *al-Sharq al-Awsat*, 15 November 2008.
61. *Al-Sharq al-Awsat*, 15 November 2008; "Intercultural Dialogue at the General Assembly of the United," accessed 13 December 2016, http://www.muslimheritage.com/article/intercultural-dialogue-general-assembly-united-nations.
62. Muslim World League, "The International Islamic Conference for Dialogue," 117.
63. Ibid. 260.
64. Muslim World League, ibid.
65. Muslim World League, "Final Communique of Dialogue and Peaceful Coexistence Conference," accessed 13 December 2016, http://en.themwl.org/final-communique-dialogue-and-peaceful-coexistence-Conference-hong-kong.
66. For more on interfaith dialogue, see Muslim World League, *Interfaith Dialogue: Cross-Cultural Views* (Riyadh: Ghainaa Publications, 2010).
67. Muslim World League, "Final Communique of Dialogue and Peaceful Coexistence Conference."

CHAPTER 15

1. For a discussion of the strategies of fundamentalist movements (including Islamist movements), see Gabriel A. Almond, R. Scott Appleby, and

Emmanuel Sivan, *Strong Religion: The Rise of Fundamentalisms around the World* (Chicago: University of Chicago Press, 2003), ch. 4.

2. Itzchak Weismann, "Framing a Modern Umma: The Muslim Brothers' Evolving Project of Daʿwa," *Sociology of Islam* 3, nos. 3–4 (2015):147, and his chapter in this volume.
3. Khalil al-Anani and Maszlee Malik, "Pious Way to Politics: The Rise of Political Salafism in Post-Mubarak Egypt," *Digest of Middle East Studies* 22 (2013):57–73; William McCants, "The Lesser of Two Evils: The Salafi Turn to Party Politics in Egypt," Saban Center at Brookings, *Middle East Memo* 23 (May 2012):1–8.
4. Mokhtar Awad, "Egypt's New Radicalism: The Muslim Brotherhood and Jihad," *Foreign Affairs*, 4 February 2016, accessed 22 October 2018, https://www.foreignaffairs.com/articles/egypt/2016-02-04/egypts-new-radicalism.
5. Francesco Cavatorta and Fabio Merone, "Moderation through Exclusion? The Journey of the Tunisian Ennahda from Fundamentalist to Conservative Party," *Democratization* 20 (2013):857–75.
6. Joseph S. Nye Jr., "The Decline of America's Soft Power," *Foreign Affairs*, May/June 2004, 16–20.
7. *Nashid* (pl. *anashid*) is an Islamic religious chant. For more on the role of *anashid* in jihadi culture, see Behnam Said, "Hymns (Nasheeds): A Contribution to the Study of the Jihadist Culture," *Studies in Conflict and Terrorism* 35 (2012):863–79.
8. On contemporary Salafism and its various manifestations, see Roel Meijer, ed., *Global Salafism: Islam's New Religious Movement* (London: Hurst, 2009); Bernard Rougier, ed., *Qu'est-ce que le Salafisme?* (Paris: Presses Universitaires de France, 2008); Itzchak Weismann "A Perverted Balance: Modern Salafism between Reform and Jihad," *Die Welt des Islam* 57 (2017), 33–66.
9. See Quintan Wiktorowicz, "Anatomy of the Salafi Movement," *Studies in Conflict and Terrorism* 29 (2006):207–39.
10. David Cook, *Understanding Jihad* (Berkeley: University of California Press, 2005).
11. Quoted in Thomas Hegghammer, "Jihadi-Salafis or Revolutionaries? On Religion and Politics in the Study of Militant Islamism," in *Global Salafism*, ed. Meijer, 253.
12. Osama bin Laden and Bruce Lawrence, *Messages to the World: The Statements of Osama bin Laden* (London: Verso, 2005), 5.
13. Weismann, "Framing a Modern Umma," 153.
14. "Biographies: Hassan al-Banna," *Ikhwan Web*, 5 July 2007, http://www.ikhwanweb.com/article.php?id=873.
15. Quoted in Abdullah al-Arian, *Answering the Call: Popular Islamic Activism in Sadat's Egypt* (New York: Oxford University Press, 2014), 190.
16. Shaul Mishal and Avraham Sela, *The Palestinian Hamas: Vision, Violence, and Coexistence* (New York: Columbia University Press, 2006), 156;

Matthew Levitt and Dennis Ross, *Hamas: Politics, Charity, and Terrorism in the Service of Jihad* (New Haven, CT: Yale University Press, 2008), 24.

17. Joas Wagemakers, *A Quietist Jihadi: The Ideology and Influence of Abu Muhammad al-Maqdisi* (Cambridge: Cambridge University Press, 2012), 228.
18. "The Disguise of the Religion," al-Waʿd Media Foundation, originally accessed 28 June 2015 (link no longer active), http://sendvid.com/e8kory2f.
19. Meir Hatina, "Redeeming Sunni Islam: Al-Qaʿida's Polemic against the Muslim Brethren," *British Journal of Middle Eastern Studies* 39 (2012):102–4.
20. A disciple of Sayyid Qutb, Faraj called for fighting the "near enemy" (the "apostate" Muslim regimes) within national borders and therefore can hardly be classified as a Salafi-Jihadist. Still, his ideas served as an important milestone in the later crystallization of the global trend.
21. Johannes J. G. Jansen, *The Neglected Duty: The Creed of Sadat's Assassins and Islamic Resurgence in the Middle East* (New York: Macmillan, 1986), 186.
22. Quoted in Daurius Figueira, *Salafi Jihadi Discourse of Sunni Islam in the 21st Century: The Discourse of Abu Muhammad al-Maqdisi and Anwar al-Awlaki* (Bloomington, IN: iUniverse, 2011), 118.
23. Omar Ashour, "Post-Jihadism and the Ideological Revisions of Armed Islamists," in *Contextualizing Jihadi Thought,* eds. Jeevan Deol and Zaheer Kazmi (New York: Columbia University Press, 2011), 123.
24. Scott Shane, "In Message, Bin Laden Praised Arab Revolt," *New York Times*, 18 May 2011, accessed 22 October 2018, http://www.nytimes.com/2011/05/19/world/middleeast/19binladen.html?_r=0.
25. For Salafi-Jihadi reactions to the "Arab Spring," see Nelly Lahoud, *Jihadi Discourse in the Wake of the Arab Spring* (West Point, NY: Combating Terrorism Center, 2013); Daveed Gartenstein-Ross and Tara Vassefi, "Perceptions of the 'Arab Spring' within the Salafi-Jihadi Movement," *Studies in Conflict and Terrorism* 35 (2012):831–48.
26. "Osama bin Laden Praises Arab Spring in Posthumous Message," *Telegraph*, May 19, 2011, accessed 22 October 2018, http://www.telegraph.co.uk/news/worldnews/al-qaeda/8522595/Osama-bin-Laden-praises-Arab-Spring-in-posthumous-message.html.
27. Ayman al Zawahiri, *General Guidelines for Jihad* (As-Sahab Media Foundation, 2013).
28. Fawaz A. Gerges, *The Far Enemy: Why Jihad Went Global* (Cambridge: Cambridge University Press, 2009).
29. Laura Mansfield, *His Own Words: A Translation of the Writings of Dr. Ayman Al Zawahiri* (Old Tappan, NJ: TLG Publications, 2006), 116.
30. Ibid., 208–9.

31. Ibid., 205.
32. Ibid., 209.
33. Zawahiri, *General Guidelines for Jihad.*
34. Joas Wagemakers, "The Transformation of a Radical Concept: *Al-Wala' wa-l-Bara'* in the Ideology of Abu Muhammad al-Maqdisi," in *Global Salafism*, ed. Meijer, 81–106.
35. One notable exception to this oversight is Aaron Y. Zelin, "When Jihadists Learn How to Help," *Monkey Cage, Washington Post*, 7 May 2014, accessed 22 October 2018, http://www.washingtonpost.com/blogs/monkey-cage/wp/2014/05/07/when-jihadists-learn-how-to-help/; Aaron Y. Zelin, "Meeting Tunisia's Ansar al-Sharia," *Foreign Policy*, 8 March 2013, accessed 22 October 2018, http://foreignpolicy.com/2013/03/08/meeting-tunisias-ansar-al-sharia/.
36. "Aspects of Daʿwah Activities Carried Out by the Guidance and Daʿwah Office in the Sahil," 26 June 2015, accessed 22 October 2018, http://jihadology.net/2015/06/26/new-video-message-from-jabhat-al-nu%E1%B9%A3rah-aspects-of-dawah-activities-carried-out-by-the-guidance-and-dawah-office-in-the-sa%E1%B8%A5il/.
37. Meir Hatina, "Martyrs as Preachers," in *Religious Knowledge, Authority, and Charisma,* eds. Daphna Ephrat and Meir Hatina (Salt Lake City: University of Utah Press, 2014), 177.
38. "Aspects of the Daʿwa Activities Carried Out by the Daʿwa and Guidance Office in the Sahel," 27 June 2015, accessed 22 October 2018, https://www.youtube.com/watch?v=jp4zze5Qkfc&feature=youtube.
39. al-Manara al-Bayda Messaging Network, "Report on the Activities of the Daʿwa and Guidance Office within the Campaign of Support of Shariʿah," *Jabhat al-Nusra*, 25 June 2015, accessed 22 October 2018, http://jihadology.net/2015/06/25/new-video-message-from-jabhat-al-nu%E1%B9%A3rah-report-on-the-activities-of-the-dawah-and-guidance-office-within-the-campaign-of-support-of-shariah/.
40. al-Manara al-Bayda Messaging Network, "Some Daʿwah and Service Work Carried out by Jabhat al-Nusrah in the City of al-Atarib and Its Surrounding Area," *Jabhat al-Nusra*, 31 March 2015, accessed 22 October 2018, http://jihadology.net/2015/03/31/new-video-message-from-jabhat-al-nu%E1%B9%A3rah-some-dawah-and-service-work-carried-out-by-jabhat-al-nu%E1%B9%A3rah-in-the-city-of-al-atarib-and-its-surrounding-area/.
41. James Denselow, "Starving Syria as a Weapon," *AlJazeera*, 10 January 2016, accessed 22 October 2018, http://www.aljazeera.com/indepth/opinion/2016/01/starving-syria-weapon-isil-assad-madaya-160110054423833.html; "Starvation by Siege Now 'Systematic' in Syria, Assistant Secretary-General Tells Security Council, amid Warnings That Tactic Could Be War Crime," *United Nations Meetings Coverage and Press Releases*, 15 January 2016, accessed 22 October 2018, http://www.un.org/press/en/2016/sc12203.doc.htm.

42. Daʿwa and Guidance Office, "Aspects of Daʿwa Activities Carried Out by the Guidance and Daʿwa Office in the Sahil," Jabhat al-Nusra, 26 June 2015, accessed 22 October 2018, http://jihadology.net/2015/06/26/new-video-message-from-jabhat-al-nu%E1%B9%A3rah-aspects-of-dawah-activities-carried-out-by-the-guidance-and-dawah-office-in-the-sa%E1%B8%A5il/.
43. "Saleel al-Sawareem [Clashing of the Swords]," *YouTube*, 29 August 2014, accessed 22 October 2018, https://www.youtube.com/watch?v=7t-Nrek3VUE.
44. Wilayat Ninawa Media Office, "Daʿwa Convoy for the Cubs of the Caliphate," Islamic State, 20 April 2015, accessed 22 October 2018, http://jihadology.net/2015/04/20/new-video-message-from-the-islamic-state-dawah-convoy-for-the-cubs-of-the-caliphate-wilayat-ninawa/.
45. Wilayat al-Raqqah Media Office, "Daʿwah Forum in al-Raqqah City," Islamic State, 16 July 2015, accessed 22 October 2018, http://jihadology.net/2015/07/16/new-video-message-from-the-islamic-state-dawah-forum-in-al-raqqah-city-wilayat-al-raqqah/.
46. Wilayat al-Barakah Media Office, "Daʿwah Tour of the Front Line Points," Islamic State, 13 June 2015, accessed 22 October 2018, http://jihadology.net/2015/06/13/new-video-message-from-the-islamic-state-dawah-tour-of-the-front-line-points-wilayat-al-barakah/.
47. Wilayat Fallujah Media Office, "Graduation of Sharia Classes from the Daʿwa and Mosques Center," Islamic State, 15 June 2015, originally accessed 7 January 2015 (link no longer active), https://dump.to/cez.
48. Wilayat Damascus Media Office, "Photographed Report on the Daʿwa for Allah in Wilayat Damascus," Islamic State, 18 December 2014, originally accessed 7 January 2015 (link no longer active), http://justpaste.it/al-da3wa.
49. Joseph S. Nye, *Soft Power: The Means to Success in World Politics* (New York: Public Affairs, 2004), 5–7.
50. Ansar al-Sharia is the name of a number of Salafi-Jihadist movements that were established in Libya, Tunisia, and Yemen following the "Arab Spring." Although not formally affiliated with al-Qaeda, they share its ideology while primarily focusing on *daʿwa* and communal activities. See Aaron Y. Zelin, "Meeting Tunisia's Ansar al-Sharia," and "Maqdisi's Disciples in Libya and Tunisia," *Foreign Policy*, 14 November 2012, accessed 7 November 2019, http://foreignpolicy.com/2012/11/14/maqdisis-disciples-in-libya-and-tunisia/.
51. Jeffrey Haynes, *Religious Transnational Actors and Soft Power* (Farnham, UK: Ashgate Publishing, 2012).
52. Joby Warrick, *Black Flags: The Rise of ISIS* (New York: Doubleday, 2015), 277.
53. Jennifer Cafarella, "Jabhat al-Nusra in Syria: An Islamic Emirate for al-Qaeda," *Middle East Security Report* 25, Institute for the Study

of War, December 2014, 37, accessed 22 October 2018, http://www.understandingwar.org/sites/default/files/JN%20Final.pdf.

54. Abu Muhammad al-Adnani al-Shami, audio statement, "O Our People Respond to the Caller of Allah," 23 June 2015, accessed 22 October 2018, https://pietervanostaeyen.wordpress.com/2015/06/23/o-our-people-respond-to-the-caller-of-allah-audio-statement-by-shaykh-abu-muhammad-al-adnani-as-shami/.
55. For more on the Islamic State's legal system, see Andrew F. March and Mara Revkin, "Caliphate of Law: ISIS' Ground Rules," *Foreign Affairs*, 15 April 2015, accessed 22 October 2018, https://www.foreignaffairs.com/articles/syria/2015-04-15/caliphate-law.
56. "Our Shariʿa," al-Ajnad Foundation for Media Production, 29 June 2015, accessed 22 October 2018, https://archive.org/details/muhd_350.
57. Hatina, "Redeeming Sunni Islam," 113.

Biblography

ʿAbd al-ʿAziz, Jamaʿa Amin. *Al-Daʿwa: Qawaʾid wa-Usul*. Alexandria: Dar al-Daʿwa, 1999.

ʿAbd al-Tawwab, Ahmad. "Baʿd Taʿrifahu, Ahl al-Sunna waʾl-Jamaʿa 'Thawra Salafiyya'ʿala Shaykh al-Azhar," accessed 26 December 2016. http://www.elyomnew.com/news/inside/2016/09/03/58598.

Abou el-Fadl, Khaled. "Islamic Law and Muslim Minorities: The Juristic Discourse on Muslim Minorities from the Second/Eighth to the Eleventh/Seventeenth Centuries." *Islamic Law and Society* 1, no. 2 (1994):141–87.

Abu ʿAbdir-Rahman, ʿAbdul-ʿAdhim. "Dawaübung." Accessed 4 January 2017. www.way-to-allah.com/unterrichte-predigten/abduladhim.html.

———. "Die Milde in der Dawa." Accessed 1 January 2017. www.way-to-allah.com/unterricht_predigten/abduladhim.html.

Abu Khadeejah, Abdul-Wahid. "Are We in a Period Similar to the Prophet in Makkah as It Relates to Fighting Jihad?" Accessed 4 January 2017. www.abukhadeejah.com/are-we-in-a-period-similar-to-the-prophet-in-makkah-as-it-relates-to-fighting-jihad/.

Abu-Lughod, Lila. *Dramas of Nationhood: The Politics of Television in Egypt*. Cairo: American University in Cairo Press, 2005.

Abu-Sahlieh, Sami A. Aldeeb. "The Islamic Conception of Migration." *International Migration Review* 30, no.1 (1996):37–57.

Adams, Charles C. *Islam and Modernism in Egypt: A Study of the Modern Reform Movement Inaugurated by Muhammad Abduh*. New York: Russel and Russel, 1968. First published 1933 by Oxford University Press (Oxford).

Adraoui, Mohamed-Ali. "Purist Salafism in France." *ISIM Review* 21 (2008):12–13.

al-Afghani, Jamal al-Din, and Muhammad Abduh. *Al-ʿUrwa al-Wuthqa*. Beirut: Dar al-Kitab al-ʿArabi, 1980.

Ahmad, Irfan. *Islamism and Democracy in India: The Transformation of Jamaat-e-Islami*. Princeton, NJ: Princeton University Press, 2009, and New Delhi: Permanent Black, 2010.

Ahmad, Khurshid, and Zafar Ishaq Ansari. "Mawlana Sayyid Abul Aʿla Mawdudi: An Introduction to His Vision of Islam and Islamic revival." In *Islamic Perspectives: Studies in Honour of Mawlana Sayyid Abul Aʿla Mawdudi*, edited by Khurshid Ahmad and Zafar Ishaq Ansari, 359–83. London: The Islamic Foundation, 1979.

Ahmad, Mirza Tahir. *Invitation to Ahmadiyyat*. Sydney: Law Book Company of Australasia, 1980.

Ahmad, Rifʿat Sayyid. *Al-Harakat al-Islamiyya fi Misr wa-Iran*. Cairo: Sayna' li'l-Nashr, 1989.

Ahmed, Chanfi. *Preaching Islamic Revival in East Africa*. Newcastle upon Tyne: Cambridge Scholars, 2018.

Ahmed, Hilal. *Muslim Political Discourse in Postcolonial India: Monuments, Memory, Contestation*. Delhi: Routledge, 2014.

———. "Muzaffarnagar 2013: Meanings of Violence." *Economic and Political Weekly* 48, no. 40 (2013):10–13.

———. "Naik, Zakir." Oxford Islamic Studies Online. Accessed 2 March 2017. http://www.oxfordislamicstudies.com/article/opr/t343/e0183.

Aishima, Hatsuki, and Armando Salvatore. "Doubt, Faith and Knowledge: The Reconfiguration of the Intellectual Field in Post-Nasserist Cairo." *Journal of the Royal Anthropological Institute* 15 (2009):41–56.

al-Albani, Muhammad Nasir al-Din. *Hadhihi Daʿwatuna*. Algeria: Dar al-Mahaja, 1434/2013.

Ali, Abdullah Yusuf. *The Holy Qur'an*. Brentwood, MD: Amana, 1989.

Ali, Muhammad. *The Founder of the Ahmadiyya Movement: A Short Study*. London: Forgotten Books, 2012.

Almond, Gabriel A., R. Scott Appleby, and Emmanuel Sivan. *Strong Religion: The Rise of Fundamentalisms around the World*. Chicago: University of Chicago Press, 2003.

Alsultany, Evelyn. "Arabs and Muslims in the Media after 9/11: Representational Strategies for a 'Postrace' Era." *American Quarterly* 65 (March 2013):161–69.

al-Alusi, Mahmud Shukri. *Tarikh Najd*. Cairo: Maktabat Madbuli, n.d.

al-ʿAlwani, Taha Jabir. *Fi Fiqh al-Aqalliyyat al-Muslima*. Cairo: Nahdat Misr, 2000.

———. "Al-Hukm al-Sharʿi fi-Musharakat al-Muslimin fi al-Haya al-Siyasiyya al-Amrikiyya." *Al-Sharq al-Awsat*, 13 November 1999.

———. "Madkhal ila Fiqh al-Aqalliyyat." *Al-Majalla al-ʿIlmiya* 4–5 (June 2004):17–92.

Ameer-e-Ahl-e-Sunnat. "72 Madani Inamaat." Dawat-e-Islami. Accessed 3 March 2017. https://www.dawateislami.net/bookslibrary/131.

al-ʿAmush, Bassam. *Fiqh al-Daʿwa*. Amman: Dar al-Nafis, 2005.

al-Anani, Khalil. "The Power of the Jamaʿa: The Role of Hasan al-Banna in Constructing the Muslim Brotherhood's Collective Identity." *Sociology of Islam* 1 (2013):41–63.

al-Anani, Khalil, and Maszlee Malik. "Pious Way to Politics: The Rise of Political Salafism in Post-Mubarak Egypt." *Digest of Middle East Studies* 22 (2013):57–73.

al-ʿAnbari, Khalid bin ʿAli bin Muhammad. *The Impact of Man-Made Laws in Determining the Judgment of an Abode as Being One of Disbelief or Islam*. Amman: Jamiah Media, 2007, originally published in Arabic in 2004.

Anderson, Lisa. "Demystifying the Arab Spring." *Foreign Affairs* 90, no. 3 (2011):2–7.

"Answering Christianity." Accessed 30 December 2016, http://www.answering-christianity.com/ac.htm.

"Answering Islam." Accessed 30 December 2016. http://www.answering-islam.org/.

al-Arian, Abdullah. *Answering the Call: Popular Islamic Activism in Sadat's Egypt*. New York: Oxford University Press, 2014.

Armbrust, Walter. "Islamists in Egyptian Cinema." *American Anthropologist* 104 (2002):922–31.

Arnez, Monika. "*Dakwah* by the Pen: Reading Helvy Tiana Rosa's *Bukavu*." *Indonesia and the Malay World* 37, no. 107 (2009):45–64.

Arnold, Thomas W. *The Preaching of Islam: A History of the Propagation of the Muslim Faith*. 2nd ed. London: Constable, 1913.

Asad, Talal. *Formations of the Secular: Christianity, Islam, and Modernity*. Stanford, CA: Stanford University Press, 2003.

Ashour, Omar. "Post-Jihadism and the Ideological Revisions of Armed Islamists." In *Contextualizing Jihadi Thought*, edited by Jeevan Deol and Zaheer Kazmi, 123–45. New York: Columbia University Press, 2011.

Assyaukanie, Luthfi. *Islam and the Secular State in Indonesia*. Singapore: Institute of Southeast Asian Studies, 2009.

Al-Atawneh, Muhammad. *Wahhabi Islam Facing the Challenges of Modernity: Dar al-Ifta in Modern Saudi Arabia*. Leiden: E. J. Brill, 2010.

———. "Wahhabi Self-Examination Post-September 11: Rethinking 'Other,' 'Otherness,' and Tolerance." *Journal of Middle Eastern Studies* 47, no. 2 (2011):255–71.

al-Awlaki, Anwar. "Was Islam Spread by The Sword—Al Shaheed, Imam

Anwar Al Awlaki (R. H.)." Accessed 24 April 2015. https://www.youtube.com/watch?v=xitkIrUvyZ8.

Atia, Mona. *Building a House in Heaven: Pious Neoliberalism and Islamic Charity in Egypt*. Minneapolis: University of Minnesota Press, 2013.

———. "'A Way to Paradise': Pious Neoliberalism, Islam, and Faith-Based Development." *Annals of the Association of American Geographers* 102 (2012):808–27.

Atkin, Douglas. *The Culting of Brands: Turn Your Customers into True Believers*. New York: Portfolio, 2004.

ʿAttar, Muhammad Ilyas. *Divine Excellence of (Causing) Invitation to Goodness*. Karachi: Maktaba al-Madina, n.d.

———. *Faizan-e Sunnat*. Karachi: Maktabat al-Madina, 2006.
Awad, Mokhtar. "Egypt's New Radicalism: The Muslim Brotherhood and Jihad." *Foreign Affairs*, 4 February 2016. Accessed 22 October 2018. https://www.foreignaffairs.com/articles/egypt/2016-02-04/egypts-new-radicalism.
Azab, Safa. "Hal Yumkin 'Akhwanat' al-Fann fi Misr ma ba'd al-Thawra?" *Al-Sharq al-Awsat*, 30 April 2013.
Aziz, T. M. "The Role of Muhammad Baqir al-Sadr in Shi'i Political Activism in Iraq from 1958 to 1980." *International Journal of Middle East Studies* 25, no. 2 (1993):207–22.
'Azzam, 'Abdallah. *Kalimat min Khat al-Nar al-Awwal*. N.p, n.d.
Baig, Noman. "God and Greed: Money and Meditation in Karachi's Marketplace." PhD diss., University of Texas, 2014.
Balala, Maha-Hanaan. *Islamic Finance and Law: Theory and Practice in a Globalized World*. London: I. B. Tauris, 2011.
al-Banna, Hasan. *Majmu'at Rasa'il*. Cairo: Iqra' Foundation, 2011.
———. *Mudhakkirat al-Da'wa wa'l-Da'iya*. Cairo: Dar al-Nashr wa'l-Tawzi' al-Islamiyya, 1986; Cairo: al-Maktaba al-Tawfiqiyya, n.d.
al-Banna, Jamal. *Istratijiyyat al-Da'wa al-Islamiyya fi'l-Qarn 21* [sic] *Kama Tuqaddimuha Da'wa al-Ihya' al-Islami*. Cairo: Dar al-Fikr al-Islami, 2000.
Baram, Amatzia. "From Radicalism to Radical Pragmatism: The Shi'ite Fundamentalist Opposition Movements of Iraq." In *Islamic Fundamentalism and the Gulf War*, edited by James Piscatori, 28–51. Chicago: American Academy of Arts and Sciences, 1991.
———. "The Impact of Khomeini's Revolution on the Radical Shi'i Movement of Iraq." In *The Iranian Revolution and the Muslim World*, edited by David Menashri, 131–54. Boulder, CO: Westview, 1990.
———. *Saddam Husayn and Islam, 1968–2003: Ba'thi Iraq from Secularism to Faith*. Washington, D.C.: Woodrow Wilson Center and Johns Hopkins University Press, 2014.
———. "Sadr the Father, Sadr the Son, the 'Revolution in Shi'ism' and the Struggle for Power in the *Hawzah* of Najaf." In *Iraq between Occupations: Perspectives from 1920 to the Present*, edited by Amatzia Baram, Achim Rohde, and Ronen Zeidel, 143–58. New York: Palgrave Macmillan, 2010.
———. "Two Roads to Revolutionary Shi'i Fundamentalism in Iraq." In *Accounting for Fundamentalism: The Dynamic Character of Movements*, edited by Martin E. Marty and R. Scott Appleby, 531–88. Chicago: University of Chicago Press and American Academy of Arts and Sciences, 1994.
Barton, Greg. *Abdurrahman Wahid: Muslim Democrat, Indonesian President*. Sydney: University of New South Wales Press, 2002.
———. "Neo-Modernism: A Vital Synthesis of Traditionalist and Modernist Islamic Thought in Indonesia." *Studia Islamika* 2 (2014):1–75.

Batatu, Hanna. *The Old Social Classes and the Revolutionary Movements of Iraq*. Princeton, NJ: Princeton University Press, 1978.

al-Bayanuni, Muhammad Abu al-Fath. *Al-Madkhal ila ʿIlm al-Daʿwa: Dirasa Minhajiyya Shamila li-Taʾrikh al-Daʿwa wa-Usuliha wa-Manahijiha wa-Asalibiha wa-Wasaʾiliha wa-Mushkilatiha fi Daw' al-Naql wa'l-ʿAql*. Beirut: Muʾassasat al-Risala, 1991.

Bayat, Asef. *Making Islam Democratic: Social Movements and the Post-Islamist Turn*. Stanford, CA: Stanford University Press, 2007.

BBC News. "Breastfeeding Fatwa Causes Stir." 22 May 2007. Accessed 12 December 2016. http://news.bbc.co.uk/2/hi/6681511.stm.

Becker, Carmen, and Nina Wiedl. "Populäre Prediger im deutschen Salafismus." In *Salafismus in Deutschland. Ursprünge und Gefahren einer islamisch-fundamentalistischen Bewegung*, edited by Thorsten Gerald Schneiders, 204. Bielefeld: transcript, 2014.

Ben-Ari, Shosh. "The Rating of Allah: Renaissance of Preaching in the Age of Globalization." In *Islamic Myths and Memories: Mediators of Globalization*, edited by Itzchak Weismann, Mark Sedgwick, and Ulrika Mårtensson, 185–207. Farnham, UK: Ashgate, 2014.

Berger, Peter L. *The Many Altars of Modernity: Toward a Paradigm for Religion in a Pluralist Age*. Berlin: De Gruyter, 2014.

Berkey, Jonathan P. *Popular Preaching and Religious Authority in the Medieval Islamic Near East*. Seattle: University of Washington Press, 2001.

Bernhardt, Florian. *Hizb ad-Daʿwa al-Islamiyya: Selbstverständnis, Strategien und Ziele einer irakisch-islamistischen Partei zwischen Kontinuität und Wandel, 1957–2003*. Würzburg: Ergon, 2012.

Bilici, Mukahit. *Finding Mecca in America: How Islam Is Becoming an American Religion*. Chicago: University of Chicago Press, 2012.

Bin Laden, Osama. "Osama bin Laden Praises Arab Spring in Posthumous Message." *Telegraph*, 19 May 2011. Accessed 22 October 2018. http://www.telegraph.co.uk/news/worldnews/al-qaeda/8522595/Osama-bin-Laden-praises-Arab-Spring-in-posthumous-message.html.

———, and Bruce Lawrence. *Messages to the World: The Statements of Osama bin Laden*. London: Verso, 2005.

Bin Radhan, Neil. "Tafsir al-Imran." HausImrans (mp3)." Accessed 4 January 2017. http://durus.de/unterrichte/tafsir/3aalimran/index.php.

Birt, Jonathan. "Wahhabism in the United Kingdom: Manifestations and Reactions." In *Transnational Connections and the Arab Gulf*, edited by Madawi al-Rasheed, 168–85. Abingdon: Routledge, 2004.

Boland, Bernard J. *The Struggle of Islam in Modern Indonesia*. The Hague: Martinus Nijhoff, 1971.

Bourdieu, Pierre. "Genesis and Structure of the Religious Field." *Comparative Social Research* 13 (1991):9–10.

Brass, Paul. *Language, Religion and Politics in North India*. Cambridge: Cambridge University Press, 1974.

Brinton, Jaquelene. "Preaching and the Epistemological Reinforcement of *Ulama* Authority: The Sermons of Muhammad Mitwalli Sha'rawi." *Intellectual Discourse* 19, no. 1 (2011):97–121.

Buchta, Wilfried. *Die iranische Schia und die islamische Einheit 1979–1996*. Hamburg: Orient Institut, 1997.

al-Bukhari, Muhammad. *Sahih al-Bukhari*. Damascus and Beirut: Dar ibn Kathir, 1423/2002.

Bundesamt für Verfassungsschutz (Federal Office for the Protection of the Constitution). Accessed 5 February 2016. https://www.verfassungsschutz.de/de/arbeitsfelder/af-islamismus-und-islamistischer-terrorismus/was-ist-islamismus/salafistische-bestrebungen.

Burns, Peter. *Revelation and Revolution: Natsir and the Panca Sila*. South-East Asian Monograph Series, no. 9. Townsville, AU: Committee of South-East Asian Studies, James Cook University of North Queensland, 1981.

Bustamam-Ahmad, Kamaruzzaman. "Contemporary Islamic Thought in Indonesian and Malay World: Islam Liberal, Islam Hadhari, and Islam Progresif." *Journal of Indonesian Islam* 5 (2011):91–129.

al-Buti, Muhammad Sa'id Ramadan. *Al-Salafiyya: Marhala Zamaniyya Mubaraka La Madhhab Islami*. Damascus: Dar al-Fikr, 1988.

Cafarella, Jennifer. "Jabhat al-Nusra in Syria: An Islamic Emirate for al-Qaeda." *Middle East Security Report 25*. Institute for the Study of War. December 2014, 1–66. Accessed 22 October 2018. http://www.understandingwar.org/sites/default/files/JN%20Final.pdf.

Cavatorta, Francesco, and Fabio Merone. "Moderation through Exclusion? The Journey of the Tunisian Ennahda from Fundamentalist to Conservative Party." *Democratization* 20 (2013):857–75.

Chalabi, Mona. "How Anti-Muslim Are Americans? Data Points to Extent of Islamophobia." *Guardian*, 8 December 2015. Accessed 24 October 2019. https://www.theguardian.com/us-news/2015/dec/08/muslims-us-islam-islamophobia-data-polls.

Chang, Leslie. "Egypt's Soap Opera Islamists." *New Yorker*, 22 July 2013.

Clark, Janine A. *Islam, Charity, and Activism: Middle-Class Networks and Social Welfare in Egypt, Jordan, and Yemen*. Bloomington: Indiana University Press, 2004.

Cockburn, Patrick. *Muqtada al-Sadr and the Battle for the Future of Iraq*. New York: Scribner, 2008.

Collins, Elizabeth F. "Islam Is the Solution: Dakwah and Democracy in Indonesia." *Kultur* 3, no. 1 (2003):151–81.

Commins, David. *The Wahhabi Mission and Saudi Arabia*. London: I. B. Tauris, 2006.

Conermann, Stephan. *Mustafa Mahmud (geb. 1921) und der modifizierte islamische Diskurs im modernen Ägypten*. Berlin: Schwarz, 1996.

Cook, David. *Understanding Jihad*. Berkeley: University of California Press, 2005.
Cook, Michael. *Commanding Right and Forbidding Wrong in Islamic Thought*. Cambridge: Cambridge University Press, 2000.
Dalacoura, Katerina. "The 2011 Uprisings in the Arab Middle East: Political Change and Geopolitical Implications." *International Affairs* 88 (2012):63–79.
Dar al-Hijrah Islamic Center. "Etiquette of Visiting a Mosque (masjid)." Accessed 26 October 2016. http://hijrah.org/media/etiquette-of-visiting-a-mosque-masjid/.
David-Secors, Sarah. "Muslims in Norman Sicily: The Evidence of Imam al-Mazari's Fatwas." *Mediterranean Studies* 16 (2007):46–66.
al-Dawish, Ahmad. *Fatawa al-Lajna al-Da'ima li'l-Buhuth al-ʿIlmiyya wa'l-Ifta' wa'l-Daʿwa wa'l-Irshad*. Riyadh: Maktabat al-ʿAbikan, 2000.
Dawud, Muhammad ʿAbd al-ʿAziz. *Al-Jamʿiyyat al-Islamiyya fi Misr wa-Dawruha fi Nashr al-Daʿwa al-Islamiyya*. Cairo: Al-Zahra li'l-Iʿlam al-ʿArabi, 1992.
Dekmejian, Hrair. "The Rise of Political Islamism in Saudi Arabia." *Middle East Journal* 48 (1994):627–43.
Demanik, Ali Said. *Fenomena Partai Kesejahtera: Transformasi 20 Tahun Gerakan Tarbiyyah di Indonesia*. Jakarta: Teraju, 2002.
Deneulin, Severine, and Masooda Bano. *Religion in Development: Rewriting the Secular Script*. London: Zed, 2009.
Denselow, James. "Starving Syria as a Weapon." *AlJazeera*, 10 January 2016. http://www.aljazeera.com/indepth/opinion/2016/01/starving-syria-weapon-isil-assad-madaya-160110544423833.html.
Deringil, Selim. "Shiʿism in Hamidian Iraq: A Study of Ottoman Counter-Propaganda." *Die Welt des Islams* 30 (1990):45–62.
Dickson, Rory. "The Tablighi Jamaʿat in Southwestern Ontario: Making Muslim Identities and Networks in Canadian Urban Spaces." *Contemporary Islam* 3, no. 2 (2009):99–112.
Die Wahre Religion. See Wahre.
Dooghan, James K. *Muslim Prison Ministry: Hindering the Spread of the Radical, Militant, Violent, and Irreconcilable Wing of Islam*. Fort Leavenworth, KS: U.S. Army Command and General Staff College, 2006.
Doumato, Eleanor Abdella, and Gregory Starrett, eds. *Teaching Islam: Textbooks and Religion in the Middle East*. Boulder, CO: Lynne Rienner, 2007.
Dudley Jenkins, Laura. "Legal Limits on Religious Conversion in India." *Law and Contemporary Problems: Galanter-Influenced Scholars* 71, no. 2 (2008):109–27.
Duhigg, Charles. *The Power of Habit: Why We Do What We Do and How to Change*. New York: Random House, 2013.
Dutton, Yasin. "Conversion to Islam: The Qur'anic Paradigm." In *Religious Conversion: Contemporary Practices and Controversies*, edited by Christopher Lamb and M. Darol Bryant, 151–65. London: Cassell, 1999.

Eaton, Richard. "Approaches to the Study of Conversion to Islam in India." In *Approaches to Islam in Religious Studies*, edited by Richard C. Martin, 107–23. Tucson: University of Arizona Press, 1985.

Edmiston, John. "Internet Evangelism and Cybermissions: Their Impact upon How We Will Do Missions in the 21st Century." Accessed 30 December 2016. http://cybermissions.org/articles/21stC_missions.pdf.

Eickelman, Dale F., and James Piscatori. *Muslim Politics.* Princeton, NJ: Princeton University Press, 1996.

Eisenlohr, Patrick. "Na't: Media Contexts and Transnational Dimensions of a Devotional Practice." In *Islam in South Asia in Practice*, edited by Barbara D. Metcalf, 101–12. Princeton, NJ: Princeton University Press, 2009.

"Eissa's 'Mowlana' to Become TV Series." *Ahram Online*. 29 July 2012. http://english.ahram.org.eg/NewsContent/5/35/48968/Arts—Culture/Stage—Street/Eissas-Mowlana-to-become-TV-series.aspx.

El-Gamal, Mahmoud A. *Islamic Finance: Law, Economics, and Practice.* Cambridge: Cambridge University Press, 2006.

Esposito, John L., and John O. Voll. *Makers of Contemporary Islam*. New York: Oxford University Press, 2001.

Fadlallah, al-Sayyid Muhammad Hussain. *Uslub al-Da'wa fi'l-Qur'an*. Beirut: Dar al-Malak, 1994.

Fahmi, George. "The Egyptian State and the Religious Sphere." Carnegie Middle East Center. 18 September 2014. Accessed 26 December 2016. http://carnegie-mec.org/2014/09/18/egyptian-state-and-religious-sphere-pub-56619.

Fandy, Mamoun. *Saudi Arabia and the Politics of Dissent*. New York: St. Martin's, 1999.

Faraj, Muhammad Abd al-Salam. *The Neglected Duty: The Creed of Sadat's Assassins and Islamic Resurgence in the Middle East*. Translated by Johannes J. G. Jansen. New York: Macmillan, 1986.

al-Faridan, 'Adil. *Al-Muntaqa min Fatawa Fadilat al-Shaykh Salih b. Fawzan b. 'Abd Allah al-Fawzan*. Beirut: Mu'assasat al-Risala, 1999.

Faridi, Iftikhar Husain. *Irshadat wa-Maktubat-e Hazrat Mawlana Shah Muhammad Ilyas Dihlawi*. Lahore: Makki Dar al-Kutub, 1997.

Farquhar, Michael. "Saudi Petrodollars, Spiritual Capital, and the Islamic University of Medina: A Wahhabi Missionary Project in Transnational Perspective." *International Journal of Middle East Studies* 47, no. 4 (2015):701–21.

Farrukh, Omar A., trans. *Ibn Taymiyya on Public and Private Law in Islam or Public Policy in Islamic Jurisprudence*. Beirut: Khayats, 1966.

al-Faruqi, Isma'il Raji. *Islam and Other Faiths*. Leicester: The Islamic Foundation, 1998.

———. "On the Nature of Islamic Da'wah," *International Review of Mission* 65, no. 260 (1976):391–409.

Faruqi, Ziya-ul-Hasan. *The Deoband School and the Demand for Pakistan*. Calcutta: Asia Publishing House, 1963.

al-Fayyad, ʿAbdallah. *Taʾrikh al-Imamiyya wa-Aslafihim min al-Shiʿa*. Baghdad: Matbaʿat Asʿad and Baghdad University, 1970.

Fealy, Greg. "Consuming Islam." In *Expressing Islam: Religious Life and Politics in Indonesia*, edited by Greg Fealy and Sally White, 15–39. Singapore: ISEAS Press, 2008.

———. "Hizbut Tahrir in Indonesia: Seeking a 'Total' Muslim Identity." In *Islam and Political Violence*, edited by Shahram Akbarzadeh, and Fethi Mansouri, 151–64. London: I. B. Tauris, 2007.

———. "Islamisation and Politics in Southeast Asia: The Contrasting Cases of Malaysia and Indonesia." In *Islam in World Politics*, edited by Nelly Lahoud and Anthony Johns, 152–69. London: Routledge, 2005.

Few, Mike. "The Untold Story of the Battle against the 'Soldiers of Heaven' (updated)." *Small Wars Journal*. Accessed 28 December 2016. http://smallwarsjournal.com/blog/the-untold-story-of-the-battle-against-the-%E2%80%98soldiers-of-heaven%E2%80%99-updated.

Figueira, Daurius. *Salafi Jihadi Discourse of Sunni Islam in the 21st Century*. Bloomington, IN: iUniverse, 2011.

al-Fiqi, Muhammad Hamid. *Athar al-Daʿwa al-Wahhabiyya fiʾl-Islah al-Dini waʾl-ʿUmrani fi Jazirat al-ʿArab wa-Ghayriha*. N.p., 1354 [ca. 1935].

Francois-Cerrah, Myriam. *My Journey to Islam*. 8 October 2012. Accessed 30 December 2016. http://www.youtube.com/watch?v=-JlkisV720s.

Freedom and Justice Party. "Barnamaj Hizb al-Hurriya waʾl-ʿAdala." *Al-Masri al-Youm*. 5 April 2011.

Gade, Anna. *Perfection Makes Practice: Learning, Emotion, and the Recited Qurʾan in Indonesia*. Honolulu: University of Hawaii Press, 2004.

Gaffney, Patrick D. *The Prophet's Pulpit: Islamic Preaching in Contemporary Egypt*. Berkeley: University of California Press, 1994.

Galal, Ehab, ed. *Arab TV-Audiences: Negotiating Religion and Identity*. Frankfurt am Main: Peter Lang, 2014.

———. "Yusuf al-Qaradawi and the New Islamic TV." In *The Global Mufti: The Phenomenon of Yusuf al-Qaradawi*, edited by Bettina Gräf and Jakob Skovgaard-Petersen, 149–80. New York: Columbia University Press, 2009.

Gardet, L. "Djamaʿa." *The Encyclopedia of Islam*, New Edition, edited by P. Bearman et al. Vol. 2, 411. Leiden: Brill, 1992.

Gartenstein-Ross, Daveed, and Tara Vassefi. "Perceptions of the 'Arab Spring' within the Salafi-Jihadi Movement." *Studies in Conflict and Terrorism* 35 (2012):831–48.

Gauvain, Richard. *Salafi Ritual Purity: In the Presence of God*. New York: Routledge, 2012.

Geaves, Ron. "The Contested Milieu of Deoband: 'Salafis' or 'Sufis'?" In *Sufis and Salafis in the Contemporary Age*, edited by Lloyd Ridgeon, 191–216. London: Bloomsbury, 2015.

Geertz, Clifford. *The Religion of Java*. New York: Free Press, 1960.

Gerges, Fawaz A. *The Far Enemy: Why Jihad Went Global.* Cambridge: Cambridge University Press, 2009.
Gershoni, Israel, and James P. Jankowski. *Redefining the Egyptian Nation, 1930–1945.* Cambridge: Cambridge University Press, 1995.
Ghalwash, Ahmad. *Al-Daʿwa al-Islamiyya: Usuluha wa-Wasaʾiluha.* Cairo: al-Risala Foundation, 1978.
al-Gharib, Abu Usama. "Abu Usama al-Gharib: Is It Not Time to Rise Up, with English Subtitles." Accessed 4 January 2017. www.youtube.com/watch?v=rfslcRj_yUk.
al-Ghazali, Muhammad. *Al-Daʿwa al-Islamiyya fiʾl-Qarn al-Hali.* Cairo: Dar al-Shuruq, 2000.
———. *Fi Mawqib al-Daʿwa.* 2nd ed. Cairo: Dar al-Kitab al-ʿArabi, 1957.
———. *Maʿa Allah: Dirasat fiʾl-Daʿwa waʾl-Duʿa.* Cairo: Dar al-Kutub al-Haditha, 1965. Reprint Cairo: Nahdat Misr, 2005.
———. *Mustaqbal al-Islam Kharij Ardihi: Kayfa Nufakkiru fihi?* Cairo: Dar al-Shuruq, 1997; first published 1984.
al-Ghazzi, ʿAsim. *Hiwarati maʿa ʿAmru Khalid.* Cairo: Arij liʾl-Nashr, 2004.
Ghubashi, Shuʿayb ʿAbd al-Munʿim. *Sihafat al-Ikhwan al-Muslimin: Dirasa fiʾl-Nashʾa waʾl-Madmun min 1933 ila 1952.* Egypt: Dar al-Tawziʿ waʾl-Nashr al-Islamiyya, 2000.
al-Ghuraba Media. "Antwort auf das Lies Projekt von Shaykh Abu Sufyan as-Sulami." Accessed 4 January 2017. www.youtube.com/watch?v=O1rJTvYkYGA.
Giddens, Anthony. *The Consequences of Modernity.* Cambridge, UK: Polity, 1990.
Gräf, Bettina, and Jakob Skovgaard-Petersen, eds. *Global Mufti: The Phenomenon of Yusuf al-Qaradawi.* New York: Columbia University Press, 2009.
Grossman, Cathy Lynn. "Number of U.S. Mosques Up 74% since 2000." *USA Today*, 29 February 2012.
Guaaybess, Tourya. "Broadcasting and Businessmen in Egypt: Revolution Is Business." In *Arab Media Moguls*, edited by Donatella della Ratta, Naomi Sakr, and Jakob Skovgaard-Petersen, 165–86. London: I. B. Tauris, 2015.
Gugler, Thomas K. *Mission Medina: Daʿwat-e Islami und Tabligi Gamaʿat.* Würzburg: Ergon, 2011.
———. "Muslim Youths on Tablighi Journeys." *Asien* 126 (2013):68–84.
———. "Sunna, Sunnaisierung und imitatio Muhammadi: Die Islamisierung der Individualsphäre als Programm der Tablighi Jamaʿat und Daʿwat-e Islami." In *Die Sunna leben: Zur Dynamik islamischer Religionspraxis in Deutschland*, edited by Paula Schrode and Udo Simon, 221–37. Würzburg: Ergon, 2012.
Habibiflo Dawah Produktion. "Abu Abdullah—Benefizveranstaltung vom 21.4.2013 Hamburg." YouTube. Accessed 4 January 2017. www.youtube.com/watch?v=uSbDObhb9Q4.
Haddad, Yvonne, and Adair Lummis. *Islamic Values in the United States: A Comparative Study.* New York: Oxford University Press, 1987.

Haddad, Yvonne Y., and Jane I. Smith, eds. *The Oxford Handbook of American Islam*. New York: Oxford University Press, 2014.

Haddad, Yvonne, Jane Smith, and Kathleen Moore, eds. *Muslim Women in America: The Challenge of Islamic Identity Today*. New York: Oxford University Press, 2006.

Haenni, Patrick. *L'islam de marché: l'autre revolution conservatrice*. Paris: Le Seuil, 2005.

al-Hakim, Muhammad Baqir. *Al-Hawza al-ʿIlmiyya*. Najaf: Matbaʿat al-Zaytun, 2005.

Halm, Heinz. *The Fatimids and Their Traditions of Learning*. London, New York: I. B. Tauris, 1997.

Hamid, Sadek. "The Development of British Salafism." *ISIM Review* 21 (2008):10–11.

Han, Byung-Chul. *Psychopolitik: Neoliberalismus und die neuen Machttechniken*. Frankfurt am Main: Fischer, 2014.

Haq, M. Anwarul. *The Faith Movement of Mawlana Muhammad Ilyas*. London: Allen and Unwin, 1972.

Haque, Amber, ed. *Muslims and Islamization in North America: Problems and Prospects*. Kuala Lumpur: A. S. Noordeen, 1999.

Hariyadi, Saja. "Islamic Popular Culture and the New Identities of Urban Muslim Young People in Indonesia: The Case of the Islamic Films and Islamic Self-Help Books." PhD diss., University of Western Australia, 2013.

Harms, Florian. *Cyberdaʿwah Islamische Mission im Internet: Voraussetzungen, Analyse und Vergleich von Daʿwa-Sites im World Wide Web*. Aachen: Shaker, 2007.

———. "Der Prophet ruft aus dem Cyberspace: Formen islamischer Mission im Internet." In *Von Chatraum bis Cyberjihad: Muslimische Internetnutzung in globaler und lokaler Perspektive,* edited by Johanna Pink and Mathias Bruckner. Würzburg: Ergon, 2009.

Haroon, Sana. "The Rise of Deobandi Islam in the North-West Frontier Province and Its Implications in Colonial India and Pakistan, 1914–1996." *Journal of the Royal Asiatic Society* 18 (2008):47–70.

Harris, Samuel Lee. "Development through Faith: the Maʿadi Life Makers and the Islamic Entrepreneurial Subject." Master's thesis, Georgetown University, 2008.

Hartung, Jan-Peter. *A System of Life: Mawdudi and the Ideologisation of Islam*. London: Hurst, 2013.

———. *Viele Wege und ein Ziel: Leben und Wirken von Sayyid Abu l-Hasan ʿAli al-Hasani Nadwi (1914–1999)*. Würzburg: Ergon, 2004.

Harvey, David. *A Brief History of Neoliberalism*. New York: Oxford University Press, 2005.

Hasan, Ehteshamul, and Ashique Elahi. *The Teachings of Tabligh*. Delhi: Idara Ishaat-E-Diniyat, 1989.

Hasan, Noorhaidi. "Islamist Party, Electoral Politics and Da'wah Mobilization among Youth: The Prosperous Justice Party (PKS) in Indonesia." *Journal of Indonesian Islam* 6 (2012):17–47.
———. *Laskar Jihad: Islam, Militancy, and the Quest for Identity in Post–New Order Indonesia*. Ithaca, NY: Cornell University Press, 2006.
———. "The Making of Public Islam: Piety, Agency, and Commodification on the Landscape of the Indonesia Public Sphere." *Contemporary Islam* 3 (2009):229–50.
———. "The Salafi Movement in Indonesia: Transnational Dynamics and Local Developments." *Comparative Studies of South Asia, Africa and the Middle East* 27, no. 1 (2007):83–94.
Hasani, Muhammad Sayyid Sani. *Sawanih Hazrat Mawlana Muhammad Yusuf Kandhalawi* [Biography of Muhammad Yusuf Kandhalawi]. Lucknow: Maktaba Dar al-'Ulum Nadwat al-'Ulama', 1982.
Hassan, Muhammad. *Khawatir 'ala Tariq al-Da'wa*. Mansura: Maktabat al-Fiyad li'l-Tijara wa'l-Tawzi', 2006.
Hatina, Meir. "Martyrs as Preachers." In *Religious Knowledge, Authority, and Charisma*, edited by Daphna Ephrat and Meir Hatina, 171–86. Salt Lake City: University of Utah Press, 2014.
———. "Redeeming Sunni Islam: Al-Qa'ida's Polemic against the Muslim Brethren." *British Journal of Middle Eastern Studies* 39 (2012):101–13.
Hawwa, Sa'id. *Ijaza Tukhassisu al-Du'a*. Cairo: Dar al-Salam, 1987.
———. *Jund Allah: Thaqafatan wa-Akhlaqan*. Cairo: Maktabat Wahbah, 1990.
Haykel, Bernard. "On the Nature of Salafi Thought and Action." In *Global Salafism: Islam's New Religious Movement*, edited by Roel Meijer, 33–57. London: Hurst, 2009.
Haynes, Jeffrey. *Religious Transnational Actors and Soft Power*. Farnham, UK: Ashgate Publishing, 2012.
Hefner, Robert. *Civil Islam: Muslims and Democratization in Indonesia*. Princeton, NJ: Princeton University Press, 2000.
———. "Islam, State and Civil Society: ICMI and the Struggle for the Indonesian Middle Class." *Indonesia* 56 (1993):1–35.
———. "Print Islam: Mass Media and Ideological Rivalries among Indonesian Muslims." *Indonesia* 64 (1997):77–103.
Hegghammer, Thomas. *Jihad in Saudi Arabia: Violence and Pan-Islamism since 1979*. Cambridge: Cambridge University Press, 2010.
———. "Jihadi-Salafis or Revolutionaries? On Religion and Politics in the Study of Militant Islamism." In *Global Salafism: Islam's New Religious Movement*, edited by Roel Meijer, 244–66. London: Hurst, 2009.
Hendrickson, Jocelyne N. "The Islamic Obligation to Emigrate: Al-Wansharisi's Asna al-Matajir Reconsidered." PhD diss., Emory University, 2009.
Hilmi, Ahmad Shalabi, and 'Abd al-'Azim Muhammad Ibrahim Ramadan. *Fusul min Ta'rikh Harakat al-Islah al-Ijtima'i fi Misr: Dirasa 'an Dawr al-Jam'iyya*

al-Khayriyya al-Islamiyya. Cairo: Al-Hay'a al-Misriyya al-ʿAmma li'l-Kuttab, 1988.

Hirschkind, Charles. *The Ethical Soundscape: Cassette Sermons and Islamic Counterpublics*. New York: Columbia University Press, 2006.

Hizb al-Daʿwa al-Islamiyya: Taʿrif Mujaz bi-Ta'sisihi wa-Masiratihi wa-Ahdafihi. Najaf: n.p., 2003.

Hoesterey, James. "Prophetic Cosmopolitanism: Islam, Pop Psychology, and Civil Virtue in Indonesia." *City and Society* 24 (2012):38–61.

———. *Rebranding Islam: Piety, Prosperity, and a Self-Help Guru*. Stanford, CA: Stanford University Press, 2015.

Hosen, Nadirsyah. "Religion and the Indonesian Constitution: A Recent Debate." *Journal of Southeast Asian Studies* 36, no. 3 (2005):419–40.

Hourani, Albert H. *Arabic Thought in the Liberal Age, 1798–1939*. New York: Oxford University Press, 1962.

Howell, Julia Day. "'Calling' and 'Training': Role Innovation and Religious De-differentiation in Commercialized Indonesian Islam." *Journal of Contemporary Religion* 28 (2013):401–19.

———. "Modernity and the Borderlands of Islamic Spirituality in Indonesia's New Sufi Networks." In *Sufism and the "Modern" in Islam*, edited by Martin van Bruinessen and Julia Day Howell, 217–41. London: I. B. Tauris, 2007.

———. "Modulations of Active Piety: Professors and Televangelists as Promoters of Indonesian 'Sufisme.'" In *Expressing Islam: Religious Life and Politics in Indonesia*, edited by Greg Fealy and Sally White, 40–62. Singapore: ISEAS Press, 2008.

Hroub, Khaled, ed. *Religious Broadcasting in the Middle East*. London: Hurst, 2012.

al-Hudaybi, Hasan Ismaʿil. *Duʿa, La Quda: Abhath fi'l-ʿAqida al-Islamiyya wa-Manhaj al-Daʿwa ila Allah*. Cairo: Dar al-Tibaʿa wa'l-Nashr al-Islamiyya, 1977.

Huq, Maimuna. "The Politics of Belief: Women's Islamic Activism in Bangladesh." PhD diss., Columbia University, 2006.

Hurgronje, C. Snouck. *Verspreide Geschriften*. 6 vols. Bonn: Kurt Schroeder, 1923–1927.

Ibn ʿAbd al-Wahhab, Muhammad. *Mu'allafat al-Imam al-Shaykh Muhammad ibn ʿAbd al-Wahhab*. Riyadh: Imam Muhammad ibn Saʿud Islamic University, 1977.

Ibn Baaz, Abdul Azeez, and Muhammad ibn Saalih al-Uthaymeen, *Muslim Minorities*. Hounslow: Message of Islam, 1998.

Ibn Baz, ʿAbd al-ʿAziz ʿAbdallah. *Al-Daʿwa ila Allah wa-Akhlaq al-Duʿa*. Riyadh: Office of Scientific Research and Ifta Administration, 2002. Online: IslamHouse, 1427/2006. www.islamhouse.com/ar/books/1886.

———. "Hukm al Safar ila al-Kharij li'l-Dirasa wa-Ghayriha." Binbaz. Accessed 19 January 2017. http://www.binbaz.org.sa/index.php?pg=mat&type=fatawa&id=1719.

———. "Hukm al-Safar Kharij al-Duwal al-Islamiyya." Binbaz. Accessed 19 January 2017. http://www.binbaz.org.sa/index.php?pg=mat&type=fatawa&id=58.

———. "Kayfa Nuharib al-Ghazw al-Thaqafi al-Gharbi wa'l-Sharqi." Binbaz. Accessed 19 January 2017. http://www.binbaz.org.sa/mat/8164.

———. *Majmu' Fatawa wa-Maqalat Mutanawwi'a.* Compiled by Muhammad ibn Sa'd al-Shuway'ir. 24 vols. Riyadh: Dar al-Qasim, 1420/1999–2000; online edition, 30 vols.: imambinbaz.org.

———. "Mudayaqa Du'at al-Batil li-Ahl al-'Ilm wa'l-Khayr." Accessed 26 January 2016. www.binbaz.org.sa/node/1816.

———. "Al-Safar ila al-Kharij." Binbaz. Accessed 19 January 2017. http://www.binbaz.org.sa\index\php?pg=mat&type=fatawa&id=41.

Ibn Baz, 'Abd al-'Aziz et al. *Fatawa 'Ulama al-Balad al-Haram.* Cairo: Dar Ibn Haytham, 2004.

Ibn Qasim, 'Abd al-Rahman. *Al-Durar al-Saniyya fi al-Ajwiba al-Najdiyya.* Riyadh: Dar al-Ifta', 1965.

'Id, Mufid Khalid 'Id Ahmad. *Al-'Alaqa bayna al-Fiqh wa'l-Da'wa.* Beirut: Dar Ibn Hazm li'l-Tiba'a wa'l-Nashr wa'l-Tawzi', 1995.

Ilyas, Muhammad, and Sayyid Abu al-Hasan 'Ali Nadwi. *Makatib, Hazrat Mawlana Shah Muhammad Ilyas.* Karachi: Dar al-Isha'at, 1982 [1952].

Imam, Muhammad Imam. "Fatwa Tujizu Shira' al-Manazil bi-Qard Ribbawi li'l-Muslimin fi Ghayr Bilad al-Islam." *Al-Sharq al-Awsat,* 3 October 1999.

International Crisis Group. *Iraq's Muqtada al-Sadr: Spoiler or Stabiliser?* Report no. 55, 11 July 2006.

———. *Pakistan: Karachi's Madrasas and Violent Extremism.* Brussels: International Crisis Group, 2007.

International Dawah. "Abu Ubayda und M. Islam über Kundgebungen Teil 1_2." 2 January 2010. Accessed 15 June 2018. www.youtube.com/watch?v=ZfcYjeze6sA&feature=related.

Iqbal, Sajid. "A House Divided." Accessed 15 June 2018. https://www.dawn.com/news/1391624/a-house-divided.

Iqtidar, Humeira. "How Long Is Life? Neoliberalism and Islamic Piety." *Critical Inquiry* 43 (2017):790–812.

———. *Secularizing Islamists? Jama'at-e-Islami and Jama'at-ud-Da'wa in Urban Pakistan.* Chicago: University of Chicago Press, 2011.

'Isa, Ibrahim. *Mawlana.* Doha: Dar Bloomsbury, 2012.

al-Islam Su'al wa-Jawab. "Ayhuma 'Ula: Da'wa Ghayr al-Muslimin li'l-Islam am Da'wa al-Muslimin Ghayr al-Multazimin li'l-Iltizam." Accessed 4 January 2017. http://islamqa.info/ar/186813.

———. "Al-Da'wa ila al-Islam." Accessed 4 January 2017. https://islamqa.info/ar/12376.

———. "Hukm al-Jihad wa-Anwa'ihi." Accessed 4 January 2017. https://islamqa.info/ar/20214.

———. "Al-Khuruj li'l-Daʿwa." Accessed 16 November 2019. https:// islamqa .info/ar/41687.

———. "La Tatruk Daʿwa Ghayr al-Muslim Khashiya Shatmih al-Din." Accessed 4 January 2017. http://islamqa.info/ar/77579.

Islamic Daʿwah Center. "History." Accessed 30 December 2016. islamicdawahcenter.org/about-us/.

The Islamic Foundation. *Christian Mission and Islamic Daʿwa: Proceedings of the Chambesy Dialogue Consultation*. Leicester: Islamic Foundation, 1982.

Islamweb.net. "Muslim Minorities in non-Muslim Countries." 20 July 2004. Accessed 20 October 2019. https://islamweb.net/en/fatwa/88291/muslim -minorities-in-non-muslim-countries.

al-Jaʿfari, Ahmad. "Al-Hukm ʿala Muhammad Hassan li-Ittihamihi bi-Izdira' al-Adyan wa-Nashr Afkar Mutattarifa." *Al-Yawm al-Sabaʿ*, 13 March 2016.

Jahangeer, Roshan A. *Towards an Inclusive Secularism and a Transformative Model of Community Engagement in Québec*. Toronto: Tessellate Institute, 2014. Accessed 30 December 2016. http://www.tessellateinstitute.com /newsite/publications/towards-an-inclusive-secularism-and-a-transformative -model-of-community-engagement-in-quebec/.

al-Jahni, Maniʿ Hamad. "Al-Islam li-Ghayr al-Muslimin: Barnamaj Muqtara li'l-Daʿwa bayna al-Aqalliyyat al-Muslima." In *al-Aqalliyyat al-Muslima fi al-ʿAlam*, 165–77. Riyadh: Al-Nadwa al-ʿAlamiyya li'l-Shabab al-Islami, 1986.

Jamaʿat-e Islami Pakistan. *The Creed*. Accessed 4 October 2019. http://jamaat.org /en/jamaatOrDawat.php?cat_id=12.

———. *Dawah*. Accessed 4 October 2019. http://jamaat.org/en /jamaatOrDawat.php?cat_id=12.

Jamil, U. "Discrimination Experienced by Muslims in Ontario." *Diversity Magazine* 9, no. 3 (2012). Accessed 22 October 2019. http://www.ohrc.on.ca/en /creed-freedom-religion-and-human-rights-special-issue-diversity-magazine -volume-93-summer-2012/discrimination-experienced-muslims-ontario.

Janson, Marloes. *Islam, Youth, and Modernity in the Gambia*. Cambridge, UK: Cambridge University Press, 2013.

Janson, Torsten. "Daʿwa: Islamic Missiology in Discourse and History." *Swedish Missiological Themes* 89 (2001):355–415.

Jiwani, Yasmin. "Colluding Hegemonies: Constructing the Muslim Other Post-9/11." In *Islam in the Hinterlands: Exploring Muslim Cultural Politics in Canada,* edited by Jasmin Zine, 115–36. Vancouver: University of British Columbia Press, 2012.

Johnstone, Ronald L. *Religion in Society: A Sociology of Religion*. 8th ed. New York: Routledge, 2006.

Jones, Linda Gale. *The Power of Oratory in the Medieval Muslim World*. Cambridge: Cambridge University Press, 2012.

Jonker, Gerdine. *Missionizing Europe: The Ahmadiyya Quest to Modernize Islam*. Leiden: Brill, 2015.

Kalam, Mohammed. "Religious Conversions in Tamil Nadu: Can These Be Viewed as Protest Movements?" *Indian Anthropologist* 20 (1990):39–48.

Kamil, Kamil. "Ta'arraf 'ala Radd fi Muhammad Hassan ba'd Bara'atihi min 'Izdira' al-Adyan." *Al-Yawm al-Saba'*, 30 October 2016.

Kantz-Feder, Rachel. "Fatima's Revolutionary Image in Fadak fi al-Ta'rikh (1955): The Inception of Muhammad Baqir al-Sadr's Activism." *British Journal of Middle Eastern Studies* 41 (2014):79–96.

Kasimi, Mufti Muhammad Rawshan Shah. *Malfuzat wa-Iqtibasat Mawlana Muhammad Yusuf.* Delhi: Rashid Publications, n.d.

al-Kawakibi, 'Abd al-Rahman. *Umm al-Qura*. Beirut: Dar al-Ra'id al-'Arabi, 1982.

Kayunga, Sallie Simba. *Islamic Fundamentalism in Uganda: A Case of the Tabligh Youth Movement*. Kampala: Center for Basic Research, 1993.

Kazim, Abbas. "The Hawza under Siege: A Study in the Ba'th Party Archive." IIBSU Occasional Paper 1. Boston: Boston University Institute for Iraqi Studies, June 2013.

Kenney, Jeffrey T. "Selling Success, Nurturing the Self: Self-Help Literature, Capitalist Values, and the Sacralization of Subjective Life in Egypt." *International Journal of Middle East Studies* 47, no. 4 (2015):663–80.

Kepel, Gilles. *Muslim Extremism in Egypt*. Berkeley: University of California Press, 1986.

———. *The Prophet and Pharaoh: Muslim Extremism in Egypt*. London: Al Saqi, 1985.

Kern, Soeren. "Muslims Converting Empty European Churches into Mosques." Gatestone Institute. 16 January 2012. Accessed 20 October 2016. https://www.gatestoneinstitute.org/2761/converting-churches-into-mosques.

Kerr, Davis A. "Islamic Da'wa and Christian Mission: Towards a Comparative Analysis." *International Review of Mission* 89, no. 353 (2000):150–71.

Khadduri, Majid, trans. *The Islamic Law of Nations: Shaybani's Siyar*. Baltimore: Johns Hopkins University Press, 1966.

———. *War and Peace in the Law of Islam*. Baltimore: Johns Hopkins University Press, 1955.

Khaled, Amr. "Amr Khaled CV." Accessed 28 December 2016. Amrkhaled.net.

———. "The Episodes of the Series Da'wa li-Ta'ayush." Accessed 28 December 2016. http://www.assabile.com/amr-khaled-141/series/daawa-litaayush-116.

———. *Integration im Islam: Über die Rolle der Muslime in Europa*. Karlsruhe: Andalusia, 2005.

———. *Suna' al-Hayat.* Television series, 50 episodes, 2005–2006.

Khan, Arsalan. "Islam and Pious Sociality: The Ethics of Hierarchy in the Tablighi Jamaat in Pakistan." *Social Analysis* 60, no. 4 (2016):96–113.

———. "Pious Masculinity, Ethical Reflexivity, and Moral Order in an Islamic Piety Movement in Pakistan." *Anthropological Quarterly* 91 (2018):53–77.

Khan, Maulana Wahiduddin. “Conversion: An Intellectual Transformation.” *Alrisala*. Accessed 19 November 2019. https://ia800806.us.archive.org/12/items/mwk-eng-book/Convertion-An-Intellectual-Transformation.pdf.

———. *The Political Interpretation of Islam*. Noida: Goodword Books, 2015.

———. “Three Stages of Da‘wah Work.” Al-Quran Mission. Accessed 2 March 2017.

Khan, Nadia. “American Muslims in the Age of New Media.” In *The Oxford Handbook of American Islam,* edited by Yvonne Haddad and Jane Smith. New York: Oxford University Press, 2014.

Khatib, Sayed. *The Political Thought of Sayyid Qutb*. New York: Routledge, 2006.

al-Khatir, ‘Abdullah. “Al-Da‘wa ila Allah: Tawajihat wa-Dawabit.” *Al-Bayan* 7 (2008).

al-Khuli, al-Bahi. *Tadhkirat al-Du‘a*. Cairo: Dar al-Kitab al-‘Arabi, 1952.

al-Kittani, ‘Ali ibn al-Muntasir. *Al-Muslimun fi Urubba wa-Amrika*. Beirut: Dar al-Kutub al-‘Ilmiyya, 2005.

Kuiper, Matthew J. *Da‘wa and Other Religions: Indian Muslims and the Modern Resurgence of Global Islamic Activism*. London: Routledge, 2018.

Kuran, Timur. *Islam and Mammon: The Economic Predicaments of Islamism*. Princeton, NJ: Princeton University Press, 2004.

Kurnaz, Murat. *Fünf Jahre meines Lebens: Ein Bericht aus Guantanamo*. Berlin: Rowohlt, 2007.

Lacroix, Stéphane. “Between Islamists and Liberals: Saudi Arabia’s New Islamo-Liberal Reformist Trend.” *Middle East Journal* 58 (2004):345–65.

———. “Between Revolution and Apoliticism: Nasir al-Din al-Albani and His Impact on the Shaping of Contemporary Salafism.” In *Global Salafism: Islam’s New Religious Movement*, edited by Roel Meijer, 58–80. London: Hurst, 2009.

———. “Egypt’s Pragmatic Salafis: The Politics of Hizb al-Nour.” *Carnegie Endowment for International Peace.* 1 November 2016. Accessed 9 October 2019. http://carnegieendowment.org/2016/11/01egypt-s-pragmatic-salafis-politics-of-hizb-al-Nur-pub-64902.

———. *The Islamic Awakening: The Politics of Religious Dissent in Contemporary Saudi Arabia*. Cambridge, MA: Harvard University Press, 2011.

———. *Sheikhs and Politicians: Inside the New Egyptian Salafism*. Brookings Doha Center, 2012.

Lahoud, Carine. “Koweït. salafisms et rapports au pouvoir.” In *Qu’est-ce que le Salafisme?* edited by Bernard Rougier, 12–135. Paris: Presses Universitaires de France, 2008.

Lahoud, Nelly. *Jihadi Discourse in the Wake of the Arab Spring*. West Point, NY: Combating Terrorism Center, 2013.

Latif, Muhammad Fahmi. “Al-Islam wa’l-Tarbiya wa’l-Ta‘lim.” *Minbar al-Islam*, April 1977/Jumada al-Ula 1397.

Lauzière, Henri. *The Making of Salafism: Islamic Reform in the Twentieth Century*. New York: Columbia University Press, 2015.

Lav, Daniel. *Radical Islam and the Revival of Medieval Theology*. Cambridge: Cambridge University Press, 2012.

Lemos, Eirini. "What Is the Festival of Bishwa Ijtema?" *Telegraph*, 7 January 2016. Accessed 16 December 2016. http://www.telegraph.co.uk/news/worldnews/asia/bangladesh/12088120/What-is-the-festival-of-Bishwa-Ijtema-and-where-is-it-held.html.

Lerman, Eran. "Mawdudi's Concept of Islam." *Middle Eastern Studies* 17 (1981):492–509.

Levitt, Matthew, and Dennis Ross. *Hamas: Politics, Charity, and Terrorism in the Service of Jihad*. New Haven, CT: Yale University Press, 2008.

Levtzion, Nehemia, ed. *Conversion to Islam*. New York: Holmes and Meier, 1979.

Lia, Brynjar. *The Society of the Muslim Brothers in Egypt: The Rise of an Islamic Mass Movement, 1928–1942*. Reading: Ithaca, 1998.

Lichter, Ida. "Misogyny in the Muslim World: Bound by Culture or Religion?" *Huffington Post*, 25 May 2011. Accessed 13 December 2016. http://www.huffingtonpost.com/ida-lichter-md/misogyny-bound-by-culture_b_803942.html.

Liddle, William. "Media Dakwah Scripturalism: One Form of Political Thought and Action in New Order Indonesia." In *Toward a New Paradigm, Recent Developments in Indonesian Islamic Thought*, edited by Mark Woodward, 323–56. Program for Southeast Asian Studies Monograph Series. Tempe: Arizona State University, 1996.

Lincoln, C. Eric. *The Black Muslims in America*. Grand Rapids, MI: Eerdmans, 1994.

Liow, Joseph Chinyong. *Piety and Politics: Islamism in Contemporary Malaysia*. New York: Oxford University Press, 2009.

Liu, Joseph. "Muslim World League and World Assembly of Muslim Youth." Pew Forum. 15 September 2010. http://www.pewforum.org/2010/09/15/muslim-networks-and-movements-in-western-europe-muslim-world-league-and-world-assembly-of-muslim-youth/.

LiveLeak.com. "Iraqi TV Airs Video Showing Leader of Jund al-Samaa (Army of Heaven)." Accessed 28 December 2016. http://www.liveleak.com/view?i=555ca47d45bG9zrma8R03vaIA1.99.

Lombardi, Clark, and Nathan Brown. "Islam in Egypt's New Constitution." *Foreign Policy*, 13 December 2012. Accessed 28 September 2016. http://foreignpolicy.com/2012/12/13/islam-in-egypts-new-constitution/.

Lynch, Marc. *The Arab Uprising: The Unfinished Revolutions of the New Middle East*. New York: Public Affairs, 2013.

Madan, T. N. "Religion of India: Plurality and Pluralism." In *Religious Pluralism in South Asia and Europe*, edited by Jamal Malik and Helmut Reifeld, 43–73. New Delhi: Oxford University Press, 2004.

Madani, Arshad, and Muhammad Sulaiman. *Preface to the Quran Sharif: Anuwad and Vyakhya*. Delhi: Jamiat Ulama e-Hind, 1992.

Mahmood, Saba. *Politics of Piety: The Islamic Revival and the Feminist Subject.* Princeton, NJ: Princeton University Press, 2005.
Mahmud, ʿAli ʿAbd al-Halim. *Fiqh al-Daʿwa ila Allah.* Cairo: Dar al-Wafaʾ liʾl-Tibaʿa waʾl-Nashr waʾl-Tawziʿ, 1990.
Maliach, Asaf. "Abdullah Azzam, al-Qaeda, and Hamas: Concepts of Jihad and Istishhad." *Military and Strategic Affairs* 2, no. 2 (2010):79–80.
Malik, Jamal. *Colonialization of Islam: Dissolution of Traditional Institutions in Pakistan.* New Delhi: Manohar, 1996.
———. "Fiqh al-Daʿwa: The Emerging Standardization of Islamic Proselytism." *Die Welt des Islams* 58 (2018):206–43.
———. *Islam in South Asia: A Short History.* Leiden: Brill, 2008.
———. "Islamic Mission and Call: The Case of the International Islamic University, Islamabad." *Islam and Christian-Muslim Relations* 9, no. 1 (1998):31–45.
———. *Islamische Gelehrtenkultur in Nordindien: Entwicklungsgeschichte und Tendenzen am Beispiel von Lucknow.* Leiden: Brill, 1997.
———. "The Luminous Nurani: Charisma and Political Mobilization among the Barelwis in Pakistan." *Social Analysis* 28 (1990):38–50.
———. "Sayyid Abu al-Aʿla al-Mawdudi, al-Jihad fi al-Islam (1930)." In *Geschichte des politischen Denkens. Das 20. Jahrhundert,* edited by Manfred Brocker, 217–32. Frankfurt am Main: Suhrkamp, 2018.
Mallat, Chibli. *The Renewal of Islamic Law: Muhammad Baqir al-Sadr, Najaf and the Shiʿi International.* Cambridge: Cambridge University Press, 1993.
al-Manara al-Bayda Messaging Network. "Report on the Activities of the Daʿwa and Guidance Office within the Campaign of Support of Shariʿah." *Jabhat al-Nusra.* 25 June 2015. http://jihadology.net.
———. "Some Daʿwah and Service Work Carried Out by Jabhat al-Nusrah in the City of al-Atarib and Its Surrounding Area." *Jabhat al-Nusra.* 31 March 2015. http://jihadology.net.
Mandaville, Peter. *Global Political Islam.* London: Routledge, 2007.
Mansfield, Laura. *His Own Words: A Translation of the Writings of Dr. Ayman al Zawahiri.* Old Tappan, NJ: TLG Publications, 2006.
al-Maqdese. See al-Maqdisi.
al-Maqdisi, Abu Muhammad ʿAsim. "An Advise [*sic*] for the American Muslims." Accessed 4 January 2017. www.al-tawhed.net.
———. "Millat Ibrahim wa-Daʿwat al-Anbiyaʾ waʾl-Mursalin." Minbar al-Tawhid wa-l-Jihad, 1984. Accessed 4 January 2017. www.tawhed.ws/r?i=iti4u3zp.
———. *Millat Ibrahim (The Religion of Ibrahim) and the Calling of the Prophets and Messengers and the Methods of the Transgressing Rulers in Dissolving It and Turning the Callers Away from It.* 2nd ed. Accessed 8 February 2016. www.kalamullah.com/al-maqdisi.html.
———. "This Is Our ʿAqidah." 2nd ed. At-Tibyan. Accessed 4 January 2017. https://archive.org/details/ThisIsOuraqidah-AbiMuhammadAl-maqdisi.

March, Andrew F., and Mara Revkin. "Caliphate of Law: ISIS' Ground Rules." *Foreign Affairs*, 15 April 2015. Accessed 22 October 2018. https://www.foreignaffairs.com/articles/syria/2015-04-15/caliphate-law.

Mårtensson, Ulrika. "'Islamic Order': Semeiotics and Pragmatism in the Muslim Brotherhood?" *Journal of Islamic Research* 9 (2015):35–57.

Martín-Sáiz, Guillermo. "Islam and the Tablighi Jamaʿat in Spain: Ghosts of the Past, Limits of Representation, and New Developments." In *Secularisms in a Postsecular Age? Religiosities and Subjectivities in Comparative Perspective*, edited by José Mapril et al., 67–85. Cham, CH: Springer International, 2017.

Mashhur, Mustafa. "Bayna al-Qiyada wa'l-Jundiyya ʿala Tariq al-Daʿwa." In *Min Fiqh al-Daʿwa*, edited by Mustafa Mashhur. Cairo: Dar al-Tawziʿ wa'l-Nashr al-Islamiyya, 1986.

———. *Min Fiqh al-Daʿwa*. 2 vols. Cairo: Dar al-Tawziʿ wa'l-Nashr al-Islamiyya, 1995.

al-Masri, Abu Hamza. "1/3 Das korrekte Dawah Verständnis—Shaikh Abu Hamza al Masri." Accessed 4 January 2017. www.youtube.com/watch?v=kzhA2OySV_s.

Masri, Fouad. "A Visit to the Mosque." Crescent Project. Accessed 26 October 2016. http://www.crescentproject.org/files/podcasts/MosqueVisit.pdf.

Masoud, Moez. Curriculum vitae. Faculty of Divinity, Cambridge University. Accessed 8 December 2015. https://www.divinity.cam.ac.uk/directory/moez-masoud.

Masʿud, Muhammad ʿAli. *Al-Jamʿiyya al-Sharʿiyya li-Taʿawun al-ʿAmilin bi'l-Kitab wa'l-Sunna al-Muhammadiyya ʿAqidatan wa-Minhajan wa-Sulukan*. Cairo: Al-Jamʿiyya al-Sharʿiyya, 1982.

Masud, Muhammad Khalid, ed. *Travellers in Faith: Studies of the Tablighi Jamaʿat as a Transnational Islamic Movement for Faith Renewal*. Leiden: Brill, 2000.

———. "Ideology and Legitimacy." In *Travellers in Faith: Studies of the Tablighi Jamaʿat as a Transnational Islamic Movement for Faith Renewal*, edited by Muhammad Khalid Masud, 79–120. Leiden: Brill, 2000.

Mattes, Hanspeter. *Die innere und äußere Mission Libyens*. Mainz: Grünwald, 1986.

Mawdudi, Abu'l-Aʿla. *A Historic Address at Madras*. Translated by Mohammad Siddiqui Naveed. Delhi: Markazi Maktaba Islami, 2009.

———. *Al-Jihad fi'l-Islam*. Lahore: Idara Tarjuman al-Qur'an, 2006.

———. *Quran Majid*. New Delhi: Maktaba al-Hasanat, 1970.

———. *Tadhkirat Duʿa al-Islam*. Damascus and Beirut: Al-Maktab al-Islami, 1983.

———. *Towards Understanding Islam*. U.K.I.M. Daʿwa Centre, 1960.

Mayaram, Shail. *Resisting Regimes: Myth, Memory, and the Shaping of a Muslim Identity*. New Delhi: Oxford University Press, 1997.

McCants, William. "The Lesser of Two Evils: the Salafi Turn to Party Politics in Egypt." Saban Center at Brookings, *Middle East Memo* 23 (2012):1–8.

McCauley, Clark. "Muslim World Outreach: The United States Intervenes in Religious Identity." *Analyses of Social Issues and Public Policy* 11 (2011):43–44.
McCloud, Aminah Beverly. *African American Islam.* New York: Routledge, 1995.
McCombs, Maxwell. *Setting the Agenda: Mass Media and Public Opinion.* 2nd ed. Cambridge, UK: Polity Press, 2014.
McDonough, Sheila, and Homa Hoodfar. "Muslims in Canada: From Ethnic Groups to Religious Community." In *Religion and Ethnicity in Canada,* edited by Paul Bramadat and David Seljak. Toronto: University of Toronto Press, 2008.
McGinty, Anna M. *Becoming Muslim: Western Women's Conversions to Islam.* New York: Palgrave Macmillan, 2006.
———. "'Faith Drives Me to Be an Activist': Two American Muslim Women on Faith, Outreach, and Gender." *The Muslim World* 102 (2012):371–89.
McLarney, Ellen. *Soft Force: Women in Egypt's Islamic Awakening.* Princeton, NJ: Princeton University Press, 2015.
Means, Gordon. *Political Islam in Southeast Asia.* Boulder, CO: Lynne Rienner, 2009.
Meijer, Roel, ed. *Global Salafism: Islam's New Religious Movement.* London: Hurst, 2009.
Memon, Nadeen. "From Mosques to Madrassas: Civic Engagement and the Pedagogy of Islamic Schools." In *Islam in the Hinterlands: Exploring Muslim Cultural Politics in Canada,* edited by Jasmin Zine. Vancouver: University of British Columbia Press, 2012.
Metcalf, Barbara Daly. *Husain Ahmad Madani: The Jihad for Islam and India's Freedom.* Oxford: OneWorld Publications, 2008.
———. *Islamic Revival in British India: Deoband, 1860–1900.* Princeton, NJ: Princeton University Press, 1982; New Delhi: Oxford University Press, 2005.
———. "Living Hadith in the Tablighi Jamaʿat." *Journal of Asian Studies* 52 (1993):584–608.
———, ed. *Making Muslim Space in North America and Europe.* Berkeley: University of California Press, 1996.
———. "Remaking Ourselves: Islamic Self-Fashioning in a Global Movement of Spiritual Renewal." In *Accounting for Fundamentalisms: The Dynamic Character of Movements,* edited by Martin E. Marty and R. Scott Appleby, 706–25. Chicago: University of Chicago Press, 1994.
———. "Tablighi Jamaʿat and Women." In *Travellers in Faith: Studies of the Tablighi Jamaʿat as a Transnational Islamic Movement for Faith Renewal,* edited by Muhammad Khalid Masud, 44–58. Leiden: Brill, 2000.
———. "'Traditionalist' Islamic Activism: Deoband, Tablighis, and Talibs." In *Islamic Contestations: Essays on Muslims in India and Pakistan,* edited by Barbara D. Metcalf, 265–84. New Delhi: Oxford University Press, 2004.
MillatuIbrahimUK. "Is Millatu Ibrahim a Group?" Accessed 4 January 2017. www.youtube.com/watch?v=Mh5aPwuhvM&feature=related.

Miller, Timothy. "Intentional Communities: The Evolution of Enacted Utopianism." In *Revisionism and Diversification in New Religious Movements*, edited by Eileen Barker, 213–26. Farnham, UK: Ashgate, 2013.

Mishal, Shaul, and Avraham Sela. *The Palestinian Hamas: Vision, Violence, and Coexistence*. New York: Columbia University Press, 2006.

Mitchell, Richard P. *The Society of the Muslim Brothers*. New York: Oxford University Press, 1969.

Mitchell, Timothy. *Colonising Egypt*. Berkeley: University of California Press, 1991.

———. "Dreamland: The Neoliberalism of Your Desires." *Middle East Report* 210 (Spring 1999):28–33.

MLYNXQUALEY. "Looking at the Longlist: Fiery Journalist Ibrahim Eissa Recognized for 'Mowlana.'" ArabLit: Arabic Literature and Translation. 8 January 2013. Accessed 1 November 2019. http://arablit.org/2013/01/08/looking-at-the-longlist/.

Moll, Yasmin. "Building the New Egypt: Islamic Televangelists, Revolutionary Ethics, and 'Productive' Citizenship." Society for Cultural Anthropology. *Fieldsights, Editors' Forum, Hot Spots*. 23 May 2013. Accessed 11 November 2019. https://culanth.org/fieldsights/building-the-new-egypt-islamic-televangelists-revolutionary-ethics-and-productive-citizenship.

———. "Islamic Televangelism: Religion, Media and Visuality in Contemporary Egypt." *Arab Media, and Society* 10 (2010):1–27.

Momen, Moojan. *An Introduction to Shiʿi Islam: The History and Doctrines of Twelver Shiʿism*. New Haven, CT: Yale University Press, 1985.

Moussa, Mohammed. *Politics of the Islamic Tradition: The Thought of Muhammad al-Ghazali*. Abingdon: Routledge, 2016.

Moussalli, Ahmad. *Radical Islamic Fundamentalism: The Ideological and Political Discourse of Sayyid Qutb*. Beirut: American University of Beirut, 1992.

Murad, Khurram. *Daʿwa among Non-Muslims in the West*. Leicester: Islamic Foundation, 1986.

Musallam, Adnan A. *From Secularism to Jihad: Sayyid Qutb and the Foundations of Radical Islamism*. Westport, CT: Praeger, 2005.

Muslim Speakers. "Tablighi Jamaat Amazing Effort." Accessed 2 September 2011. https://www.youtube.com/watch?v=KaJdwA8cdQI.

Muslim World League. "Final Communique of Dialogue and Peaceful Coexistence Conference." Accessed 4 January 2017. http://en.themwl.org/final-communique-dialogue-and-peaceful-coexistence-Conference-hong-kong.

———. *Interfaith Dialogue: Cross-Cultural Views*. Riyadh: Ghainaa Publications, 2010.

———. "The International Islamic Conference for Dialogue: Makkah al-Mukarramah." Accessed 4 January 2017. http://en.themwl.org/content/international-islamic-conference-dialogue.

———. "Objectives and Methods of MWL." Accessed 4 January 2017. http://en.themwl.org/content/objectives-methods-mwl.

al-Musnad, Muhammad bin ʿAbd al-ʿAziz, comp. *Fatawa Islamiyya*. Vol. 4. Riyadh: Dar al-Watan: 1415/1994–1995.

———, comp. *Fatawa Islamiyya*. Vol. 8. Riyadh: Darussalam, 2002.

Mustafa, Faizan. "Freedom of Religion in India: Contemporary Challenges." 4th AAE Memorial Lecture. Accessed 19 November 2019. https://csss-isla.com/wp-content/uploads/2019/08/Prof.-Faizan-Mustafas-4th-AAE-Memorial-Lecture.pdf.

Muttaqi, Salwa. "34,000 Americans Converted to Islam." Tell Me about Islam. Accessed 17 December 2016. http://tellmeaboutislam.com/34000-american-entered-islam.html.

Muzakki, Akh. "The Islamic Publication Industry in Modern Indonesia: Intellectual Transmission, Ideology, and the Profit Motive." PhD diss., University of Queensland, 2009.

Nadwi, Syed Abul Hasan ʿAli. *Daʿwah in the West: The Quranic Paradigm*. London: Islamic Foundation, 1996.

———. *Hazrat Mawlana Muhammad Ilyas awr Unki Dini Daʿwat* [Mawlana Muhammad Ilyas and His Religious Mission]. Lucknow: Tanvir, 1964 [1946].

———. *Hindustani Musalman Aik Drishti Main* [An Overview of Indian Muslims]. Lucknow: Academy of Islamic Research and Publication, 2014.

———. *Inviting to the Way of Allah*. London: Ta-Ha Publishers and UK Islamic Society, 1992.

———. *Karwan-e Zindagi*. Lucknow: Maktaba-ye Islam, 2001.

———. *Life and Mission of Maulana Mohammad Ilyas*. Translated by Muhammad Asif Kidwai. Lucknow: Academy of Islamic Research and Publications, 1979.

———. *Live to Lead: A Call to Indian Muslims*. Lucknow: Academy of Islamic Research and Publications, 1980.

———. *Muslims in India*. Translated by Mohammad Asif Kidwai. Lucknow: Academy of Islamic Research and Publications, 1976.

———. *Try to Understand the Problems and Sentiments of Indian Muslims: A Pre-requisite of Peaceful Co-existence*. Lucknow: All India Solidarity Forum, n.d.

Nadwi, Abul Lais Islahi. *Bharat ka Nawnirman awr Hum* [Rebuilding India and Our Role]. Translated by Afzal Husain. Delhi: Markazi Maktaba Islami, 2014.

Naik, Zakir. "The Foregone Conclusion: The Second Letter to India." *India Today*. Accessed 2 March 2017. http://indiatoday.intoday.in/story/zakir-naik-open-letter-to-india-facing-the-foregone-conclusion/1/819726.html.

Najaf, A. *Al-Shahed al-Shahid*. Tehran: n.p., early 1980s.

Najib,ʿImara. "Nazra Islamiyya fi Mushkilat al-Taʿlim." *Al-Daʿwa*, January 1978/Safar 1397.

al-Najjar, ʿAbd al-Majid. *Fiqh al-Muwatana liʾl-Muslimin fi ʾUrubba*. Beirut: Al-Majlis al-ʾUrubbi liʾl-Iftaʾ waʾl-Buhuth, 2009.

Nakash, Yitzhak. *The Shiʿis of Iraq*. Princeton, NJ: Princeton University Press, 1994.

Nasr, Seyyed Vali Reza. *Islamic Leviathan: Islam and the Making of State Power*. New York: Oxford University Press, 2001.

———. *Mawdudi and the Making of Islamic Revivalism*. New York: Oxford University Press, 1996.

———. *The Vanguard of the Islamic Revolution: The Jamaʿat-i Islami of Pakistan*. Berkeley: University of California Press, 1994.

Nasser, S. "Paris Attacks Backlash 'Nothing New,' Canadian Muslims Say, but Public Also Supportive." *CBC News*. 24 November 2015. Accessed 30 December 2016. http://www.cbc.ca/news/canada/toronto/paris-attacks-backlash-nothing-new-canadian-muslims-say-but-public-also-supportive-1.3331724

National Council of Canadian Muslims. *ODIHR Hate Crime Report*. Ottawa, 2014. Accessed 17 December 2016. http://www.nccm.ca/wp-content/uploads/2014/11/Hate-Crime-Report-2013-National-Council-of-Canadian-Muslims.pdf.

al-Nayfar, Muhammad al-Shadhili. "Al-Tajannus bi-Jinsiyya Ghayr Islamiyya." *Majallat al-Majmaʿ al-Fiqhi al-Islami* 2, no. 4 (1989):177–252.

Nedza, Justyna. "Salafismus: Überlegungen zur Schärfung einer Analysekategorie." In *Salafismus: Auf der Suche nach dem wahren Islam,* edited by Behnam T. Said and Hazim Fouad, 80–105. Freiburg im Breisgau: Herder, 2014.

Nielsen, Jorgen S. *Muslims in Western Europe*. 3rd ed. Edinburgh: Edinburgh University Press, 2004.

Noer, Deliar. *The Modernist Muslim Movement in Indonesia, 1900–1942*. Singapore: Oxford University Press, 1973.

Noor, Farish. *Islam on the Move: The Tablighi Jamaʿat in Southeast Asia*. Amsterdam: Amsterdam University Press, 2012.

———. *The Malaysian Islamic Party, 1951–2013: Islamism in a Mottled Nation*. Amsterdam: Amsterdam University Press, 2014.

North American Imam's Federation. "Visiting an Islamic Center." Accessed 26 October 2016. http://imamsofamerica.weebly.com/visiting-a-mosque.html.

Noth, Albrecht. *The Early Arabic Historical Tradition: A Source-Critical Study*. Princeton, NJ: Darwin Press, 1994.

Nye, Joseph S., Jr. "The Decline of America's Soft Power." *Foreign Affairs* May/June 2004.

———. *Soft Power: The Means to Success in World Politics*. New York: Public Affairs, 2004.

Paris Dawah. "L'importance de la dawah (partie 1)." Accessed 4 January 2017. www.paris-dawah.fr/dawah-2/article-6-limportance-de-la-dawah/.

———. "Les qualités d'un prédicateur." Accessed 4 January 2017. www.paris-dawah.fr/news/article-9-les-qualites-dun-predicateur/.

———. "Qui peut faire dawah?" Accessed 4 January 2017. www.paris-dawah.fr /news/qui-peut-faire-la-dawah/.

———. "La sincérité (partie 1)." Accessed 4 January 2017. www.paris-dawah.fr /news/la-dawah-est-une-science-la-sincerite-partie-1/.

Peter, Frank. "Tariq Ramadan." In *Islamic Movements in Europe: Public Religion and Islamophobia in the Modern World,* edited by Frank Peter and Rafael Ortega, 274–77. London: I. B. Tauris, 2014.

Peters, Rudolph. *Jihad in Classical and Modern Islam*. Princeton, NJ: Markus Wiener, 1996.

Peterson, Roger, Gordon Aeschliman, and R. Wayne Sneed. *Maximum Impact Short-Term Mission: The God-Commanded Repetitive Deployment of Swift, Temporary Non-Professional Missionaries*. Minneapolis: Stempress, 2008.

Pew Research Center. "5 Facts about the Muslim Population in Europe." Pew Research. Accessed 19 July 2016. http://www.pewresearch.org/fact-tank /2016/07/19/5-facts-about-the-muslim-population-in-europe.

———. How Americans Feel about Religious Groups." 16 July 2014. Accessed 24 October 2019. http://www.pewforum.org/2014/07/16/how-americans -feel-about-religious-groups/.

———. "Religion in Prisons: A 50-State Survey of Prison Chaplains." Pew Research Center. 22 March 2012. Accessed 23 October 2019. http://www .pewforum.org/2012/03/22/prison-chaplains-exec/.

Pfeifer, Karen. "How Tunisia, Morocco, Jordan and Even Egypt Became IMF 'Success Stories' in the 1990s." *Middle East Report* 210 (1999):23–27.

Philips, Abu Ameena Bilal. *The Fundamentals of Tawheed*. 2nd ed. Riyadh: International Islamic Publishing House, 2005.

Pieri, Zacharias P. *Tablighi Jamaat and the Quest for the London Mega Mosque: Continuity and Change*. London: Palgrave Macmillan, 2015.

Pink, Johanna, and Matthias Brückner, eds. *Muslimische Internetnutzung in globaler und lokaler Perspektive*. Würzburg: Ergon, 2009.

Platzdasch, Bernhard. *Islamism in Indonesia: Politics in the Emerging Democracy*. Singapore: Institute of Southeast Asian Studies, 2009.

The Pluralism Project. "Muslim Chaplaincy in the U.S." Cambridge, MA: Harvard University. Accessed 30 December 2016. http://pluralism.org/religions /islam/issues-for-muslims-in-america/muslim-chaplaincy-in-the-u-s/.

Poston, Larry. "The Future of Da'wah in North America." In *Muslims and Islamization in North America: Problems and Prospects*, edited by Amber Haque. Kuala Lumpur: A. S. Noordeen, 1999.

———. *Islamic Daʿwah in the West: Muslim Missionary Activity and the Dynamics of Conversion to Islam*. New York: Oxford University Press, 1992.

Pranowo, M. Bambang. "Islam and Party Politics in Rural Java." *Studia Islamika* 1, no. 2 (1984):1–19.

Preckel, Claudia. "Islamische Bildungsnetzwerke und Gelehrtenkultur im Indien des 19. Jahrhunderts: Muhammad Siddiq Hasan Han (st. 1890) und die

Entstehung der Ahl-e hadit-Bewegung in Bhopal." PhD diss., Bochum University, 2005.

Press Association. "Study Shows 'Demonisation' of Muslims." *Guardian.* 14 November 2007. Accessed 30 December 2016. http://www.theguardian.com/media/2007/nov/14/pressandpublishing.religion.

al-Qadiri, Arshad. *Tablighi Jamaʿat: Haqaʾiq wa-Maʿlumat.* Lahore: Maktaba Nabawiyya, n.d. [1969].

al-Qadri, Arshad. *Tableeghi Jamaat.* Mumbai: Sunni Youth Federation, 2000.

al-Qaradawi, Yusuf. "Athar Ustadhuna al-Bahi al-Khuli." Accessed 28 December 2016. www.qaradawi.net/new/Articles-3427.

———. "Duties of Muslims Living in the West." 7 May 2006. Originally posted on Islamonline.net. Accessed 10 January 2007.

———. *Fi Fiqh al-Aqalliyyat al-Muslima.* Cairo: Dar al-Shuruq, 2006 [2001].

———. *Al-Halal wa'l-Haram fi'l-Islam.* Cairo: Matkabat Wahba, 2004 [1960].

———. "Shiraʾ Buyut al-Sukna fi al-Gharb ʿan Tariq al-Bunuk." In *Fi Fiqh al-Aqalliyyat al-Muslima*, edited by Yusuf al-Qaradawi, 154–91.

———. *Taʾrikhuna al-Muftara ʿalayhi.* Cairo: Dar al-Shuruq, 2008 [2005].

———. *Thaqafat al-Daʿiya.* 2nd ed. Beirut: Muʾassasat al-Risala, 1979.

al-Qasim, Khalid. *Al-Hurriyya al-Diniyya bayna al-Muslimin wa-Ahl al-Kitab.* Riyadh: Kursi al-Amir Sultan li'l-Dirasat al-Islamiyya al-Muʿasira, 2009.

Qasmi, Mufti Inam Haq. *Injunctions Pertaining to the Traveller.* New Delhi: Adam, 2003.

Qureshi, M. Naeem. *Pan-Islam in British Indian Politics: A Study of the Khilafat Movement, 1918–1924.* Leiden: Brill, 1999.

Qureshi, Regula B. "Transcending Space: Recitation and Community among South Asian Muslims in Canada." In *Making Muslim Space in North America and Europe*, edited by Barbara Metcalf, 46–64. Berkeley: University of California Press, 1996.

Qutb, Muhammad. *Kayfa Naduʿ al-Nas?* Cairo: Dar al-Shuruq, 2001.

Racius, Egdunas. "The Multiple Nature of the Islamic Daʿwa." PhD diss., University of Helsinki, 2004.

al-Rafiʿi, Salim b. ʿAbd al-Ghani. *Ahkam al-Ahwal al-Shakhsiyya li'l-Muslimin fi al-Gharb.* Beirut: Dar Ibn Hazm, 2002.

Rahnema, Ali, ed. *Pioneers of Islamic Revival.* London: Zed, 2005.

Ramadan, Tariq. "Daʿwa in the West." Accessed 28 December 2016. http://www.tariqramadan.com/spip.php?article72.

———. "Europeanization of Islam or Islamization of Europe?" In *Islam, Europe's Second Religion*, edited by Shireen T. Hunter, 207–19. Westport, CT: Praeger, 2002.

———. *Western Muslims and the Future of Islam.* New York: Oxford University Press, 2004.

al-Rasheed, Madawi. *Contesting the Saudi State: Islamic Voices from a New Generation.* Cambridge: Cambridge University Press, 2007.

Raza, Imam Ahmad. *Husam al-Haramain*. Stockport, UK: Raza Academy Publication, 2005 [1906].

Reetz, Dietrich. "The 'Faith Bureaucracy' of the *Tablighi Jama'at*: An Insight into Their System of Self-Organisation (*Intizam*)." In *Colonialism, Modernity, and Religious Identities: Religious Reform Movements in South Asia*, edited by Gwilym Beckerlegge, 98–124. New Delhi: Oxford University Press, 2008.

———. *Islam in the Public Sphere: Religious Groups in India, 1900–1947*. New Delhi: Oxford University Press, 2006.

———. "Laïcité and Piety: The Tablighi Jama'at in France." In *Islamic Movements of Europe: Public Religion and Islamophobia in the Modern World*, edited by Frank Peter and Rafael Ortega, 195–98. London: I. B. Tauris, 2014.

Report of the National Commission for Religious and Linguistic Minorities. Delhi: Ministry of Minority Affairs, 2007.

Ricklefs, M. C. *Islamisation and Its Opponents in Java: A Political, Social, Cultural and Religious History, c. 1930 to the Present*. Singapore: NUS Press, 2012.

Rida, Rashid. "Al-Islam fi Inkaltra." *Al-Manar* 18, no. 14 (14 February 1915):73–79.

———. "Jama'at al-Da'wa wa'l-Irshad." *Al-Manar* 14, no. 2 (1 March 1911):114–20.

———. *al-Manar wa'l-Azhar*. Cairo: Dar al-Manar, 2007.

———. *Tafsir al-Qur'an al-Shahir bi-Tafsir al-Manar*. Cairo: al-Manar, 1911.

Riexinger, Martin. *Sana'ullah Amritsari (1868–1948) und die Ahl-i Hadis im Punjab unter britischen Herrschaft*. Würzburg: Ergon, 2004.

Rock-Singer, Aaron. "Amr Khaled: From Da'wa to Political and Religious Leadership." *British Journal of Middle Eastern Studies* 37, no. 1 (2010):15–37.

———. "Prayer and the Islamic Revival: A Timely Challenge." *International Journal of Middle East Studies* 48, no. 2 (2016):293–312.

Rosyad, Rifki. *A Quest for True Islam: A Study of the Islamic Resurgence Movement among the Youth of Bandung*. Canberra: ANU E-Press, 2006.

Rougier, Bernard, ed. *Qu'est-ce que le Salafisme?* Paris: Presses Universitaires de France, 2008.

Rudnyckyj, Daromir. "Spiritual Economies: Islam and Neoliberalism in Contemporary Indonesia." *Cultural Anthropology* 24, no. 1 (2009):104–41.

Ryad, Umar. "Islamic Reformism and Great Britain: Rashid Rida's Image as Reflected in the Journal al-Manar in Cairo." *Islam and Christian-Muslim Relations* 21 (2010):263–85.

———. "A Prelude to Fiqh al-Aqalliyat: Rashid Rida's Fatwas to Muslims under non-Muslim Rule." In *In-Between Spaces: Christian and Muslim Minorities in Transition in Europe and the Middle East*, edited by Christiane Timmerman et al., 239–70. London: Peter Lang, 2009.

al-Sadr, Muhammad Baqir. "Hawla al-Ism wa'l-Shikl al-Tanzimi li-Hizb al-Da'wa al-Islamiyya." In *Min Fikr al-Da'wa al-Islamiyya: al-Shahid al-Rabi' al-Imam al-Sadr*, edited by Muhammad Baqir al-Sadr. Tehran: Hizb al-Da'wa al-Islamiyya al-I'lam al-Markazi, 1980.

———. *Ikhtarna Laka*. Beirut: Dar al-Taʿaruf li'l-Matbuʿat, 1975.

———. *Lamha Fiqhiyyah Tamhidiyya ʿan Mashruʿ Dustur al-Jumhuriyya al-Islamiyya fi Iran*. Silsilat al-Islam Yaqudu al-Hayat 1. Beirut: Dar al-Nahar li'l-Matbuʿat, 1979.

———. *Muqaddimat fi'l-Tafsir al-Mawduʿi li'l-Qur'an*. Beirut: Dar al-Taʿaruf li'l-Matbuʿat, 1980.

al-Sadr, Muhammad Sadiq. *Fiqh al-ʿAsha'ir: Hiwar Fatawa maʿa Marjaʿ al-Muslimin Zaʿim al-Hawza al-ʿIlmiyya Samahat Ayat Allah al-ʿUzma al-Sayyid Muhammad al-Sadr*. Beirut: Dar al-Najwa, 1997.

Said, Behnam T. "Hymns (Nasheeds): A Contribution to the Study of the Jihadist Culture." *Studies in Conflict and Terrorism* 35 (2012):863–79.

———. "Salafismus und politische Gewalt unter deutscher Perspektive." In *Salafismus: Auf der Suche nach dem wahren Islam,* edited by Behnam T. Said and Hazim Fouad, 193–228. Freiburg im Breisgau: Herder, 2014.

Sakr, Naomi. *Arab Television Today*. London: I. B. Tauris, 2007.

"Saleel al-Sawareem [Clashing of the Swords]." YouTube. Published 29 August 2014. https://www.youtube.com/watch?v=LomJ322yZds.

Salvatore, Armando. "Social Differentiation, Moral Authority, and Public Islam in Egypt: The Path of Mustafa Mahmud." *Anthropology Today* 16, no. 2 (April 2000):12–15.

al-Samman, Muhammad ʿAbdallah. "Istratijiyyat al-Daʿwa al-Islamiyya fi Duwal Ghayr Islamiyya." *Al-Aqalliyyat al-Muslima fi al-ʿAlam*, 181–93. Riyadh: al-Nadwa al-ʿalamiyya lil-shabab al-islami, 1986.

Sanyal, Usha. *Devotional Islam and Politics in British India: Ahmad Riza Khan Barelwi and His Movement, 1870–1920*. New Delhi: Oxford University Press, 1996.

Sayeed, Khalid B. "The Jamaʿat-i-Islami Movement in Pakistan." *Pacific Affairs* 30 (1957):59–68.

Sayeed, Sarah, Aisha al-Adawiya, and Ihsan Bagby. "Women and the American Mosque." *The American Mosque 2011*. Plainfield, IN: Islamic Society of North America, 2013.

al-Sayyid, ʿAdl, ed. *Al-Hakimiyya wa'l-Siyasa al-Sharʿiyya: ʿInda Shuyukh Jamaʿat Ansar al-Sunna al-Muhammadiyya*. Cairo: Dar al-Ibana, 2009.

Schulze, Gerhard. *Die Erlebnisgesellschaft: Kultursoziologie der Gegenwart*. Frankfurt am Main: Campus, 1992.

Schulze, Reinhard. *Islamischer Internationalismus im 20. Jahrhundert: Untersuchungen zur Geschichte der Islamischen Weltliga*. Leiden: Brill, 1990.

Schumann, Christoph. "A Muslim "Diaspora" in the United States?" *The Muslim World* 97 (2007):11–32.

"Shahid Afridi Official." Accessed 15 June 2018. https://www.facebook.com/ShahidAfridiOfficial10/.

Shaikh, Farzana. *Community and Consensus in Islam: Muslim Representation in Colonial India, 1860–1947*. Cambridge: Cambridge University Press, 1991.

Shaltut, Mahmud. *Al-Da'wa al-Muhammadiyya wa'l-Qital fi'l-Islam*. Cairo: al-Matba'a al-Salafiyya, 1933.
Shanahan, Rodger. "Shi'a Political Development in Iraq: The Case of the Islamic Da'wa Party." *Third World Quarterly* 25 (2004):943–54.
Shane, Scott. "In Message, Bin Laden Praised Arab Revolt." *New York Times*, 18 May 2011. Accessed 22 October 2018. http://www.nytimes.com/2011/05/19/world/middleeast/19binladen.html?_r=0.
al-Sha'rawi, Muhammad Mutawali. *Usul al-Da'wa*. Cairo: al-Matba'a al-Tawfiqiyya, n.d.
Sharon, Moshe. *Revolt: The Social and Military Aspects of the 'Abbasid Revolution*. Jerusalem: Hebrew University, 1990.
Shavit, Uriya. *The New Imagined Community*. Brighton: Sussex Academic Press, 2009.
Shavit, Uriya, and Frederic Wiesenbach. "Muslim Strategies to Convert Western Christians." *Middle East Quarterly* 16, no. 2 (2009):3–14.
al-Shaybani, Muhammad. *Hayat al-Albani wa-Atharuhu wa-Thana' al-'Ulama' 'alayhi*. N.p.: Maktabat al-Sirrawi, 1986.
Shukr, Abd al-Ghaffar, ed. *Al-Jam'iyyat al-Ahliyya al-Islamiyya fi Misr*. Cairo: Dar al-Amin li'l-Nashr wa'l-Tawzi', 2002.
Siddiqi, Bulbul. *Becoming "Good Muslim": The Tablighi Jamaat in the UK and Bangladesh*. Singapore: Springer Singapore, 2018.
Siddiqui, Muzzamil. "Muslims in a Non-Muslim Society." *Islamic Horizons* (May–June 1986):22–25.
Sikand, Yoginder. "Arya Shuddhi and Muslim Tabligh: Muslim Reactions to Arya Samaj Proselytization (1923–30)." In *Religious Conversion in India: Modes, Motivations, Meanings*, edited by Rowena Robinson and Sathianathan Clarke, 98–117. New Delhi: Oxford University Press, 2003.
———. *The Origins and Development of the Tablighi Jama'at, 1920–2000: A Cross-Country Comparative Study*. New Delhi: Orient Longman, 2002.
———. "Reformist Sufism of the Tablighi Jama'at: The Case of the Meos of Mewat, India." In *Sufism and the "Modern" in Islam*, edited by Martin van Bruinessen and Julia Day Howell, 129–48. London: I. B. Tauris, 2007.
Sirriyeh, Elisabeth. "Wahhabis, Unbelievers and the Problem of Exclusivism." *Bulletin of the British Society for Middle Eastern Studies* 16, no. 2 (1989):123–132.
Sisler, Vit. "The Internet and the Construction of Islamic Knowledge in Europe." *Masaryk University Journal of Law and Technology* 1 (2007):205–18.
Sivan, Emmanuel. "The Enclave Culture." In *Fundamentalisms Comprehended*, edited by Martin M. Marty, 11–68. Chicago: University of Chicago Press, 1995.
Skovgaard-Petersen, Jakob. "The Global Mufti." In *Globalization and the Muslim World*, edited by Birgit Schaebler and Leif Stenberg, 153–65. Syracuse: Syracuse University Press, 2004.

———. "New Media in the Muslim World." In *The Oxford Encyclopedia of Islam and Politics*, edited by Emad El-Din Shahin, Vol. 2, 183–88. New York: Oxford University Press, 2014.

Smelser, Neil J. *The Odyssey Experience: Physical, Social, Psychological, and Spiritual Journeys*. Berkeley: University of California Press, 2009.

Somin, Ilya. *Democracy and Political Ignorance: Why Smaller Government Is Smarter*. Palo Alto, CA: Stanford University Press, 2013.

Spellberg, Denise A. *Thomas Jefferson's Qur'an: Islam and the Founders*. New York: Vintage, 2013.

Spence, D. "Why Online Islamophobia Is Difficult to Stop." *CBC News*, 1 November 2014. Accessed 30 December 2016. http://www.cbc.ca/news/why-online-islamophobia-is-difficult-to-stop-1.2810242.

Stark, Rodney. "Why Religious Movements Succeed or Fail: A Revised General Model." *Journal of Contemporary Religion* 11, no. 2 (1996):133–46.

Starrett, Gregory. "The Political Economy of Religious Commodities in Cairo." *American Anthropologist* 97 (1995):51–68.

———. *Putting Islam to Work: Education, Politics, and Religious Transformation in Egypt*. Berkeley: University of California Press, 1998.

Steinback, Robert. "The Anti-Muslim Inner Circle." *Intelligence Report—Southern Poverty Law Center*. 17 June 2011. Accessed 30 December 2016. http://www.splcenter.org/fighting-hate/intelligence-report/2011/anti-muslim-inner-circle.

Student Association of the University of Cairo. "Mawqaʿ Kull al-Taliba." All-talaba. Accessed 28 December 2016. http://www.alltalaba.com/tegara.php.

Tadros, Samuel. *Mapping Egyptian Islamism*. Washington, D.C.: Hudson Institute, 2014.

al-Tahir, Ahmad Muhammad. *Jamaʿat Ansar al-Sunna al-Muhammadiyya: Nash'atuha, Ahdafuha, Manhajuha, Juhuduha*. Cairo: Jamaʿat Ansar al-Sunna al-Muhammadiyya—al-Markaz al-ʿAmm, 2006.

Tammam, Husam. "Yusuf al-Qaradawi and the Muslim Brothers: The Nature of a Special Relationship." In *The Global Mufti: The Phenomenon of Yusuf al-Qaradawi*, edited by Bettina Gräf and Jakob Skovgaard-Petersen, 55–83. New York: Columbia University Press, 2009, and London: Hurst, 2009.

Tarres, Sol. "The Tablighi Jamaʿat in Spain." In *Islamic Movements of Europe: Public Religion and Islamophobia in the Modern World*, edited by Frank Peter and Rafael Ortega, 195–98. London: I. B. Tauris, 2014.

Thanwi, Maulana Ashraf Ali. *Islamic Renaissance: Muslim Revival and Awakening*. Delhi: Adam, 1997.

Thompson, Mark. *Saudi Arabia and the Path to Political Change: National Dialogue and Civil Society*. London: I. B. Tauris, 2014.

al-Tikriti, Anas Usama, and Shakir Nasif al-ʿUbaydi, trans. *Fatwas of European Council for Fatwa and Research*. Cairo: Islamic INC, 2002.

Timol, Riyaz. "Religious Travel and Tablighi Jamaʿat: Modalities of Expansion in Britain and Beyond." In *Muslims in the UK and Europe (I)*, edited by Yasir

Suleiman, 194–206. Cambridge: Center of Islamic Studies, University of Cambridge, May 2015.

al-Tirmidhi, Abu ʿIsa Muhammad. *Al-Jamiʿ al-Kabir*. Beirut: Dar al-Gharb al-Islami, 1996.

Toktogulova, Mukaram. "The Localization of the Transnational Tablighi Jamaʿat in Kyrgyzstan: Structures, Concepts, Practices, Metaphors." Crossroads Asia Working Paper Series 17, edited by Ingeborg Baldauf et al., 2014. http://hdl.handle.net/20.500.11811/144.

Tripp, Charles. "Sayyid Qutb: The Political Vision." In *Pioneers of Islamic Revival*, edited by Ali Rahnema, 154–83. London: Zed, 1994.

Troll, Christian W. "Two Conceptions of Daʿwa in India: Jamaʿat-i Islami and Tablighi Jamaʿat." *Archives de sciences sociales des religions* 87 (1994):115–33.

ʿUkasha, Tawfiq. "Yakshif Haqiqat ʿAmr Khalid Daʿiya Ikhwani wa-Tajir Din." Accessed 28 December 2016. https://www.youtube.com/watch?v=WIyjF4mKX2k.

al-ʿUmrani, Muhammad al-Kadi. *Fiqh al-Usra al-Muslima fi'l-Muhjar*. Beirut: Dar al-Kutub al-ʿIlmiyah, 2001.

United Nations Meetings Coverage and Press Releases. "Starvation by Siege Now 'Systematic' in Syria, Assistant Secretary-General Tells Security Council, amid Warnings That Tactic Could Be War Crime." 15 January 2016. Accessed 22 October 2018. http://www.un.org/press/en/2016/sc12203.doc.htm.

ʿUrfa, Ahmad. "Abu Ishaq al-Huwayni li-Haraka Salafiyya: Iʿtaziltu hatta La Yuqalu ʿani Kha'in wa-ʿAmil." *Al-Yawm al-Sabaʿ*, 30 October 2015.

U.S. Department of Justice. "Confronting Discrimination in the Post-9/11 Era: Challenges and Opportunities Ten Years Later." 19 October 2011. Accessed 30 December 2016. http://www.justice.gov/sites/default/files/crt/legacy/2012/04/16/post911summit_report_2012-04.pdf.

U.S. Equal Employment Opportunity Commission. "What You Should Know about the EEOC and Religious and National Origin Discrimination Involving the Muslim, Sikh, Arab, Middle Eastern, and South Asian Communities." Accessed 30 December 2016. http://www.eeoc.gov/eeoc/newsroom/wysk/religion_national_origin_9-11.cfm.

al-ʿUthaymin, Muhammad ibn Salih. "Inviting to Allah in Communities Where There Are Muslim Minorities." In *Muslim Minorities: Fatawa Regarding Muslims Living as Minorities*, edited by ʿAbd al-ʿAziz ibn ʿAbdallah bin Baz, and Muhammad ibn Salih al-ʿUthaymin, 43–59. London: Message of Islam, 1998.

———. "Al-Iqama fi Bilad al-Kuffar." In *Fatawa al-Balad al-Haram*, edited by Muhammad ibn Salih al-ʿUthaymin, 189–91. Cairo: Dar al-Tawfiqiyya, n.d.

———. *Majmuʿ Fatawa wa-Rasa'il*, compiled by Fahd ibn Nasir al-Sulayman. Vol. 3. Riyadh: Dar al-Watan, 1413/1992–1993.

———. *Zad al-Daʿiya ila Allah*. 3rd ed. Riyadh: Dar al-Watan, 1413/1993–94.

ʿUthman, Wa'il. *Asrar al-Haraka al-Islamiyya fi Misr, 1968–1975*. Cairo: al-Shirka al-Misriyya li'l-Tibaʿa, n.d.

Vahed, Goolem. "Contesting 'Orthodoxy': The Tablighi-Sunni Conflict among South African Muslims in the 1970s and 1980s." *Journal of Muslim Minority Affairs* 23, no. 2 (2003):313–34.

Valentine, Simon Ross. *Islam and the Ahmadiyya Jama'at: History, Belief, Practice*. New York: Columbia University Press, 2008.

van Bruinessen, Martin. "Genealogies of Islamic Radicalism in Post-Suharto Indonesia." *Southeast Asia Research* 10 (2002):117–54.

———. "Islamic State or State Islam? Fifty Years of State-Islam Relations in Indonesia." In *Indonesien am Ende des 20. Jahrhunderts*, edited by Ingrid Wessel, 19–34. Hamburg: Abera, 1996.

———. "Liberal and Progressive Voices in Indonesian Islam." In *Reformist Voices of Islam*, edited by Shireen Hunter, 187–207. London: Routledge, 2008.

Van Nieuwkerk, Karin. "Of Morals, Missions, and the Market: New Religiosity and 'Art with a Mission' in Egypt." In *Muslim Rap, Halal Soaps, and Revolutionary Theatre: Artistic Developments in the Muslim World*, edited by Karin van Nieuwkerk, 177–205. Austin: University of Texas Press, 2011.

Verskin, Alan J. *Oppressed in the Land? Fatwas on Muslims Living under Non-Muslim Rule from the Middle Ages to the Present*. Princeton, NJ: Markus Wiener, 2013.

Vidino, Lorenzo. *The New Muslim Brotherhood in the West*. New York: Columbia University Press, 2010.

Vogel, Pierre. "1/5 Dawa Kurs 5 (Teil 1): Friede Freude Eierkuchen." Accessed 4 January 2017. www.youtube.com/watch?v=lLHOlKOuqcA&playnext=1&list=PL168E55663BFC3EE0&index=43.

———. "Dawa-Kurs 1 (Einführung) Pierre Vogel." Accessed 4 January 2017. www.youtube.com/watch?v=9wU26e1D5hc.

———. "Einführung in die Methodik der Koran Interpretation (Teil 2/3)." Accessed 4 January 2017. www.ezpmuslimportal.de/index.php?option=com_hwdvideoshare&task=viewvideo&Itemid=1&video_id=816&lang=de.

———. "Die Reaktionen der Mushrikun auf die Dawah zur Zeit des Propheten Muhammed." Accessed 12 September 2015. www.youtube.com/watch?v=Mfs5hzq09fg.

———. "Tipps zur Verbesserung der Dawa (DawaKursFolge 2)—Pierre Vogel, Teil 2/8." Accessed 4 January 2017. www.youtube.com/watch?v=0MIASsK08-0&feature=PlayList&p=FB56DAFBF22AA964&playnext_from=PL&playnext=2&index=1.

———. "Verbreite die Botschaft." Einladung zum Paradies. Accessed 4 January 2017. www.einladungzumparadies.de/videos/kategorien/dawah/verbreite-die-botschaft-625.html625.

al- Wa'd Media Foundation. "The Disguise of the Religion." Accessed 17 October 2018 (link no longer active). http://sendvid.com/e8kory2f.

Wagemakers, Joas. "Framing the 'Threat to Islam': *al-Wala' wa-l-Bara'* in Salafi Discourse." *Arab Studies Quarterly* 30, no. 4 (2008):1–22.

———. *A Quietist Jihadi: The Ideology and Influence of Abu Muhammad al-Maqdisi*. Cambridge: Cambridge University Press, 2012.

———. "Salafistische Strömungen und ihre Sicht auf al-wala' wa-l-bara' (Loyalität und Lossagung)." In *Salafismus: Auf der Suche nach dem wahren Islam*, edited by Behnam T. Said and Hazim Fouad, 55–79. Freiburg im Breisgau: Herder, 2014.

———. "The Transformation of a Radical Concept: *Al-Wala' wa-l-Bara'* in the Ideology of Abu Muhammad al-Maqdisi." In *Global Salafism: Islam's New Religious Movement*, edited by Roel Meijer, 81–106. London: Hurst, 2009.

Die Wahre Religion. "Islamische Da'wah Pflicht." Accessed 4 January 2017. www.diewahrereligion.de.

———. "Das vollständige Interview mit dem DWR-Team (ZDF)—Abu Dujana und Ibrahim Abou-Nagie (1/4)." Accessed 4 January 2017. www.youtube.com/watch?v=wIt71PnfJw4&NR=1.

———. "Wir hoffen dass ihr anhand von Beispielen erklären könnt, was mit der Aussage gemeint ist: Die Kuffar als enge Freunde oder Beschützer zu nehmen ist haram." Accessed 4 January 2017. www.diewahrereligion.de.

Wa'il, Lutfi. *Zahirat al-Du'a al-Judud: Tahlil Ijtima'i: al-Da'wa, al-Tharwa, al-Shuhra*. Cairo: al-Hay'a al-Misriyya al-'Amma li'l-Kitab, 2005.

al-Wa'ili, Isma'il. *Dustur (Muhammad Sadiq) al-Sadr*. Najaf: Mu'assasat Baqiyyat Allah li-Nashr al-'Ulum al-Islamiyya, Maktabat Dar al-Mujtaba, 2004/1434.

Walker, Paul E. "Da'wah: Qur'anic Concepts." In *The Oxford Encyclopedia of the Modern Islamic World*, edited by John Esposito. Vol. 1, 343–46. New York: Oxford University Press, 1995.

Warrick, Joby. *Black Flags: The Rise of ISIS*. New York: Doubleday, 2015.

Weber, Max. *The Sociology of Religion*. Boston: Beacon, 1993.

———. *Wirtschaft und Gesellschaft*. Tübingen: Mohr, 1922.

Webman, Esther. "The Jew as a Metaphor for Evil in Arab Public Discourse." *Journal of the Middle East and Africa* 6 (2015):275–92.

Weismann, Itzchak. "Framing a Modern Umma: The Muslim Brothers' Evolving Project of Da'wa." *Sociology of Islam* 3, nos. 3–4 (2015):146–69.

———. "Modernity from Within: Islamic Fundamentalism and Sufism." *Der Islam* 86 (2011):142–70.

———. "A Perverted Balance: Modern Salafism between Reform and Jihad." *Die Welt des Islam* 57 (2017), 33 66.

———. "Sa'id Hawwa and Islamic Revivalism in Ba'thist Syria." *Studia Islamica* 85 (1997):131–54.

Why Islam. "Visit a Mosque." 10 August 2010. http://www.whyislam.org/services/visit-a-mosque/.

Wickham, Carrie R. "Interests, Ideas, and the Islamic Outreach in Egypt." In *Islamic Activism: A Social Movement Theory Approach*, edited by Quintan Wiktorowicz, 231–49. Bloomington: Indiana University Press, 2004.

———. *Mobilizing Islam: Religion, Activism, and Political Change in Egypt*. New York: Columbia University Press, 2002.

———. *The Muslim Brotherhood: Evolution of an Islamist Movement*. Princeton, NJ: Princeton University Press, 2013.

Wiedl, Nina. "Daʿwa and the Islamist Revival in the West." *Current Trends in Islamist Ideology* 9 (2009):120–50.

———. *Daʿwa: Der Ruf zum Islam in Europa*. Berlin: Hans Schiler, 2008.

———. *The Making of a German Salafiyya: The Emergence, Development and Missionary Work of Salafi Movements in Germany*. Aarhus, DK: Centre for Studies in Islamism and Radicalisation, 2012.

———. *Zeitgenössische Rufe zum Islam. Salafitische Daʿwa in Deutschland, 2002–2011*. Baden-Baden: Nomos, 2017.

Wiktorowicz, Quintan. "Anatomy of the Salafi Movement." *Studies in Conflict and Terrorism* 29 (2006):207–39.

———. *Islamic Activism: A Social Movement Theory Approach*. Bloomington: Indiana University Press, 2004.

Winkelmann, Mareike Jule. *From Behind the Curtain: A Study of a Girls' Madrasa in India*. Amsterdam: Amsterdam University Press, 2005.

Wise, Lindsay. "Amr Khaled: Broadcasting the Nahda." *Transnational Broadcasting Studies* 13 (2004). Accessed 28 September 2016. www.tbsjournal.com/Archives/Fall04/wiseamrkhaled.html.

World Assembly of Muslim Youth. "Al-Nadwa al-ʿAlamiyya li'l-Shabab al-Islami." Accessed 4 January 2017. http://www.wamy.org/.

Wrogemann, Henning. *Missionarischer Islam und gesellschaftlicher Dialog*. Frankfurt am Main: Lembeck, 2006.

Yahya, Harun. "The Rapid Spread of Islam in America." The Rise of Islam.com. Accessed 26 October 2016. http://www.riseofislam.com/islam_in_america_02.html.

Yakan, Fathi. *Kayfa naduʿ ila al-Islam*. 3rd ed. Beirut: Mu'assasat al-Risala, 1977.

———. *Mushkilat al-Daʿwa wa'l-Daʿiya*. Beirut: Mu'assasat al-Risala, 1987.

al-Yassini, Ayman. *Religion and State in the Kingdom of Saudi Arabia*. Boulder, CO: Westview, 1985.

Zakariya, Muhammad, Ihtishamul Hasan Kandhalawi, and ʿAshiq Ilahi. *Faza'il-e Aʿmal*. New Delhi: Idara Ishaat-E-Diniyat, 1994.

———. *Tablighi Nisab*. Delhi: n.p., 1940.

Zaman, Muhammad Qasim. *The Ulama in Contemporary Islam: Custodian of Change*. Princeton, NJ: Princeton University Press, 2007.

al-Zawahiri, Ayman. *General Guidelines for Jihad*. As-Sahab Media Foundation, 2013. https://azelin.files.wordpress.com/2013/09/dr-ayman-al-e1ba93awc481hirc4ab-22general-guidelines-for-the-work-of-a-jihc481dc4ab22-en.pdf.

Zaydan, ʿAbd al-Karim. *Usul al-Daʿwa*. n.p., 1976.

Zeghal, Malika. *Gardiens de l'Islam: les oulémas d'al-Azhar dans l'Egypte contemporaine*. Paris: Presses de Sciences Po, 1996.

Zelin, Aaron Y. "Maqdisi's Disciples in Libya and Tunisia." *Foreign Policy*, 14 November 2012. Accessed 7 November 2019. http://foreignpolicy.com/2012/11/14/maqdisis-disciples-in-libya-and-tunisia/.

———. "Meeting Tunisia's Ansar al-Sharia." *Foreign Policy*, 8 March 2013. http://foreignpolicy.com/2013/03/08/meeting-tunisias-ansar-al-sharia/.

———. "When Jihadists Learn How to Help." *Monkey Cage*, *Washington Post*, 7 May 2014. Accessed 22 October 2018. http://www.washingtonpost.com/blogs/monkey-cage/wp/2014/05/07/when-jihadists-learn-how-to-help/.

Zine, Jasmin, ed. *Islam in the Hinterlands: Exploring Muslim Cultural Politics in Canada*. Vancouver: University of British Columbia Press, 2012.

———. "Redefining Resistance: Towards an Islamic Subculture in Schools." *Race Ethnicity and Education* 3 (2000):293–316.

Zollner, Barbara H. E. *The Muslim Brotherhood: Hasan al-Hudaybi and Ideology*. Abingdon: Routledge, 2009.

Contributors

Hilal Ahmed is associate professor at the Center for the Study of Developing Societies (CSDS). He works on political Islam, Muslim modernities/representation, and the politics of symbols in South Asia. His book *Muslim Political Discourse in Postcolonial India: Monuments, Memory, Contestation* (Routledge 2014), engages these thematic concerns. His latest book, *"Siyasi Muslims": A Story of Political Islam in India* (Penguin 2019) is the second major outcome of his long-term intellectual engagements with postcolonial Islam(s) and Muslim communities. Ahmed is associate editor, *South Asian Studies*, journal of the British Association of South Asian Studies.

Muhammad Al-Atawneh is associate professor at Ben-Gurion University of the Negev. He has published extensively on Islamic law and society in contemporary Arab and Islamic worlds. Among his publications are *Wahhabi Islam Facing the Challenges of Modernity: Dar al-Ifta in the Modern Saudi State* (Brill 2010); (with Nuhad Ali) *Islam in Israel: Muslim Communities in Non-Muslim States* (Cambridge University Press 2018); and *Rethinking Islam at the Turn of the 21st Century: Liberal Trends, Agents of Change and Reassessments of Classical Traditions* (forthcoming).

Amatzia Baram is professor emeritus and director of the Center for Iraq Studies at the University of Haifa, Israel. He was resident senior fellow three times at the Woodrow Wilson Center and twice at the U.S. Institute for Peace, both in Washington, D.C., and at the Rockefeller Foundation at Bellagio. Among his many academic appointments, he was senior associate member at Saint Antony's College, Oxford. His fields of research are intellectual history in the Arab world, radical Sunni, Shiʿi, and nationalist-secular movements, and the history of Iraq. His latest book is *Saddam Husayn and Islam, 1968–2003* (Johns Hopkins University Press 2014).

Richard Gauvain is currently associate professor of Islamic studies in the British University in Egypt. With a background in the fields of cultural anthropology, Middle Eastern studies, and comparative religions, his research explores creative intersections between notions of religion, culture, and tradition in specific Middle Eastern communities. Drawing on several years of fieldwork, he has published a series of articles and one full monograph, *Salafi Ritual Purity: In the Presence of God* (Routledge 2012), on the subject of Egyptian Salafism.

Thomas K. Gugler is a member of the Frankfurt Research Center of Global Islam (FFGI) and the Cluster of Excellence "The Formation of Normative Orders" at Goethe University in Frankfurt am Main. He graduated in South Asian studies, religious studies, and psychology from LMU Munich and received his PhD with distinction from Erfurt University. His monographs include *Mission Medina* (Ergon 2011) and *Ozeanisches Gefühl der Unsterblichkeit* (Lit 2009).

Elysia Guzik is a researcher and educator in Toronto, Ontario, and holds a PhD from the Faculty of Information at the University of Toronto. She has published on religious reading practices (with Iulian Vamanu in the *Journal of Religious and Theological Information*, 2015), autoethnographic approaches to information science research (*Canadian Journal of Information and Library Science*, 2013), and Muslim veiling in Quebec (with Meena Sharify-Funk in *Everyday Sacred: Religion in Contemporary Quebec*, McGill-Queen's University Press 2017).

Adam Hoffman is a lecturer at the Rothberg International School of the Hebrew University of Jerusalem, and a junior researcher at the Middle East Network Analysis Desk, Moshe Dayan Center (MDC), Tel Aviv University. His research focuses on the ideology and political behavior practices of global jihadi groups, with a particular focus on ISIS. His most recent article was published in *The New East* (Journal of The Middle East and Islamic Studies Association of Israel), and his publications have appeared in *The Centre for Religion and Geopolitics*, *Strategic Assessment*, *Tel Aviv Notes,* and *Beehive*.

Julia Day Howell is professor of the sociology of religion at the Religion and Society Research Centre, University of Western Sydney. She has studied religious reform movements in Indonesia since the 1970s. Since the 1990s, her work has focused on Sufism amid the wider Islamic revival and on new forms of Islamic piety in modern, media-saturated social settings. Together with Indonesian colleagues, she pioneered the sociological study of cosmopolitan "urban Sufism" in Southeast Asia. Her work on Sufism and Islamic seeker spirituality among urbanites has appeared in such publications as the *Journal of Asian Studies* and *Modern Asian Studies* and in her edited volume (with Martin van Bruinessen), *Sufism and the "Modern" in Islam* (I. B. Tauris 2007).

Jamal Malik is professor of Islamic studies at the University of Erfurt. A member of the European Academy of Sciences and Arts, Vienna, and a fellow of the Royal Asiatic Society of Great Britain and Ireland, he works on Islam in South Asia and Muslims in Europe. He has published widely on Islamic education, religious pluralism, Sufism, and the mobilization of religion. His most recent monograph is *Islam in South Asia* (Brill 2008 and Orient Blackswan 2012). Together with Saeed Zarrabi-Zadeh (Erfurt), he has coedited *Sufism East and West: Mystical Islam and Cross-Cultural Exchange in the Modern World* (Brill 2019).

Larry Poston was professor of religious studies at Nyack College (Nyack, NY) for nearly three decades. He is presently adjunct professor of religion at Messiah College (Pennsylvania), Stevenson University (Maryland), and Morgan State University (Baltimore). He holds a PhD in the history of religions from Northwestern University and has written *Islamic Daʿwah in the West* (Oxford University Press 1992), *The Changing Face of Islam in America* (Wingspread Publishers 2007), and numerous articles.

Dietrich Reetz is senior research fellow at Leibniz Zentrum Moderner Orient, Berlin, and external faculty member of the Department of Political Science and PI, Berlin Graduate School of Muslim Cultures and Societies, Free University Berlin. He has researched and widely published on Islam and Muslims in South Asia, including their global entanglements. He covers South Asia in his monograph *Islam in the Public Sphere: Religious Groups in India, 1900–1947* (Oxford University Press 2006).

Aaron Rock-Singer is visiting assistant professor, Department of Near Eastern Studies, Cornell University. His research draws on mass and small media to trace the changing relationship among religion, politics, and society in the Middle East. His publications include *Practicing Islam in Egypt: Print Media and Islamic Revival* (Cambridge University Press 2018) and a number of articles in peer-reviewed journals. His next book project explores the transnational emergence of Salafism as a social movement during the second half of the twentieth century, with a particular focus on Salafi networks in Egypt and Saudi Arabia.

Uriya Shavit is chair of the Department of Arabic and Islamic Studies, as well as chair of the Graduate Program in Religious Studies, Tel Aviv University. He specializes in the study of modern Islamic theology and law and the sociology of Muslim minorities in the West. His most recent books are *Islamism and the West* (Routledge 2014), *Shariʿa and Muslim Minorities* (Oxford University Press 2015), *Zionism in Arab Discourses* (Manchester University Press 2016), and *Scientific and Political Freedom in Islam* (Routledge 2017)

Jakob Skovgaard-Petersen is associate professor of Islamic and Arabic studies, University of Copenhagen. He works on the modern Muslim public sphere and the role of ulama in modern Arab states. Lately, his research has focused on Islam in new pan-Arab television networks. Key publications include *Defining Islam for the Egyptian State: Muftis and Fatwas of the Dar al-Ifta* (Brill 1997); *Global Mufti: The Phenomenon of Yusuf al-Qaradawi*, coedited with Bettina Gräf (Hurst/Columbia University Press 2009); *Islam on Arab TV* (Vandkunsten 2013); and *Arab Media Moguls*, coedited with Donatella della Ratta and Naomi Sakr (I. B. Tauris 2015).

Itzchak Weismann is professor of Islamic studies and former director of the Jewish-Arab Center at the University of Haifa. His research interests focus on modern Islamic movements and ideologies. He has published widely on the Muslim Brotherhood, Salafism, Sufism, and jihadi organizations in the Middle East (especially Syria, Egypt, and Saudi Arabia), South Asia, and worldwide. His latest monograph is *Abd al-Rahman al-Kawakibi: Islamic Reform and Arab Nationalism* (Oneworld 2015). He is also scientific editor of the Sahar (Crescent) series of translations into Hebrew of major modern Islamic texts.

Nina Wiedl has studied Islamic and Middle Eastern Studies in Hamburg and Be'er Sheva. She completed her PhD at the Ben-Gurion University of the Negev, Be'er Sheva, with a thesis on contemporary Salafi *daʿwa*, in 2016. She works as an independent researcher and consultant and has published on modern Salafi thought and movements, *daʿwa,* (counter-) radicalization, and Islam in Europe. Her last monograph is *Zeitgenössische Rufe zum Islam: Salafitische Daʿwa in Deutschland, 2002–2011* (Nomos 2017).

Index